Miniature Marvels

The Book Cover Art of James E McConnell

Miniature Marvels

The Book Cover Art of James E McConnell

STEVE CHIBNALL

First published in England by:
Telos Publishing Ltd, 139 Whitstable Road, Canterbury, Kent CT2 8EQ
www.telos.co.uk

Telos Publishing Ltd values feedback. Please e-mail any comments you might have about this book to: feedback@telos.co.uk.

ISBN: 978-1-84583-210-0

Miniature Marvels: The Book Cover Art of James E McConnell © 2023 Steve Chibnall

The moral right of the author has been asserted.

Design, typesetting and layout by Stephen James Walker.

Printed and bound in the UK by Short Run Press, Exeter, Devon

British Library Cataloguing in Publication Data.
A catalogue record for this book is available from the British Library.

This book is sold subject to the condition that it shall not, by way of trade or otherwise, be lent, resold, hired out or otherwise circulated without the publisher's prior written consent in any form of binding or cover other than that in which it is published and without a similar condition including this condition being imposed on the subsequent purchaser.

'If you are a collector of modern books, don't throw away these gay covers in which they are generally encased. One day they may be of considerable value ... Yet how many preserve these jackets? I know of only one other collector besides myself. A few careful souls cut out the picture, if they are attracted by the design, and paste it inside the boarded covers, but in general it is looked at and thrown away. I am convinced that the jacket in some form or another will be required at future book sales, and perhaps some ingenious collector will devise a new plan for its preservation.'

Ralph Straus, literary critic, 1924[1]

James McConnell, pictured in the late 1930s.

ACKNOWLEDGEMENTS

A book may usually be attributed to a single author, but one like this cannot be produced by a lone writer sitting at a solitary desk. Although I am responsible for the words and any mistakes that may remain, many people have helped with my research. Thanks are due to fellow McConnell collector and enthusiast Jim Kealy; two 'friends in the North', Ian Farrier at the West Newcastle Photograph Collection and Ruth Taylor at the Pendower Good Neighbour Project; John and Elsie Munday, rescuers of Corgi artwork; my colleague and ace ancestry researcher, Justin Smith; the indefatigable staff at the British Library, the National Library of Wales, the University of Oxford's Bodleian Library and the De Montfort University's Special Collections; and especially Alex Fisher and her colleagues at the University of Cambridge Library.

The book would also have been a 'whiter shade of pale' without all the encouragement, technical mastery and research ability of one of my publishers, Stephen James Walker. But the lion's share of my gratitude is reserved for James McConnell himself, who allowed me an interview not long before his death; and for his youngest daughter, Ann, who supplied invaluable reminiscences and family photos. It is to Ann, and the memory of her wonderfully-talented father, that this book is respectfully dedicated.

James, Maureen and (in the barrow with their dog Taffy) Ann McConnell in their garden, circa 1960.

The Limping Wolf by E T Portwin (Featherstone Press, 1946); painted October 1945. A very scarce McConnell cover for a horror novel from an obscure small press.

CONTENTS

1: Painting with a Purpose 11
    Gallery 18
2: A Painter's Life 27
    Gallery 60
3: Fancy Jackets: The First Ten Years 73
    Gallery 96
4: Depicting the Detectives: Crime Thrillers and Mysteries 115
    Gallery 124
5: A Gunman on a Horse: Imagining the Old West 171
    Gallery 178
6: A Lass, a Lad and a Landscape: Picturing the Perfect Romance 221
    Gallery 228
7: Thrills A-Plenty: Fantasy, War and Adventure 267
    Gallery 274
8: Doing It for the Kids 303
    Gallery 306
Epilogue 317
References 319
Bibliography 321

Original artwork for *Westering* by Irwin R Blacker (Corgi GW838, 1960); painted October 1959. (Author's collection.)

1: PAINTING WITH A PURPOSE

'Book cover designing can be considered as a means of advertising the book. Therefore, it must be treated as such. Your design should convey, as strikingly as possible, the "atmosphere" of the book (in the same way as a play poster should denote the "spirit" of the show). Boldness in style and colour is essential. On a bookstall there are many books in direct competition. People are influenced to buy by the picture they see on the outside of a book. Often they buy without looking inside.'

V L Danvers, 1926[2]

The 20th Century was a time of ceaseless artistic upheaval. New movements came and went at an unprecedented pace: post-impressionism, expressionism, cubism, Dadaism, constructivism, art deco, the international style, surrealism, neo-romanticism, abstract expressionism, situationism, pop art, post-modernism … the list goes on and on. James McConnell was a 20th-Century artist whose course was hardly deflected by this constant stylistic churn. His work was commercial, made on commission for clients who knew what he could supply and valued the particular style of figurative art that he had evolved. They trusted him to satisfy their needs, free of fads and fashionable foibles, and came to him because of his exceptional ability to paint people, animals and landscape in a totally convincing way. His hand could conjure the scene imagined in his mind's eye with unerring speed and accuracy, fixing it in gouache on board for photo-reproduction. This instant visual translation of imagined scenarios was a minor miracle that he achieved on a daily basis, year after year.

James McConnell liked to think of himself as an action painter – not the kind who threw paint on canvas and then wheeled a bike over it to emphasize the process of artistic labour, but the kind who could create the illusion of movement in his tableaux. His paintings carry a sense of narrative: the ghost of what has gone before and the hint of what is to follow, movement 'arrested for contemplation' to use a phrase of Marshall McLuhan's. The contemplative gaze of the book buyer and reader was what McConnell's art craved, and the drama of his compositions coupled with the life-like quality of his renderings ensured the sympathetic attention of his audience.

By the time that commercial illustration became a primary source for the vibrant pop-

Original artwork for *Racers to the Sun* by James B Hall (Corgi GN1099, 1961); painted July 1961.

art of the 1960s, McConnell had largely abandoned the fast-contracting field of book cover illustration in favour of bringing history to life for children in the weekly paper *Look and Learn*. The young luminaries of pop-art struck sparks from the magma of popular culture, but the sources of the paintings that graced the white walls of their galleries were left anonymous, undifferentiated, unheralded, decontextualized and too often appropriated as kitsch. McConnell's paintings did not make it onto a gallery wall until 1976, five decades after his extraordinary stream of production began; but his work had been constantly presented to the public in newsagents', bookshops, toy shops, playgrounds, market stalls and a myriad of other venues where printed products were viewed and passed between consumers. His was art for every day, accessible to all, not reserved for the special visit to a rarefied, declamatory environment. He painted modestly and he painted small. Not for him the giant environment-filling canvases of the 'situation' artists; his work was intimate, designed to be viewed at arm's length or closer, like the miniatures of previous centuries. The paintings themselves were rarely much more than half a meter high, and could therefore be accomplished quickly, and a living made. McConnell's talent turned them into miniature marvels.

The size and the medium employed distinguish McConnell's cover paintings, and those of most other British illustrators, from those produced by American artists for the pulp magazines presenting genre fiction not unlike many of the novels that McConnell illustrated. The pulp covers shared much of the iconography and atmosphere of McConnell's genre paintings, but they were generally executed in oils on canvases that were approximately 30" x 20", or double crown in British printing terminology. Consequently, they took two or three times longer to paint.

Of course, McConnell's work extended beyond the confines of the book cover. He illustrated sales brochures, press and point-of-sale advertising for leading commercial brands, jigsaws and box-tops for puzzle manufacturers, posters for films, coming-attractions booklets for picture palaces, promotional materials for estate developers, frontispieces and internal illustrations for publishers, and almost 100 covers for larger-format weekly educational magazines such as *Ranger* and the aforementioned *Look and Learn*. Indeed, some of his later work for 1,000-piece jigsaws and picture papers is on a grander scale, influenced by cinema epics, with their casts of thousands. He was particularly proud to be commissioned to illustrate the commemorative American Roll of Honour, which lies in the American Chapel of London's St Paul's Cathedral. Sadly, this document also has a cast of thousands: 28,000 servicemen and women killed in the European campaign of World War Two. The dedication of the 473-page Roll in 1958 was attended by Royal family

Original artwork for *Trail of the Blood-Mark* by Claude Rister (Western Library # 50, 1952); painted January 1952. (Image courtesy Jim Kealy.)

The romance of painting: *Love Me For Ever* by Lydon Snow (Collins, 1955); painted February 1955.

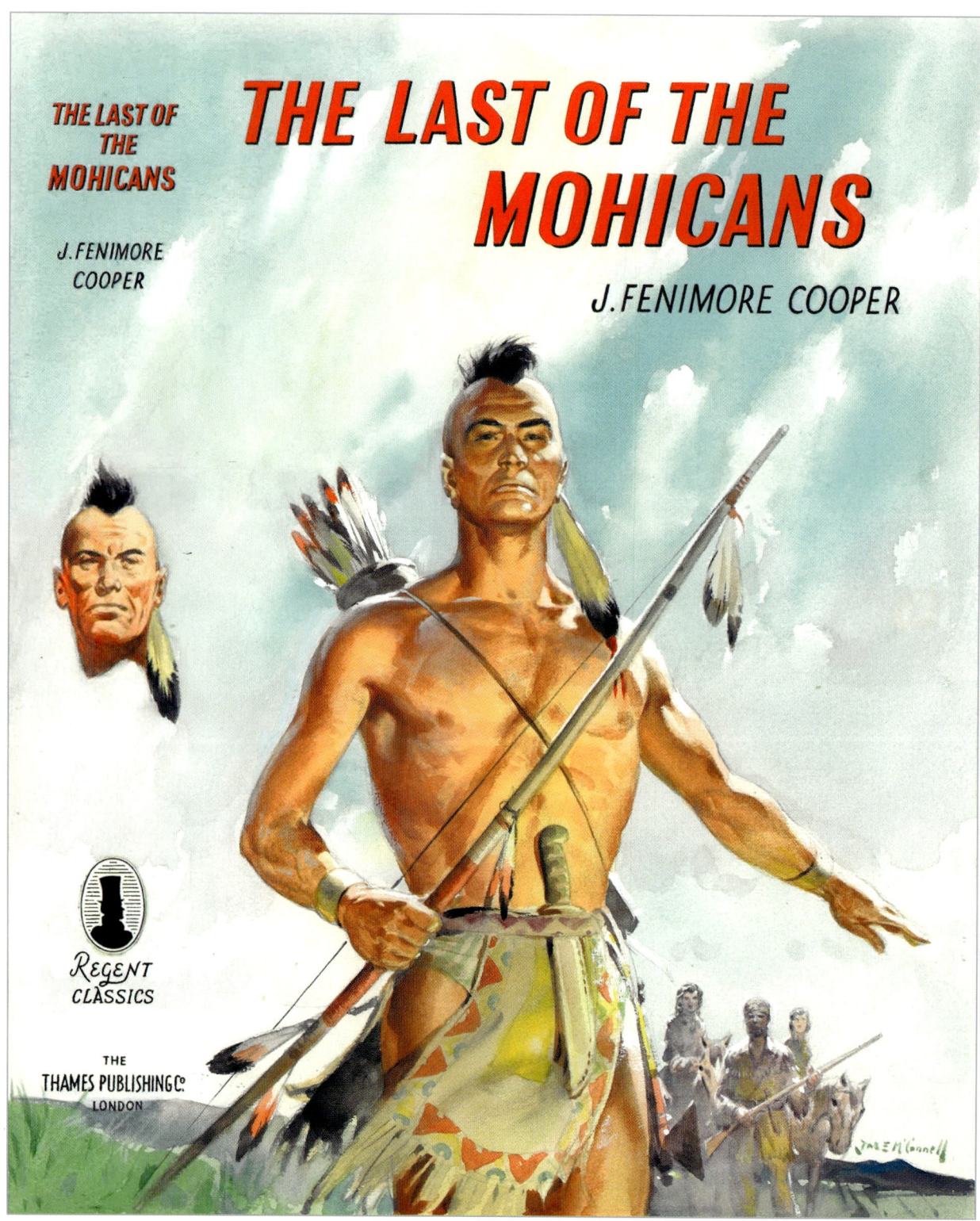

Original artwork for *The Last of the Mohicans* by James Fenimore Cooper (Thames Publishing, 1957); painted April 1957. (Image courtesy Jim Kealy.)

members and seen by 2.5 million viewers on television. But as impressive as much of this alternative work might be, this debut study of McConnell's art will concentrate on his book cover pieces, which number over 2,000.

The book's principal primary sources, besides the collections of the author and others, are an interview that the author conducted with McConnell in 1991, four years before his death, and the artist's workbook containing details of almost all of his commissions from his first day as a freelancer in 1933 until his retirement in the mid-1970s. McConnell's interview reveals that his *modus operandi* as an illustrator was fairly typical for a mid-century commercial painter working via an agent on commissions from publishers. The process and methods of producing 'camera-ready' artwork have been admirably described by former art-director Colin Larkin in his book *Cover Me* (Telos Publishing, 2020) on the cover paintings used by Pan in the 1950s and 1960s, so it is probably sufficient here to quote McConnell's own comments on his practice:[3]

> 'I worked in gouache – opaque watercolour – sometimes in oils, but not very much because they wouldn't dry in time for the customers, you see. It was mostly watercolour, I wasn't very keen on "body colour", although I did use it. Always twice-up – Corgi insisted on it being twice the size [of the published book cover]. I never touched the lettering, I just left the space for it.'[4]

The endless repetition of genre paintings inevitably led to some of the stylistic clichés that make an artist's work identifiable, even without a signature:

> 'I got in trouble on occasions for drawing the same figure all the time, the same face, very square-jawed. I had an idea in my mind for the face. I suppose I should have used models more, but it's such a waste of time working with models. I used to hire costumes from a shop in Holborn and work with the model in the costume, rather than take photographs, as a rule. I used photographs sometimes just to get the position right. I never used women as models, of course; I was always too frightened, too shy.'

Surprisingly, this shy man, unlike his celebrated contemporary Reginald Heade, never even used his wife as a model. Instead he liked to read the books that he was asked to summarise and promote in his cover paintings. Using his vivid imagination, he would visualise a scene and authenticate its details by drawing upon a wide range of reference material, both from the libraries in the art departments of publishers such as Pan, and from the American

Contemplating a miniature marvel: *Brief Hour* by Don Portbury (Cassell, 1939).

and British weekly magazines and the monthly Western-story pulp that he bought regularly.

> 'I used to buy *Picturegoer* – there used to be a lot of stuff in that that I could use. I was careful not to make the stars recognisable; I changed them a bit. I also took one of the Western magazines. I would always buy the *Saturday Evening Post*. I admired Norman Rockwell – very photographic, jolly good composition, and he produced plenty of ideas in his time. Illustrators are still considered artists in America. There were some very fine illustrators in the *Saturday Evening Post*.'

This comment betrays a lingering resentment about the low status given to illustrators, and commercial art in general, in Britain. McConnell worked at a time when stylistic innovation, abstract expressionism and various iconoclastic movements such as Op and Pop Art set the critical tone. In truth, 'fine' art became another

Come Back Miranda by Anne Duffield (Cassell, 1955); painted December 1954.

form of commercialism, marketed and sold competitively through an expanding network of private galleries. 'I never liked exhibitions,' he commented dryly. 'I was never one for competing, even in my gardening. I was never fussed about that sort of thing. I was quite happy to do anything. I never tried to cultivate it, I just drew!'

The kind of ebullient, dramatic narrative illustration in which McConnell specialised was widely despised by critics, who believed that they knew what was in good taste and what was not. Christian Barman, for example, condemned the colourful illustrations used by publishers to sell popular fiction as an abuse of the craft that had given the whole field of illustration a bad name. To Barman, they constituted 'the shameless vulgarisation of four-colour process illustration.' But then he also believed that story illustration should be used *only* very sparingly, criticising popular magazines for their excessive use of pictorial elements: 'I know I am not the only person who finds many illustrated magazines altogether

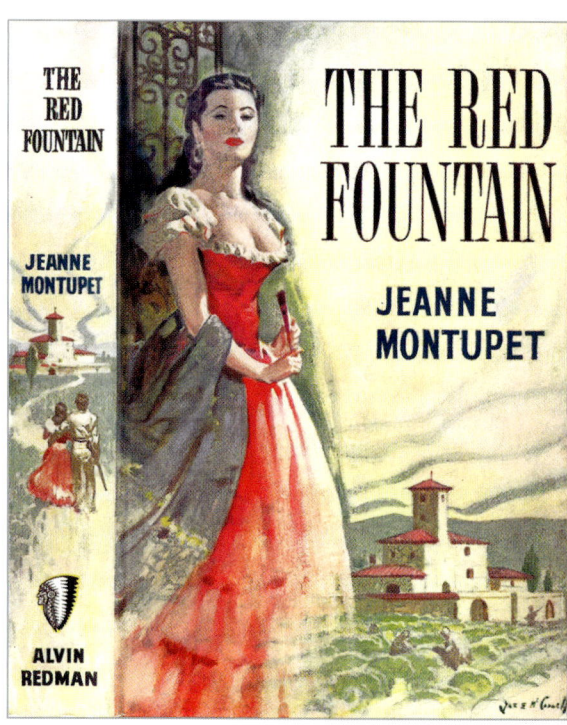

The Red Fountain by Jeanne Montupet (Alvin Redman, 1963)

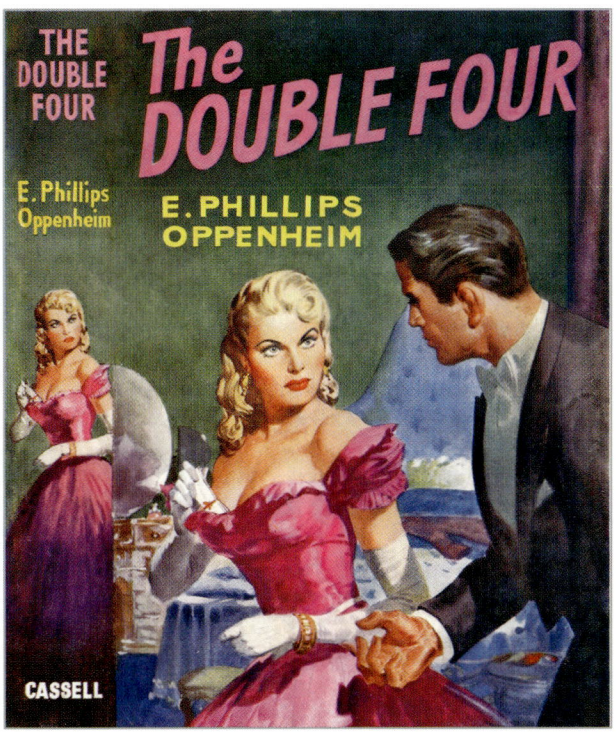 

There are some occasions when it is possible to see through McConnell's disguises. The Edwardian beauty who is retrieving a letter from her pink décolletage on the cover of E Phillips Oppenheim's *The Double Four* (Cassell, 1956) is Rank's rising star Belinda Lee. The source for the December 1955 painting was the Cornel Lucas publicity photograph of Lee playing the vamp in the Norman Wisdom comedy *Man of the Moment* (1955) that had graced the cover of *Picturegoer* on 22 October 1955.

unreadable; to try and focus one's attention on the printed words is like trying to carry on an intimate conversation on a tube railway.'[5] But from the very beginning of his work on book jackets, there was little doubt that the illustrative style favoured by McConnell and others of his school was appreciated by the consumers of popular fiction. In the early 1930s, a book retailer wrote to *The Publisher and Bookseller* to indicate the preferences of his customers:

> 'I find that the majority of books sell better by having an artistic jacket such as H V Morton's books and Jenkins', Ward Lock's and Hodder's publications. This style of jacket is more sales compelling than the crude [typographical] ones of Gollancz, Benn and Faber. Having a circulating library, I find subscribers much prefer to take a book with a picture jacket.'[6]

McConnell and his publishers understood that, for most consumers, the book cover was not an intrusion on the reading experience. Instead, the cover was an invitation to open and purchase the novel; an invitation that indicated the emotions that the reader might access through the story contained within, and then offered a reminder to return to the experience every time the book was temporarily closed. In mid-century Britain, the bookshop, the railway station stall and the local newsagent were art exhibitions for folk who rarely visited municipal museums or private galleries. James McConnell was a master of his craft, whose pocket-sized images could be collected by connoisseurs of modest means. His covers were indivisible from the stories they wrapped, and a permanent aid to the book-reader's imagination. If they were impressively rendered, beautifully composed, and full of excitement, then the same might well apply to the narratives within. His were truly paintings with a purpose.

GALLERY

THE WOMEN'S WESTERN: *Slow White Oxen* by Vingie E Roe (Cassell, 1950); painted July 1949. Vingetta Roe (1879-1958) was a doctor's child of the Old West, born in Kansas. She wrote more than 30 female-centred novels, many of them featuring strong and active women. Some were adapted for the silent cinema. McConnell painted nine covers for her books; another four are shown opposite.

GALLERY

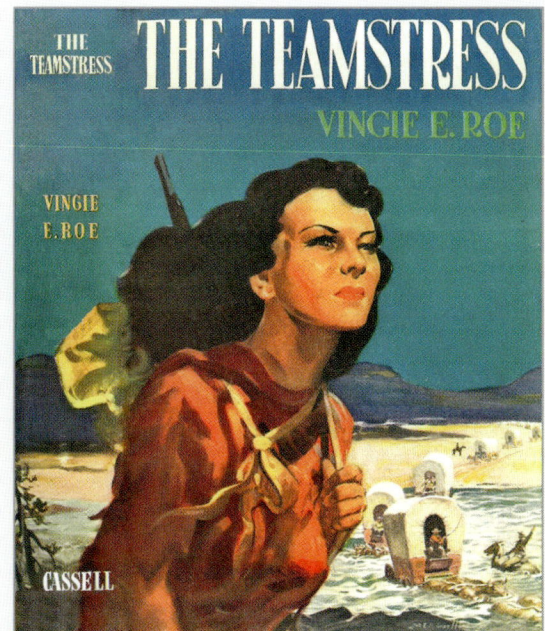
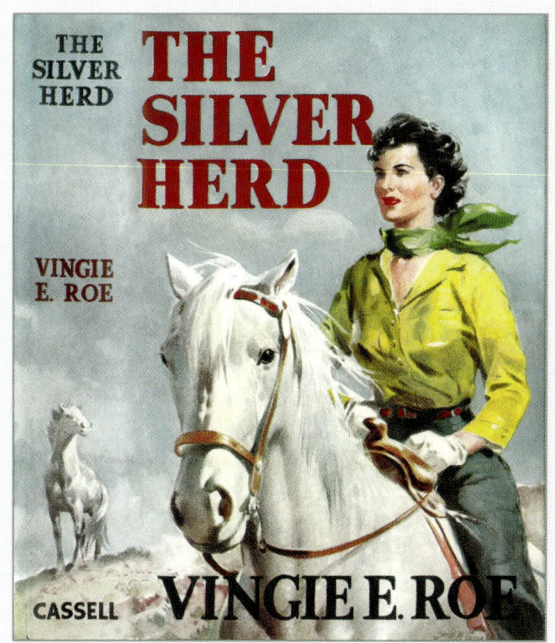

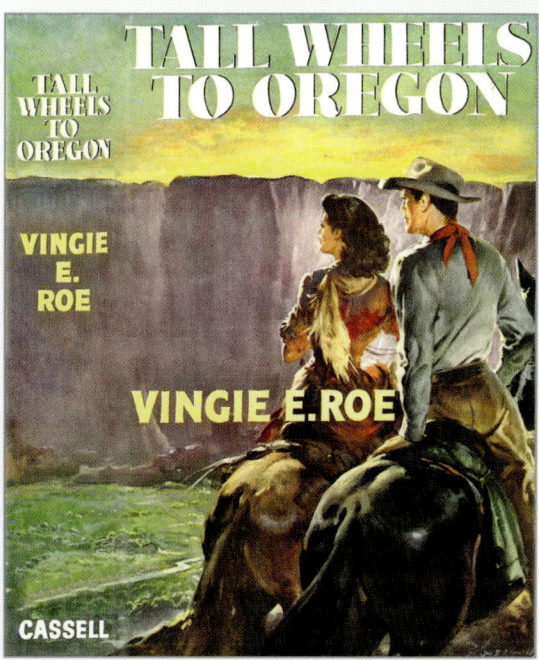

THE WOMEN'S WESTERN: Four further McConnell jackets for Vingie E Roe Western novels, all published by Cassell:

Top left: *The Teamstress* (1949); painted November 1948. Top right: *The Silver Herd* (1957); painted January 1957. Bottom left: *West of Abilene* (1952); painted October 1951. Bottom right: *Tall Wheels to Oregon* I1955); painted November 1954.

MINIATURE MARVELS

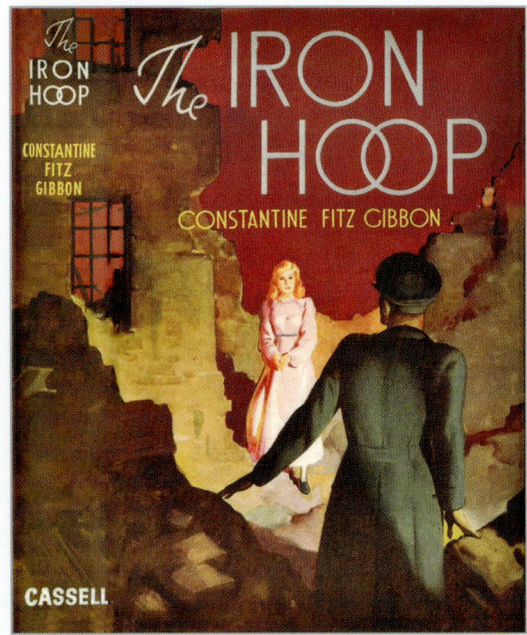

THE STAND-OFF: This page: four of McConnell's cover paintings presenting a variation on a theme: Top left: *The Iron Hoop* by Constantine Fitz Gibbon (Cassell, 1950); painted June 1949. Top right: *The Tilted Moon* by Barry Perowne (Cassell, 1949); painted April 1948. Bottom left: *The Spiral Road* by Jan de Hartog (Four Square #173, 1959); a paperback cover painted March 1959. Bottom right: *After the Glory* by Helen Topping Miller (Alvin Redman, 1959); painted February 1959.

THE STAND-OFF: *From Here to a Star* by Betty Trask (Collins, 1941).

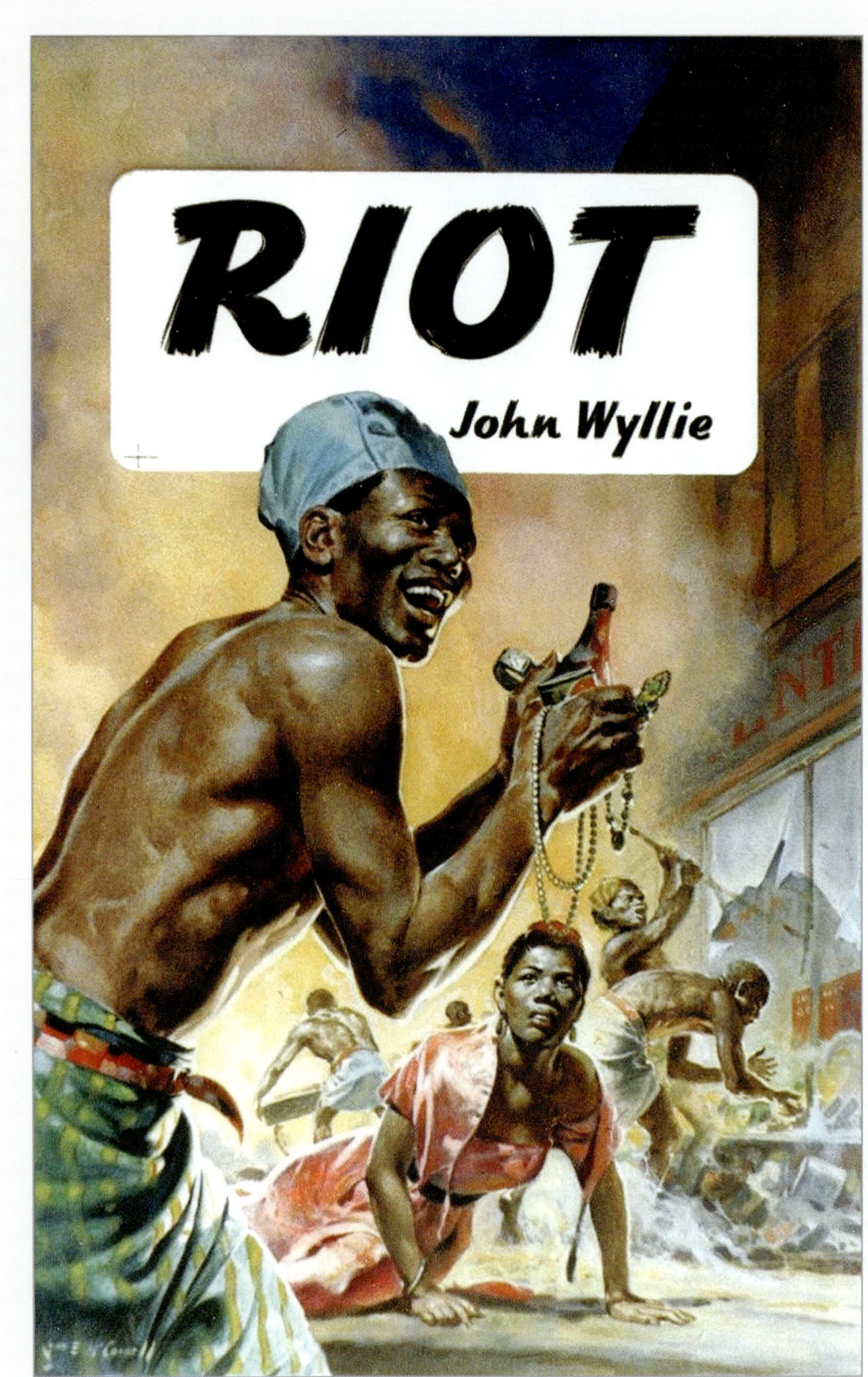

BLACK SUFFERING AND RESISTANCE: Original artwork for *Riot* by John Wyllie (Pan G159, 1958); painted November 1957. (Author's collection.)

GALLERY

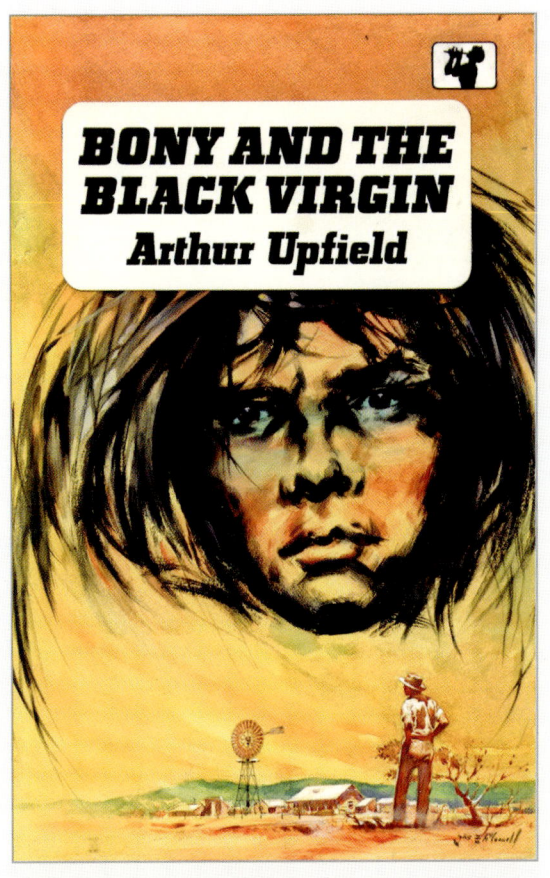

BLACK SUFFERING AND RESISTANCE: Top left: *The Golden Valley* by Frank O'Grady (Cassell, 1955); painted January 1955. Top right: original artwork for *Bony and the Black Virgin* by Arthur Upfield (Pan G574, 1962); a paperback cover painted October 1961. Bottom left: *Black Saga* by Peter Bourne (Arrow, 1955); a paperback cover painted January 1955. Bottom right: *Kiboko* by Daniel Mannix (Cassell, 1959); painted October 1958.

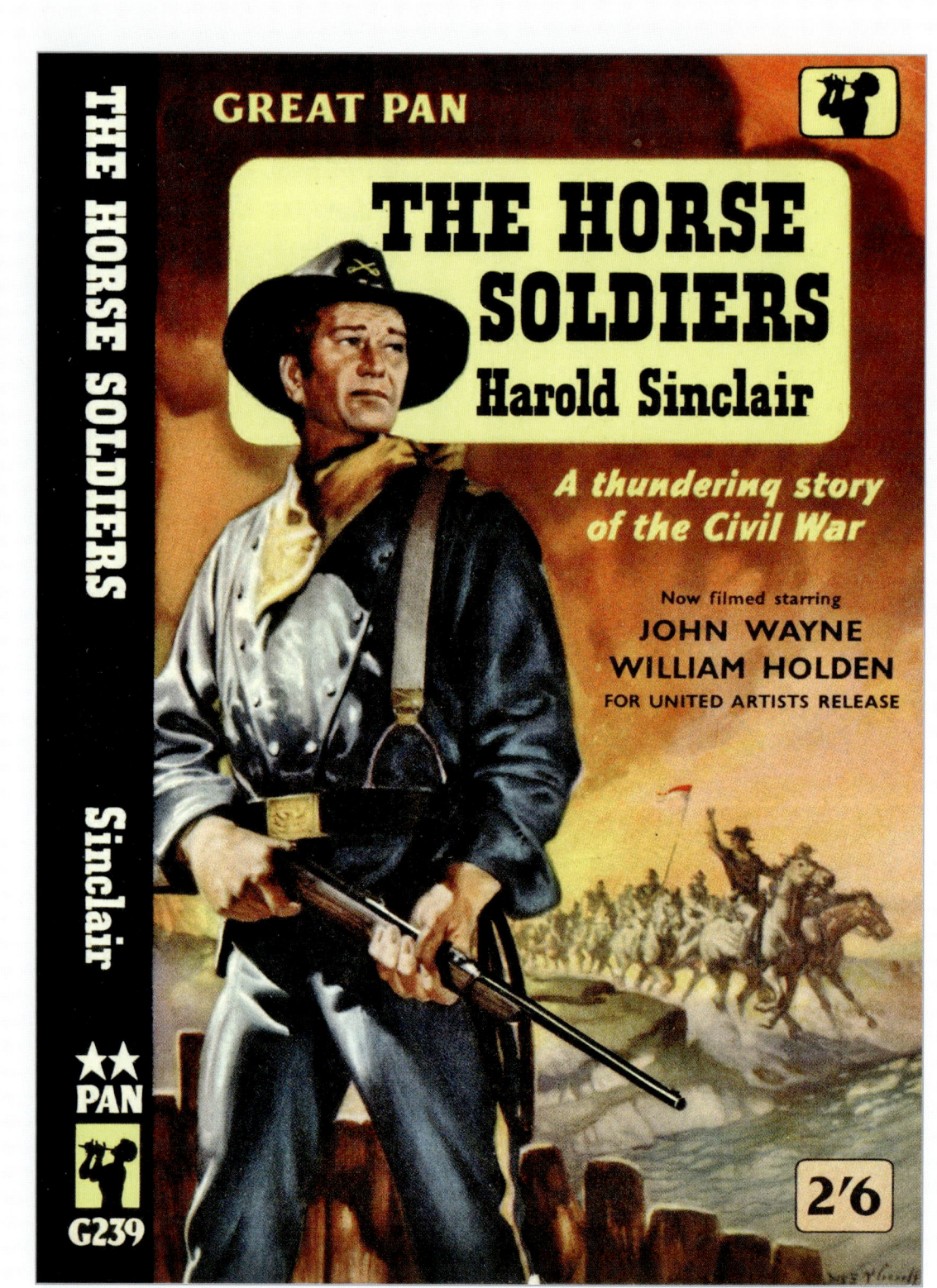

HOLLYWOOD STARS: A portrait of movie star John Wayne on the cover of a film tie-in paperback of *The Horse Soldiers* by Harold Sinclair (Pan G239, 1959); painted November 1959. (Advance cover distributed to wholesale buyers; author's collection.)

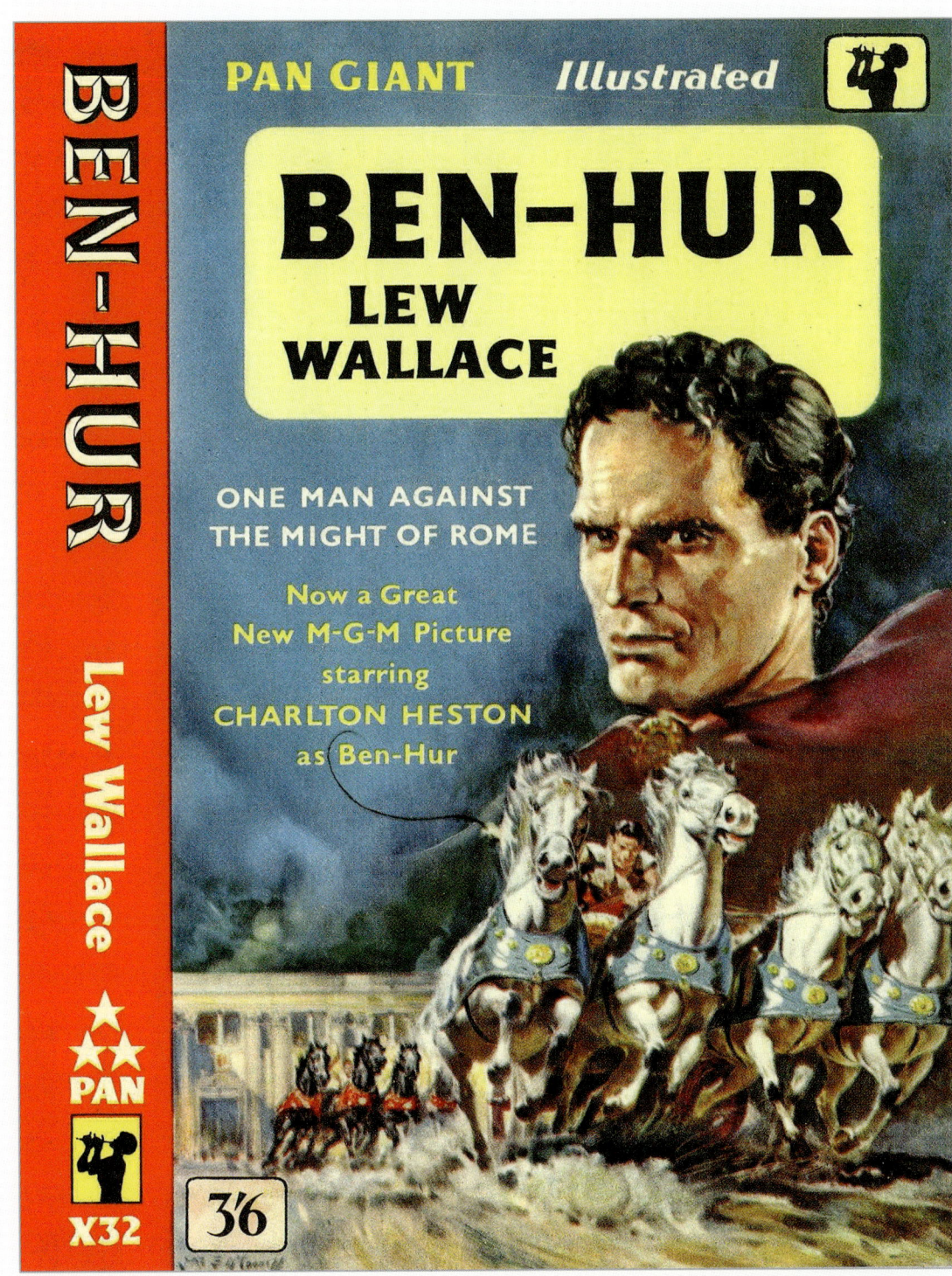

HOLLYWOOD STARS: A portrait of movie star Charlton Heston on the cover of a film tie-in paperback of *Ben-Hur* by Lew Wallace (Pan X32, 1959); painted October 1958. (Advance cover distributed to wholesale buyers; author's collection.)

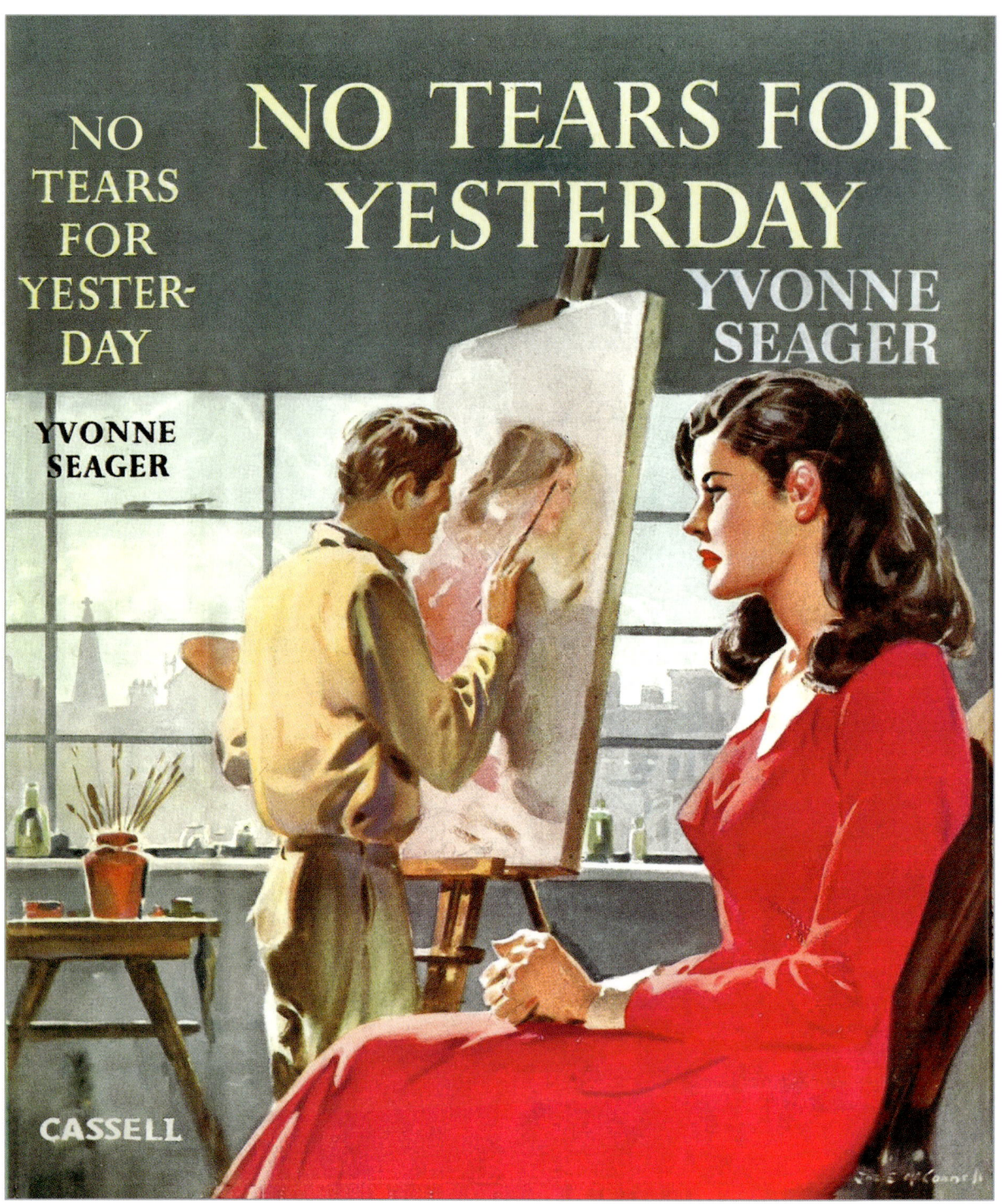

No Tears for Yesterday by Yvonne Seager (Cassell, 1954); painted June 1954.

2: A PAINTER'S LIFE

'It was just a hard-working life.'

James McConnell

Hometown Story

James Edwin McConnell was born on 15 July 1903 in the Netherton district of the small market town of Bedlington in Northumberland, ten miles north of the city of Newcastle-on-Tyne in England's North-East corner. Bedlington, which gave its name to the famous breed of terrier dogs, was a town built on coal and steel. Although it may be best known now as the birthplace of model and *Top of the Pops* presenter Jayne Middlemiss, at the turn of the 20th Century its reputation rested on its sons rather than its daughters: Victorian engineers like the Isambard Kingdom Brunel protégé Daniel Gooch, who ended his career as a Conservative MP with a knighthood; his brothers John and Thomas, who also contributed manfully to the development of the early railway network; and John Birkinshaw, who invented iron rails. Miners, railway workers or engineers were what sons of Bedlington were expected to be; but the son of Margaret Loadman (born c1871) and Thomas McConnell (born c1875) became an artist. James McConnell would later recall:

> 'My father was a policeman ... The nearest my family got to art was that my uncle played the violin! I had three brothers and a sister, but I was the only one to enter a profession really.[7] But my father let me go whichever way I wanted to.'

This was an unusually *laissez faire* attitude for a member of the constabulary. His father would never rise above the rank of constable; his eldest brother became a locomotive fitter; and the others entered the developing motor trade as a driver and a mechanic respectively.

Above: Benwell police station where McConnell's father was based when he moved to Newcastle. (Image courtesy the West Newcastle Photograph Collection.)

Around 1905, the McConnells moved south to Old Benwell in Newcastle, where the 1911 census recorded the family of seven living in a three roomed cottage, part of a small complex of buildings behind the Fox and Hounds Inn on Benwell Bank Top. The Inn fronted onto West Road, which runs parallel to the famous Scotswood Road, north-west out of Tyneside. The Fox and Hounds (licensee Anne Burn) would later become the terminus of the new electrified tramway, but in the Edwardian years it stopped short of the McConnell homestead. By the time the trams arrived in 1925, the pub had been demolished and rebuilt (in 1909).[8]

Below: West Road, Benwell, showing the Fox and Hounds c1900. (Image courtesy the West Newcastle Photograph Collection.)

Above left: The Fox and Hounds, showing the cottages at the rear, where it is believed that the McConnell family lived. Above right: The 'White Cottage', Old Benwell, in winter c1920. (Both images courtesy the West Newcastle Photograph Collection.)

At some point between 1911 and 1921, as the McConnell children outgrew the small dwelling house on Benwell Bank Top, the family moved about a quarter of a mile south to Old Benwell. They occupied the larger, detached 'White Cottage', which stood in its own grounds and is thought to have been built in the mid-19th Century. The ancient village of Benwell had been almost overrun by the spiralling urbanisation that spilled west from the city centre along the Scotswood Road, and rows of terraced houses had been thrown up to accommodate the ever-increasing army of industrial workers. The Benwell terrace has been immortalised as the Carter family home in Mike Hodges' grim thriller, *Get Carter*, made in 1970, when the old back-to-backs and their outside lavatories were finally being demolished. It was a rough and deprived neighbourhood, and a challenge for any copper. The McConnells were fortunate to live at the beginnings of a greener belt, on rising ground at the edge of the Pendower estate, owned by the Lloyds banker J W Pease.

We do not know for sure which elementary school the young James McConnell attended, but there were plenty being built in his locality to meet the educational needs of the rapidly-expanding Benwell population. The nearest were at Delaval (built 1893), Canning Street (built 1903), and Denton Road (built 1908); but whichever one it might have been, McConnell was a lucky kid, because his headmaster recognised and nurtured his rare talent, as he remembered: 'I always liked art. I was always drawing on the slates at school – we had slates in those days – and the headmaster, who was an artist himself, used to keep an eye on my slates, and he encouraged me.' The support of his headmaster was probably vital to McConnell's future career. The start of his schooling also coincided with the opening of a public lending library in Benwell, paid for by the philanthropist Andrew Carnegie, and one wonders if young James was invited to view its collection of books on art.

Schooling in Benwell was significantly disrupted by the First World War. The West End of Newcastle was a national centre for the production of armaments and warships, and a magnet for factory workers, with the Armstrong factory alone employing 78,000 by the end of hostilities; but the schools also played their part, with many of their buildings being commandeered for military use. The architectural design of schools was mindful of the need to contain any childish impulse to truant, and they therefore made good prisons. Some were used for German prisoners of war. Others became convalescent homes or hospitals for the wounded, or venues for military instruction. One of the Benwell history websites suggests the general level of disruption at one of the schools that McConnell might well have attended:

Above: School photograph c1910 and (inset) a detail of McConnell. The shyness that would be part of his personality is clearly evident. Below: School photograph c1912 and (inset) a detail of McConnell. A study in the concentration that would be vital to his career. (Images courtesy D F Higgins, Elswick Road, Newcastle.)

'The Log Book for Canning Street School records in detail the impact of the outbreak of war. An entry for 25 August 1914 records that owing to the "school premises being used by soldiers, the children are meeting for afternoon session only at Elswick Road Council School". From September 1914 the pupils were transferred to Atkinson Road School and the Benwell Parish Hall on Atkinson Road, both temporary measures that actually lasted until Canning Street School was handed back and reopened in January 1918.'9

The school was closed again in February 1919 by the deadly 'Spanish Flu' influenza outbreak, but by that time, McConnell had left.

When his period at elementary school ended in 1917, the First World War was still raging, but McConnell was too young for the trenches. He might have gone to aid the war effort in the pits or on the railways, but he managed to win a scholarship to Newcastle's Armstrong College, an affiliate college of Durham University, with a School of Arts that had opened in 1894. During the War, much of the grand building and its additional wings had been requisitioned as a military hospital. McConnell, who was known to his friends as 'Ted' (presumably a diminutive of his middle name), was a student there until 1921. At about

Armstrong College, Newcastle, pictured in 1911.

The West Road tramway at the Fox and Hounds, as it was in 1930. (Image courtesy the West Newcastle Photograph Collection.)

this time, too, the McConnell family became one of the early beneficiaries of a pioneering council house estate built on what had been the grounds of the Pendower mansion. The family, which by now had four teenage children all in employment and needed extra space, moved back to the West Road, but slightly closer to Newcastle City Centre at number 315: one of the earliest houses of the Pendower scheme to be completed, and handily placed for the tram into town. The progressive new housing included gardens, and it may have been here that the young James McConnell was first bitten by the gardening bug, leaving him with green fingers for the rest of his life.

His family's house move and McConnell's emergence into the world of work came at a buoyant time for employment in the printing industry, the young male population having been severely depleted by the war and the subsequent influenza pandemic: 'I had six jobs to choose from when I left school,' McConnell later recalled. 'You wouldn't get that now, would you? I started work for a local block-maker. Block-makers were the only people who employed artists.'

His employer was Philipson & Son, an up-and-coming process printing business based in large premises on Lisle Street in Newcastle, about two miles from his home. The 'Son', James Philipson, would eventually be elected President of the Federation of Master Process Engravers. In the 1921 Census the 17-year-old

McConnell is already described as an 'artist'. At Philipson's he learnt to use the relatively-new American invention the airbrush, but found that it was not his cup of tea: 'I hate the thing,' he complained passionately. 'I only used it for backgrounds sometimes.'

Jobs for people who could draw may have been plentiful in Newcastle at the time, but they had limited prospects. A few years later, in 1928, W R Maxwell-Foster would write a book of advice for budding commercial artists in which he would declare: 'London is the hub of the publishing world, and sooner or later the artist who would come to the front must live in London and make use of its terrific advantages, even if he again retires to the country when he has won his spurs.'[10] But the young McConnell already knew that if he wanted to advance in his chosen profession, he needed to go south:

'I stayed at the block-makers in Newcastle until I was 21 or 22, and then I came down to London. I always wanted to come down to London. I got a job with John Swains' block-makers. I started just before the General Strike in 1926, and I stayed quite a long time, until 1933.'

John Swain & Son was a leading photo-engraving and wood-block making company that had recently moved from Farringdon Street in Islington to Columbia House in Shoe Lane, close to the newspaper publishing hub in Fleet Street. They specialised in designing and illustrating trade catalogues and point-of-sale advertising materials. 'It was all advertising,' McConnell recalled. 'Pears Soap, that sort of thing.' The artist was now known by his given name, James, as he sought to forge a strong professional identity in the metropolis.

Below: dating from 1926, a Philipson-produced local press advert of the type to which McConnell would have leant his artistic talents during the years he worked for the firm.

Below: a 1920s trade advertisement for John Swain & Son.

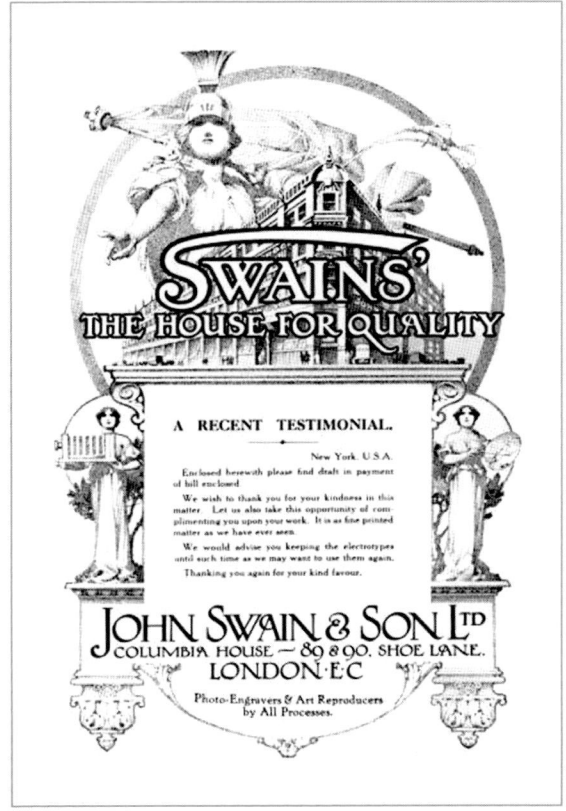

The famous Foyles bookstore in London's Charing Cross Road, pictured in the 1950s.

Although he had landed a good job with a prestigious employer, McConnell was still learning his craft, and he enrolled for evening classes at one of London's premier art schools, Saint Martin's in London's Charing Cross Road, a thoroughfare famous for its book shops. It would not be long before the road's flagship store, and the School of Art's neighbour, Foyles, would be stocking scores of McConnell's cover designs on its shelves. 'I used to go to St Martin's after I joined Swain's,' he later recalled. 'I used to go to the evening classes with an artist friend for two or three years.'

By the late-1920s, London had thoroughly entered the 'jazz age'. In the West End clubs, close to St Martin's, men in dinner suits and women in beaded 'shimmy' dresses with scandalously short skirts were trying out the Charleston and sometimes experimenting with the fashion drug cocaine. Graphic and interior design had been rocked by the new geometric decorative styles, inspired by ancient Egyptian and tribal art and unveiled at the influential Paris exhibition of 1925. Soon the magazine press was full of *sans serif* lettering, ziggurats, flappers, elongated profiles and long, lean limousines. In fine art, the idea of avant-gardism as a key strategy of value was beginning to find some purchase amongst critics and practitioners. However, England's art schools, including those in the capital, retained a traditional curriculum: life drawing, still-life painting, portraiture, the copying of old masters and classical sculpture, focusing on the honing of representational skills. The libertarian revolution of the late 1950s and the 1960s had yet to sweep through art education.

First and foremost, the art school offered training in 'commercial' art, tailored to the needs of the expanding magazine press and advertising industry. Typography, lithography, calligraphy and illustration by hand were the required techniques, and the study of these skills, in the context of the fashionable change in commercial tastes, was the primary conduit by which students absorbed the style of the age. Even so, trade publications still carried articles expressing concern that art education paid insufficient attention to the principles and needs of publicity. Maxwell-Foster, in his manual for the young professional artist, agreed that the arts schools were not doing enough to prepare students for the world of work.[11] Illustration, which was McConnell's speciality, was still the dominant mode of representation in the 1920s, even in much of the newspaper press, and the quotidian needs were met by an army of journeymen practitioners. As emphasised in another contemporary training manual, by author V L Danvers, the key skill for commercial artists was the realistic rendering of the human figure: 'Good figure artists are none too plentiful. Those who are well known and recognised as such are never out of work. If you are a good figure artist, your future success is assured. If you are not, then the sooner you "get down to it" the better.'[12] Nonetheless, the school of realistic figure representation in which McConnell had been trained was already under attack from the heralds of modernism, who championed the stylised and abstracted mode of representation that was emerging in France and especially in Germany and Austria. McConnell's more naturalistic approach had evolved from the Italian 'old masters' via the more secular storytelling of Victorian pictorial moral fables. Even in the mid-1920s, this school of figurative art was being routinely referred to as the 'English' style, and its leading commercial exponent widely thought to be Septimus E Scott. Defending the work of Scott in *Commercial Art*, John Harrison pointed to its honesty, national identity and utility as mass communication:

V L Danvers' *Training in Commercial Art* (Sir Isaac Pitman & Sons, 1926).

> 'On the whole his advertising work is a reminder to artists that if you are English it is well to be English, and that the world is not yet sufficiently international for any standard pattern to be freely interchanged and used amongst all countries as some attempt to use it. From the point of view of art, Septimus Scott's work is not flawless by any means. It is excellent as a serious effort to say something and it is excellent as advertising. It is borrowed neither from Germany nor France. It is strong honest work performing its task efficiently, appealing to the people to whom it is intended to appeal.'[13]

McConnell was not a man for manifestos, but he would have recognised his own practice in Harrison's praising of Scott. In later years,

Scott's paintings would line up alongside McConnell's 'strong, honest and efficient' efforts on the covers of Amalgamated Press's picture library series. Scott's may not have been a household name in the 1920s, but it was distinctive and relatively well-known at a time when becoming famous beyond the trade was not so easy for illustrators, because their work, particularly in advertising, was largely anonymous. Except for established stars such as the 'poster boys' Tom Purvis and E McKnight Kauffer, signing work was generally discouraged by clients and publishers, who wanted a stylish but standardised product. It was a strategy designed to keep payment rates common and low. The consequence was that, to ensure that they made a decent living, illustrators learned to produce work at speed. McConnell was faster than most.

McConnell may have been fast with a paintbrush and pen, but he was not a devotee of the 'fast life'. Despite adopting a new signature, 'Jas E McConnell', that suggested he was part of London's 'jazzy' culture, he resisted most of the city's temptations and its clubland. He later portrayed himself as something of a recluse – although his statement that he 'never met anybody anywhere, I just did my work, I sat down and did my drawing' was doubtless an exaggeration. He remained a countryman at heart: 'I used to enjoy gardening. I bought a house with a big garden.' That house was 'Katina', Nork Hill, Reigate Road in Epsom, a large commuter village in Surrey, 13 miles south-west of London, with regulation Surrey half-timbered and thatched buildings. This would become McConnell's marital home in December 1933 when he led his first bride, Adelaide Godfrey Bambridge, down the aisle;

A 1930s trade advertisement for Swains'.

and leafy Surrey would be his adopted county for the rest of his life. He moved from one village or small town to another over the years, and finally to 'Low Barbary', Amberley Lane, Milford.

By the early 1930s, as Britain went into recession following the American Stock Market crash, companies like Swains began to shed their costlier in-house illustrators in favour of commissioning work from the new art agencies, such as the fashionably modernist Clement Dane Studio, peopled largely by young male and female graduates of St Martin's, Chelsea, and of the Royal College of Art. 'I got the sack from Swains,' McConnell later recounted. 'All the block-makers started dismissing their artist staff. The studios started creeping up, and they were too much competition; so I went on my own then, freelance.'

The studios in question were groups of freelance artists working usually in their own or collective premises and using a central commissioning agent. Their work was praised in the annual *Posters and Publicity* in 1928:

McConnell's portrait of British cinema star Jack Buchanan, distributed as a film magazine insert in the early 1930s.

> 'In England the high standard of the work produced is to a considerable degree to the credit of the service agencies. They evince a power of co-ordinating various forms of advertising activity, of arranging campaigns and schemes with an expert knowledge of the value of each step and keen discrimination and good taste in their choice of designers to carry out their schemes. The high quality of the past year's work is one of the greatest evidences that the agencies have yet given in their own justification.'[14]

For the rest of the decade, McConnell rented a series of properties suitable for an artist's studio, none of them very far from his former workplace and all within walking distance of Fleet Street and the publishing quarter. The first was at 53-54 Chancery Lane, a couple of doors down from the studio that his contemporary Reginald Heade had recently vacated and almost adjacent to the paperback publishers Mellifont at number 60. (Perhaps surprisingly, Mellifont appear not to have made use of the services of either local artist.) One of the previous tenants was the illustrator Nat (Nathaniel) Long, with whom McConnell would soon share an agent. The Electoral Register for 1933 suggests that McConnell briefly used the studio as an official residence with Adelaide, his wife-to-be, before they moved into their Surrey home; but it remained McConnell's primary place of work throughout the 1930s.

> 'I had four or five different studios: I started in Chancery Lane, then New Court, then King Street, and then Queen Street. New Court was a big complex behind the Law Courts; all the artists' studios were on the top floor, and all the rest down below were solicitors' offices.'

It is notable that at least two of the properties

McConnell used as studios had associations with the legal profession. It is known that he joined the brotherhood of Freemasonry, perhaps following in the footsteps of his policeman father, and this may have enhanced his acceptability as a tenant for fellow Lodge members.

For a freelancer, a studio somewhere not far from the publishing hubs of Bloomsbury, Fleet Street and Paternoster Row was almost as essential as moving to London. 'The freelance artist will find it very difficult to keep busy if he works at home,' advised Maxwell-Foster. 'He is never handy when wanted for an urgent order, and, unless he takes a studio in a central position and installs the telephone, he will find that gradually he will drop out of the running as the men on the spot are more in evidence.'[16] For a while, McConnell managed without an artists' agent, continuing to fulfil commissions from Swains for its advertising clients. These included food and drink brands such as Chivers, Corona, Thorley's, Bird's and Dewars, as well as Salisbury's (accessories), Murphy's (radios) and the developers of Saltdean, the neo-village near Brighton. He illustrated a number of promotional and sales brochures for the latter development, including one for the now Grade-II listed, art-deco Saltdean Lido. He also turned his hand to 'story illustration in cheap women's magazines'. There were many of these weekly story magazines, printed on pulp paper and

Examples of the promotion of Saltdean in the 1930s. It is unknown if these particular pieces were painted by McConnell, but he worked extensively on the campaign.

illustrated with black-and-white line drawings: *Horner's Stories*, *Red Letter Magazine*, *Peg's Paper* and others. The illustrations were often unsigned, and it is difficult now to distinguish McConnell's contributions, as he was yet to develop a distinctive style.

McConnell's freelance workbook begins on 8 June 1933, with designs for 36 laundry marks for John Swain; illustrations for a 'Sea Shore' fashion spread for a women's magazine commissioned by Byron Studios of Farringdon Street; and a variety of advertising work for Creighton Griffiths, which appears to have been a Cardiff-based agency. After three weeks, he had earned almost £30, less £4 agent's commission; equivalent to about £1,300 today. At the time, it was just about a living wage for a man with two properties to pay for and a Christmas wedding in the offing. But his income began to increase in March 1934, when his advertising work was suddenly supplemented by earnings from a new source. By that summer, he was banking £50 to £60 per month, and more than two-thirds of his income was from commissions secured by a new agent, William Partridge.

Jackets to Suit

Based at 28 Rosebery Avenue in Clerkenwell, less than a mile north of McConnell's studio, before moving a few years later to Museum Mansions in Great Russell Street, Partridge was a book-trade insider. He received commissions for book jackets from London publishing houses such as Collins, Cassell and Hutchinson, who paid six to eight guineas for finished pieces of colour artwork. It may now sound paltry, but it was good remuneration at the time – an average week's wages for a couple of day's work or less. The increasingly lucrative nature of this emerging market for illustration had been noted in the journal *Commercial Art* in 1929:

Partridge's business card, late 1940s.

'To the commercial artist, the designing of book jackets opens a wide and welcome field, for the payment of many firms is generous and, when one comes to think of it, the general adoption of illustrated jackets has meant extra work for the illustrator, the block-maker and the printer, all of whom have been paid by the publisher and yet not one penny is added to the price of the book. An example of sales being increased through advertising giving you better value at no increase in cost.'[17]

Although he had painted a few film posters for Swains', the colourful book cover was a new type of work for McConnell, who had previously executed his commissions mainly in monochrome to suit the needs of the newspaper and magazine press. 'I was never a natural colourist,' he confessed. 'I had to work very hard at it. I worked on the ads for a long time with the old customers and then Partridge came along and saw me and got me entangled and I started to work on the book jackets.'

These remarks might suggest that the artist embarked on this new direction in his career without much confidence and largely out of necessity; but there is evidence to suggest that he had already dabbled in jacket illustration while still at Swains', either as part of his employment or as additional work in his spare time. Nevertheless, the advantages of having a well-connected agent are evident from this account from a publishing executive:

'A major trouble which the publisher suffers from to-day is the constant applications for work which are made by artists as a result of the increased use of designs on wrappers. My firm is asked to see half-a-dozen new artists every week and inspect their work; and the standard of work is indeed very good, although one should add that it usually is standard work and not very original. Nevertheless, it is rather heart-breaking to have to put off these young artists, for they are all under the illusion that having taken a course in commercial art they have only to call on the publishers and commissions for wrapper designs at remunerative rates will shower upon them.'[18]

But shower they did upon McConnell. As he became 'entangled' with William Partridge, the production of paintings for book covers took over his working life. Within a couple of years, his old freelance work for John Swain and Creighton Griffiths was only about 20 per cent of his output. McConnell was not the only artist in Partridge's web. The roster also included: two celebrated painters of women, Reginald Heade and Arthur Ferrier; the flower and still-life painters Laurence Biddle and E J Detmold; the cartoonist John Cameron; and jack-of-all-trades Nat Long.[19] Partridge was born in Salcombe, Devon in 1893, the son of a master mariner. He founded his agency in the 1920s and later diversified into children's book publishing. 'Partridge's was one of the premier agencies,' remembered McConnell. 'Partridge was a funny bloke. He used to lead a double life. I only found that out when he died. He had another bird he used to keep somewhere else. They only discovered it when they went through his stuff after he died.'

McConnell quickly built a reputation as a leading exponent of dust-jacket art. By the late 1930s, he was well enough regarded to be featured in a trade press advertisement endorsing the use of Reeves' gouache poster paint; an advertisement that supplied a rare portrait photograph of the artist. It was a relatively privileged position for an illustrator, as most of his contemporaries relied on line drawings for magazines and newspapers for their basic income, as an illustrator's agent pointed out:

'Almost every young artist, it seems to me, when he leaves art school, thinks he is an embryonic McKnight Kauffer ... If our youth were taught at

The late 1930s trade advertisement for Reeves' paints with a 'celebrity' endorsement from McConnell.

art school that for every one colour design sold there are innumerable black-and-white drawings of some sort or another, perhaps our art students would pay a little more attention to this branch of commercial art rather than concentrate on poster design, the supply of which is already more than adequate.'[20]

While he would produce the occasional line drawing throughout his subsequent career, McConnell would be lucky enough to receive a steady stream of commissions for colour work until his retirement in the 1970s. By then, his total output would number at least 2,500 paintings. He achieved this by staying mostly in good health (apart from a sensitive stomach) and by adopting a very disciplined attitude toward his life as an artist, working regular, if unsociable, hours. Maxwell-Foster, who recommended that 'an artist should tackle his job in the way any other professional man tackles his – that is, with clearness, purpose, and efficiency,' would have been proud of him.[21]

Having relocated to Surrey, McConnell joined the army of weekday commuters to the city, arriving at the street beside the Royal Courts of Justice before the host of lawyers and their clerks had even left home. This routine gave him an opportunity to familiarise himself with the novels that were the subjects of his covers:

> 'I used to read the books. I loved a book to read on the train. I particularly liked Westerns, because of the action. I never liked the love stories or gangsters, that sort of thing. Westerns I could read pretty quickly. There were some very good ones, too. I kept the good ones.'

By the late 1930s, McConnell was regularly earning around £550 per annum. Statistically equivalent to an average wage today, it might seem absurdly little for the amount of work involved and the exceptional talent required, but it was two to three times the average wage back then, at a time when a new Austin Seven motor car cost less than £200. Its property-buying power was very considerable when a semi in London's suburbia could be bought for less than £1,000. His was an income appropriate to a member of the middle class, above the average salary of a teacher. He had achieved social mobility, something still rare for the son of a working-class family. He also had a settled lifestyle as a happily married man who derived great pleasure and satisfaction from his freelance work and his gardening hobby. But, of course, the clouds of war were gathering, and McConnell responded to the growing threat by volunteering for the Air Raid Precautions (ARP) organisation, established by the Home Office in 1935. It would become the Civil Defence Service in 1941, incorporating air raid wardens, first aiders, firemen and fire watchers. Almost two million citizens would 'do their bit' in the Civil Defence Service by the end of the war, and it was particularly vital to London when the Blitz began. 'I was in civil defence before the war,' McConnell recalled, 'and I stayed in civil defence when the war started. I went full-time instead of joining the bloody army.' One wonders if he whiled away time reading (or even illustrating) Sutherland Scott's *The ARP Mystery*, published by Stanley Paul in the summer of 1939 and described by the *National Newsagent, Bookseller and Stationer*'s Tom Bookman (a pseudonymous J J Seeley) as a 'thoroughly up-to-date' story of 'death and mystery among the gas-masks in a London suburb'.[22]

Tom Bookman knew that the First World War had created a boom in the reading of novels, and when the new war with Germany was declared, he quickly detected an instant response to the publishing trade's slogan 'Books Brighten Blackouts'. 'Everywhere the libraries are getting an increased demand,' he

Above left: reading through the Blitz, London 1940. Above right: books for the blackout.

enthused, 'The newsagent never had so good an opportunity of making extra profit in these war days.'[23] McConnell was suddenly dealing with a rush of demand for his services, from the Collins publishing house in particular. His workbook reveals that between August and December 1939 he received more than £250 from the Partridge agency, suggesting that he may have painted more than 40 covers during that five-month period. He was probably still part-time with the ARP, but duties during the 'phoney war' months were lighter than they would soon become. His garden must have suffered some neglect, however. There were another 20-plus covers in the first three months of 1940. Nonetheless, his earnings for the year ending May 1940 were down by 20 per cent. It was the Dunkirk moment, and things were about to get very serious for the ARP. McConnell discontinued his workbook on 5 July 1940, at a point when his earnings from his work for Partridge constituted more than 95 per cent of his income. He would resume his records five years later in June 1945 when, presumably, he left the Civil Defence Service and was once again a full-time freelance artist.

But conveniently, and notwithstanding the onerous and frightening duties involved, Civil Defence was a service with a working pattern that actually allowed McConnell to carry on illustrating. His double life at that time is most appropriately commemorated by an eerily beautiful painting of barrage balloons floating above the cityscape for *London Front*, a book of letters to America in the months before the Blitz, published in late 1940 by Constable. There was a continuing but subdued demand from a publishing industry increasingly beset by paper restrictions. By VE Day, the number of titles being published in Britain was only a third of the pre-war figure; and the relatively small number of McConnell covers that have been identified from this period suggests that his volume of production was, understandably, significantly reduced. 'Civil defence was a day off and a day on,' he recalled, 'so I could work. I kept illustrating right through the war.' On the mornings of those days off, for much of the war, McConnell must have approached his

London Front by F Tennyson Jesse and H M Harwood (Constable, 1940)

studio with considerable trepidation: the City of London and the East End were the epicentre of the Luftwaffe's night-time bombing campaign, and he must have wondered if the latest raid had spared his workplace. Author Virginia Woolf recorded seeing damage to Chancery Lane in her diary in 1941: 'We went on to Gray's Inn. Left the car and saw Holborn. A vast gap at the top of Chancery Lane. Smoking still. Some great shop entirely destroyed: the hotel opposite like a shell. Heaps of blue green glass in the road at Chancery Lane.'[24]

The raid on Sunday 29 December 1940 was a devastating one for the publishing industry. The incendiary bombs rained on Paternoster Row near St Paul's Cathedral, the historic hub for publishers, packed with warehouses and offices, most notably those of Hutchinson, Collins and the book wholesalers Simpkin Marshall. Not only were thousands of books with McConnell jackets destroyed that night, but most likely dozens of pieces of his original artwork. It was estimated that five million books went up in flames in Paternoster Row; and another fifteen million were reduced to ashes in the rest of the London Blitz. The massive raid that sparked what was dubbed 'the Second Great Fire of London' also brought down buildings in Shoe Lane, the home of McConnell's erstwhile employer, Swains. The event is commemorated in the painting by a fellow artist, Leonard Rosoman, who was working as a fireman on the spot where the two firefighters depicted lost their lives. In all, fourteen of Rosoman's colleagues died that night, and his painting captures just the kind of dangers that would have been faced at times by ARP men like McConnell, whose principal task was to make bombed houses

Below left: *A House Collapsing on Two Firemen in Shoe Lane, London EC4*, a 1940 painting by fireman artist Leonard Rosoman. (Image courtesy the Imperial War Museum.) Below right: *Carol's Love Affair* by Rob Eden (Robert Hale, 1941): swirling smoke, damaged vehicles and injured women were part of the everyday experience of ARP workers.

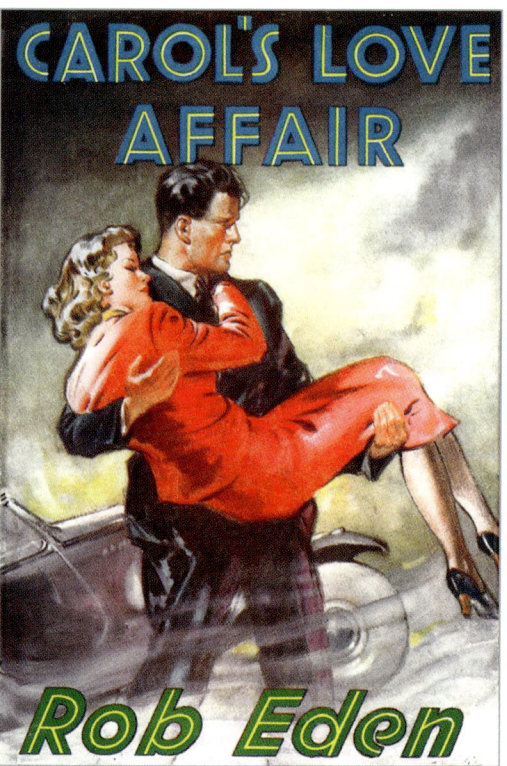

safe. 'Friendships from those days were long-lasting', his daughter Ann notes, 'and Dad frequently met his old friends for a pint. And he outlived them all.'

Painting in Peace

> 'Life itself has been so exciting during the past few years, so much more thrilling in many cases that almost any story hitherto written, that quite obviously the story that is going to provide an escape into unreality ... has got to be sufficiently colourful to hold a jaded mind.'
>
> Christine Campbell Thomson, 1946.[26]

John Sutherland, a leading historian of popular literature, has observed that, in the immediate post-war years, 'the British population wanted a Technicolor world where they might escape the grimly monochrome world outside the window.'[27] When material shortages allowed, McConnell's bright cover paintings would invite just this sort of escapist fantasy. Nevertheless, at the time, there were conservative elements in British society that came stumbling out of the wartime gloom and resented the dazzle created by painters of book covers. The venerable Sir Max Beerbohm, for instance, complained:

> 'To stand by any book-stall or to enter any book-shop is to witness a terrific scene of internecine warfare between the innumerable latest volumes, almost all of them violently vying with one another for one's attention, fiercely striving to outdo the rest in crudity of design and colour. It is rather like visiting the parrot-house in the Zoological Gardens, save that there one can at least stop one's ears with one's fingers, whereas here one merely wants to shut one's eyes.'[28]

But, for McConnell, the peacetime began with privation and tragedy. In 1946, the artist lost his wife, Adelaide, to cancer after 13 years of childless marriage, and his grief extended into the pitiless winter that followed. The coldest start to a year on record saw Britain's countryside frozen to a standstill for weeks, at a time of fuel shortages and all the other limitations of post-war austerity. Happily, the floods that inevitably accompanied the great thaw were dried by a hot summer, and McConnell's grief was assuaged by the love of a woman he had met during the war, when they were civil defence colleagues working from the same depot next to the Bricklayers Arms pub on Walton Heath, Surrey.

Rosina Lince was the daughter of a carter, whose team of horses carried him regularly between Tadworth, a picturesque village just south of McConnell's home, and the City of London. He died young from cancer but left his daughter Rosina with an abiding love for horses. She was 19 when the war began and was assigned to jobs previously thought of as 'men's work', specifically as a train guard and an ambulance driver, while her sister joined the WRENs. McConnell married the now 27-year-old Rosina in Tadworth on 27 September 1947. The couple would have three children – Patrick born in 1948, Maureen born in 1950 and Ann born in 1953 – and would live in 'Little Holland' on Church Road, Great Bookham, Surrey, less than five miles from McConnell's previous home and just a short walk from the railway station. It was ideal for his commute, and he made the most of it: 'I used to really enjoy work. I used to get the 5.59 train in the morning from Bookham and the two o'clock train back.' He spent the rest of the afternoon doing his gardening, and lavished considerable time and energy on his new home, as Ann recalls:

> 'The house in Bookham was originally fairly small – hall, three bedrooms, bathroom, kitchen and lounge – but

Above: Rosina McConnell, pictured in the late 1940s. Below: Wedding day for James and Rosina in Tadworth, 1947. (Both images courtesy Ann McConnell.)

he extended it on all sides and built a garage. The old windows were made into a summerhouse. He also built a greenhouse, the horse's stable, then his studio and woodshed. He could turn his hand to anything and was always the perfectionist. It's incredible looking back, just how much work he did there, along with an immaculate pond and garden and an incredibly productive vegetable garden. I can remember wheelbarrow-loads of runner beans being given to all the neighbours.

'What can I say about our childhood days except that they were idyllic, with a third of an acre garden and the huge expanse of Bookham Common right on our doorstep. Family days out to the coast and holidays, usually at Bognor Regis or Felpham. It really was another world then.'

The family would ride horses on the Common, every year crossing it to attend the annual sports day at McConnell's favourite public house, The Cricketers, a 17th Century, half-timbered inn at Downside, near Cobham. There, he and his drinking buddy, Bob, kept their own ceramic tankards for a beer after a long day's work.

McConnell's main publisher clients in the first two years of the peace were Collins and Martin & Reid. A publishing phoenix risen from the ashes of Paternoster Row, Collins, like Cassell, was a staple client of his throughout most of his working life. Between them, they commissioned more than 300 dust jacket paintings from him. Martin & Reid, on the other hand, was a new publishing venture, established in the second half of 1945, which could indicate that it was one of many businesses set up by demobilised servicemen. Certainly one of its principal writers, illustrators

The McConnells at the christening of their first child, Patrick, at Bookham in 1948. Seated in front of James and Rosina are Rosina's mother and James's father. (Image courtesy Ann McConnell.)

and editors, Mick Anglo, had just been demobbed from the army. The Martin of the partnership may have been an ex-employee of Partridge, the same man who would establish the agency John Martin and Artists with Bill Bowen-Davies, the brother of another ex-Partridge employee, the young Tony Bowen-Davies, after the death of his employer in the early 1950s. Martin & Reid launched Arrow Books, a larger-format pulp-paperback imprint anticipating the deluge of British pulp fiction that would flood newsagents' shelves over the next few years. Partridge began to cast his net into this flow of low-cost genre fiction (Western, crime, romance and space) for a primarily working-class readership: 120-page quick reads that sometimes pushed the boundaries of propriety in their treatment of sex and violence. Like Reginald Heade, another Partridge artist, McConnell was also soon illustrating covers for Raymond and Lillian Locker's Archer Books, but specialising in

scenes for Westerns, which he also supplied for Hamilton, Scion, T V Boardman and Hector Kelly's Robin Hood Press. In this way, he differentiated his work from that of Heade, who found that his special talent for the erotic or romantic depiction of women was in increasing demand.

In six years, McConnell would paint upwards of 170 covers for the pulp paperback trade. His specialisation in Western covers meant that he avoided the predicament of his fellow illustrator Len Gard, who was prosecuted at The Old Bailey in 1954 for painting the covers for *Soho Street Girl*, *Academy of Love* and *The Big Sin*, all published by Kaye Books. The prosecution contended: 'What goes on the outside of a book – namely the picture on the cover – has an important bearing in connection with the book itself'; but the jury was unconvinced, and may have accepted Gard's defence that he had painted the covers before the books were written. He was acquitted of conspiracy to publish obscene libels, while the Kaye brothers went to jail and the authors and printers were fined.[29]

Ironically, McConnell did paint the cover for a book that was the subject of a successful obscenity prosecution around the same time as the Gard case, but it was a dust jacket for a hardback novel from a 'respectable' publisher rather than a cover for a pulp paperback. In December 1952, McConnell painted a Headean pin-up cover for *Julia*, a spicy romance involving a married American GI and a British woman, written under the pseudonym Margot Bland by Kathryn Dyson-Taylor, the American wife of an insurance broker living in London's Berkeley Square. The book was first the subject of a prosecution of Boots lending library at Douglas on the Isle of Man, where a nominal fine of £1 was imposed because of the high reputation of the publisher, T Werner Laurie. Typically, Boots removed the dust jackets from its books, so the issue of McConnell's cover illustration did not arise. But 1953-54 was a highly censorious period for the book trade, and a further

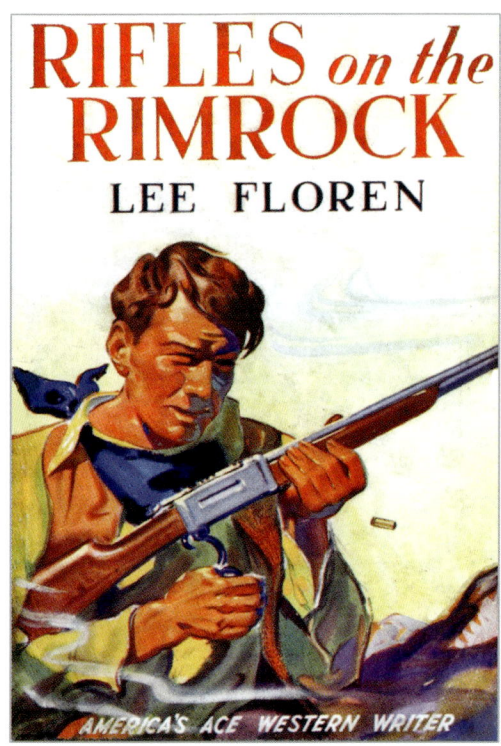

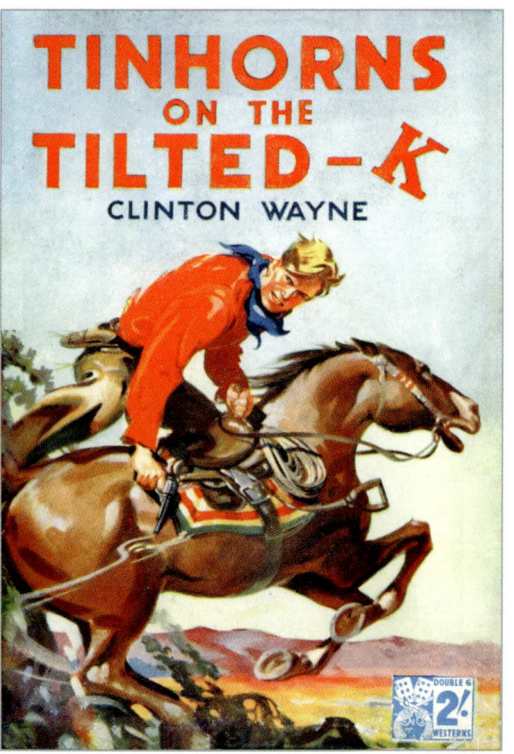

Four of McConnell's celebrated paperback covers: Top left: *Complete Stories* (Martin & Reid, 1946); painted February 1946. Top right: *Rifles on the Rimrock* by Lee Floren (Archer, 1948); painted August 1948. Bottom left: *Drygulched!* by Webb Anders (Scion, 1952); painted June 1951. Bottom right: *Tinhorns on the Tilted-K* by Clinton Wayne (Robin Hood, 1949); painted December 1948. (Latter image courtesy Jim Kealy.)

Julia by Margot Bland (T Werner Laurie, 1953); painted December 1952. The book had first and second edition print runs of 3,500, considerably lower than those ordered by the pulp paperback publishers.

the stewardship of Tony Bowen-Davies. When Tony became art director at Pan, his artists were passed to John Martin and Artists, run by brother Bill.

With the slow easing of paper restrictions, book production had struggled back to pre-war levels in the 1950s, but the number of fiction titles never matched the 5,000 per year published in the 1930s. However, the trade statistics excluded much of the output of those fiction publishers that distributed their wares exclusively through newsagents and market traders, rather than through bookshops. The prime example was Amalgamated Press, a leading periodical publisher with a portfolio of digest-size 'story papers', fortnightly novellas mostly aimed at teenagers – the Sexton Blake Library, Thriller Picture Library, Super Detective Library, Western Library and Cowboy Comics Library – often accompanied annually by larger format hardbacks. From early in 1950, and for the following 11 years, painting covers for these libraries provided McConnell's staple income. His tireless brush strokes created

prosecution against the author and publisher was brought at Clerkenwell Court in May 1954, a fate that was probably ensured when the publisher provocatively printed a second edition after the Douglas verdict. Even so, the guilty pleas submitted by the accused parties resulted not in the prison sentences handed down to the less respectable Kaye brothers, but in relatively light fines. It was a shot across the bows for the mainstream publishing trade, lest it decided to take a leaf out of the book of the pulp fictioneers.[30]

The response of McConnell, Heade, and some of their fellow artists to the hostile environment created by police persecution was to set up a new agency, Artists Ltd, under

Below: an October 1957 trade advert for Amalgamated Press annuals; both had McConnell covers.

A September 1955 trade advert for the Amalgamated Press libraries.

more than 250 covers for Amalgamated Press, peaking during 1957 and 1958 with 91.

A Plenitude of Paperbacks

> 'More people than ever will be going on holidays this year, and buying paper-backs to read as they travel, or take things easy … Start now, and keep up stocks and displays, to make the most of this profitable market. Big development in recent months in the paper-back market has been the ousting of the bosoms brigade by non-fiction war books of all kinds. Novels with scantily-clad females on the jacket are being pushed into the background by sales of war books, and this development is likely to continue, for this season at least, stimulated by such films as *The Dam Busters*.'
>
> Stephen Mogridge, 1955.[31]

The obscenity prosecutions of 1954 caused the pulp fiction publishers to adjust their commissioning policies and business plans. Hamilton & Co enhanced its branding of Panther Books; Brown Watson launched its Digit imprint; and all virtually eliminated the spicy romances from their lists and shifted the format of their products to the smaller size already popularised by Penguin, Pan and Corgi. After ten years of post-war recovery, there was also a vogue for revisiting the events and untold stories of the war. McConnell was not much in demand for military subjects, but toward the end of 1954, among the handful of film posters recorded in his workbook were two for *The Dam Busters* (1955) – although it appears that the film's producers, Associated British Picture Corporation (ABPC), did not use these for the general release campaign.

Despite accounting for less than a quarter of the almost 20,000 books published in 1955, paperbacks had by then come to dominate

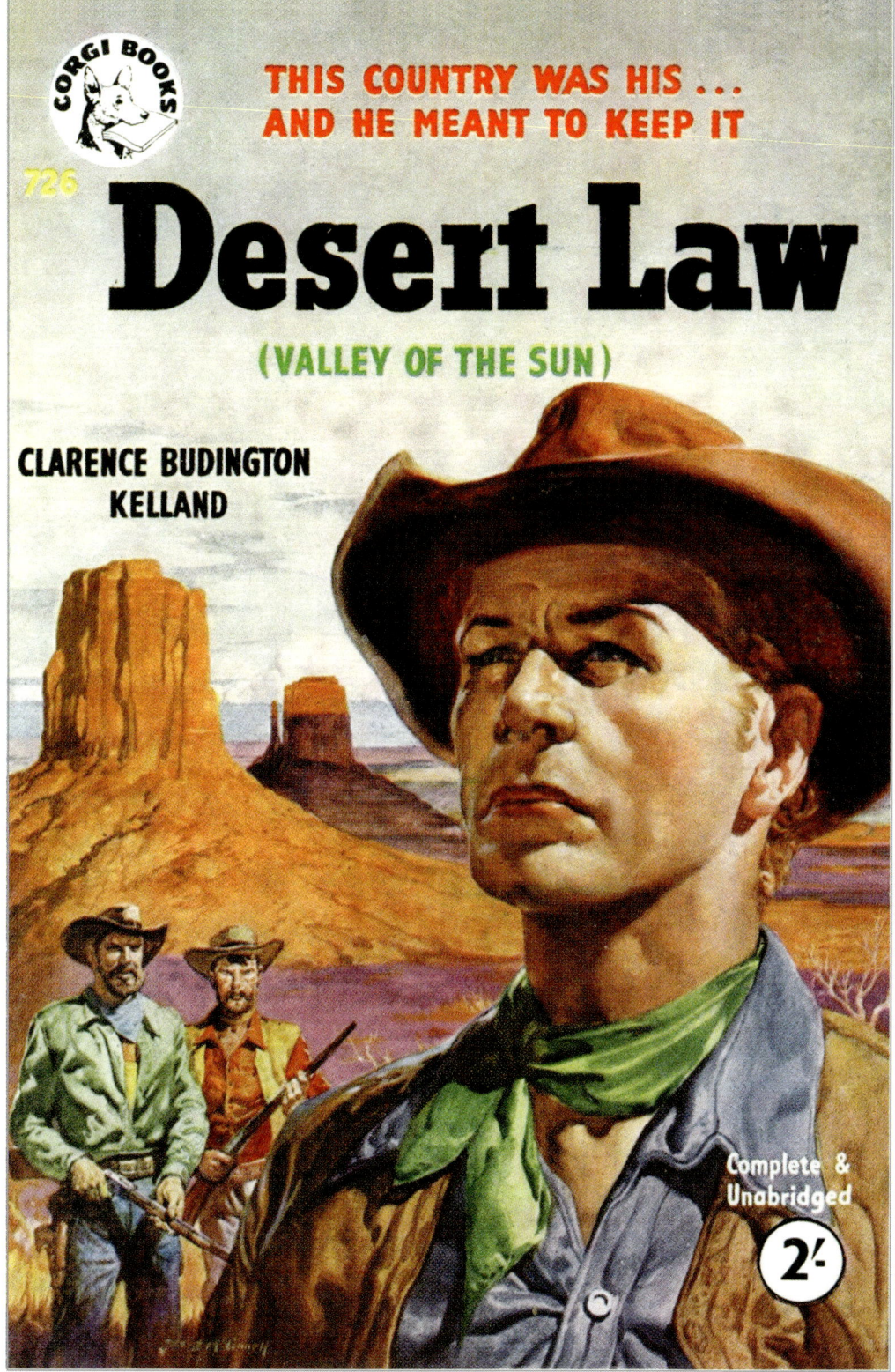

Desert Law by Clarence Budington Kelland (Corgi 726, 1954); painted October 1953. McConnell's second cover for Corgi, commissioned a year after his first.

A very rare poster promoting Corgi's July 1959 publications, including an image of McConnell's cover for *Unarmed Killer* by C William Harrison (Corgi T708, 1959), painted January 1959 (see opposite). (Author's collection.)

volume sales in the trade. A survey in the *Financial Times* revealed that more than half the books sold in the UK were softcovers, and they were the format of choice for younger customers. When it came to novels, the vast majority of sales were of paperbacks. Penguin and Pan led the field with annual sales of around ten million books each. Corgi was not far behind with six million. These companies were publishing fifteen or twenty new titles per month, often with print runs of 250,000, dwarfing the 10,000 to 50,000 runs of the now largely defunct pulp publishing houses.[32] Established publishers, such as Collins and Hutchinson, who had reprinted their more successful novels as pulp paperbacks during the inter-war years, were also now launching new, carefully-branded paperback imprints (Fontana and Arrow respectively). Cover art was regarded as even more important to the inexpensive paperback than it was to the pricier first edition hardback, and it was appropriately remunerated. 'Corgi used to pay £50 a cover,' McConnell remembered. 'I was a very fast worker, and I used to do two or three a week sometimes for Corgi. But I was very conscientious – I didn't get many turned down. Hardly any at all, in fact.'

In the course of ten years, McConnell painted at least 118 covers for Corgi, nearly three-quarters of them between 1957 and 1960. In that four year period he also supplied 30 covers for Pan; and in the following two he added a further 15 – although not all of his paintings were used. As Colin Larkin has explained in his book *Cover Me*, painting for Pan was possible only if the artist was signed to the agency, John Martin and Artists, that was favoured by Pan's art editor, Tony Bowen-Davies. McConnell's first paintings for Pan via that agency came in November 1957, a month after the death of Reginald Heade, who had been one of the imprint's premier illustrators for the previous year or two. Essentially, McConnell became a replacement for Heade, painting in painstaking detail and adopting a similar subdued and muted colour palette.

He also inherited commissions that might well have gone to the other artist, had he lived: *Eliza Callaghan*, *Riot* and *Opium Venture*, for example. For both artists, their work for Pan demonstrated their range and versatility, as well as their impressive painterly ability in a subtler register. Nevertheless, it was his work for Corgi that McConnell found more memorable and enjoyable, probably because the subject matter, with its preponderance of rugged cowboys and galloping horses, was more to his taste.

Somehow, though, in 1957 and 1958 McConnell managed to take time out from his increasingly lucrative work for this expanding paperback market to meticulously illustrate the American Roll of Honour for St Paul's Cathedral. It was a demanding commission, as he recalled:

Unarmed Killer by C William Harrison (Corgi T708, 1959); painted January 1959.

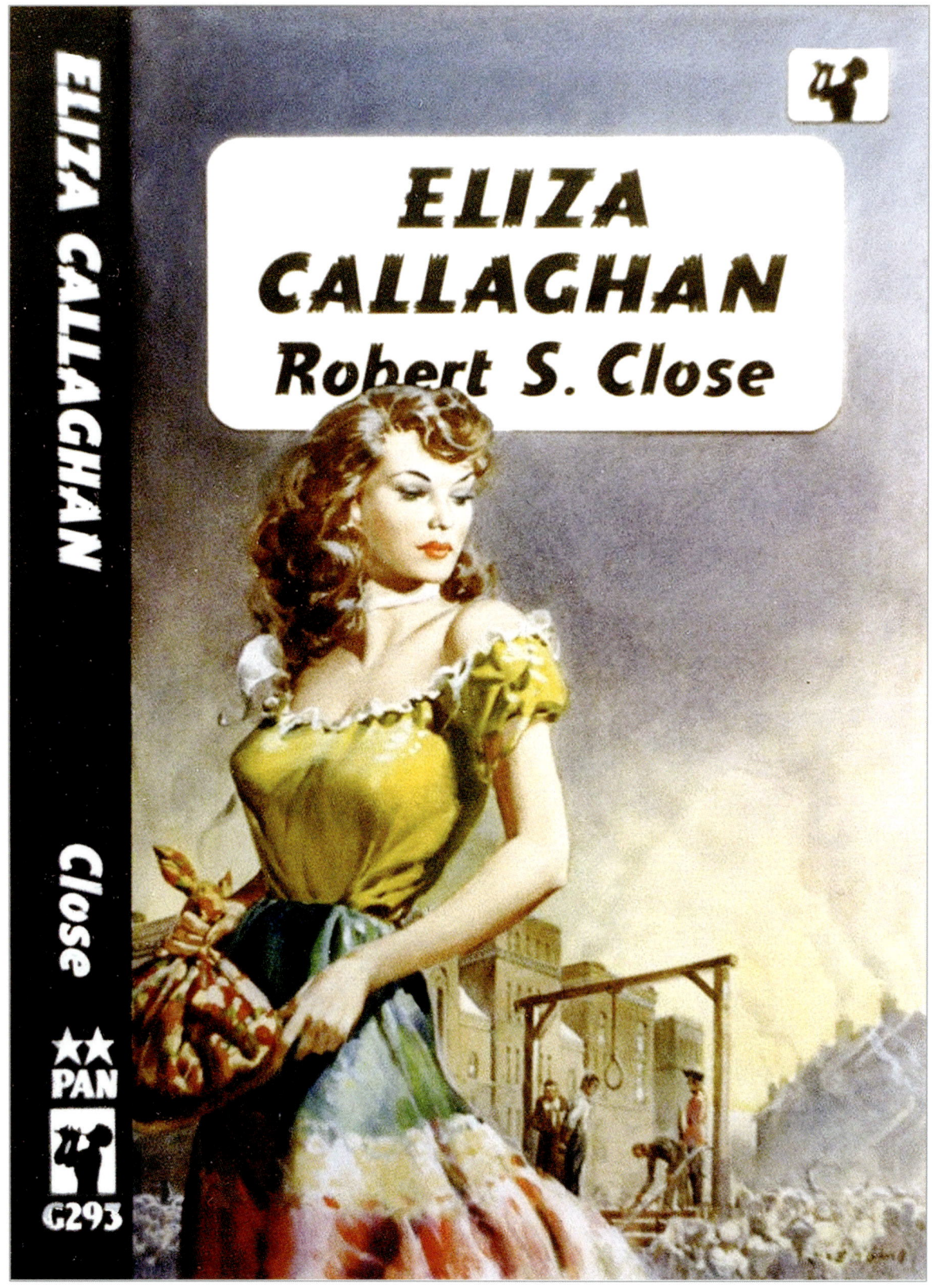

Original artwork for *Eliza Callaghan* by Robert S Close (Pan G293, 1959); painted November 1958. (Author's collection.)

'The American Government got in touch with me through an artist in America. It's a bound book that illustrates all different aspects of the war. They turn a page every day in St Paul's. I haven't seen the book at all since it was finished. It was all done on vellum, and very hard work that was. Painting on vellum: you couldn't do anything twice, you had to let it dry first.'

McConnell had also begun to diversify outputs, working on more expansive paintings for jigsaw puzzles from Philmar (Amex), Tower Press and Strome, together with box-tops for other kinds of children's puzzles and games. This had started in 1952, but the commissioning rate grew significantly from 1959, when Philmar in particular were increasing the size and number of pieces of their jigsaws and seeking more 'cinematic', wide-screen scenes. McConnell supplied images of modern ceremonials and historical pageantry, full of epic splendour, no doubt inspired by the CinemaScope version of *Ben-Hur* released that same year; we have already noted that he painted the cover for Pan's paperback edition of the latter (see page 25), but that piece was in standard 'portrait' format. The jigsaws were the gateway to the final phase of McConnell's career as an illustrator for young people.

By June 1960, the paperback revolution had thoroughly transformed the publishing world. There were 6,337 paperback titles in print in Britain, almost half of which total was

Example pages from the American Roll of Honour, held in St Paul's Cathedral, London.

Old Hampton Court, a Criterion jigsaw puzzle (Philmar, 1960); painted February 1960. Just one of numerous jigsaw illustrations that McConnell completed.

accounted for by fiction titles, including books from 34 British-based publishers of popular fiction. Crime was the dominant genre (23% of all paperback fiction titles), followed by Westerns, war stories, historical fiction and love stories, with science fiction providing the fewest titles (2%) (see table).

Within 12 months, there were 7,882 paperbacks in print. On the face of it, these were good times for the cover artist; but there were problems ahead.[33] Traditional figurative representation of the type at which McConnell excelled was increasingly held in low esteem. By around 1963, even the publishers that had encouraged its refinement into something resembling hyper-realism – Pan and Corgi, for example – had decided that it was yesterday's style, and were replacing it with faster and cheaper photography, stylised vignettes, or simply typography. Television viewing was steadily eating into the leisure time the public had available for book reading, and publishers' profit-margins were under threat. Panther was not the only imprint to make economies by

PAPERBACK FICTION TITLES IN PRINT, JUNE 1960	
General fiction	934 (32%)
Crime fiction	665 (23%)
Western fiction	245 (8%)
War fiction	183 (6%)
Historical fiction	104 (4%)
Romantic fiction	96 (3%)
Children's fiction	76 (3%)
Science fiction	62 (2%)
Short stories	53 (2%)

Total: 2,918

importing second-hand imagery from abroad, as its early 1960s art director, Peter Green, recalled: 'We started to buy in transparencies of American covers for Westerns. The Americans had some very good artists, and at £17 to £20 they were cheaper than commissioning a jacket. We even used some Spanish material.'[34]

Throughout the late 1940s and into the early 1960s, McConnell continued to rent his London studio at 6 New Court, where the large majority of his book covers were produced. Day in, day out, he would rise before dawn and catch the early train to London's Waterloo Station and cross the Thames to the city's law courts district between the Strand and the river. New Court was a pleasant and sequestered area away from the hustle and bustle, where for a decade and a half the artist was able to pursue a commercial fantasy life that transported him to the prairies and deserts of the old West; the jungles of Africa; the dark streets of Chicago and New York; and on to the mountains of Mars. All were imagined and brought vividly to life by a brush wielded in an upper room above the wigs and gowns of law practitioners.

But arrangements were about to change, as his daughter Ann recalled: 'Dad moved from the studio around about 1965 to another, top floor again (Mum and I helped him move), in King Street in Covent Garden.' The street was at the North-East corner of what was then still a wholesale vegetable and flower market, before its conversion to a tourist attraction. McConnell would briefly move again to Queen Street, South of St Paul's; but this lengthened a commute for which he had a steadily dwindling appetite. As he reached his mid-sixties, the conventional age for retirement, he could no longer tolerate the daily separation from his beloved Surrey flora: 'I built a studio in my garden and worked from there,' he remembered. 'I used to start at 5.00 or 6.00 in the morning, first thing. I always worked better in the mornings, and gradually faded out. I got mentally tired after five or six hours – I could not do any more, it would have been a waste of time to do any more.' His daughter dates his working from the home studio to around 1969. 'It was like a fridge in there in the winter,' she recalls, 'and how he managed to work is beyond me!'

McConnell's commissions changed with the times. By the 1960s, his dust jackets were largely restricted to a few companies without paperback imprints, such as Alvin Redman; and as the entire market for illustrated book covers continued to contract through the early years of the decade, his only refuge was publications for children and young people. This readership, it was believed, were prepared to study the detailed image and valued the imaginary world it evoked. The Look and Learn Picture Archive

Original artwork for *Opium Venture* by Gerald Sparrow (Pan G333, 1959); painted February 1959. (Author's collection.)

Above: McConnell's ambitious composition for a piece entitled *The Money Lenders*, which appeared in *Bible Stories* #3 (Fleetway Publications, 21 March 1964). Below: the original artwork for one of McConnell's two black-and-white illustrations accompanying a story called *Bear Trap!* in *Look and Learn* #303 (Fleetway Publications, 4 November 1967). (Both images courtesy Jim Kealy.)

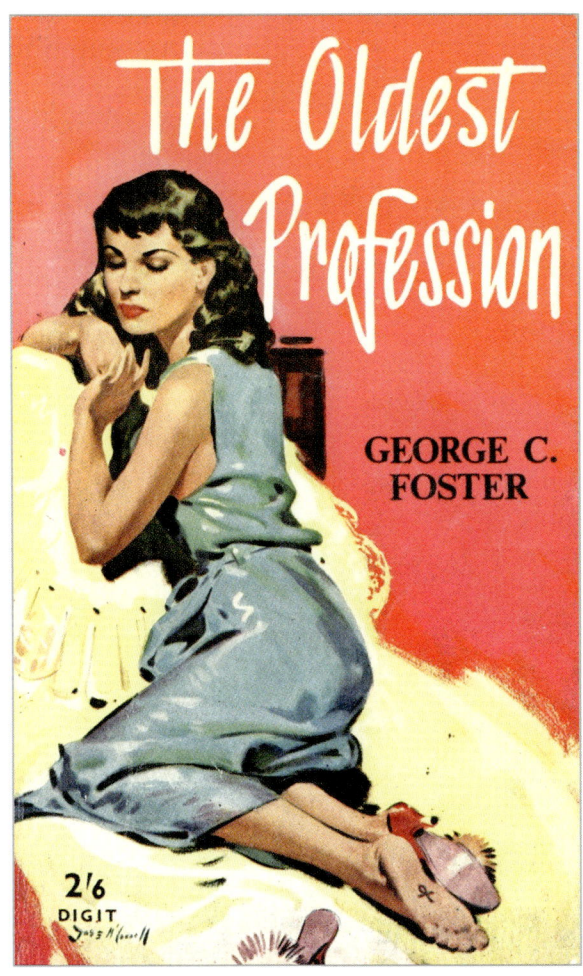

Digit was another leading paperback imprint that regularly used McConnell's services. For *The Oldest Profession* by George C Foster (Digit R510, 1961), painted February 1961, he cleverly undercut the subject's eroticism with poignancy by allowing the discarded slipper to reveal the foot tattoo.

and Learn's regular weekly circulation of about 300,000 brought McConnell's talent to a huge audience, most of them young people aged 10 to 15 years. With additional work on Fleetway's children's annuals and further jigsaw designs, the regular and demanding historical illustrations – which always required robust research – took McConnell through to retirement. Corgi gave him nostalgic send-off by repurposing some of his paintings for a short series of cowboy novels by Frank O'Rourke.

It was a fitting conclusion to a career for a man from the North, who had moved to the more genteel South, but had spent so much of his time imagining the Wild West.

After the Fine Weather by Michael Gilbert (Hodder, 1965), painted February 1965, was probably McConnell's final paperback cover painting. (Image courtesy Jim Kealy.)

contains in excess of 500 illustrations that McConnell produced during the 1960s and 1970s for the *Bible Stories, Ranger* and *Look and Learn* titles of Fleetway Publications (formerly Amalgamated Press). Close to 100 of these were cover pieces.[35] Of course, the artist had illustrated for younger consumers before, especially with his work on the Amalgamated Press's pocket-sized picture libraries in the 1950s; but the paintings for these Fleetway educational papers were often in larger format and with a wider-ranging subject-matter. *Look*

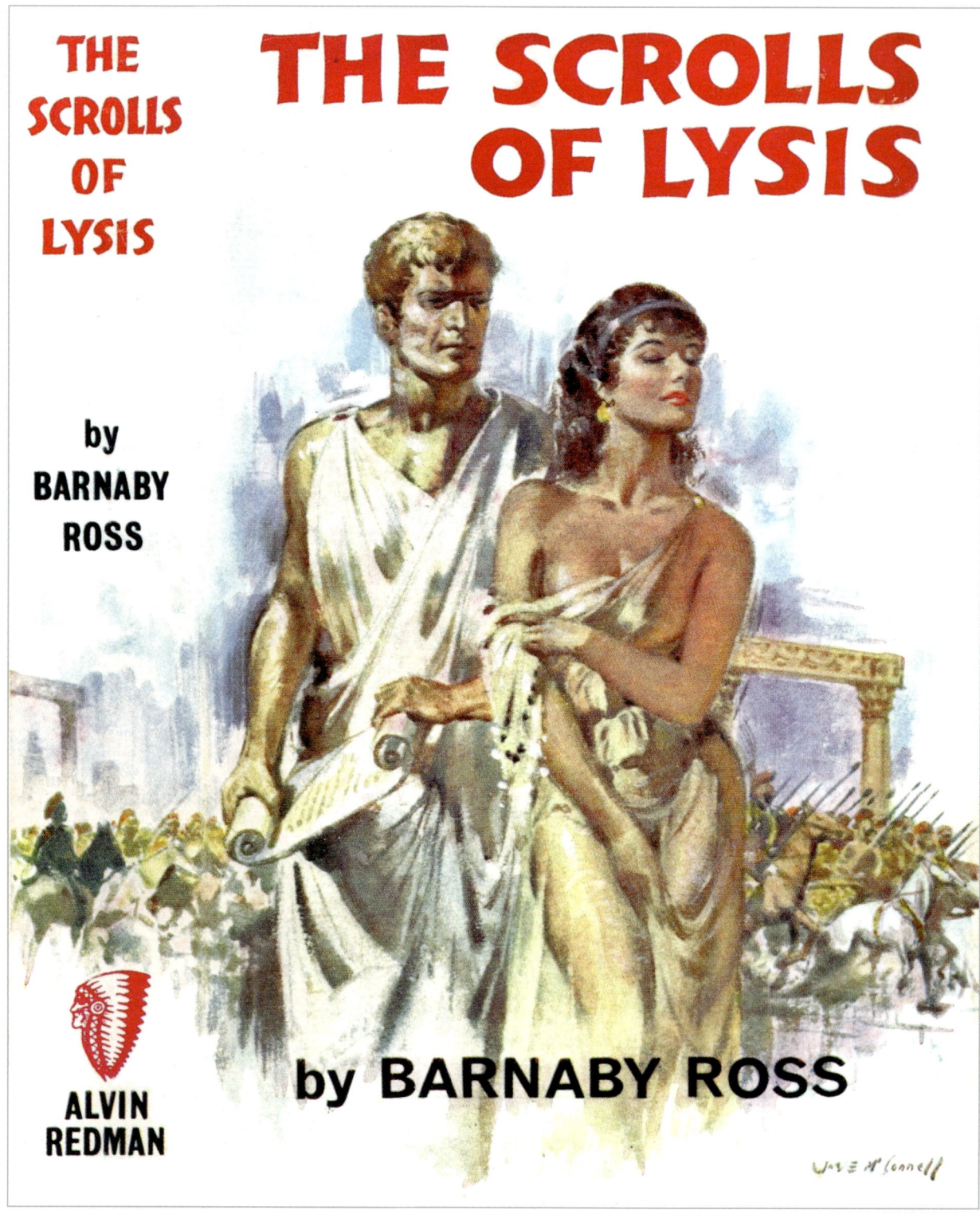

The Scrolls of Lysis by Barnaby Ross (Alvin Redman, 1964); painted October 1963. A typical example of McConnell's mid-1960s dust jackets.

PUBLISHER	McCONNELL'S POST-WAR BOOK COVER PAINTINGS (publication years 19...)												TOTAL
	45/46	47/48	49/50	51/52	53/54	55/56	57/58	59/60	61/62	63/64	65/66	67/68	
W H Allen				20	29	6	11						66
Amalgamated Press			21	50	25	54	91	11	4	1	1		258
Ernest Benn						1							1
Birn Brothers		3	1	2	1								7
Boardman			13	38	6								57
Bodley Head						3							3
Cassell	4	14	17	16	23	35	14	5	9	6		1	144
Chapman and Hall	1												1
Collins	31	26	24	24	22	11		3					141
Corgi (Transworld)				1	4	12	25	57	20				119
Dakers				2	1								3
John Dennis				2									2
Digit							11	7	22				40
Eldon	1		1										2
Fiction House				43	28	20	4						95
Foulsham	1	1	2	4	4	3	2						17
Four Square							5	8	5				18
Gannet					9								9
Gaywood		1											1
John Gifford					6	5	2						13
Guild				1	6								7
Robert Hale				1	19	25	9	5	4	2			65
Hamiltons / Panther			21	12			2		1				36
Harrap / Hennel Locke			4	8	1	2	1						16
Hodder & Stoughton	1		1			1					1		4
Grant Hughes		2	3										5
Hulton / Eagle							1	1					2
Hutchinson Group	2		2	8	32	53	23	7	19	6	7	4	163
Kemsley / Cherry Tree				4									4
Livingstone		1											1
R & L Locker / Archer		13	2										15
Longmans Green	1												1
Lutterworth			2										2
Macdonald					2	3							5
Martin & Reid	10	2											12
Mills & Boon				1	18	20	1		1				41
Alexander Moring						2							2
Frederick Muller	2												2
John Murray								2					2
Museum Press					4								4
Peter Nevill						1							1
News of the World / Pocket					8								8
Pan							9	21	15				45
Partridge	6			1	4								11
Arthur Pearson							16	8					24
Pickering & Inglis	1		1										2
Alvin Redman						4	1	7	12	17	4		45
Robin Hood / Peveril		1	9	1									11
Scion			12	28									40
Selwyn & Blount	1												1
Thames / Juvenile	4	6	5	7	5	1	3						31
Rafael Tuck	2												2
Ward Lock				4	18	20	7	2					51
Warne					6								6
Werner Laurie			1	1	1								3
WDL / Consul									4				4
World's Work			1	1					1				3
Other / unidentified	4	2	9	6	1	1		1	6				30
TOTAL	72	73	156	303	283	268	233	143	123	32	13	5	1704

GALLERY

PAINTING IN WARTIME: *Straight Runs Harley Street* by Philip Inman (Chapman and Hall, 1942). Exquisitely rendered in perspective and sensitively lettered. (Image courtesy Jim Kealy.)

GALLERY

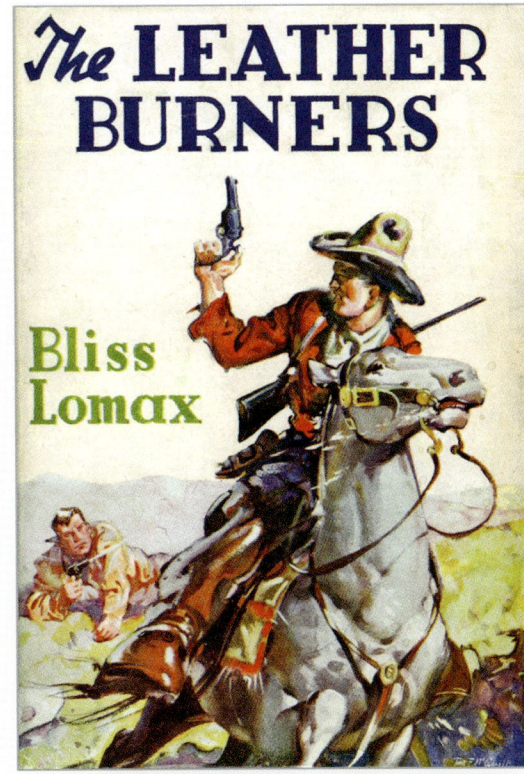

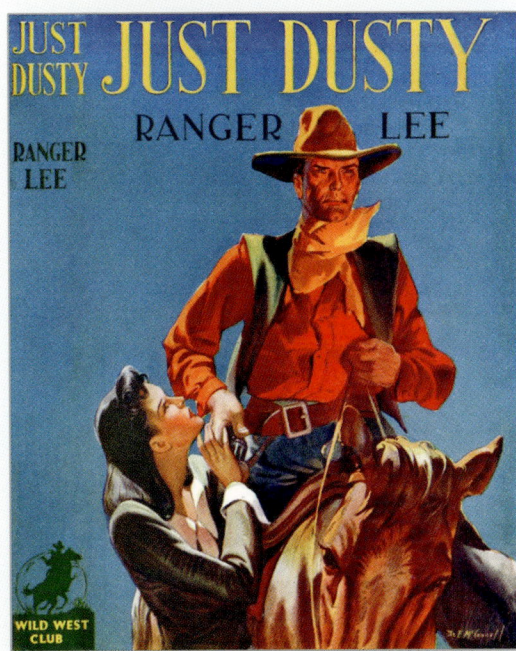

PAINTING IN WARTIME: Top left: *Murder in the Coal Hole* by Miles Burton (Collins Crime Club, 1940), showcasing McConnell's talent for dramatic lighting. Top right: *The Leather Burners* by Bliss Lomax (Frederick Muller, 1941), depicting action in the pulp tradition, with flying horse sweat. Bottom left: *Trapped by Love* by Rob Eden (Robert Hale, 1941), a scene of sadness and cityscape, with the removed hat enhancing the realism of the composition. Bottom right: *Just Dusty* by Ranger Lee (Collins Wild West Club, 1944), with 'magic hour' lighting and a man on a mission. (*Trapped by Love* and *Just Dusty* images courtesy Jim Kealy.)

PAINTING IN WARTIME: *Mail for McNair* by Sanford Lock (Hutchinson, 1940) employs the back-lighting effect that McConnell sometimes used in the 1940s.

GALLERY

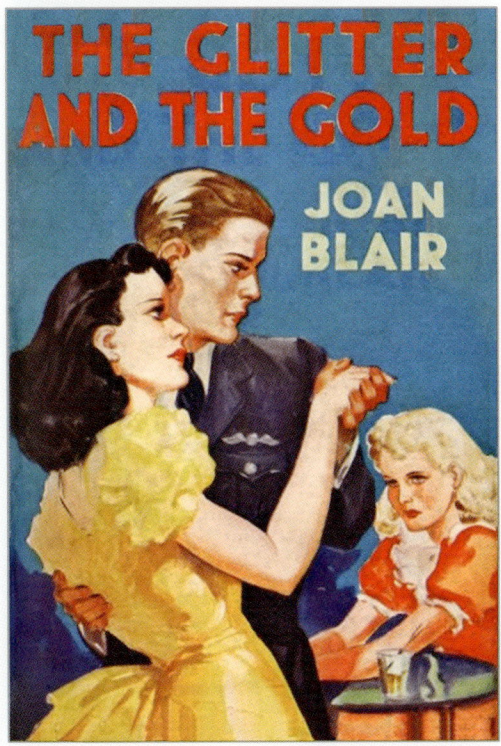

PAINTING IN WARTIME: Top: two paintings that adopt very different techniques for Anne Duffield novels, *The Inscrutable Nymph* (Cassell, 1942) (left) and *Sunrise* (Cassell, 1944) (right). Bottom: two romance covers depicting love triangles involving very similar blondes, Joan Blair's *The Glitter and the Gold* (Mills & Boon 1940) (left) and Lilian Chisholm's *Afraid to Dream* (Mills & Boon, 1941) (right).

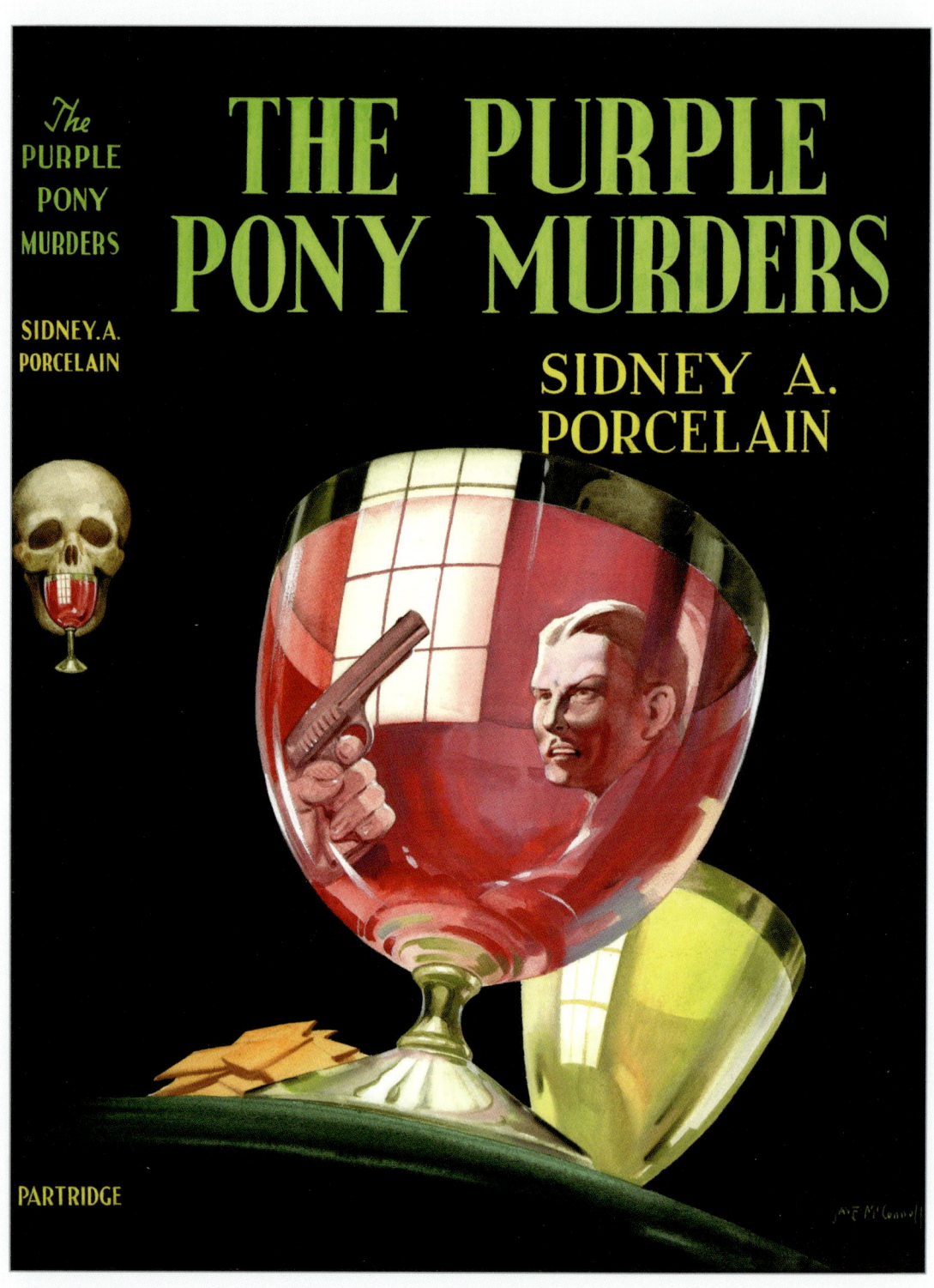

PAINTING IN PEACETIME: Original artwork for *The Purple Pony Murders* by Sidney A Porcelain (Partridge, 1948); painted April 1946. An unusual composition and highly accomplished technique. (Author's collection.)

GALLERY

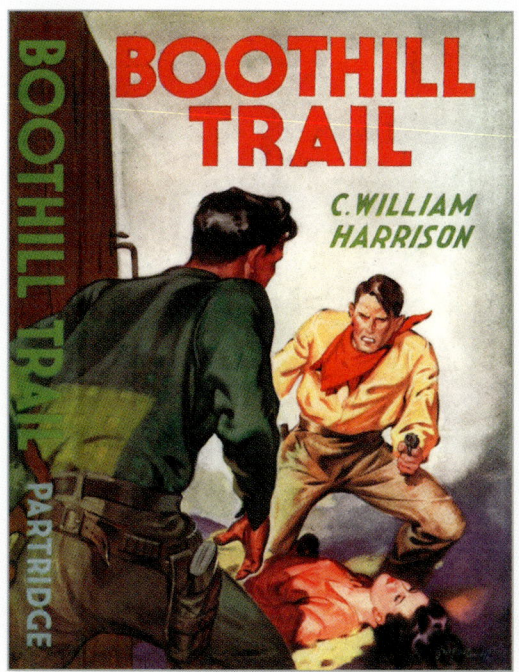
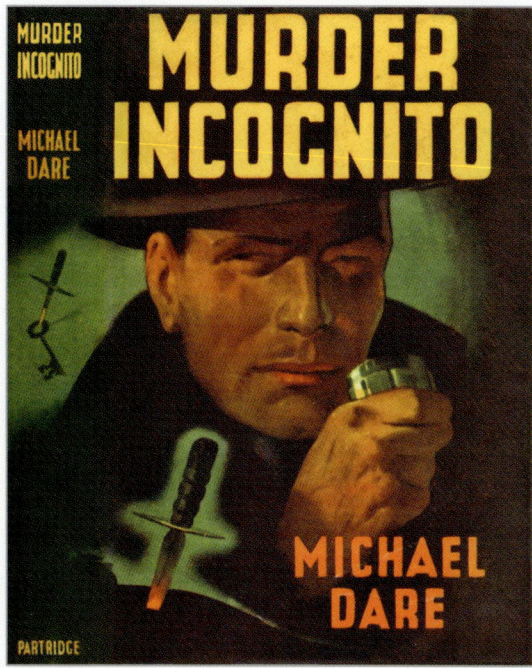

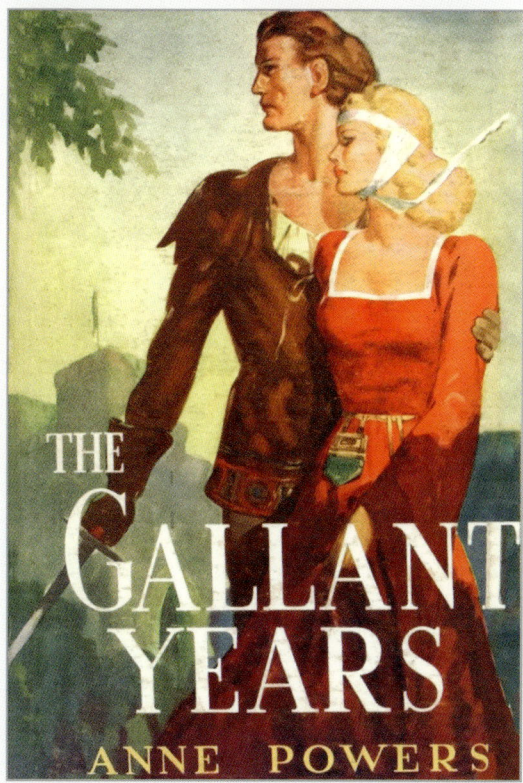

PAINTING IN PEACETIME: Further examples of McConnell's work for Partridge, demonstrating his versatility and willingness to experiment with style and composition. Top left: *Boothill Trail* by C William Harrison (1946); painted September 1945. Top right: *Murder Incognito* by Michael Dare (1947); painted April 1946. Bottom left: *Trouble at Hanard* by Vivian Beynon-Harris (1948); painted September 1946. Bottom right: *The Gallant Years* by Anne Powers (1949); painted June 1946.

PAINTING IN PEACETIME: Martin & Reid was one of the first of the post-war 'mushroom' publishers. The Arrow and Mascot series were thin booklets that evidenced the paper rationing of the time. Above: *The Case of the Innocent Wife* by Nigel Morland (Martin & Reid, 1947), painted November 1945.

GALLERY

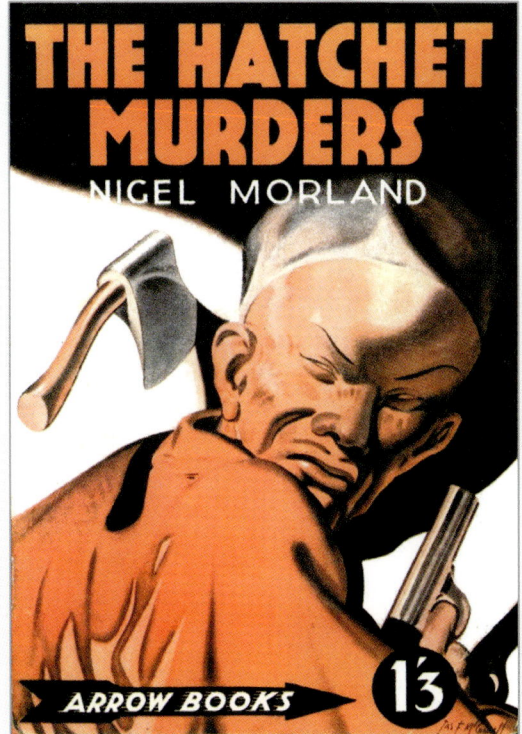
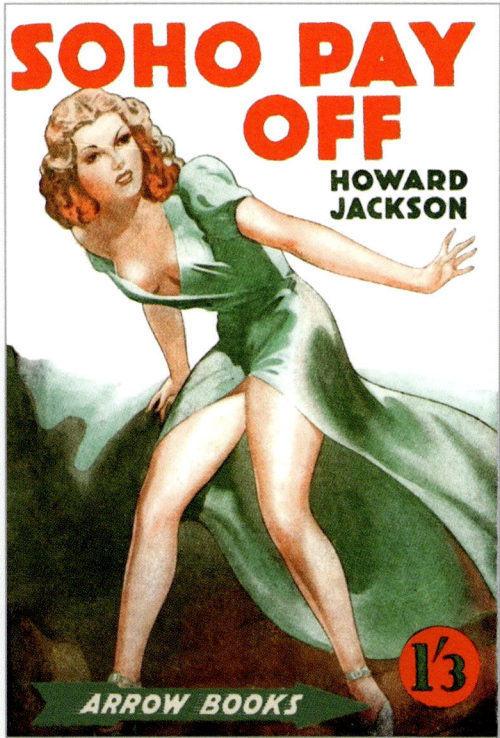
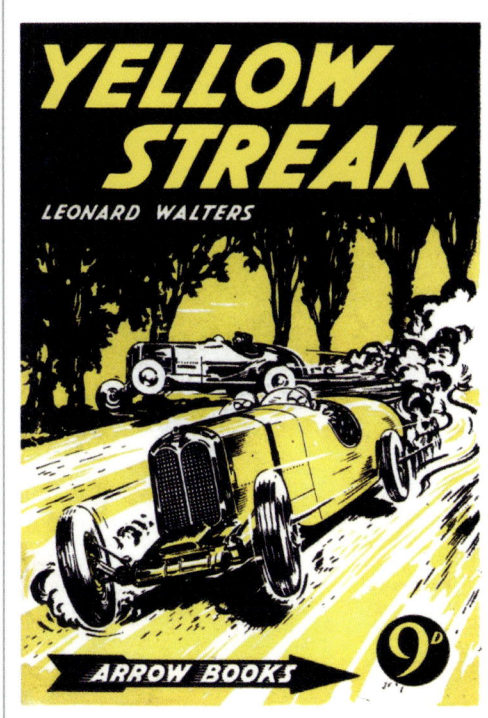

PAINTING IN PEACETIME: Top left: *The Hatchet Murders* by Nigel Morland (Martin & Reid, 1947); painted October 1945. Top right: *Soho Pay Off* by Howard Jackson (Martin & Reid, 1946); painted December 1945. Bottom left: *Yellow Streak* by Leonard Walters (Martin & Reid 1946); painted March 1946. Bottom right: *Dead Man's Spread* by John Theydon (Martin & Reid 1948); painted August 1948.

VARIATIONS ON A THEME: THE CARRYING KIND. *No Peace for Archer* by Hugh Clevely (Guild, 1953); painted April 1953. McConnell began supplying cover illustrations for the Maxwell Archer series in the 1930s, but this explosive composition is the star.

GALLERY

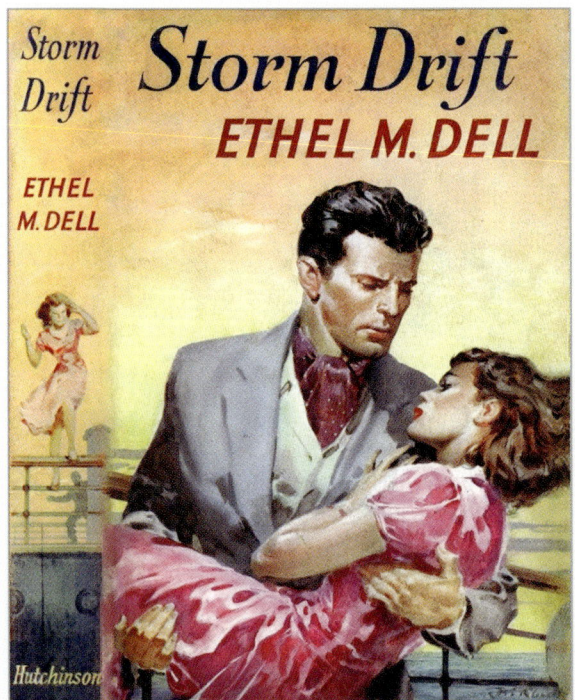

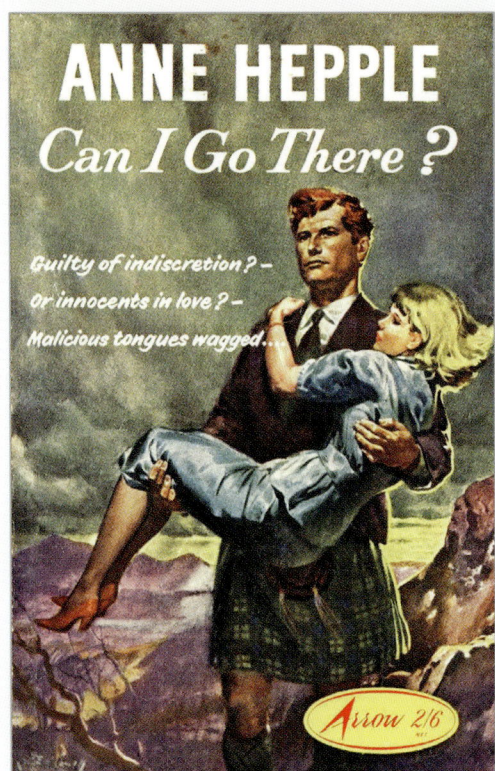
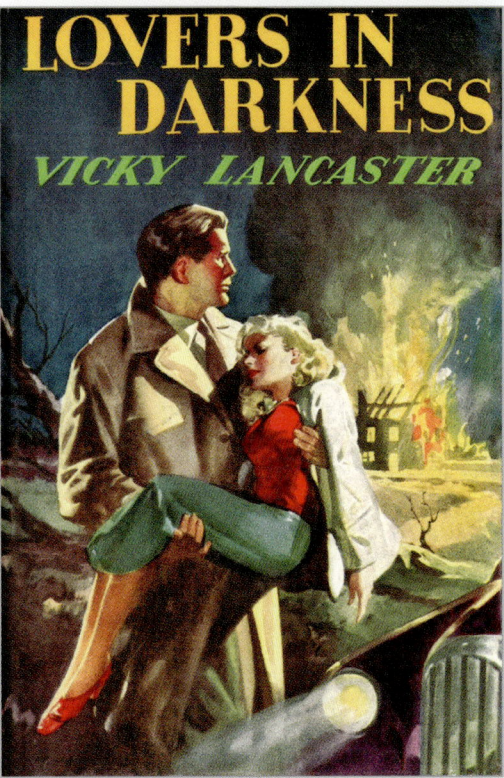

VARIATIONS ON A THEME: THE CARRYING KIND: Top left: *Storm Drift* by Ethel M Dell (Hutchinson, 1954); painting date not recorded. Top right: *The Sea Lady* by H G Wells (Digit R592, 1962); painting unsigned and unrecorded, but probably by McConnell. Bottom left: *Can I Go There?* by Anne Hepple (Arrow, 1962); painted November 1961. Bottom right: *Lovers in Darkness* by Vicky Lancaster (Robert Hale, 1955); painted October 1954.

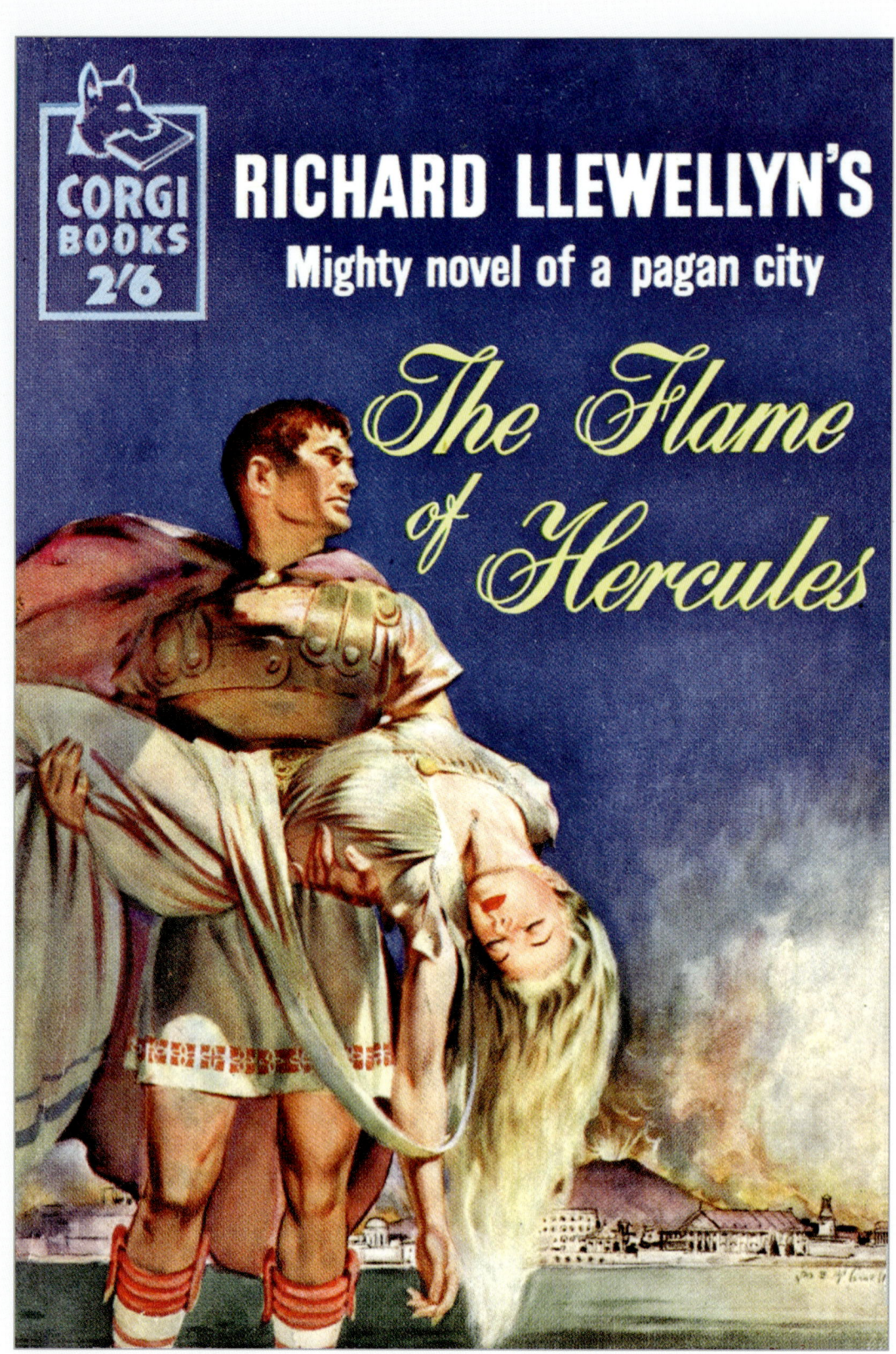

VARIATIONS ON A THEME: THE CARRYING KIND: *The Flame of Hercules* by Richard Llewellyn (Corgi S623, March 1959); painted September 1958. (Image courtesy Jim Kealy.)

VARIATIONS ON A THEME: THE CARRYING KIND: *The Velvet Hand* by Helen Reilly (Museum Press, 1955); painted May 1954.

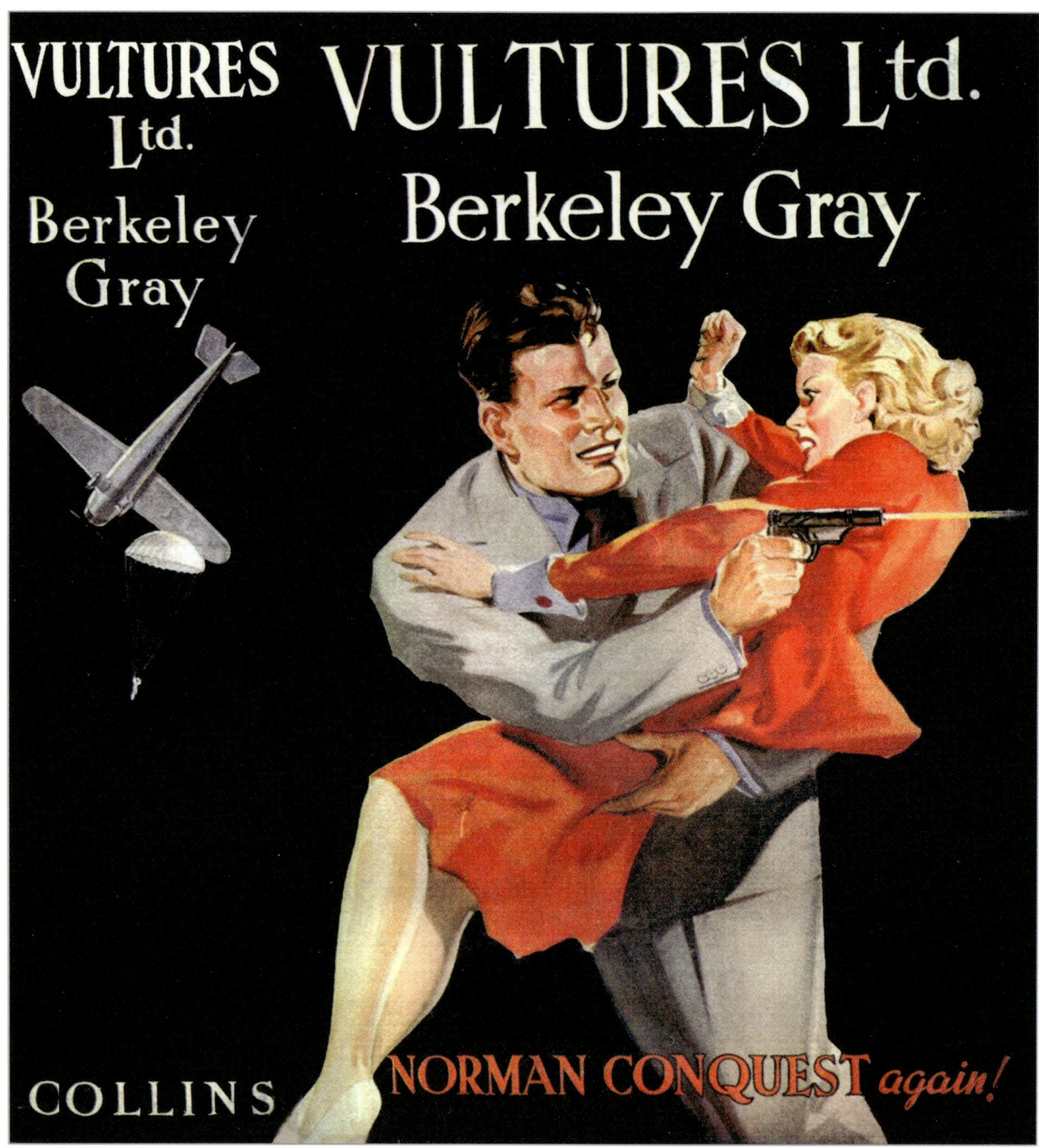

Vultures Ltd by Berkeley Gray (Collins, 1938)

3: FANCY JACKETS: THE FIRST TEN YEARS

'An attractive jacket can be of distinct advantage to a book by an unknown author, creating interest and so sales.'

K O Fearon, 1929[36]

In the early 1930s, when McConnell entered the field, the illustrated book jacket was still a new application for painterly skills. Although pictorial front covers had for been enlisted to market the paperback novels sold on railway station bookstalls more than half a century, the gaudy, eye-catching cover image had been generally considered distasteful for the first publication of literary works. A few popular publishers – most notably Mills & Boon – had begun using pictorial wrappers even before the First World War, but it was really not until the 1920s that the book jacket fully transitioned from simply a utilitarian protector against dust and dirt for the cover boards to a confident, even strident advertisement for the contents of the book it wrapped. 'To-day a bookseller's window is as many-coloured as a flower show,' wrote a librarian in 1924, 'due to the large number of pictorial paper covers, wrappers or "jackets" – as they are variously termed – on the books exposed for sale.'[37]

In *Commercial Art*, K O Fearon related the tale of a publisher's representative who visited an important book-buyer and asked why a good novel by a new author had not been ordered by them. 'Not with a poor jacket like that,' came the reply. 'Give it a first-class jacket, and I will at once order 500 copies.' According to Fearson, the sales rep, who had been schooled to believe in the word rather than the image, 'could hardly believe his ears.' A new jacket was duly designed, the order secured and then advertised to buyers from smaller firms to solicit further orders. G S Sandilands' contemporary article 'Book Jackets' provides corroboration, quoting a publisher: 'This novel was first published without a jacket, and its sales stopped at 400. We then issued it with this wrapper, and we sold 4,000 in a few weeks.'[38]

Fearon also offered advice to artists and publishers, suggesting that purely decorative covers and abstract designs failed to convey the 'atmosphere' of the book's story:

'The object of a book-jacket should be to tell the story of the book, or to suggest its special atmosphere as quickly and as simply as possible. To achieve its purpose a jacket must attract and hold the fleeting glance – against the competition of perhaps dozens of other jackets. It is obvious, therefore, that the designs should be simple, striking and straightforward. The thin, the "busy", the finicky designs do not hold their own in the company of bold and direct work. Therefore, the design of a book-jacket should be as much like a poster as possible.'

What Fearon neglected to mention, though, was that posters are designed to be seen from afar, whereas cover illustrations lend themselves to close and repeated study. Greater detail is therefore possible and, perhaps, desirable. To develop a design language and style, the illustrated wrapper for popular genre fiction drew upon two more ephemeral examples of applied art: namely, the monthly magazine cover, which supplied the inspiration for a fashionable blend of typography and image; and the lower status film poster, which frequently appropriated the conventions of Victorian narrative painting. Above all, in transferring the site of illustration from the cover board and spine to the jacket, the new art form quickly learned to be bold, in its use of colour, symbolism and composition. This came as quite a shock to some observers and critics. Take, for example, A J A Symons, writing in *Art and Industry* in 1937, the year that book production reached a record peak of over 17,000 titles that would not be surpassed for 14 years:

> 'Gradually [the pictorial dust jacket] has become more flaunting, more dramatic, more highly coloured and more expensive, until now, forgetting its former modesty completely, it has become the most noticeable, and sometimes the most agreeable feature of the book that it at once adorns and protects ... I must confess that for several years I regarded the book-jacket as the enemy of the cover it conceals ... Beneath the gayer and gayer jackets I foresaw duller and duller books ... Fortunately I was wrong.'[39]

The mention of 'more expensive' is significant, because the publisher incurred new design and printing fees that, unless passed on to the consumer, would reduce profit margins. The illustrator and art director had to be paid, and multiple-colour printing was a costly luxury.[40] Together, they might add 20 per cent to the production cost of a first edition and more to a budget-priced reprint. Most public libraries, and even some private circulating libraries such

Splendour of Love by Pamela Wynne (Collins, 1940). The book jacket not only provided insight into the book's story, but also often located it within a series and genre, while offering further opportunity to promote the publisher's wares.

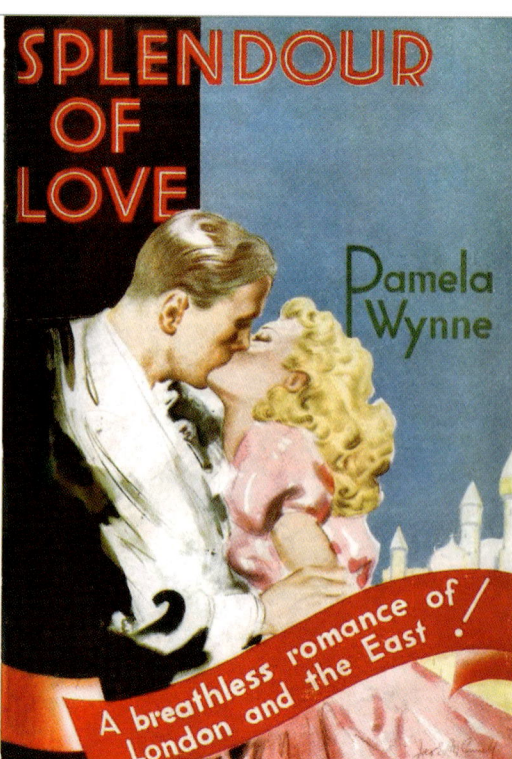

as Boots, would promptly remove the dust jackets, although others, such as W H Smith, enthusiastically retained them. Nevertheless, in an increasingly competitive fiction market, publishers began to rely on cover art to get their products noticed at point of sale. A publisher seeking a mark of distinction for his latest product might employ a famous artist who might, in turn, charge up to £100 for the privilege; but most professional illustrators could be hired for less than £10 per painting.

This expanding field of illustration was easy to enter with a talent like McConnell's and a well-connected agent like Partridge. McConnell's leading competitors included: Frank Marston, who illustrated for Methuen, Herbert Jenkins and Ward Lock; the brothers Salomon Van Abbe (1883-1955) and Joseph Van Abbe (1889-1954), who under the name 'Abby' illustrated regularly for Ward Lock, and also for Methuen, Collins, Hodder & Stoughton, Skeffington, Nelson, Hale, Unwin and others, between the two World Wars; Pip Youngman Carter (1904-1969), a gifted graphic artist (and husband of writer Margery Allingham) who produced many covers for Collins Crime Club, Heinemann, Constable and Hamish Hamilton during the 1930s; G P Micklewright (1893-1951), who began his career as a cover artist around the same time as McConnell and whose atmospheric pulp-style covers were a feature of the lists of Modern Publishing and Wright & Brown; and Eugene Hastain (1887-1957), the Anglo-French designer of the Saint logo for Leslie Charteris, whose often macabre work mainly materialised on the yellow jackets of Hodder & Stoughton. One of the few female illustrators was Ellen Edwards, who worked principally for Collins and Hodder & Stoughton in the 1920s. Another was Bip Pares (1904-1977), who is best known for the jackets that she painted throughout the 1930s and 1940s for Hodder & Stoughton, but who also worked for Thornton & Butterworth as well as a number of publishers in the Hutchinson group. Perhaps most gifted of all, at least compositionally, was the Glasgow-based Nina Miller-Davidson (1895-1957), whose distinctive and imaginative paintings sometimes graced the wrappers of Ward Lock novels.

While, like McConnell, these artists achieved a degree of fame in their field, there were also dozens of others who worked competently and conscientiously, but largely unrecognised, on the job of enticing the reader to the story. Artists' agent, Donovan Candler, offered his advice:

> 'The function of a story illustration is to whet the interest, and to persuade the observer to read the story and find out more about the people the artist has portrayed; in other words, his design must be full of interest – but must not tell the story. This point is very important, and marks the fundamental difference between an illustration for a story and [one] for an advertisement.'

Candler also pointed out that the successful illustrator must know how to draw 'types', not just coalmen, tramps and crooks, but 'the normal type of person: the doctor, the clerk, the schoolmistress, the housewife'. He or she (though it was always 'he' for Candler) 'must learn to compose a picture, and to centralise the interest where most interest lies.'[41]

At the time when McConnell was starting to forge a long-term career in cover illustration, Allen Lane was planning the revolution of book design and marketing that arrived with his Penguin imprint. The apostles of modernism hailed his 'clean', simplified, colour-coded cover designs for mass-market paperbacks, and the way in which the 'brand' conferred dignity and a sense of quality control on his selected texts. Soon, other publishers were experimenting with stark typography on colour-saturated backgrounds for new releases aimed at making a splash in bookshop window displays. Elements of the trade welcomed the distinctiveness, 'economy and orderliness' of the new trend, but thankfully for McConnell's livelihood, others took a different view. In the 1938 *Penrose Annual*, I M Parsons jumped to the defence of the illustrated book jacket:

> 'The typographical jacket can never, it seems to me, perform all the functions of a good wrapper. It may attract the eye, and it can convey a message quickly and forcibly. But that isn't enough. The perfect wrapper must not only attract the eye but hold the attention and … convey something more than the very limited message possible in a few words of display copy. And this, I contend, can only be done with a pictorial design, with a design that not only tells you the name of the book and author, but at the same time summarises graphically the particular character, quality, atmosphere – call it what you will – of the work in question.'[42]

Frustratingly, McConnell did not record the quantity or titles of the book covers that he painted prior to World War Two, but it is possible to estimate the number by studying his receipts from William Partridge, which *are* recorded in his workbook. There will have been other illustration commissions from Partridge that were not cover paintings – such as line drawings and interior plates – but looking at the total receipts from Partridge between 1934 and 1940 and dividing by the typical commission value of six guineas, it is reasonable to assume that McConnell painted between 250 and 350 covers in the period. Less than half have so far been identified, the majority being for crime fiction, the genre that dominates the collectors' market. He completed further commissions during the war in his time off from the ARP.

Fiction from Faber

The output of the distinguished publishing house of Faber & Faber in the 1930s is now chiefly remembered for modernist poetry and prose by the likes of Eliot, Auden, Spender and Pound. Their slim volumes often included illustrations by fine artists such as Edward Bawden, Eric Ravilious and Graham Sutherland; but more populist painters from the Partridge stable also made regular contributions to the company's fiction list. McConnell was one of them, and actually began painting Faber covers before his formal association with the Partridge agency. His first signed cover – a classic portrait of a Trilby-hatted sleuth peering through a magnifying glass – graced *My Best Detective Story*, a 1931-published anthology. His striking, confrontational cover for *Death Rattle*, a political thriller by Hanns Gobsch, wraps a book with a first publication date of March 1932; while the first cheap edition of *The Ghost Book*, an anthology of supernatural stories,

Terror in the Thames by A D Divine (Collins, 1938)

My Best Detective Story (Faber & Faber, 1931). McConnell's earliest book cover yet identified.

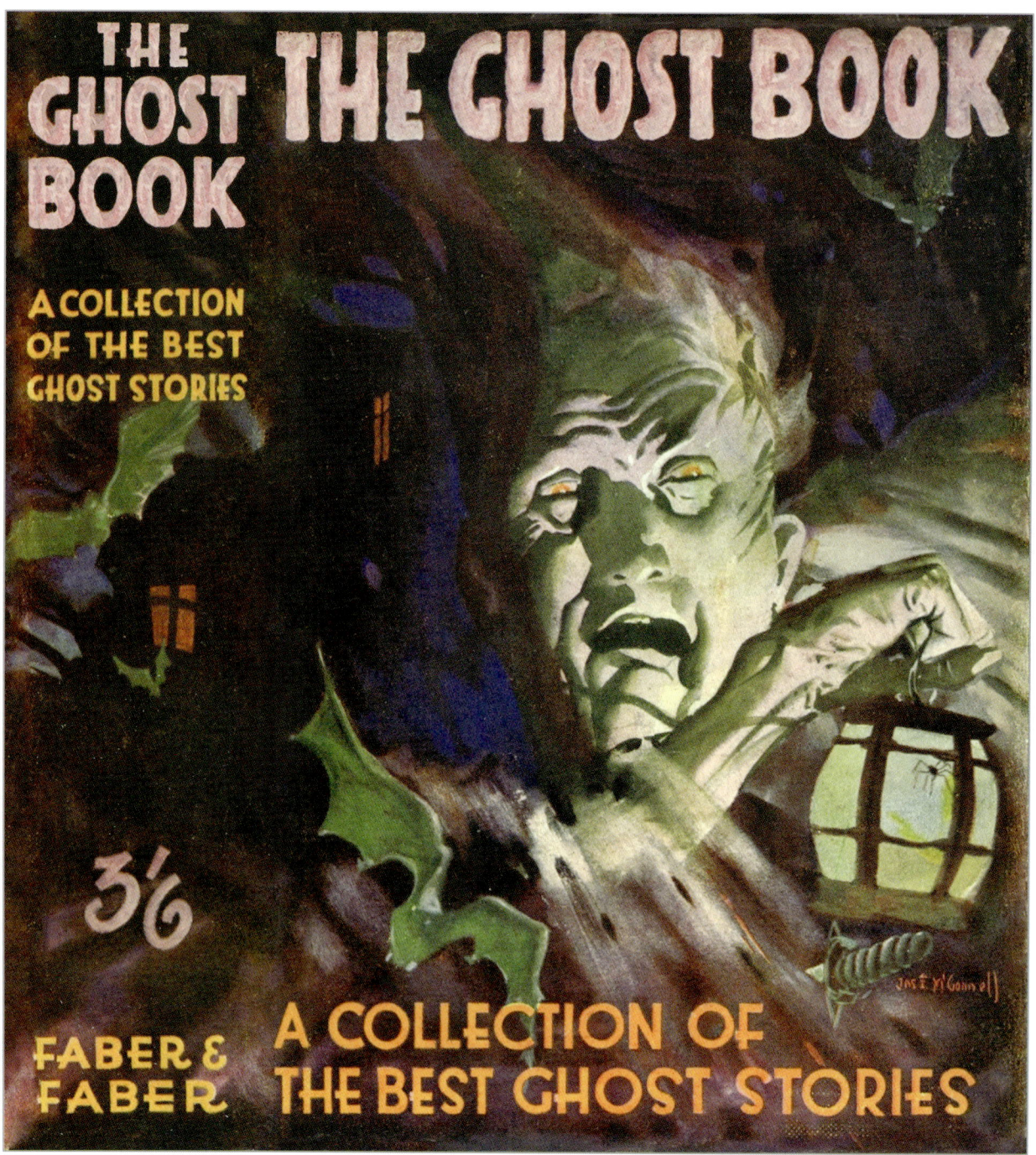

The Ghost Book (Faber & Faber, 1932)

bearing a McConnell portrait of a none-too-friendly spirit, appeared in September 1932. The inescapable conclusion is that McConnell was 'moonlighting' for Faber while still working at Swains. This would have been a way of testing the waters before going fully freelance, and of demonstrating his artistic powers to his prospective agent. The cheap edition of the publisher's best-selling *First Series* of *Best Detective Stories* debuted in September 1933, with the sort of action-packed cover that would become McConnell's trademark. The book trade used the term 'omnibus' to describe these collections, which were a regular feature of the publisher's lists. Partridge must have been thrilled, because here evidently was an illustrator to challenge the established exponents of cover art, painting in a way that conveyed the excitement of the text beyond

Young George by F O Mann (Faber & Faber, 1934). The contemplative figure in a landscape. The cover for the second printing of Mann's *Albert Grope* (February 1931) had been painted by Reginald Heade – his earliest known commercial work.

Death Rattle by Hanns Gobsch (Faber & Faber, 1932). (Image courtesy Jim Kealy.)

the covers.

McConnell contributed covers for at least two further detective mystery omnibuses (many of which were popular enough to be regularly reprinted for twenty years), as well as a few for single-author novels. One of the latter was a painting for F O Mann's *Young George* (1934), which was, appropriately for the artist, the story of a young man from humble origins making his way in London. The composition set a contemplative George in a rural landscape. The motif of a figure in a landscape would become typical of McConnell's compositional style, but this particular example was unusually static, and rendered in muted colours that the artist presumably thought appropriate to a title from a publisher of 'serious' literature like Faber. There is a lot more action in the landscape depicted in his cover painting for the following year's *Famous Crimes* by William Roughead. And he succeeded in generating a good deal of romantic tension in the more industrial landscape of the cover for Norman Lindsay's novel *Redheap*, which was probably the first of his many jackets for historical romances.

Below: the jacket for *Famous Crimes* by William Roughead (Faber & Faber, 1935). (Image courtesy Jim Kealy.)

Top right: *Redheap* by Norman Lindsay (Faber & Faber, 1934) may be McConnell's first cover for an historical romance novel.

Bottom right: the *Second Series* volume of *Best Detective Stories* (Faber & Faber, 1933). (Image courtesy Jim Kealy.)

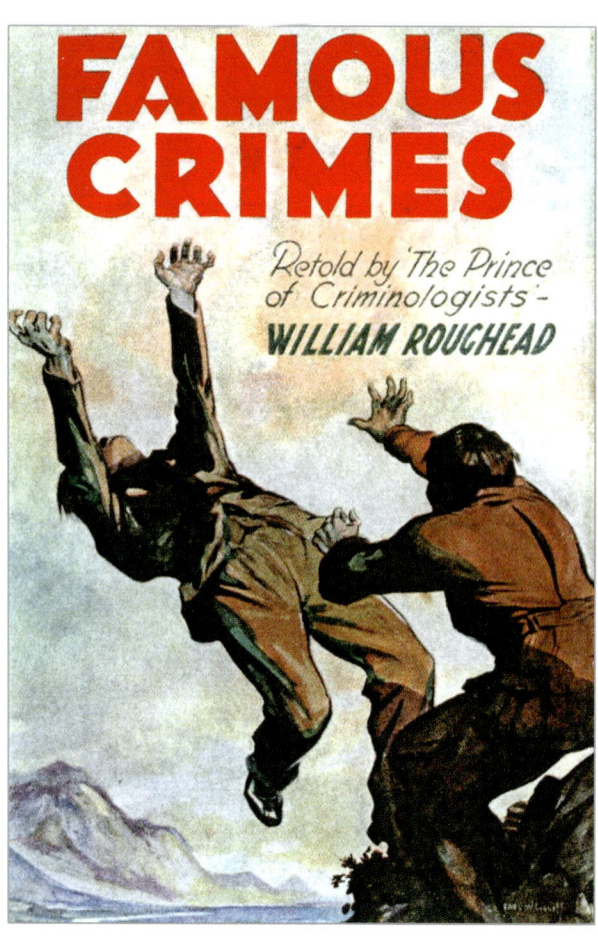

Best Detective Stories – First Series (Faber & Faber, c1932)

Publishers Galore

The work for Faber & Faber ended before the outbreak of the War, but by that time, McConnell's art was in constant demand from a range of other publishers, whose patronage lasted throughout the 1940s and 1950s. The first of these was the Hutchinson group, for whom he first painted covers in 1934. One of the company's ads announced, 'It has been estimated that three out of five library books are published by Hutchinson or one of its Allied Houses'; and J J Seeley, the literary editor of *National Newsagent, Bookseller and Stationer* supported the claim:

> 'Their list of authors and the many popular books they issue form the strongest combination on the market. Frankau, Sabatini, Stacpoole, Gibbs,

A striking composition for *Sanderson: Master Rogue* by John Jay Chichester (Hutchinson, c1934).

> Savi, Sandys, Pillpotts, Wallace and Dell — these are but a few of the famous names under the Hutchinson imprint. At 2/6 and 3/6 there is a great array of first-class and full-length reprints, well printed, strongly bound *and strikingly wrapped*.'[43] (emphasis added)

There are doubtless many McConnell covers for this publishing group that have yet to be attributed, but the earliest that have so far been identified — for John Jay Chichester's *Sanderson: Master Rogue* and Sydney Horler's *The Man from Scotland Yard* — both drip with Oriental menace in compositions that more closely resemble film posters than his work for Faber. Soon he was also painting stunning covers for romantic stories like Isabel C Clarke's *Roman Year* with its fluttering white doves, and

McConnell's jacket for *The Man from Scotland Yard* by Sydney Horler (Hutchinson, c1934).

Roman Year by Isabel C Clarke (Hutchinson, 1935)

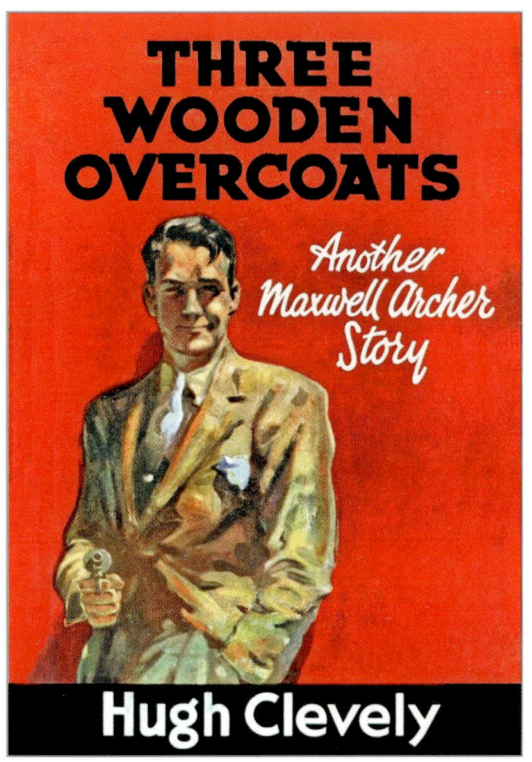
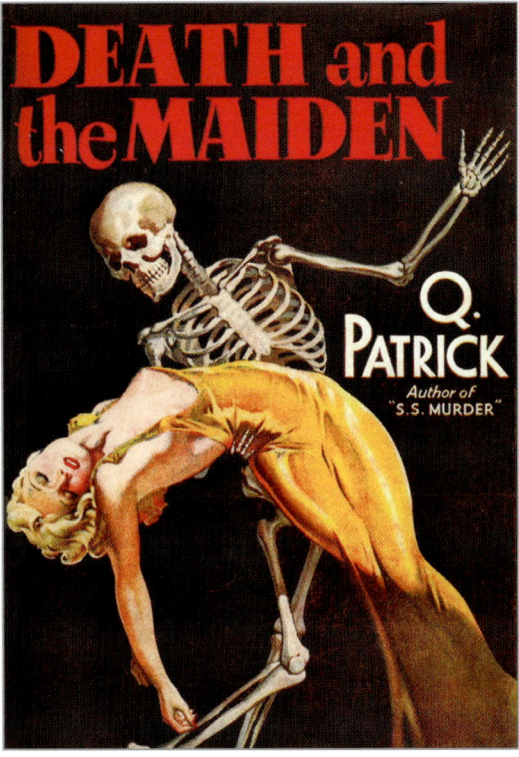
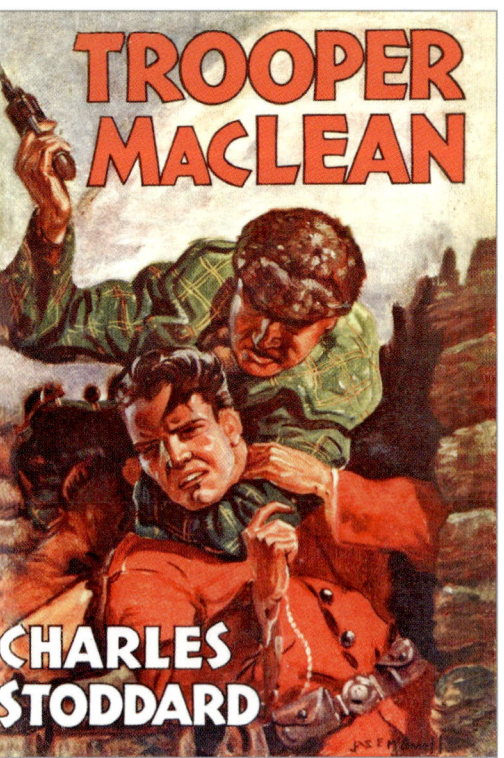

Top left: *The Case of the Monday Murders* by Christopher Bush (Cassell, 1936). Top right: *Three Wooden Overcoats* by Hugh Clevely (Cassell, 1939) (top right), reusing McConnell's artwork for another Clevely novel, *Zero the 14th*. Bottom left: *Death and the Maiden* by Q Patrick (Cassell, 1939). Bottom right: *Trooper MacLean* by Charles Stoddard (Cassell, 1938). (Top two images courtesy Jim Kealy.)

discovering that his evocative compositions were in demand for a variety of genres from two giants of fiction industry: Cassell and Collins.

The first identified McConnell painting for Cassell is his 1936 cover for *The Case of the Monday Murders* by Christopher Bush – an author of detective mysteries for whose novels he would supply a further two covers. He also contributed jackets for books by the thriller author Hugh Clevely, whose Maxwell Archer protagonist reached the cinema screen in 1940 in a movie directed by John Paddy Carstairs; and for Q Patrick's 1939 novel *Death and the Maiden*, with a chillingly memorable depiction of the bony symbol of death carrying off an unfortunate feminine victim.

Cassell had a sizable crime fiction list, but were perhaps the first publisher to recognise McConnell's talent for tackling North American subjects. They put him to work on jackets for Charles Stoddard's tales of the Royal Canadian Mounted Police and on various other American scenarios. These were often the first British editions, marketed by Cassell at reprint prices, and were enthusiastically received by 'Tom

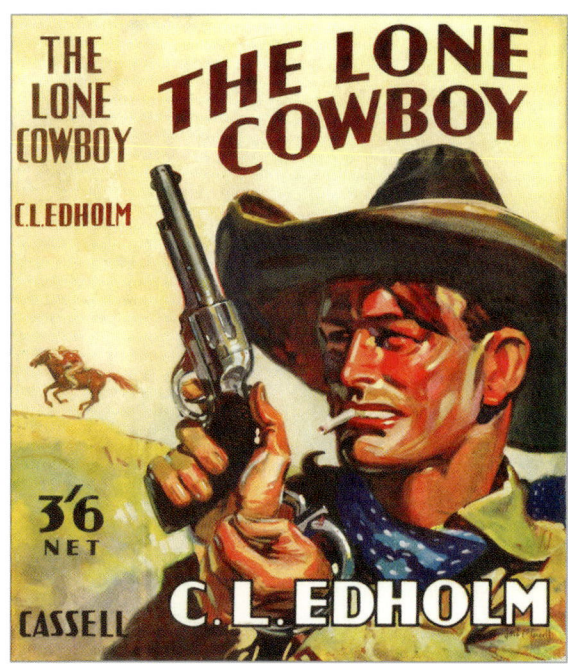

The Lone Cowboy by C L Edholm (Cassell, 1937)

Bookman' (J J Seeley) in *National Newsagent*. Charles Stoddard's *Trooper McLean* (1938) was described as a 'stirring and exciting story, running at top speed and with many thrills,' while the same author's *North of the Stars* (1938) was 'a murder mystery of the great northland, with many adventures before its solution.' These books were further praised for their 'vigorous picture-wrappers in four colours.'[44] McConnell's jacket for C L Edholm's *The Lone Cowboy* (1937), with its confidently-rendered sun-reddened gunslinger portrait, is a classic example. Cassell's Western covers of this period were frequently eye-catching, but many were unsigned, and attribution is often uncertain and relies on the similarity of the artwork to other signed examples.

Collins also requested Western covers, not least for their Wild West Library, as well as a wagon-train cover for Stuart Cloete's historical saga of settlers in South Africa, *Turning Wheels* (1937), which became a critical and commercial success. Although the novel's reputation has dimmed over the years, and McConnell's jacket is not one of his finest, Tom Bookman singled

North of the Stars by Charles Stoddard (Cassell, 1938)

Mine Inheritance by Frederick Niven (Collins, 1940)

it out as 'such a book as we only get once in a decade.'[45] Three years later, McConnell painted the cover for another best-seller for Collins, Frederick Niven's *Mine Inheritance* (1940), an exciting 'epic of our Empire' that chimed with the times and was selected by the Book Society as its monthly 'Choice'. Collins took out a whole-page advertisement in *The Bookseller* to sing its praises and announce that it had sold 15,000 copies in a week. McConnell's jacket painting was suitably heroic, and must have helped to establish his enduring reputation as a painter of historical scenes. He had already demonstrated his capabilities with his moving painting for the cover of Clifford Dowdey's American Civil War story *Bugles Blow No More* (1937). *The Abbot's Heel* (1939) by Neil Bell was another historical; set in 14th Century Bury St Edmunds, it was considered by Tom Bookman 'a fine, realistic story of old time, crammed with rich and exciting incident.'[46]

McConnell seems to have been given fewer opportunities to show his talents on the romantic subjects that were one of Collins' staple genres – Reginald Heade provided stiff competition – but when the opportunity did arise, he rose to the challenge, such as with his achingly passionate painting for Mary Howard's *Partners for Playtime* (1937). He also effectively evoked an elegiac mood for bucolic nostalgia like James Barke's *The Land of the Leal* and David Rame's *Wine of Good Hope* (both 1939) at a time when the country was on the brink of war. At the same time, he could startle the viewer with a vibrant image of a woman in a flaming scarlet dress for Thelma Strabel's *Reap the Wild Wind* (1941). Unlike some of his contemporaries, McConnell had the versatility not only to tackle a range of genres, but also to adapt his style to suit the subject matter.

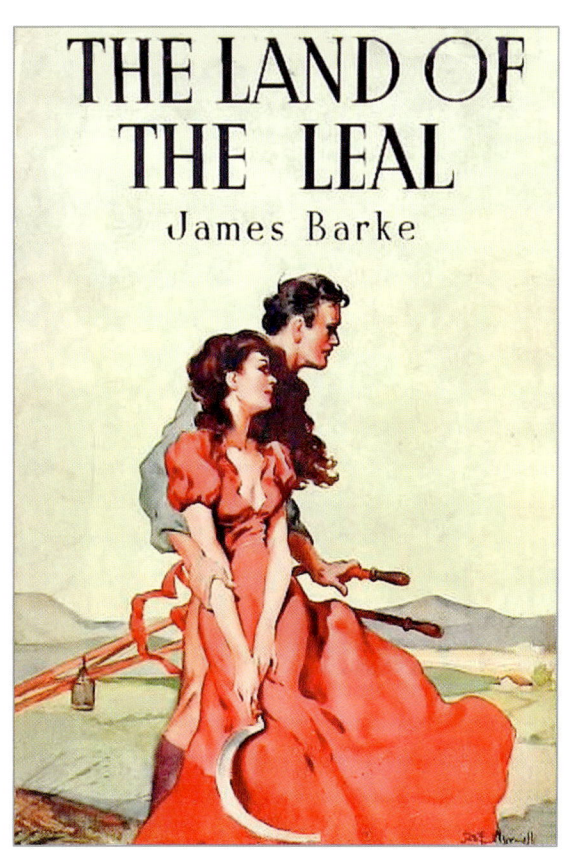

Top right: *Turning Wheels* by Stuart Cloete (Collins, 1937)

Bottom right: *The Land of the Leal* by James Barke (Collins, 1939)

Bugles Blow No More by Clifford Dowdey (Collins, 1937)

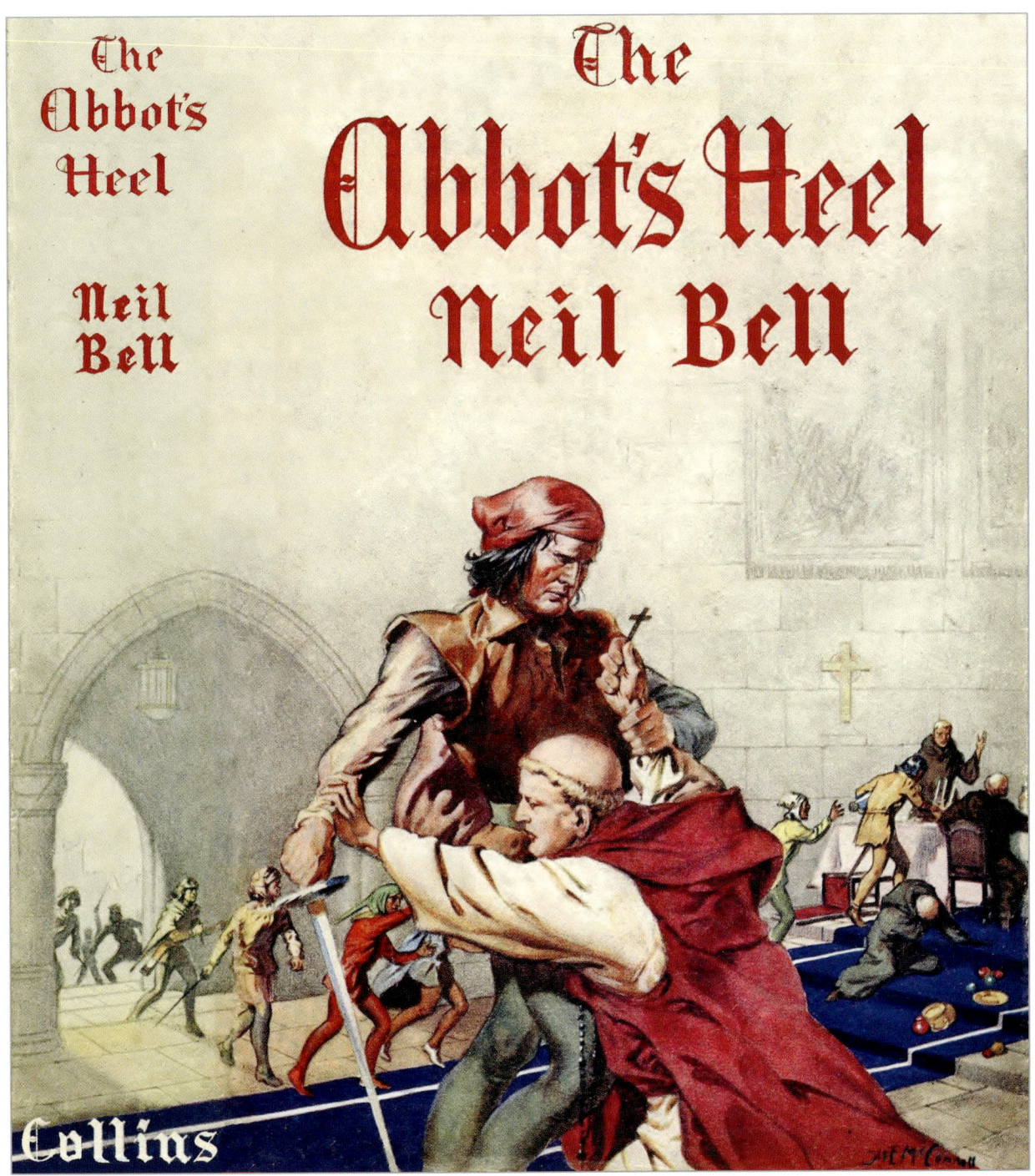

The Abbot's Heel by Neil Bell (Collins, 1939). (Image courtesy Jim Kealy.)

Partners for Playtime by Mary Howard (Collins, 1937)

Wine of Good Hope by David Rame (Collins, 1939)

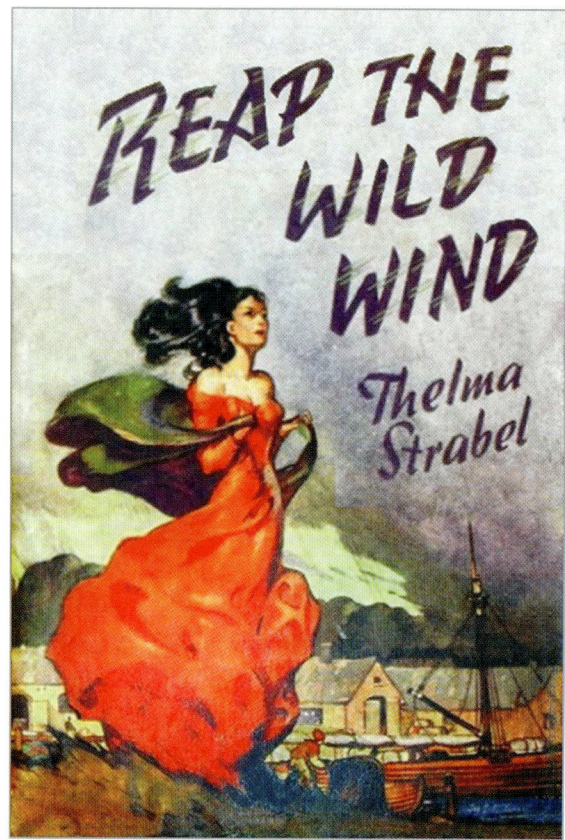

Reap the Wild Wind by Thelma Strabel (Collins, 1941). (Image courtesy Jim Kealy.)

Historical subjects would ultimately be McConnell's future, but in the late 1930s, his most enduring work adorned crime fiction by Berkeley Gray, a pseudonym of the London-based writer Edwy Searles Brooks (1889-1965), who was born in Hackney. A veteran of the Sexton Blake and Nelson Lee Library series, Brooks wrote his first of more than fifty stories of the 'gay desperado' named Norman Conquest in *The Thriller* story paper. McConnell began providing distinctive covers for these when the stories were published by Collins in 1938, an assignment that continued (with a break during the war) until the mid-1950s. He also looks to have painted the first two covers of Brooks' series of Chief-Inspector William 'Ironsides' Cromwell stories published under the pseudonym Victor Gunn. The paintings are unsigned, but are thought to be the work of McConnell, who did sign his post-war Ironsides covers.

The lack of the artist's signature also dogs the attribution of some covers for the crime novels of David Hume (John Victor Turner, 1900-1945), until McConnell's name finally pops up on 1940's *Five Aces*. Although other hands were responsible for the majority of the earlier titles in the long-running Hume series, the impossible poker hand for the latter was surely not McConnell's first contribution.

While Norman Conquest became almost as much McConnell's character as Brooks', the same cannot be said of Slim Callaghan, the creation of the extraordinary and flamboyant author Peter Cheyney (1896-1951). McConnell appears to have painted only three covers for Cheyney's novels, which Collins began to publish in 1938:

> 'I put two left hands on a girl once, a girl with a revolver behind her back, for a Peter Cheyney book. I did Peter

Five Aces by David Hume (Collins, 1940)

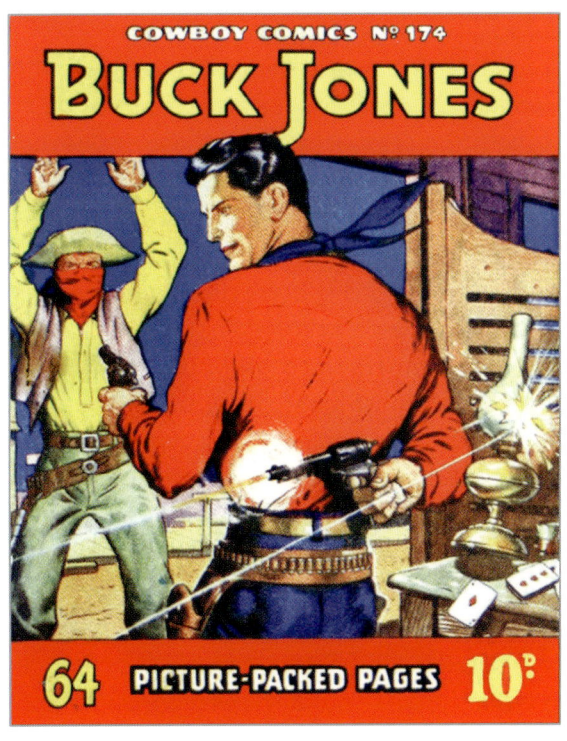

Cheyneys for quite a while until I put two left hands on the girl and that was the end of it. I worked with Cheyney direct. He had me go over there to see him.'

The girl with two left hands (or rather, right hands – McConnell misremembered that detail) appeared on the cover for *You'd Be Surprised*, a Lemmy Caution story published in 1940. Sixteen years later, the artist had a chance to correct his rare anatomical error, accurately depicting Buck Jones firing a revolver from behind his back on the cover of *Cowboy Comics* #174 (1956). He

Above: *Mr. Mortimer Gets the Jitters* by Berkeley Gray (Collins, 1938); McConnell's first Norman Conquest cover.

Top right: Peter Cheyney's *You'd Be Surprised* (Collins, 1940); a reprint edition here but with artwork uncorrected.

Bottom right: *Buck Jones* (Cowboy Comics #174, published by Amalgamated, 1956); painted April 1956.

Dangerous Curves by Peter Cheyney (Collins, 1939)

probably first encountered Cheyney while still working at Swains, because the printers' Shoe Lane premises neighboured those of Cheyney's Editorial and Literary Services (London) Ltd. The artist could hardly have missed a man with a monocle, smoking from a cigarette holder, dressed in a flowing black cloak with scarlet silk lining and a wide-brimmed hat cocked to shade the side of his face without the monocle. McConnell must surely have been responsible for the unsigned cover of *This Man is Dangerous* (1936), Cheyney's first novel for Collins, as well as the signed one for *Dangerous Curves* (1939).

The other major publishers of McConnell's artwork in the early days were Robert Hale, who appear to have used his talents almost exclusively for their romantic fiction list. Perhaps most notably, McConnell supplied covers for the British editions of a number of books by 'Rob Eden', the pseudonym used by American authors Robert and Eve Burkhardt. Indeed, his earliest identified Robert Hale cover was for the Burkhardts' *Love or Money* (1936). He also painted jackets for books by the world's most prolific female author, Ursula Bloom (1896-1984), making a particularly fine job of *Marriage in Heaven* (1943). The exquisite watercolour piece for Joan Kennedy's *Paradise Calling* (1939) is not signed, but a comparison of this with the composition used in the earlier signed painting for E W Savi's *A Question of Honour* (1937), published by Hutchinson, suggests that both illustrations are by the same hand – and a very accomplished hand it certainly is.

Love or Money by Rob Eden (Robert Hale, 1936)

FANCY JACKETS: THE FIRST TEN YEARS

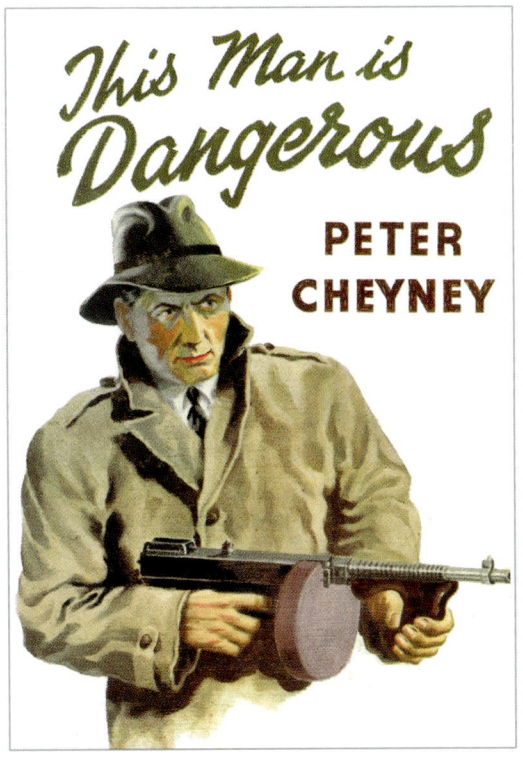

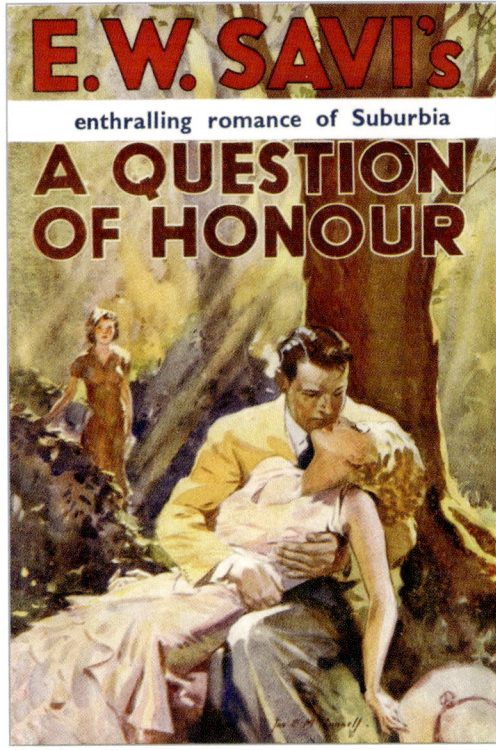

Top left: *This Man is Dangerous* by Peter Cheyney (Collins, 1936). Top right: *Marriage in Heaven* by Ursula Bloom (Robert Hale, 1943). Bottom left: *Paradise Calling* by Joan Kennedy (Robert Hale, 1939). Bottom right: *A Question of Honour* by E W Savi (Hutchinson, 1936).

GALLERY

THE NORMAN CONQUESTS: *Miss Dynamite* by Berkeley Gray (Collins, 1939). A year prior to his error on the cover of Peter Cheney's *You'd Be Surprised* (see page 93), McConnell demonstrates that he *can* execute an anatomically correct painting of a woman with a handgun held behind her back. (Image courtesy Jim Kealy.)

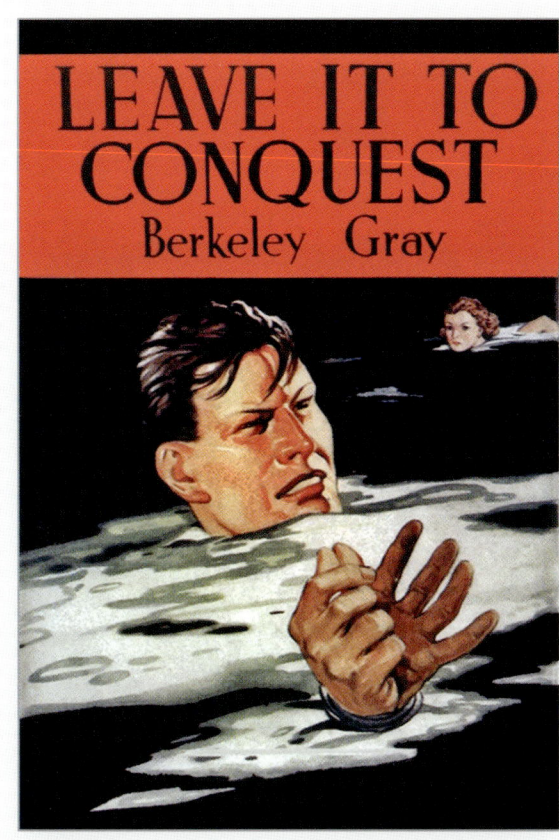
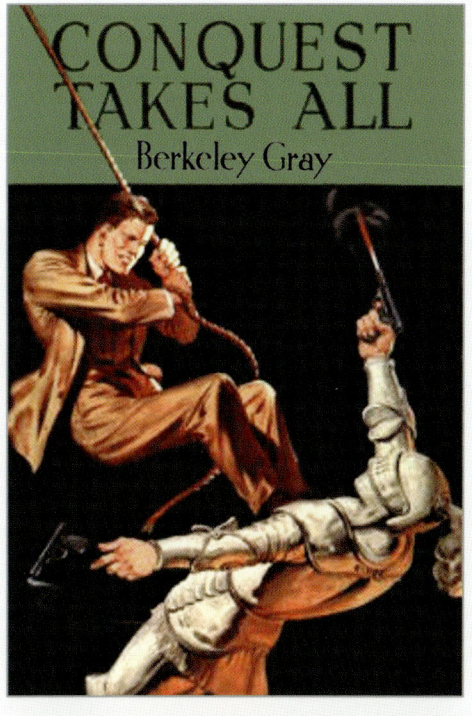
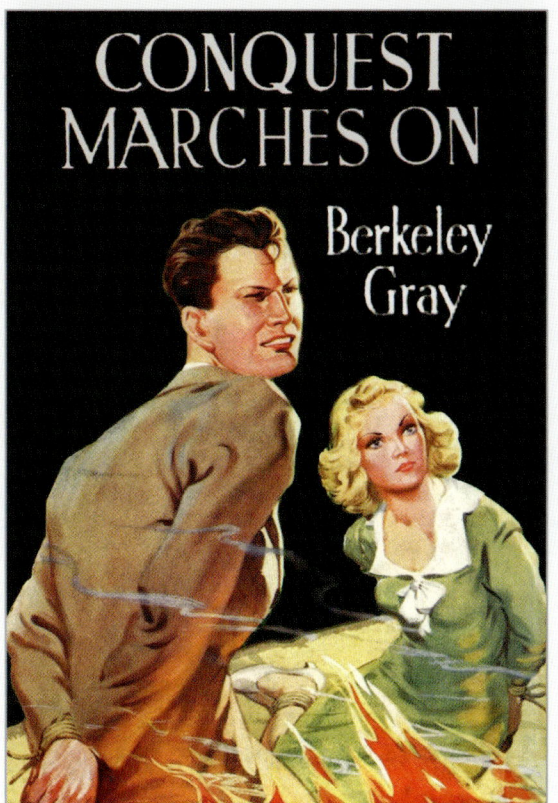

THE NORMAN CONQUESTS: McConnell's covers for Berkeley Gray novels. Top left: *Leave It to Conquest* (Collins, 1939). Bottom left: *Conquest Marches On* (Collins, 1939). Above top: *Conquest Takes All* (Collins, 1940). Above bottom: *Meet the Don* (Collins, 1940). (*Leave It to Conquest* and *Conquest Marches On* images courtesy Jim Kealy.)

HEARTS AND FLOWERS: *She Grew Up* by Grace Elliott Taylor (Ivor Nicholson and Watson, 1934)

GALLERY

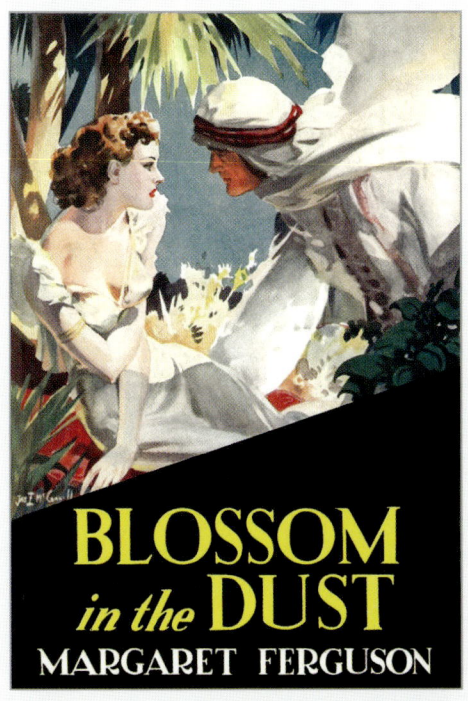
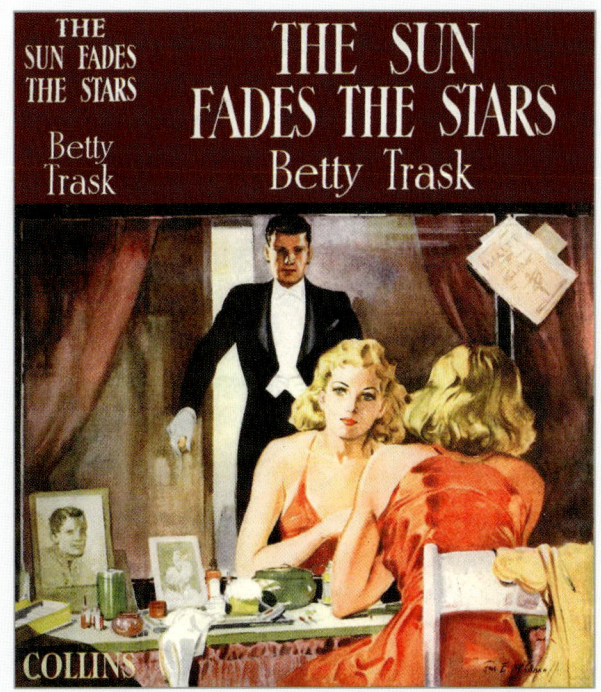
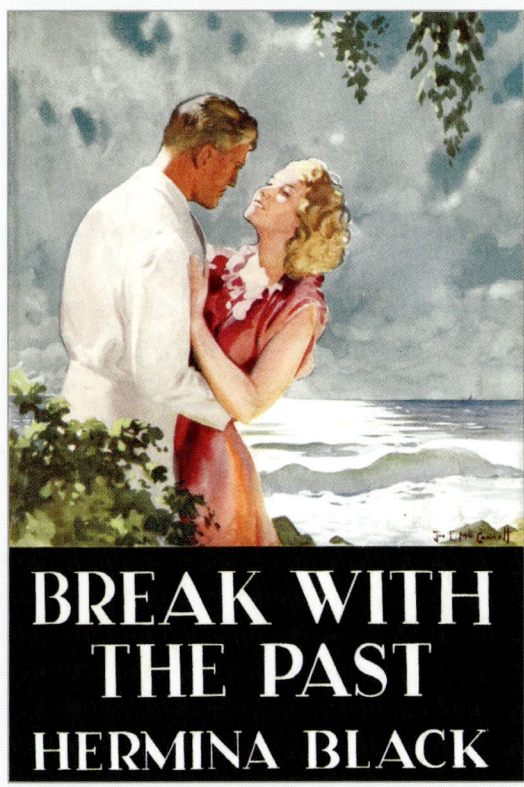

HEARTS AND FLOWERS: Top left: *Blossom in the Dust* by Margaret Ferguson (Robert Hale, 1939); McConnell picked the better bottom corner for his signature on this seductive sheik-in-the-oasis image. Top right: *The Sun Fades the Stars* by Betty Trask (Collins, 1940); a beautifully detailed composition in which the framed 'photo' on the spine confirms that her love is visiting. Bottom: *Break with the Past* by Hermina Black (Robert Hale, 1939) and *Joy's Bonfire* by Hilda Hewett (Robert Hale, 1942); a revealing example of the repurposing of artwork, probably due to the shortage of wartime labour: the publisher reused McConnell's painting within three years.

PERILOUS PURSUITS: *Mr. Hyde* by Hugh Arnott (Chapman and Hall, 1939). Fascinating depth of field in this almost 3-D downhill racer image.

GALLERY

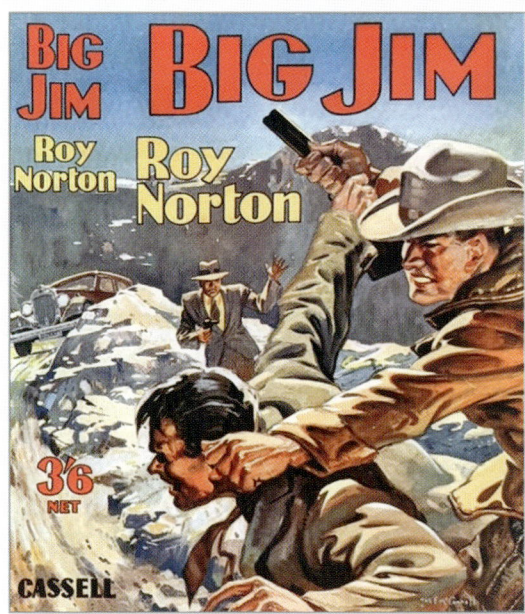
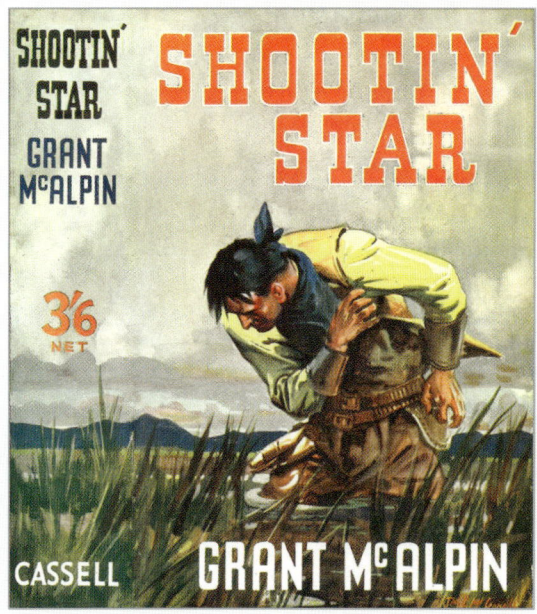
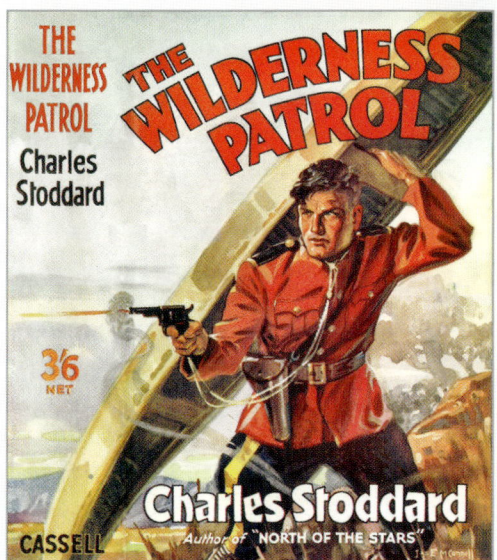

PERILOUS PURSUITS: Top left: *Big Jim* by Roy Norton (Cassell, 1937). Top right: *Shootin' Star* by Grant McAlpin (Cassell, 1939). Bottom left: *The Wilderness Patrol* by Charles Stoddard (Cassell, 1939). Bottom right: *Thirsty Land* by Joan Sutherland (Cassell 1937).

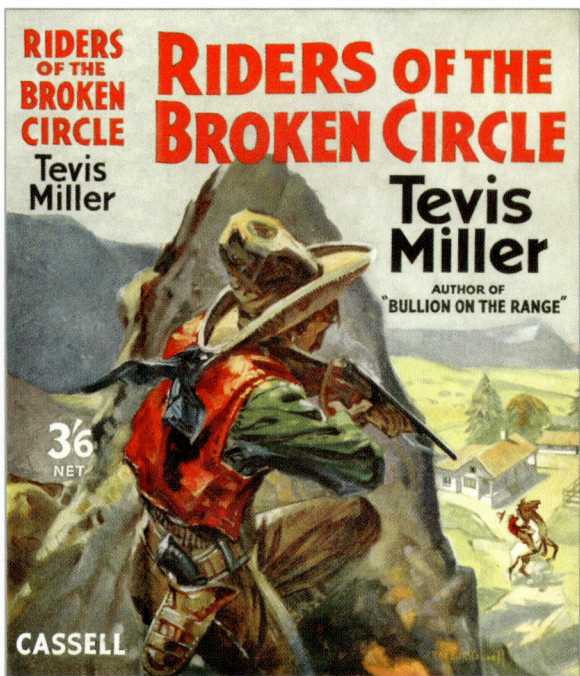

PERILOUS PURSUITS: Top left: *King's Enemies* by J M Walsh (Collins, 1939). Top right: *Riders of the Broken Circle* by Tevis Miller (Cassell, 1937). Bottom left: *Obstruction-Danger* by John Thomas (Blackwood, 1937). Bottom right: *Guns of Silver Valley* by Jackson Cole (Cassell, 1937).

GALLERY

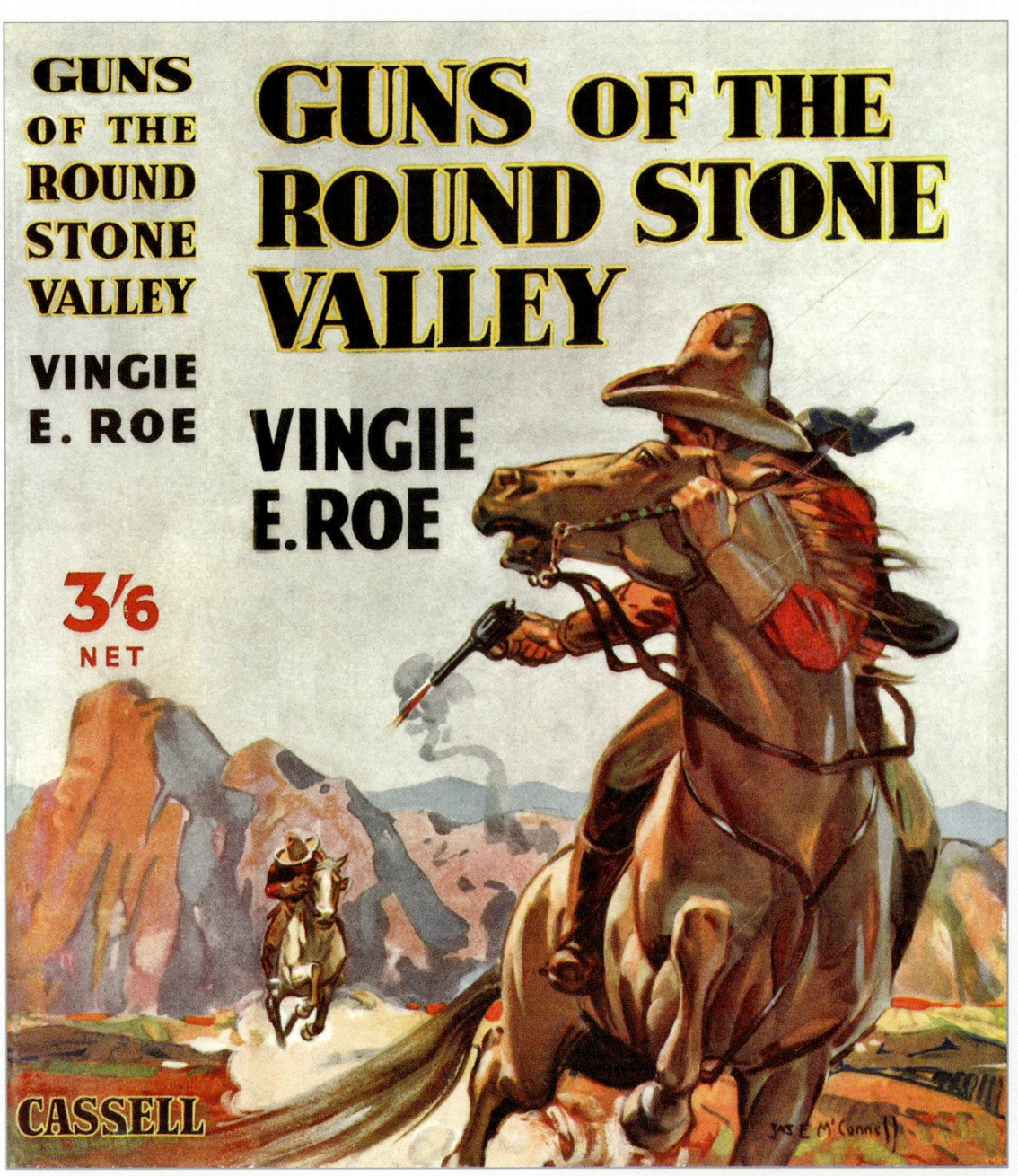

PERILOUS PURSUITS: *Guns of the Round Stone Valley* by Vingie E Roe (Cassell, 1937). McConnell is not afraid to make the horse the dominant element in his composition.

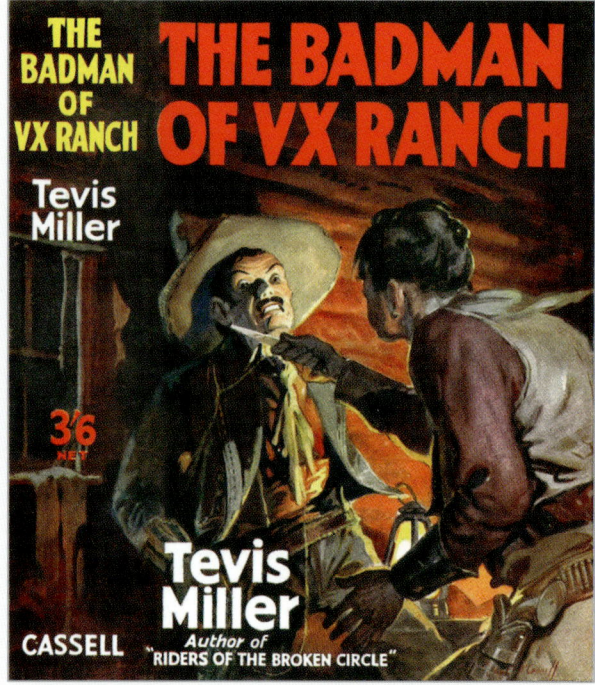

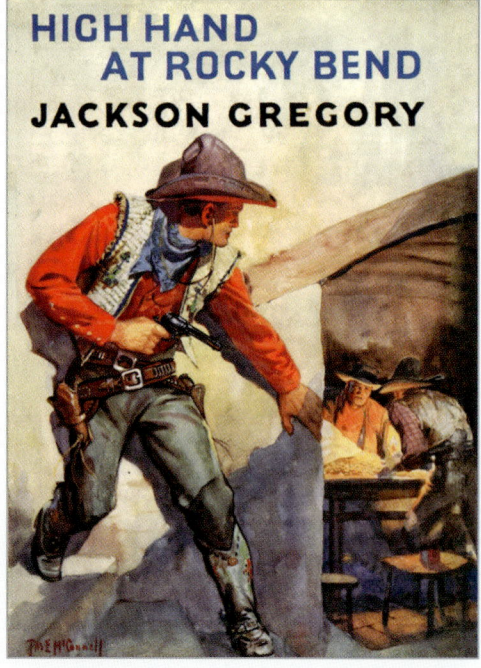

PERILOUS PURSUITS: Top left: *The Badman of VX Ranch* by Tevis Miller (Cassell, 1937). Top right: *Bullets for Breakfast* by J M Walsh (Collins, 1940). Bottom left: *High Hand at Rocky Bend* by Jackson Gregory (Hodder & Stoughton, 1939) – McConnell was not a regular artist for Hodder, but the publisher extracted full value from this painting by frequent reuse. Bottom right: *No Less Renowned* by Gilbert Hackforth-Jones (Blackwood, 1935) – McConnell was usually hired for his prowess in rendering humans and animals, so this was an exception to the rule. (*High Hand at Rocky Bend* image courtesy Jim Kealy.)

PERILOUS PURSUITS: Two youngsters are confronted by a cowboy in McConnell's artwork for the front cover and colour frontispiece of the children's novel *Jerky* by Ned Andrews (Cassell, 1939); an early painting for a juvenile readership by an illustrator predominantly associated at that time with work for adults. (Image courtesy Jim Kealy.)

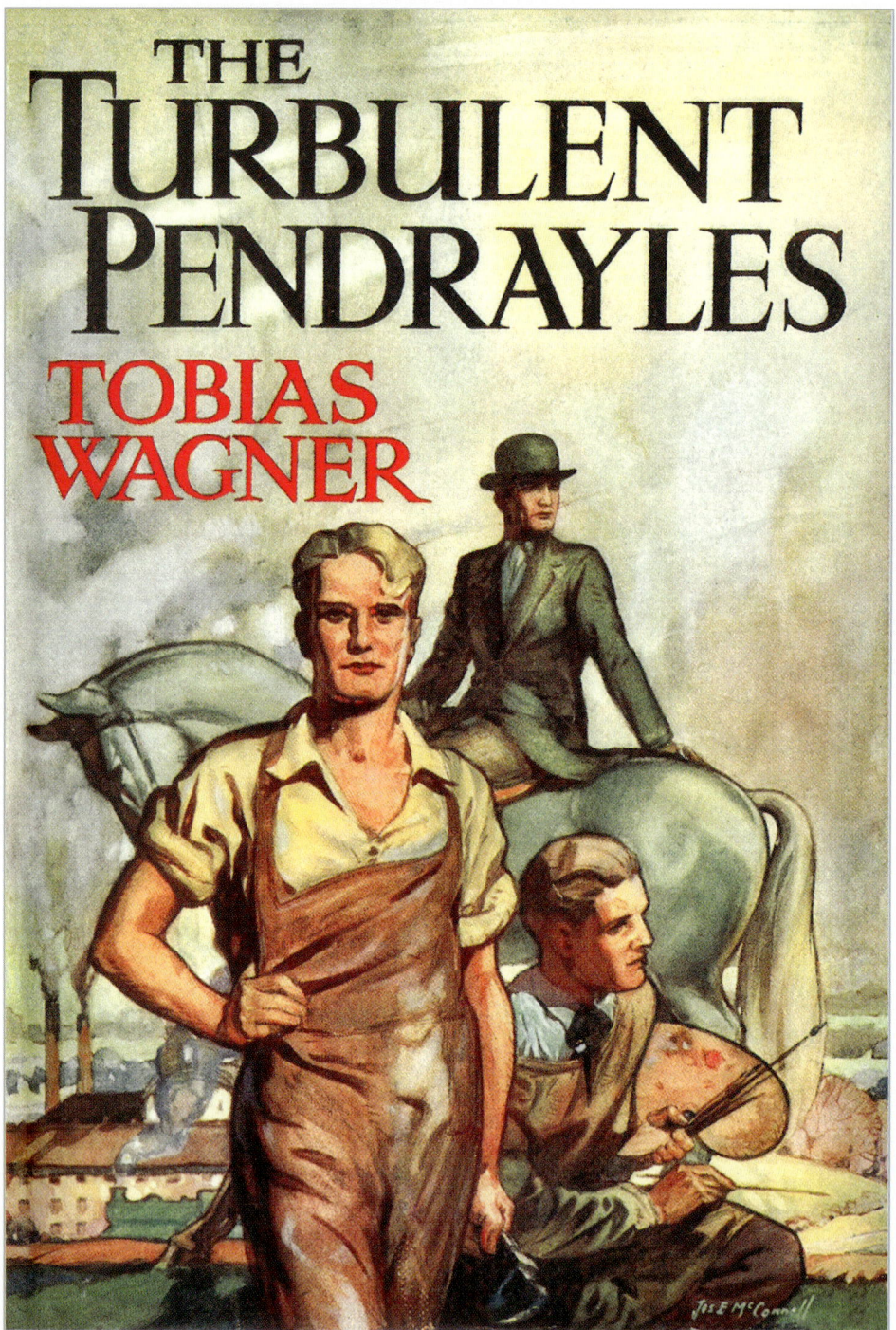

EXPERIMENTS WITH STYLE: *The Turbulent Pendrayles* by Tobias Wagner (Cassell, 1939). An unusually static and stately composition and a muted colour palette consciously invoke the conventions of society portraiture for a book that is essentially a family portrait. Its blurb described it thus: 'Mr Wagner has had the courage to tell a frankly romantic story of clean, healthy people who have a code and who stick to it. It is one of those so-called old-fashioned stories that a host of readers hunt for hopefully, apologetically, despairingly, and which they discover with unalloyed delight.'

GALLERY

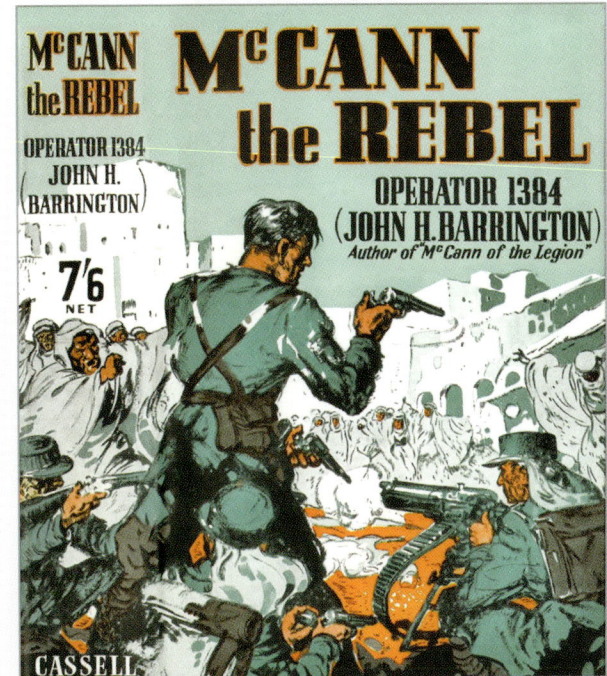

EXPERIMENTS WITH STYLE: Top left: *The Case of the Green Felt Hat* by Christopher Bush (Cassell, 1939), executed in colour-block, poster style, that produces a dramatic atmosphere without being entirely successful. Top right: *McCann the Rebel* by Operator 1384 (John H Harrington) (Cassell, 1941), a Foreign Legion battle cover rendered in the two-colour process usually reserved for interior illustration. Bottom left: *Out of the Dog House* by Charles North (Cassell, 1940), a drawing with background colour fill possibly indicating that, in the difficult circumstances of wartime, Cassell was already repurposing pre-existing file material. Bottom right: *Time to Go* by Renée Shann (Collins, 1938), the signature on which seems to have dissolved in the pen and ink wash, although the boy is very much one of McConnell's stock 'types'.

EXPERIMENTS WITH STYLE: *Dinah's Husband* by Ursula Bloom (Cassell, 1941). Tension by candlelight.

EXPERIMENTS WITH STYLE: *The Case of the Flying Ass* by Christopher Bush (Cassell, 1939). Searching for the signature.

WOT NO SIGNATURE?: *Marine Parade* by Ivor Brown (Robert Hale, 1937). Despite the lack of signature, there can be little doubt that the miniature marvel at the centre of this delightful watercolour is McConnell's work.

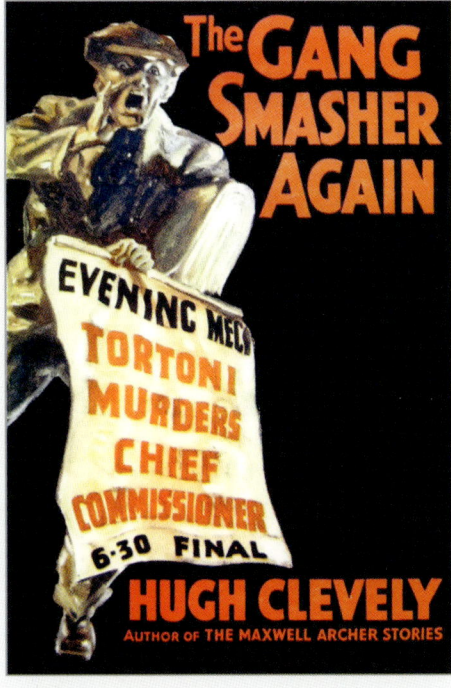

WOT NO SIGNATURE?: Top left: *Call in the Yard* by David Hume (Collins, 1936). At one time suspected to be by Reginald Heade, this is now thought much likelier to be McConnell's work; both artists supplied other Hume covers for Collins. Top right: *Naked Gold* by S t'Serstevens (Constable, 1937). This was attributed to McConnell by another collector; but only one other, confirmed, McConnell painting for Constable is known, and this author doubts the attribution. Bottom left: *The Gang Smasher Again* by Hugh Clevely (Cassell, 1939). This is quite likely to be McConnell's work, as he painted covers for Clevely's Maxwell Archer stories. Bottom right: *The Spring Returns* by Dorothy Black (Hutchinson 1935). McConnell was being commissioned by Hutchinson at the time, and the bouquet certainly recalls a similar one for Grace Elliott Taylor's *She Grew Up* (see page 98).

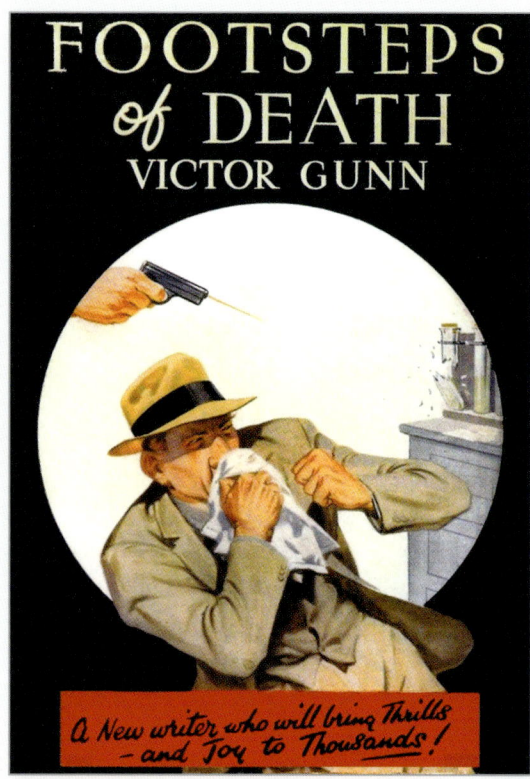

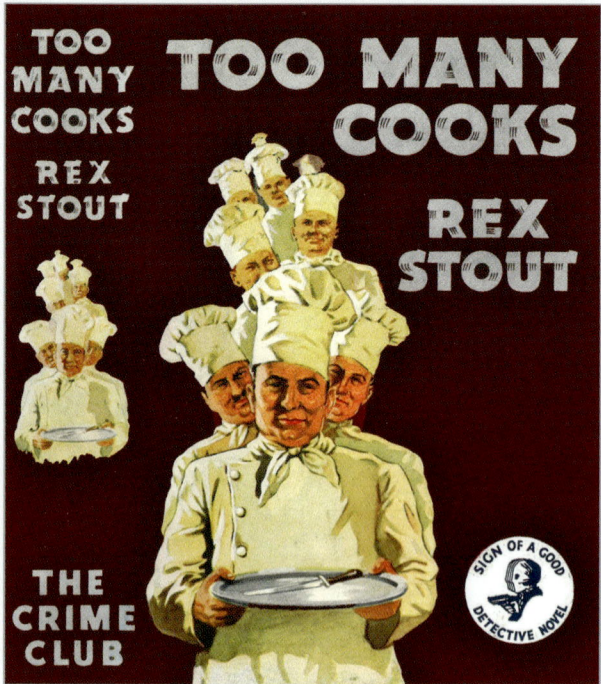

WOT NO SIGNATURE?: Top: *Footsteps of Death* (left) and *Ironsides of the Yard* (right) by Victor Gunn (Collins, 1939, 1940). McConnell would go on to paint another dozen covers for Victor Gunn novels, and everything points to these unsigned examples being the others' precursors. Bottom left: *Death Before Honour* by David Hume (Collins, 1939). Another unsigned David Hume cover; and whoever painted the Victor Gunn ones probably did this one too. McConnell would begin signing his Hume covers the following year. Bottom right: *Too Many Cooks* by Rex Stout (Collins, 1938). But the chefs looks like McConnell's to me.

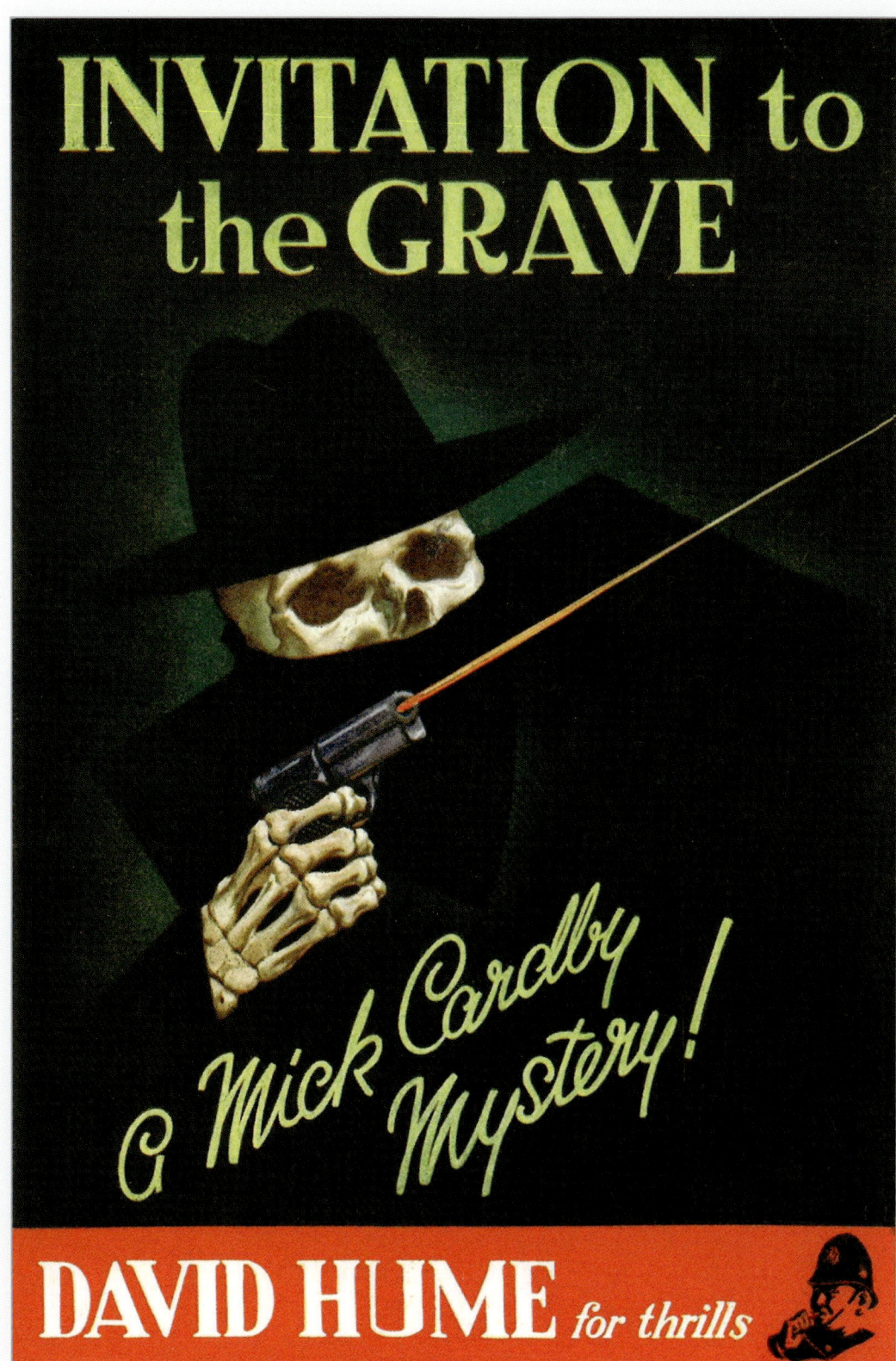

WOT NO SIGNATURE?: *Invitation to the Grave* by David Hume (Collins, 1940). One more unsigned cover for a thriller from this author; but here the style really leaves no room for doubt that it is McConnell's work.

Original artwork for *Murder by Arrangement* by William Beyer (Partridge, 1947); painted April 1946. (Author's collection.)

4: DEPICTING THE DETECTIVES: CRIME THRILLERS AND MYSTERIES

'I remember once reading a story by a writer of experience whose work I had always liked because he told a good story and held the interest to the last page. But in a lapse of appreciation – or so it seemed to me – he produced in one of his novels a scene in which a tommy-gun shooting episode took place in Piccadilly, the villains firing from the back of a car. That seemed to me to be going rather beyond the range of possibility – a thing like this doesn't happen in Piccadilly.'

Christine Campbell Thomson, 1946.[48]

McConnell, the artist who painted a Tommy-gun-toting figure for the jacket of the Peter Cheyney novel *This Man is Dangerous* (see page 95), began his career in book-cover illustration in the middle of the 'golden age' of detective fiction. Colin Wilson has noted that, by the arrival of World War Two, murder mysteries constituted a quarter of all new fiction: 'Novels of detection flowed from the presses month after month, year after year, in an ever-increasing tide,' he writes, 'the appetite for them seemed to be insatiable.'[49] Wilson also disparagingly points out that covers for these novels quickly achieved a high degree of standardisation so that avid readers could spot books in their favourite genre on sight, and not be set a puzzle before confronting the one set in the novel's pages.

> 'Jackets were of a more or less standard character. Their common features being crude colour, ill-designed type, and the display, often in defiance of a book's actual contents, of a sprawled corpse in expensive-looking clothes. The inclusion of a weapon of some kind (not necessarily that mentioned in the story) was another pictorial convention, curiously wrought daggers and great liquorice-coloured automatics being top-favourites.'[50]

The challenge for a new entrant to this field of illustration, such as McConnell, was to bend and stretch the conventions without frustrating his art director. Covers for the top authors, such as Christie and Sayers, were already 'sown up' by his more established competitors, but he was given a chance with new British thriller authors like Cheyney and Edwy Searles Brooks, as well as Americans like Erle Stanley Gardner.

McConnell's jacket for Erle Stanley Gardner's *The Case of the Rolling Bones* (Cassell, 1940).

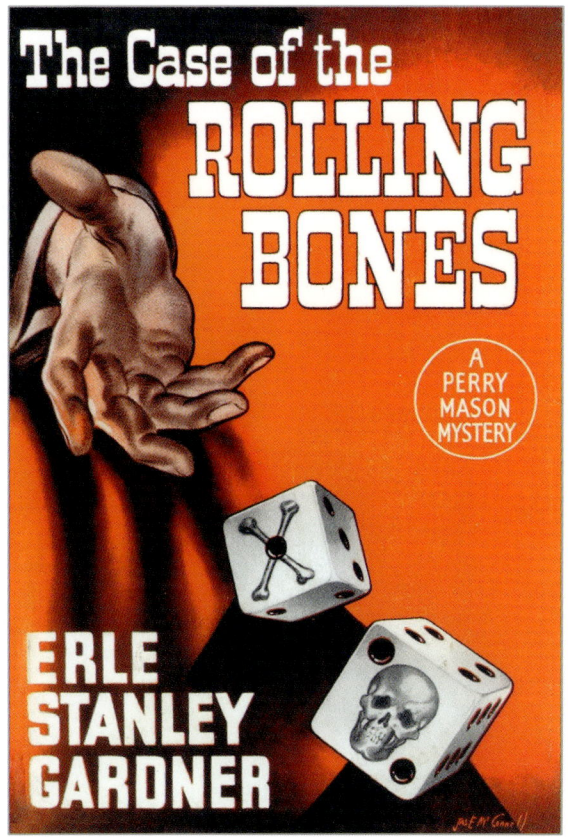

In fact, Gardner's *The Case of the Buried Clock* was his first post-war cover assignment from Cassell, whose art director instructed him to produce an approximation of the American first edition jacket.

In January 1946, McConnell resumed work for Collins on Brooks' Berkeley Gray and Victor Gunn series with the cover for Gray's *Mr. Ball of Fire*. Over the next ten years, he painted a further fifteen Grays and a dozen Gunns (and many more guns of course). Crime fiction was perhaps this publisher's strongest suit, and McConnell's commissions also included books by Laurence Meynell, Stephen Maddock, Arthur Hobart Mills, J M Walsh, Ben Benson, Hartley Howard and the golden-age wordsmith J Jefferson Farjeon, with a cover for one of his final novels, *The Double Crime*. But McConnell's most numerous crime covers, after those for novels by Brooks, were five for thrillers by the hard-boiled American writer Bart Spicer (Albert Samuel Spicer 1918-1978). Perhaps the most striking of these was the skeletal trombonist for *Blues for the Prince*.

Above: *The Double Crime* by J Jefferson Farjeon (Collins, 1953); painted March 1953.

Lleft: McConnell's cover for Erle Stanley Gardner's *The Case of the Buried Clock* (Cassell, 1945); painted August 1945. Below: the inspiration: the cover of the US edition, published by Morrow earlier the same year (artist unknown).

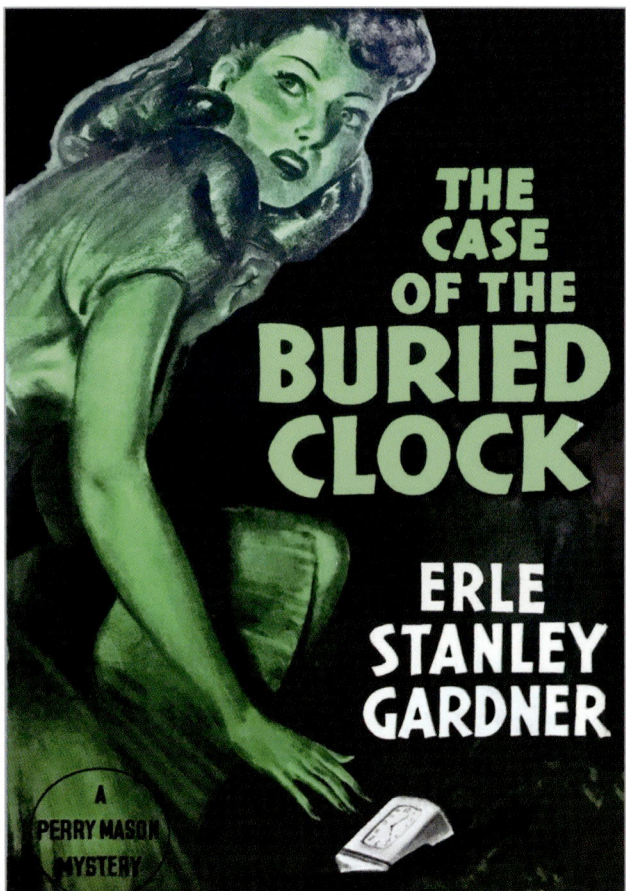

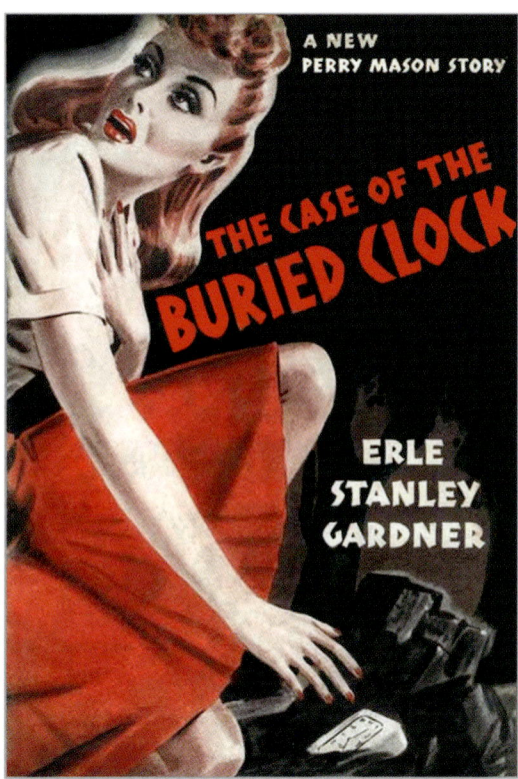

Blues for the Prince by Bart Spicer (Collins, 1950); painted June 1950. (Image courtesy Jim Kealy.)

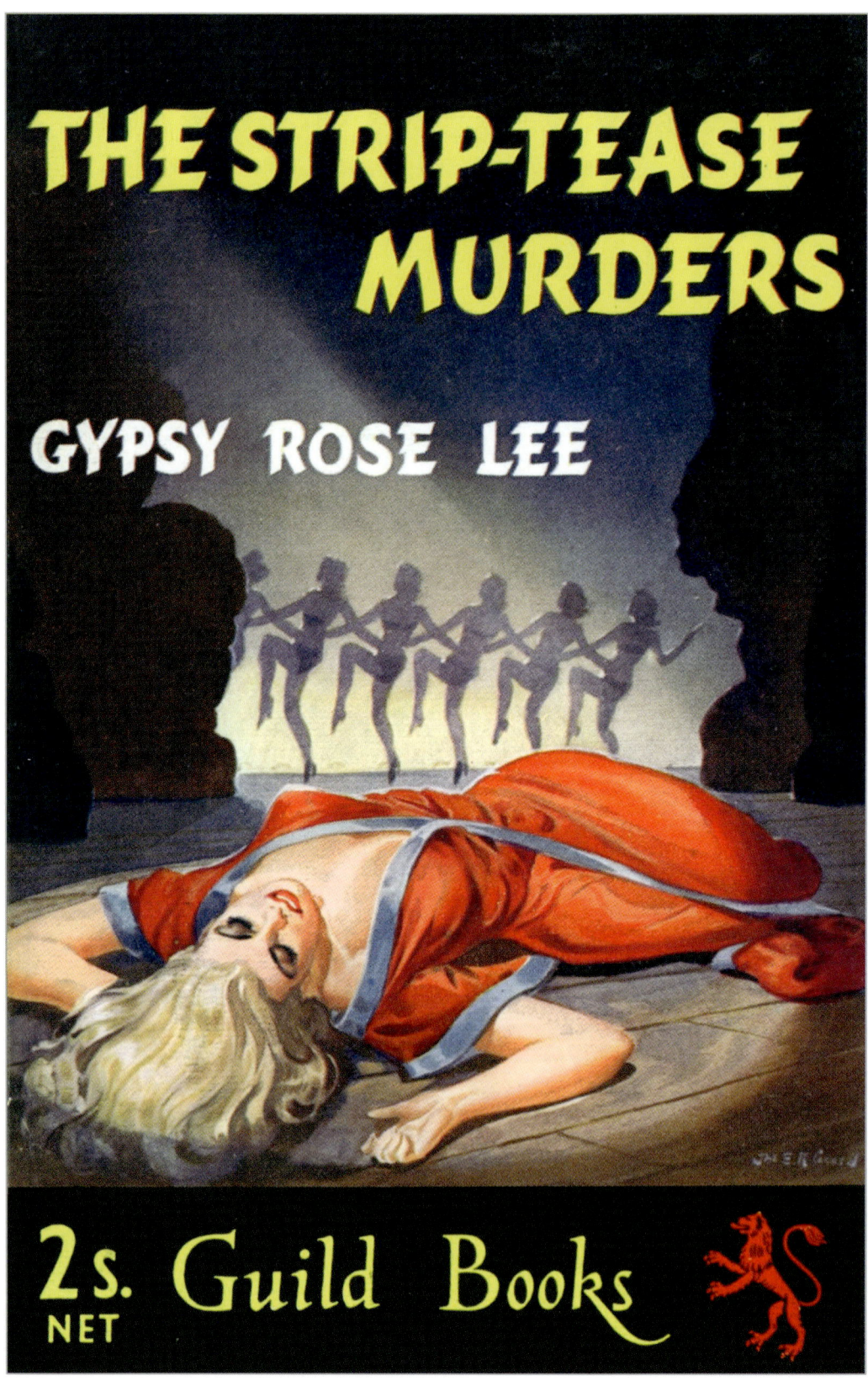

The Strip-Tease Murders by Gypsy Rose Lee (Guild, 1953); painted March 1953. (Image courtesy Jim Kealy.)

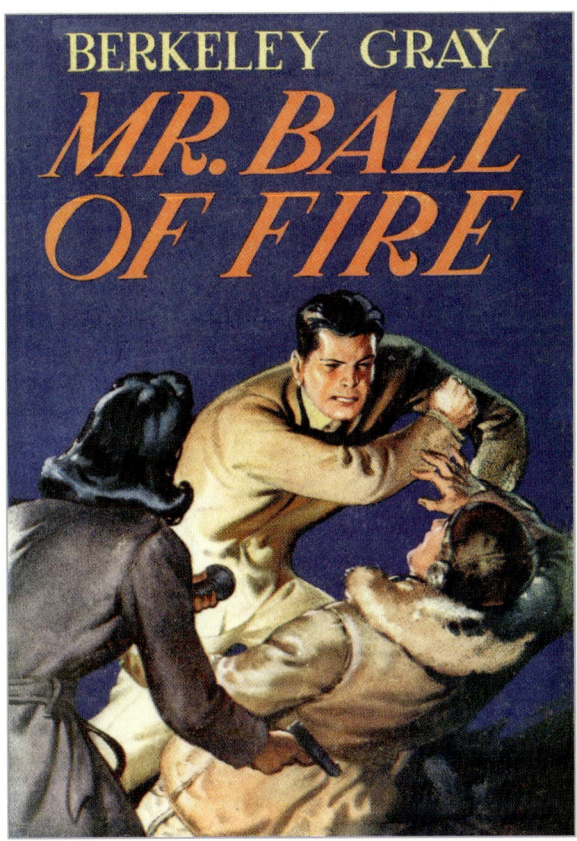

Mr. Ball of Fire by Berkeley Gray (Collins, 1946); painted January 1946.

had requested mostly romantic fiction covers from McConnell, also entrusted him with commissions for American crime novels. These included not only a trio of covers for classics by James M Cain (the most successful of which, for *Jealous Woman*, was a riff on that of the American Avon paperback edition published in 1951) but also five jackets for the British editions (and first hardback editions of Dell paperback originals) of John D MacDonald thrillers.[51] These mid-1950s volumes, including appropriately *The Price of Murder*, are now amongst the most valuable post-war books featuring McConnell's art. British detective stories were not entirely neglected, though, and there was a brace of accomplished covers for stories featuring the popular radio sleuth Dr Morelle, created by Ernest Dudley (Vivian Ernest Coltman-Allen 1908-2006).

However, McConnell's most ubiquitous crime covers remain those illustrating tough thrillers by Vernon Warren (John Warren Vernon Chapman 1925-96), a British author who had previously worked for Lloyds of London but set his fiction in the USA, where he

Callers for Dr. Morelle by Ernest Dudley (Robert Hale, 1957); painted August 1956.

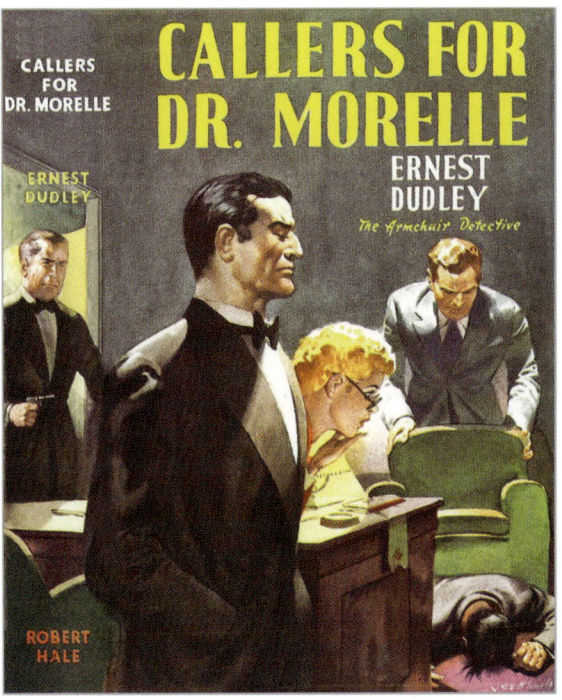

Cassell's post-war crime list was less extensive than Collins', and a pair of Nigel Morland covers in 1952 were the highlights of only a handful of criminous commissions they gave McConnell in the first decade after the war – until he was selected to replace Reginald Heade in furnishing the covers for their mid-1950s reprints of the Fu Manchu canon. McConnell painted half-a-dozen of these, often adapting the covers of earlier editions for a new readership. He had already proved his worth with an earlier Fu Manchu cover for the publishing consortium Guild Books, for which he also painted the memorable corpse-and-chorines cover for Gypsy Rose Lee's *The Strip-Tease Murders*. In the 1930s and during World War Two, Sax Rohmer (Arthur Henry Ward 1883-1959), the creator of Fu Manchu, the 'Devil Doctor', actually lived just down the road from the artist in Reigate, Surrey.

Robert Hale, a publisher that previously

Dr. Morelle Takes a Bow by Ernest Dudley (Robert Hale, 1957); painted May 1956. (Image courtesy Jim Kealy.)

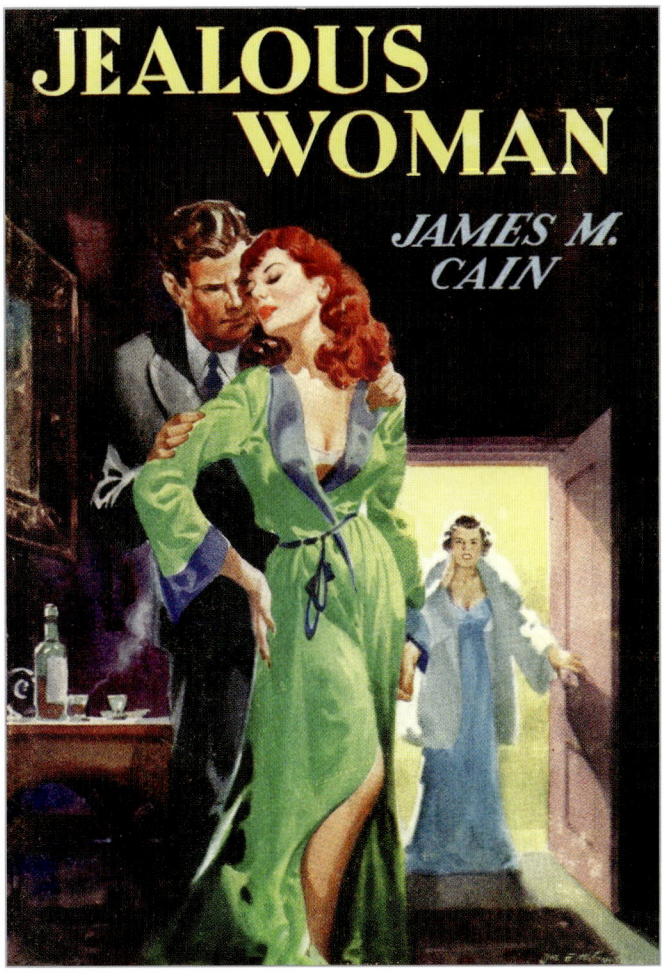

Jealous Woman by James M Cain (Robert Hale, 1956); painted September 1955. (Image courtesy Jim Kealy.)

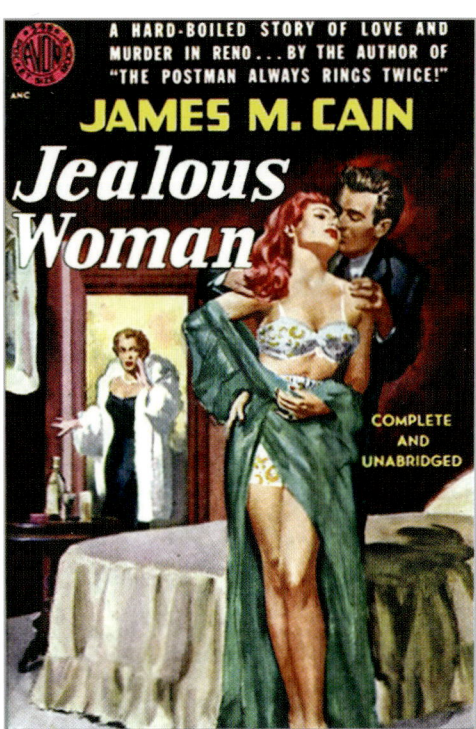

Above: the inspiration for McConnell's *Jealous Woman* painting: the US edition from Avon, published in 1951 (artist unknown).

Below: *The Wages of Fear* by Georges Arnaud (Guild, 1953); painted February 1953.

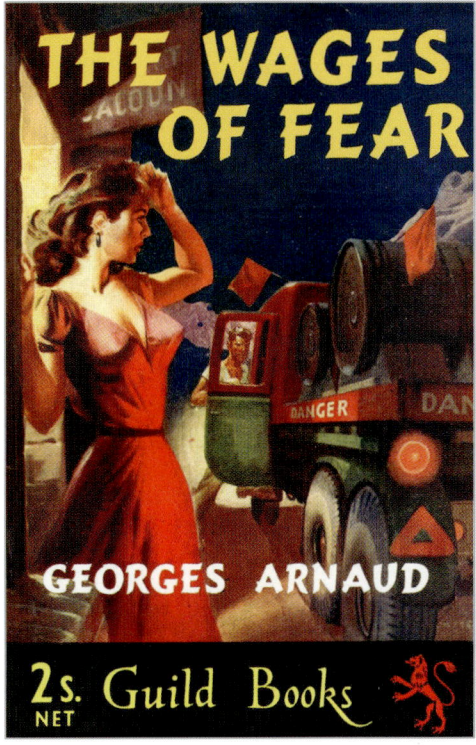

eventually spent his retirement. His books, and McConnell's hard-boiled covers, were adopted by the Thriller Book Club. McConnell supplied striking action covers for eleven Warren titles between 1953 and 1957. Three of the paintings – *Brandon Takes Over* (originally painted January 1953), *Brandon Returns* (originally painted July 1953) and *Appointment in Hell* (originally painted November 1955) – were extended, possibly by another hand, to fit the wraparound cover format of early Digit paperbacks published by Brown Watson. McConnell contributed at least 38 covers for the Digit imprint, of which about 20 per cent were for crime stories, including three Edgar Wallace reprints.

McConnell also painted a few crime covers for the Hutchinson group of publishers. These included two now rare jackets for books by the prolific and multi-pseudonymous T C H Jacobs (painted in July 1954 and April 1956, for Stanley Paul); another pair for scarce Gordon Ashe (John Creasey) novels (painted in July 1954 and February 1955, for John Long); and an appropriately menacing wrapper for Ruth Alexander's 1920s railway thriller *The Wrecker* (1951, for Eldon). There were two handfuls of crime novel covers for W H Allen, perhaps most notably the gaslight ghoulishness of the now hard-to-find *Jack the Ripper* paperback (Pinnacle Books, 1952); but – in common with T V Boardman – this publisher generally offered McConnell other subjects. Nevertheless, this did not stop his work becoming emblematic of English crime cover art during the 1950s, the age when the detective story and the police procedural dominated the British 'B' film.

The Wrecker by Ruth Alexander (Eldon, 1951); painted May 1951.

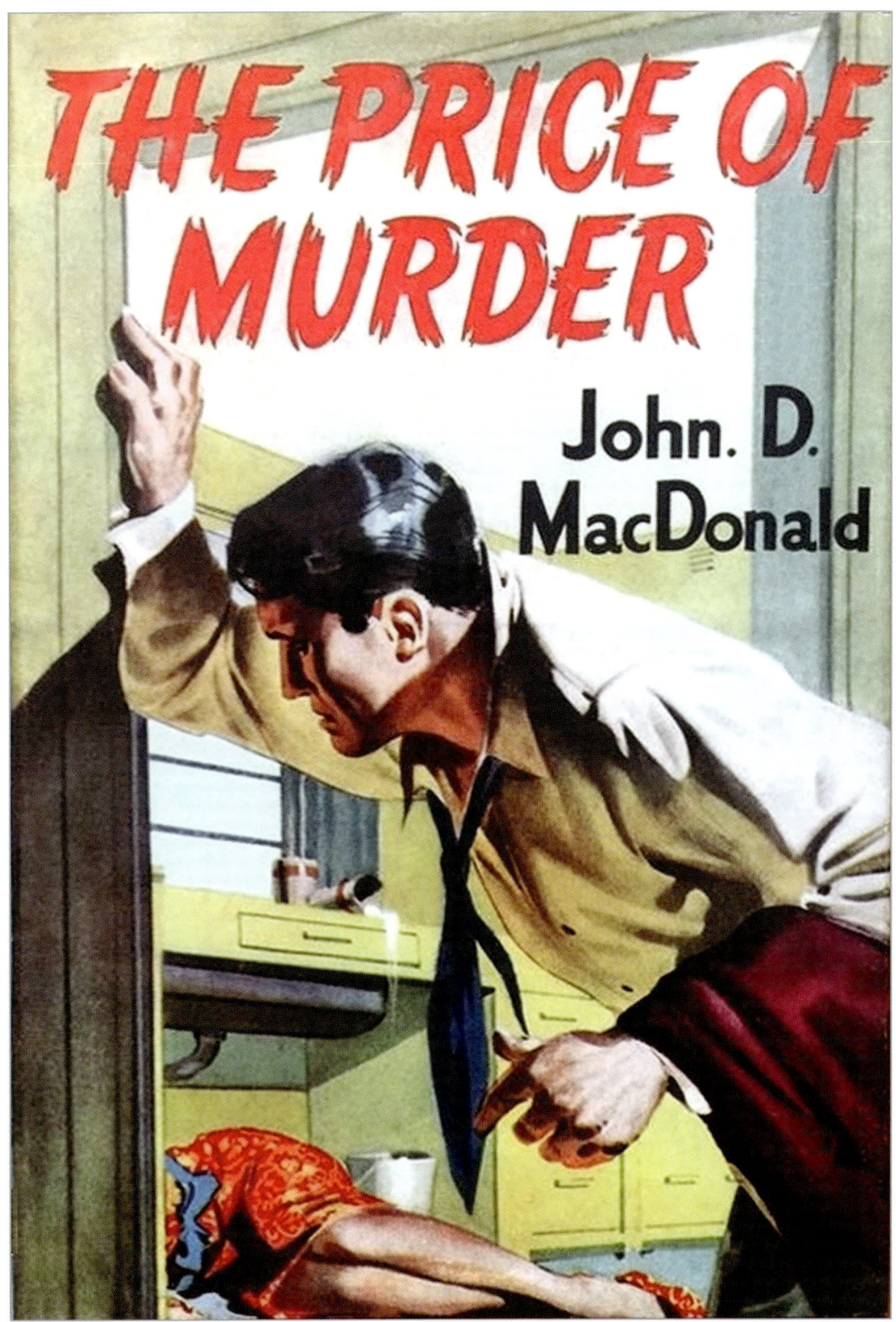

The Price of Murder by John D MacDonald (Robert Hale, 1958); painted February 1958.

GALLERY

THE VERNON WARRENS: *Mister Violence* by Vernon Warren (John Gifford, 1957); painted March 1957; Thriller Book Club edition.

GALLERY

THE VERNON WARRENS: Top left: *Brandon Takes Over* by Vernon Warren (John Gifford, 1953; painted January 1953; Thriller Book Club edition. Top right: *Brandon in New York* by Vernon Warren (John Gifford, 1953); painted April 1953; Thriller Book Club edition. Bottom left: *Brandon Returns* by Vernon Warren (John Gifford, 1954); painted July 1953. Bottom right: *Appointment in Hell* by Vernon Warren (John Gifford, 1956); painted November 1955. All four of these titles were subsequently reissued as Digit Books paperbacks, with McConnell's artwork reused in adapted form (see overleaf). (*Brandon Takes Over* and *Brandon in New York* images courtesy Jim Kealy.)

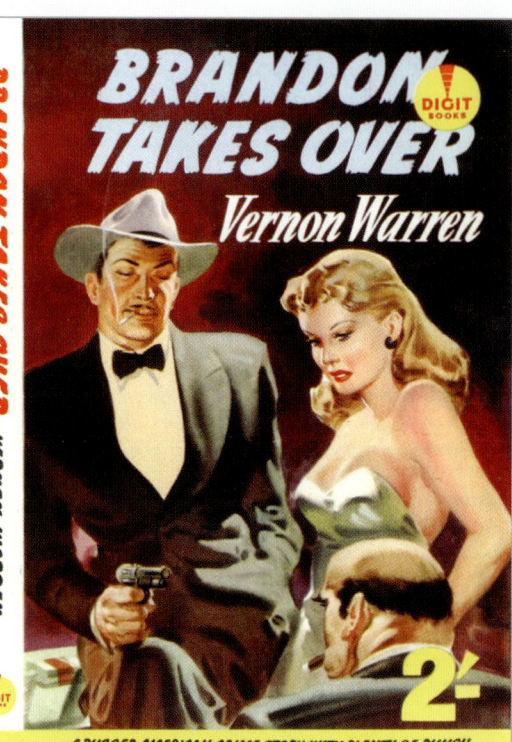

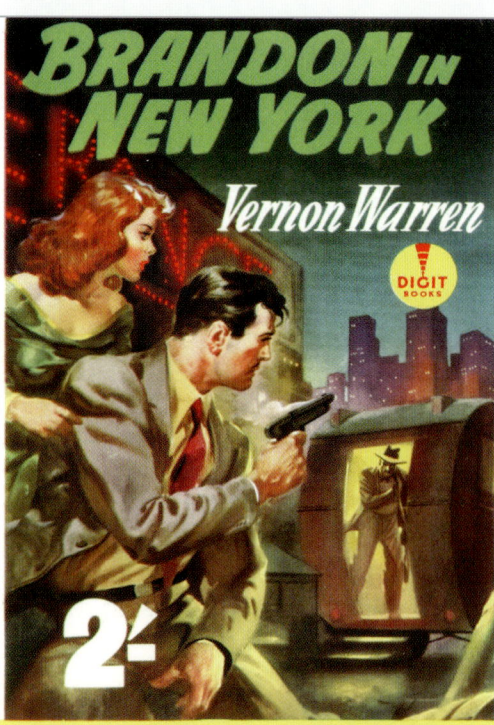

THE VERNON WARRENS: Advance covers for the Digit paperback editions of Vernon Warren's *Brandon Takes Over* (top) and *Brandon in New York* (bottom), both published in 1957. (Author's collection.)

GALLERY

THE VERNON WARRENS: The Digit paperback edition of *Brandon Returns* (top); and the advance cover for the equivalent edition of *Appointment in Hell* (bottom), both published in 1957. (Latter from Author's collection.)

THE VERNON WARRENS: Top left: *Bullets for Brandon* by Vernon Warren (John Gifford, 1955); painted March 1955; Thriller Book Club edition. Top right: *No Bouquets for Brandon* by Vernon Warren (John Gifford, 1955); painted October 1954. Bottom: an advance cover for the Digit paperback edition of *No Bouquets for Brandon*, published in 1957. (Top two images courtesy Jim Kealy; bottom image from author's collection.)

GALLERY

THE VERNON WARRENS: Top left: *The Blue Mauritius* by Vernon Warren (John Gifford, 1954); painted September 1953. Top right: *By Fair Means or Foul* by Vernon Warren (John Gifford, 1956); painted April 1956. Bottom left: *Three Steps to Hell* by Vernon Warren (John Gifford, 1957); painted November 1955; Thriller Book Club edition. Bottom right: *Runaround* by Vernon Warren (John Gifford, 1958); painted August 1957; the last book in the series. (*Three Steps to Hell* image courtesy Jim Kealy.)

THE JOHN D MacDONALDS: *Contrary Pleasure* by John D MacDonald (Robert Hale, 1955); painted October 1954. Another portrait of Belinda Lee.

THE JOHN D MacDONALDS: *Hurricane* by John D MacDonald (Robert Hale, 1957); painted December 1956. It is easy to miss the man on the car roof!

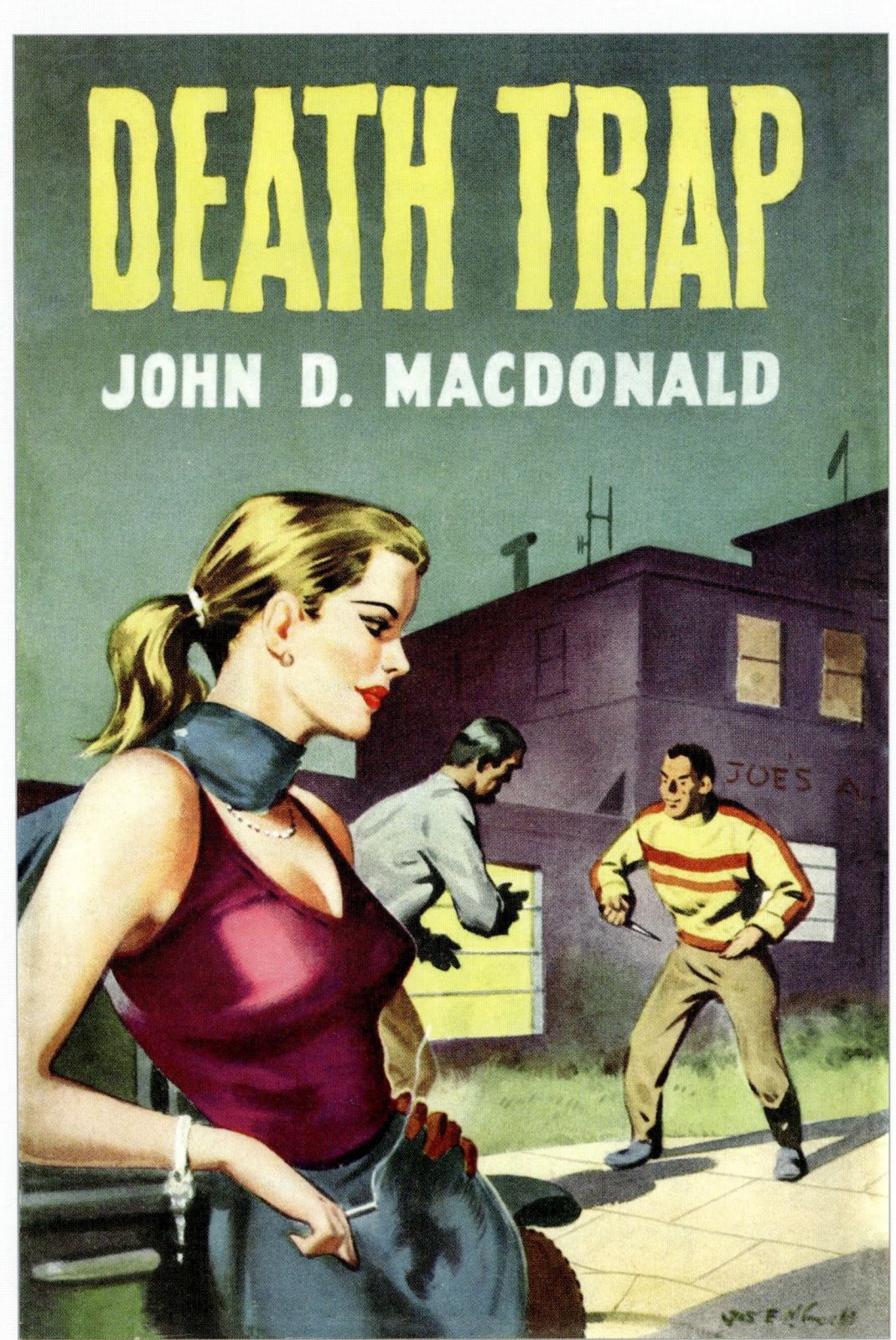

THE JOHN D MacDONALDS: *Death Trap* by John D MacDonald (Robert Hale, 1958); painted June 1957.

THE JOHN D MacDONALDS: *A Man of Affairs* by John D MacDonald (Robert Hale, 1958); painted February 1958.

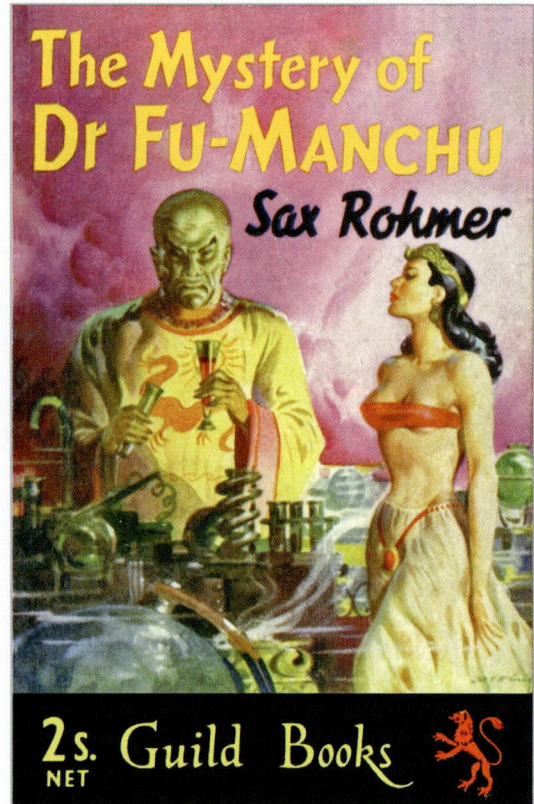

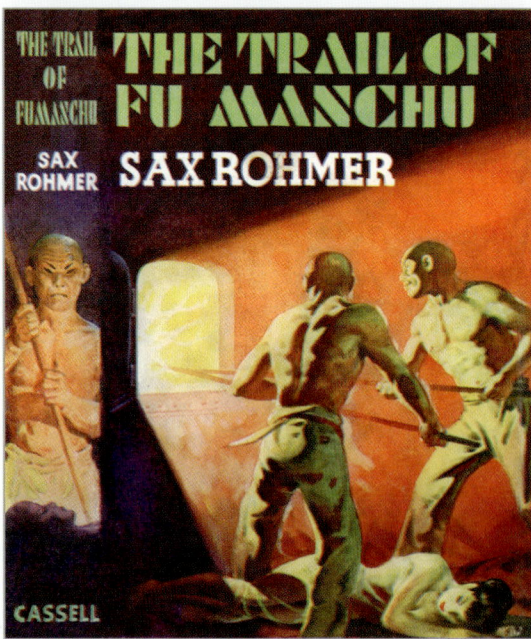

THE SAX ROHMERS: Top left: *The Mystery of Dr Fu-Manchu* by Sax Rohmer (Guild, 1953). A heady concoction of Oriental menace and eroticism. Signed, but not recorded in McConnell's workbook, it would have been painted in the run-up to the Queen's Coronation. Top right: *The Island of Fu Manchu* by Sax Rohmer (Cassell, 1956); painted January 1956. Bottom left: *The Trail of Fu Manchu* by Sax Rohmer (Cassell, 1957); painted August 1956. Bottom right: *Daughter of Fu Manchu* by Sax Rohmer (Cassell, 1963); painted August 1962. An earlier Cassell edition, published in 1955, had had a Reginald Heade cover. (*The Trail of Fu Manchu* image courtesy Jim Kealy.)

THE SAX ROHMERS: *The Drums of Fu Manchu* by Sax Rohmer (Cassell, 1956); painted February 1956. McConnell's inspiration for this piece was another, unidentified artist's jacket painting for the first Cassell edition of the same title, published in 1939 (see thumbnail image to the right). The basing of new jacket paintings on those produced for earlier editions of the same titles – including American editions – was fairly common practice at the time, and McConnell was just one of a number of artists who occasionally did this, Reginald Heade being another. This would doubtless have been on the instructions or at the suggestion of the publisher's art editor. (Main image courtesy Jim Kealy.)

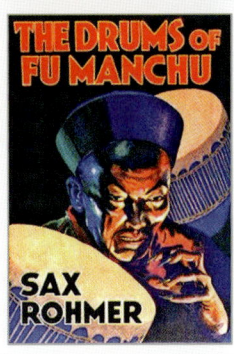

THE SAX ROHMERS: Original artwork for *The Bride of Fu Manchu* by Sax Rohmer (Cassell, 1956); painted January 1956. (Image courtesy Stephen James Walker.)

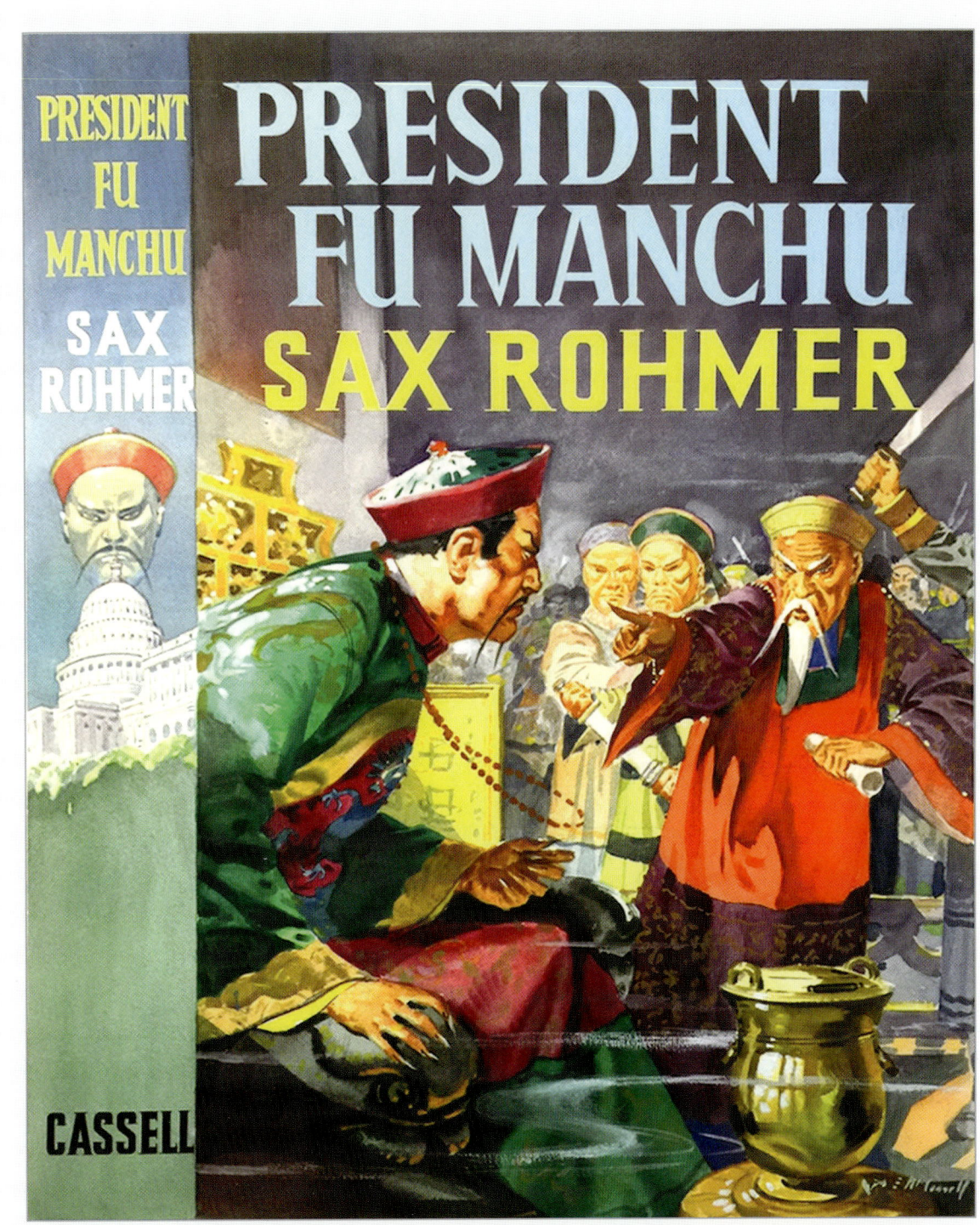

THE SAX ROHMERS: Original artwork for *President Fu Manchu* by Sax Rohmer (Cassell, 1957); painted August 1956. (Image courtesy Stephen James Walker.)

THE COLLINS MYSTERIES: THE BERKELEY GRAYS: *Dare-Devil Conquest* by Berkeley Gray (Collins, 1950); painted July 1949. (Image courtesy Jim Kealy.)

GALLERY

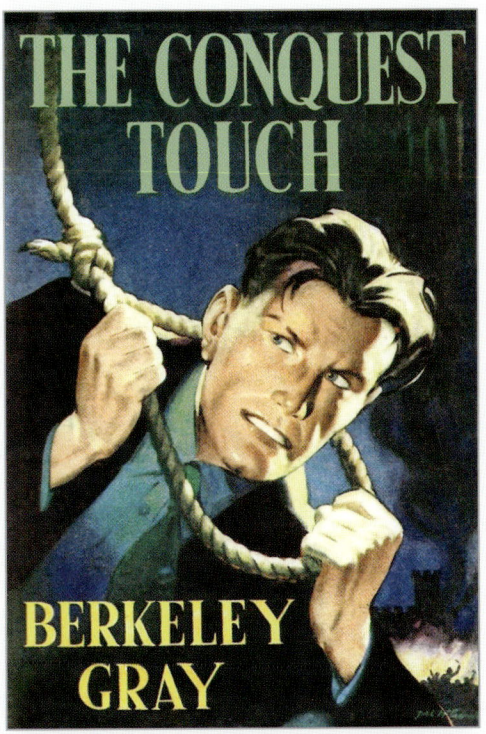
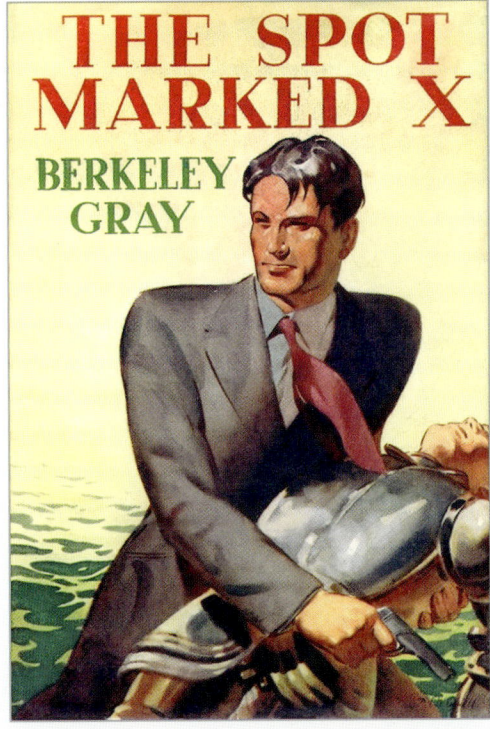
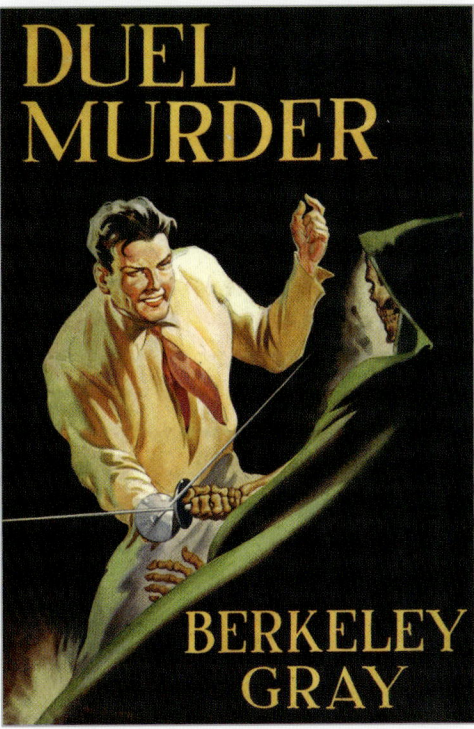

THE COLLINS MYSTERIES: THE BERKELEY GRAYS: Top left: *Killer Conquest* by Berkeley Gray (Collins, 1947); painted November 1946. Top right: *The Conquest Touch* by Berkeley Gray (Collins, 1948); painted August 1947. Bottom left: *The Spot Marked X* by Berkeley Gray (Collins, 1948); painted February 1948. Bottom right: *Duel Murder* by Berkeley Gray (Collins, 1949); painted November 1948. (*The Spot Marked X* Image courtesy Jim Kealy.)

THE COLLINS MYSTERIES: THE BERKELEY GRAYS: *Conquest in Scotland* by Berkeley Gray (Collins, 1952); painted March 1951. (Image courtesy Jim Kealy.)

GALLERY

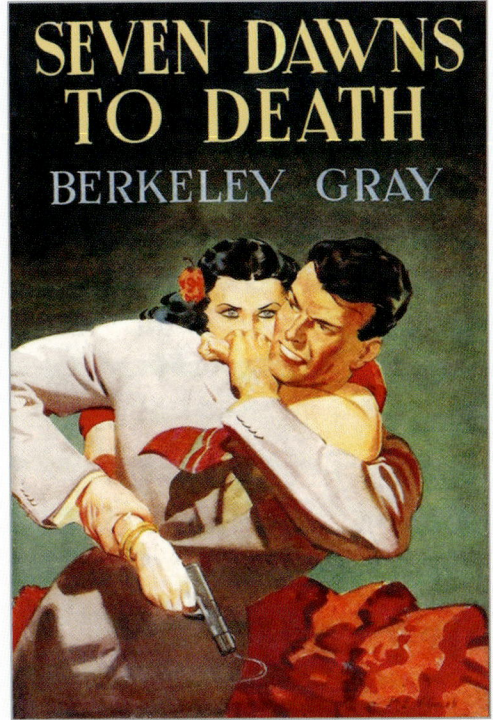

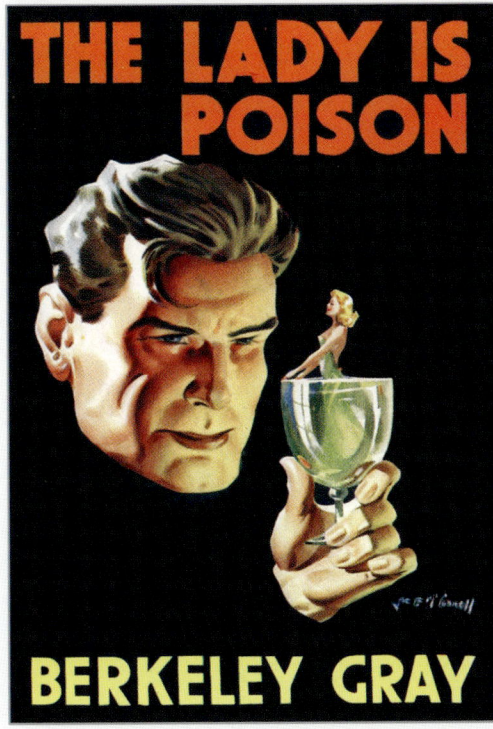

THE COLLINS MYSTERIES: THE BERKELEY GRAYS: Top left: *Seven Dawns to Death* by Berkeley Gray (Collins, 1950); painted March 1950. Top right: *Operation Conquest* by Berkeley Gray (Collins, 1951); painted September 1950. Bottom left: *The Lady is Poison* by Berkeley Gray (Collins, 1952); painted October 1951. Another miniature marvel, this time in a wine glass. Bottom right: *Target for Conquest* by Berkeley Gray (Collins, 1953); painted March 1953. (All images except *Target for Conquest* courtesy Jim Kealy.)

MINIATURE MARVELS

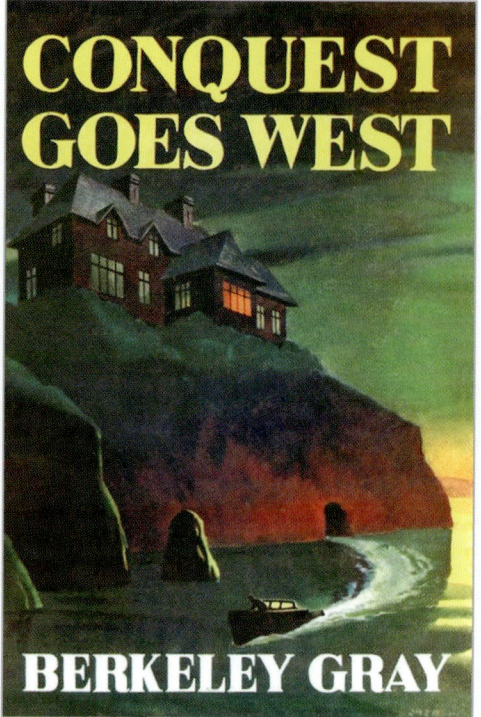
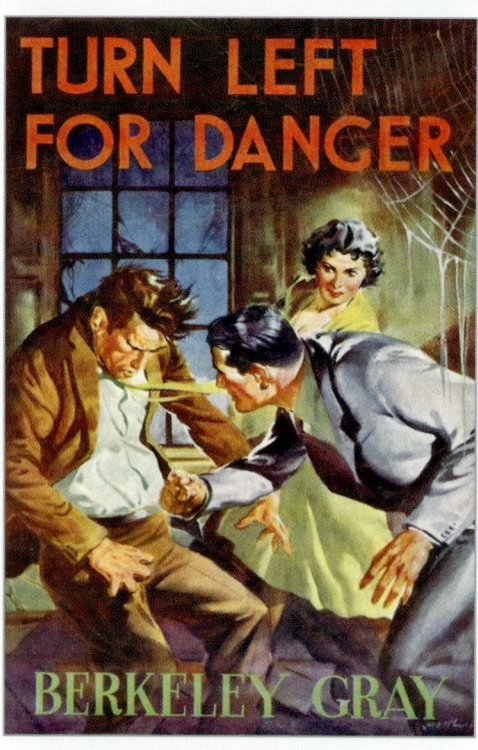

THE COLLINS MYSTERIES: THE BERKELEY GRAYS: Top left: *The Half-Open Door* by Berkeley Gray (Collins, 1953); painted June 1952. Top right: *Conquest Goes West* by Berkeley Gray (Collins, 1954); painted June 1954. Bottom left: *Turn Left for Danger* by Berkeley Gray (Collins, 1955); painting not recorded in McConnell's workbook. Bottom right: *Conquest in Command* by Berkeley Gray (Collins, 1956); painted June 1955. (All images courtesy Jim Kealy.)

THE COLLINS MYSTERIES: THE BERKELEY GRAYS: *Follow the Lady* by Berkeley Gray (Collins, 1954); painted November 1953. (Image courtesy Jim Kealy.)

MINIATURE MARVELS

THE COLLINS MYSTERIES: THE VICTOR GUNNS: *Death on Shivering Sand* by Victor Gunn (Collins, 1947); painted June 1946.

GALLERY

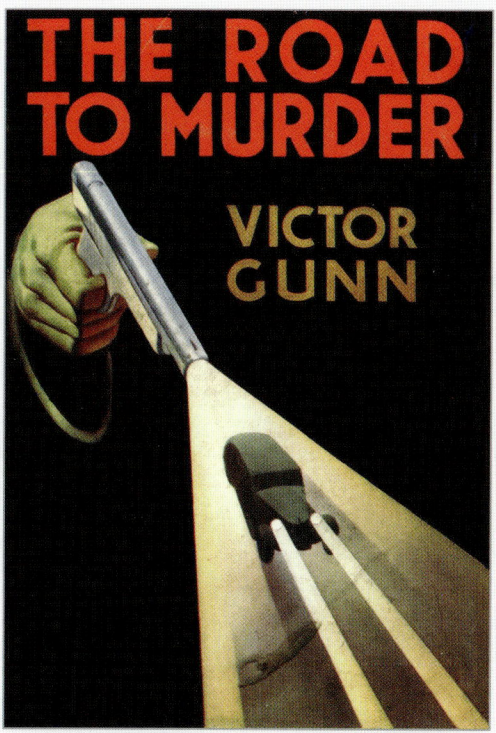

THE COLLINS MYSTERIES: THE VICTOR GUNNS: Top left: *Ironsides on the Spot* by Victor Gunn (Collins, 1948); painted February 1948. Top right: *The Road to Murder* by Victor Gunn (Collins, 1949); painted June 1948. An unusual experiment in composition. Bottom left: *Murder on Ice* by Victor Gunn (Collins, 1951); painted June 1950. Bottom right: *The Whistling Key* by Victor Gunn (Collins, 1953); painted December 1952. A moonlight Gothic composition. (*Ironsides on the Spot* and *The Road to Murder* images courtesy Jim Kealy.)

THE COLLINS MYSTERIES: THE VICTOR GUNNS: *Death Comes Laughing* by Victor Gunn (Collins, 1952); painted February 1952.

THE COLLINS MYSTERIES: THE VICTOR GUNNS: *The Crooked Staircase* by Victor Gunn (Collins, 1954); painted June 1953. (Image courtesy Jim Kealy.)

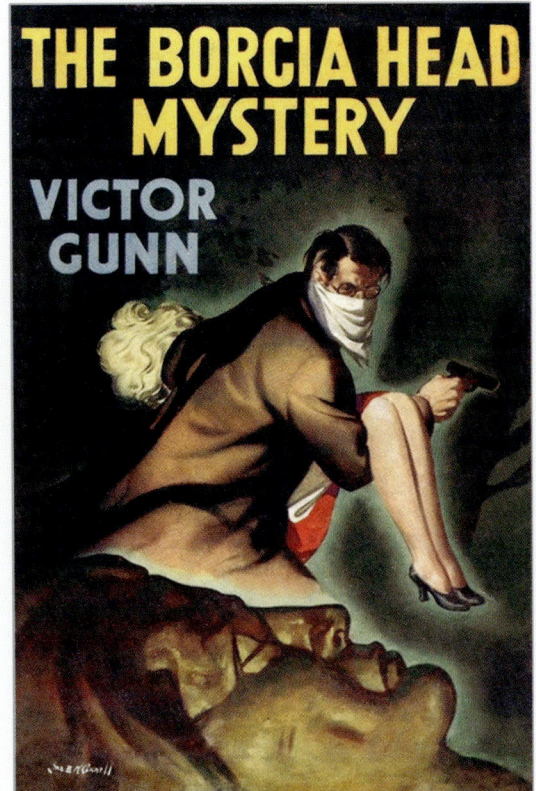
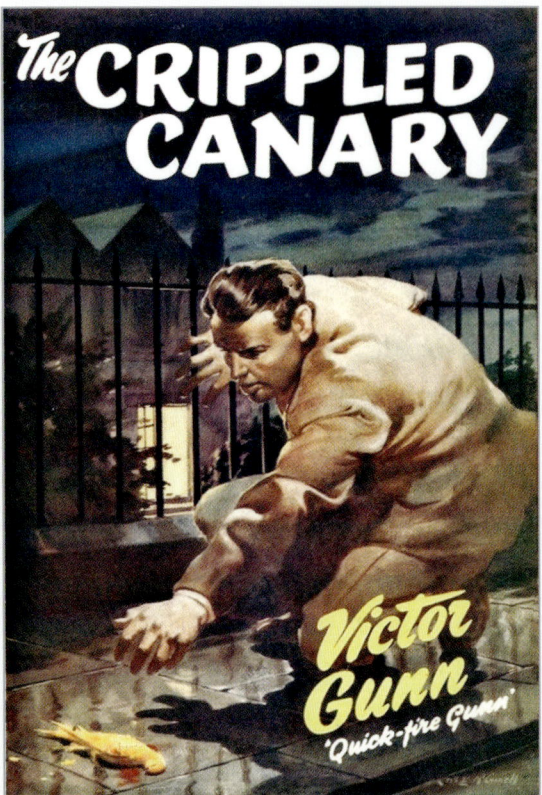

THE COLLINS MYSTERIES: THE VICTOR GUNNS: Top left: *The Borgia Head Mystery* by Victor Gunn (Collins, 1951); painted January 1951. Top right: *The Crippled Canary* by Victor Gunn (Collins, 1954); painted February 1954. Bottom left: *The Laughing Grave* by Victor Gunn (Collins, 1955); painted September 1954. More moonlight Gothicism. Bottom right: *The Painted Dog* by Victor Gunn (Collins, 1955); painted March 1955. (*The Painted Dog* image courtesy Jim Kealy.)

THE COLLINS MYSTERIES: THE VICTOR GUNNS: *Dead Men's Bells* by Victor Gunn (Collins, 1956); painted October 1955. (Image courtesy Jim Kealy.)

MORE COLLINS CRIME AND MYSTERY: *Public Mischief* by Stephen Maddock (Collins 1951), painted June 1950.

GALLERY

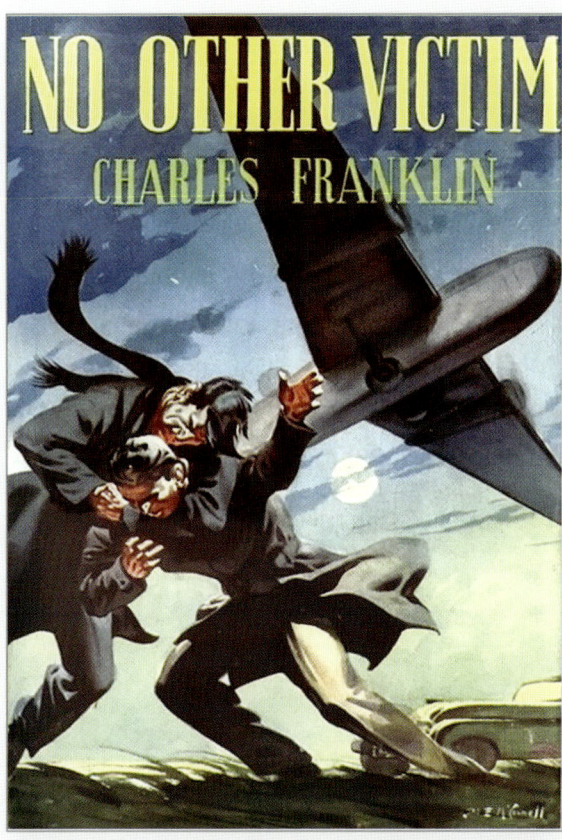

MORE COLLINS CRIME AND MYSTERY: Top left: *The Evil Hour* by Laurence Meynell (Collins, 1947); painted November 1946. Top right: *No Other Victim* by Charles Franklin (Collins, 1952); painted October 1951. Bottom left: *Black Sheep, Run* by Bart Spicer (Collins, 1952); painted December 1951. Bottom right: *Shadow of Fear* by Bart Spicer (Collins, 1953); painted June 1952. (All images except *No Other Victim* courtesy Jim Kealy.)

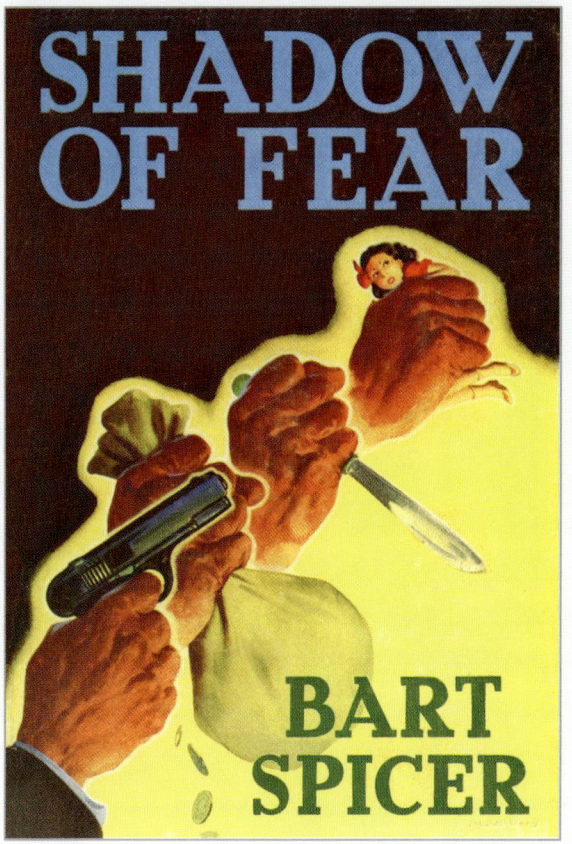

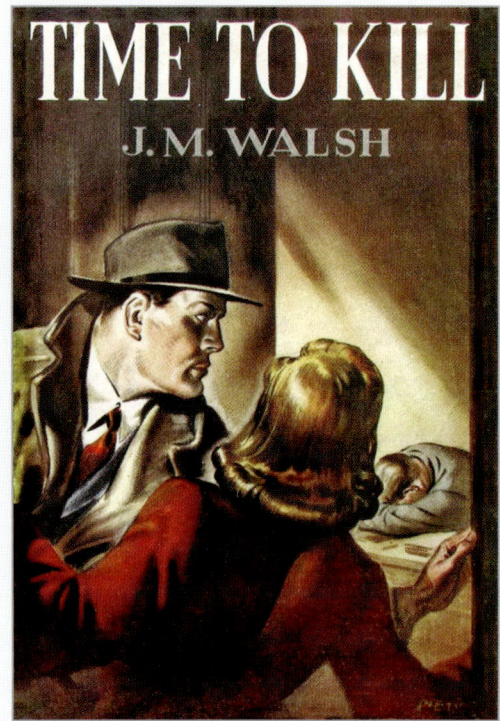

MORE COLLINS CRIME AND MYSTERY: Top left: *Time to Kill* by J M Walsh (Collins, 1949); painted February 1949. Top right: *Perchance to Kill* by Charles Franklin (Collins, 1954); painted November 1953. Bottom left: *Target in Taffeta* by Ben Benson (Collins, 1955); painted February 1955. Bottom right: *The Bowman Touch* by Hartley Howard (Collins, 1956); painted June 1955.

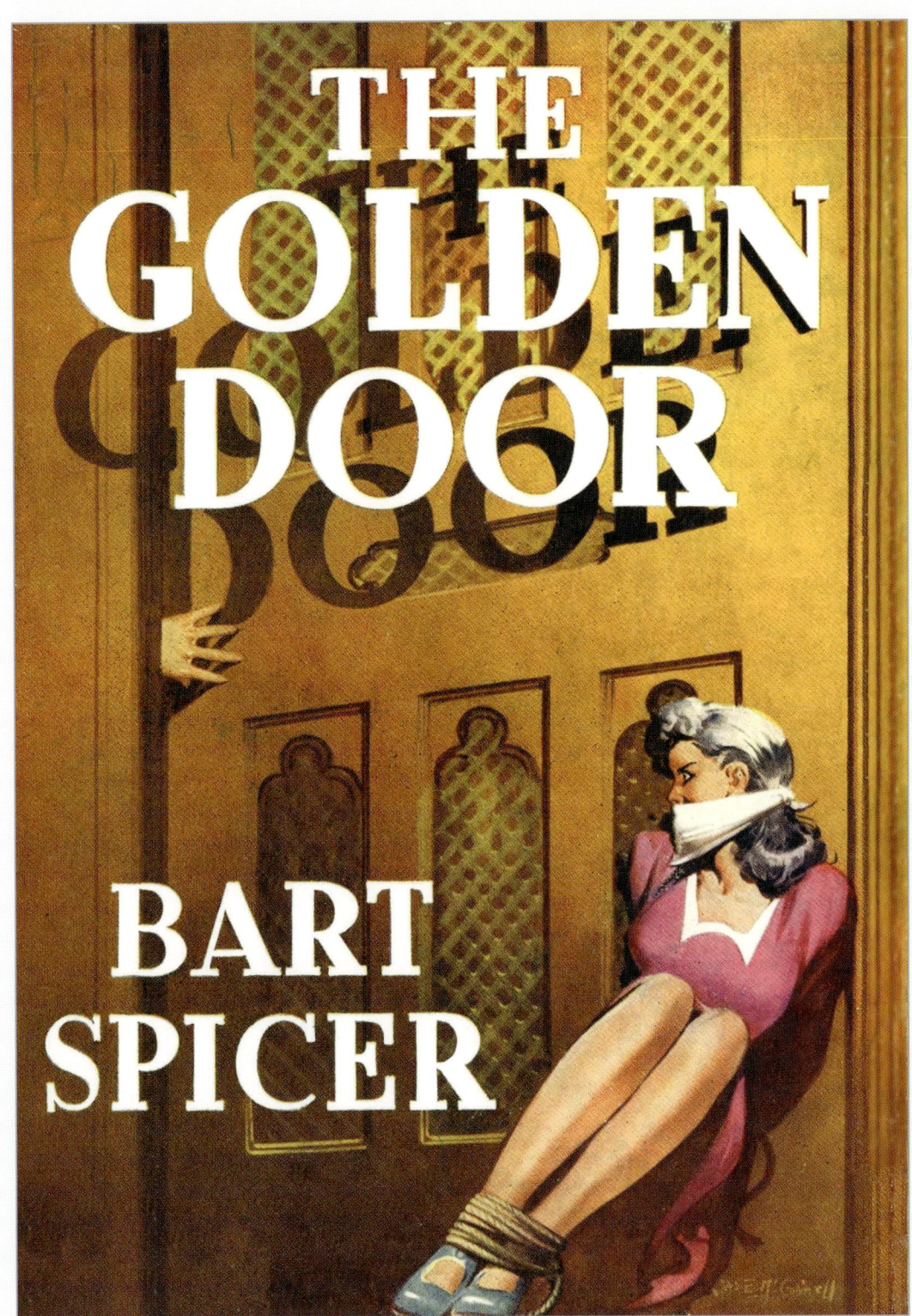

MORE COLLINS CRIME AND MYSTERY: *The Golden Door* by Bart Spicer (Collins, 1951); painted May 1951. The incorporation of the shadow of the title into the body of the painting suggests that McConnell must have executed the lettering on this cover, and perhaps on others. (Image courtesy Jim Kealy.)

THE EDGAR WALLACES: *The Hand of Power* by Edgar Wallace (Arrow Books 413JL, 1956); painted March 1961.

GALLERY

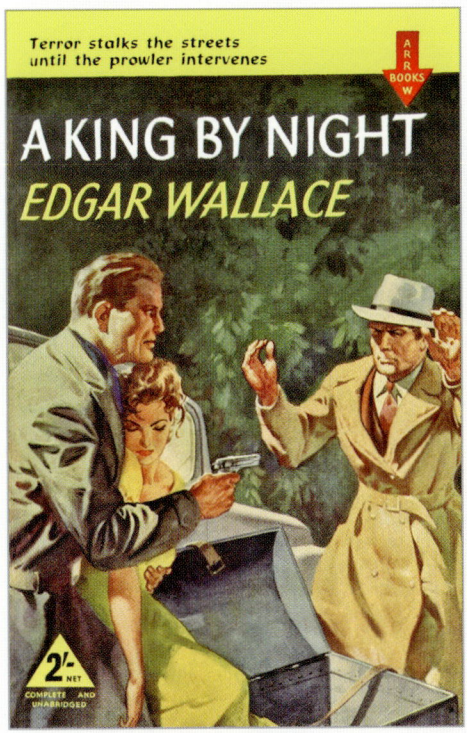
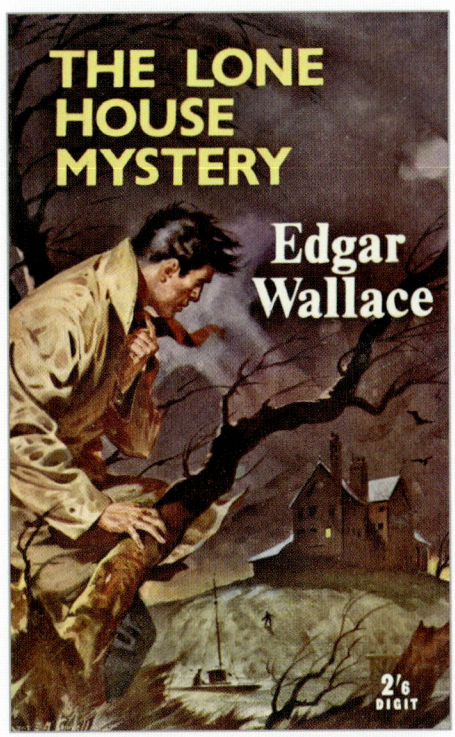
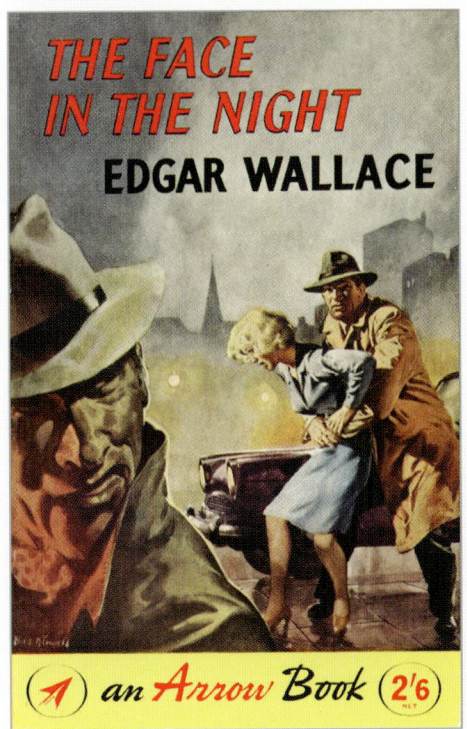
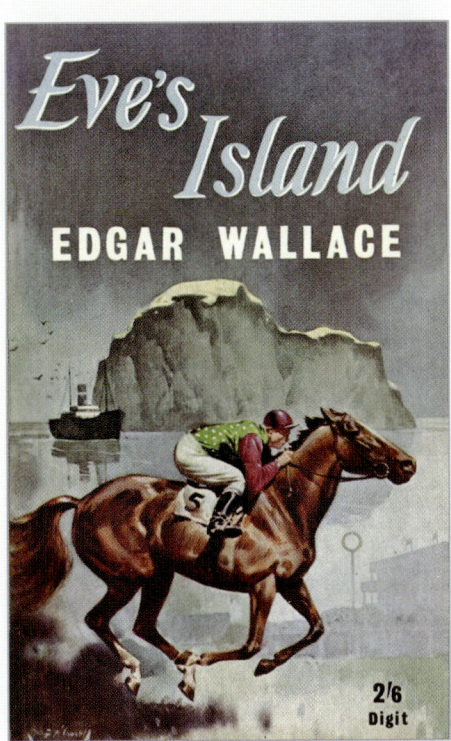

THE EDGAR WALLACES: Top left: *A King by Night* by Edgar Wallace (Arrow Books 441JL, 1957); painted August 1956. Top right: *The Lone House Mystery* by Edgar Wallace (Digit R517, 1961); painted March 1961. Bottom left: *The Face in the Night* by Edgar Wallace (Arrow Books 593, 1961); painting not recorded. Bottom right: *Eve's Island* by Edgar Wallace (Digit R528, 1962), painted May 1961.

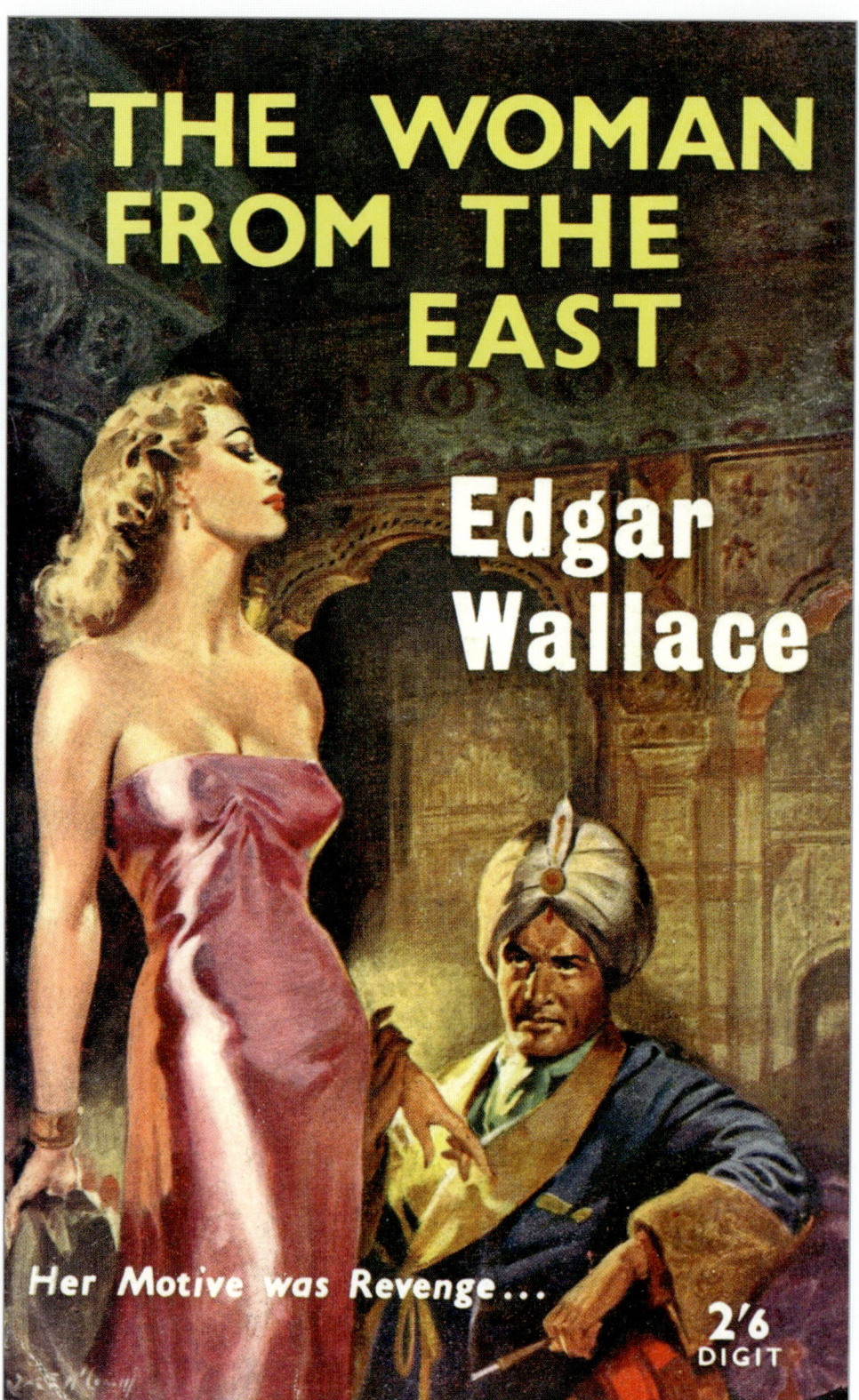

THE EDGAR WALLACES: *The Woman from the East* by Edgar Wallace (Digit R566, 1962); painted October 1961.

GALLERY

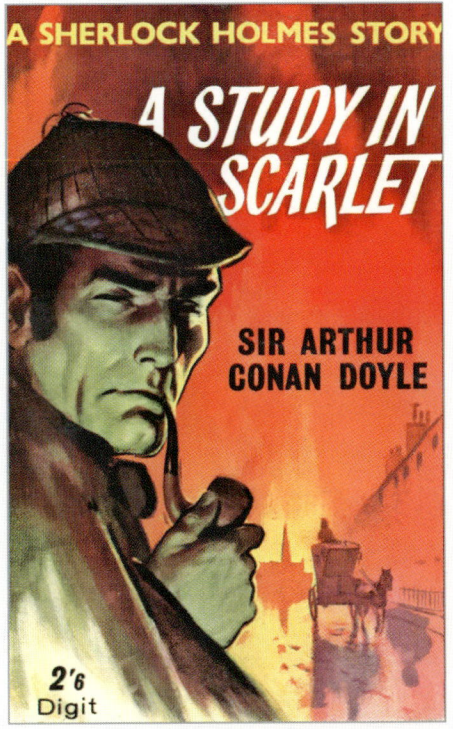
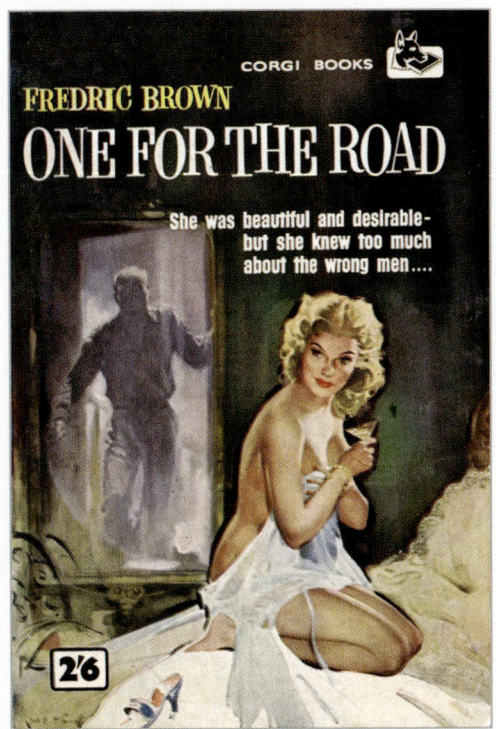
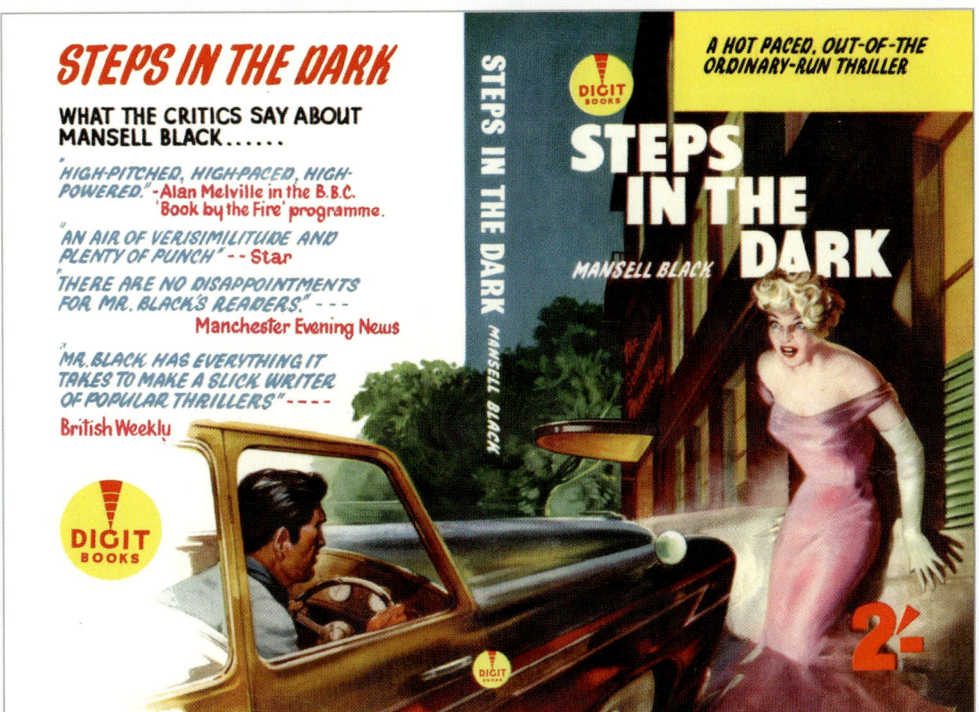

THE BEST OF THE REST: Top left: *A Study in Scarlet* by Sir Arthur Conan Doyle (Digit R604, 1962), painting unrecorded but signed. McConnell's classic study of the great detective in all his steely meditative glory. Top right: *One for the Road* by Fredric Brown (Corgi SC884, 1961), painted January 1961 in the fashionable paperback-cover style popularised by Barryé Phillips and Robert Maguire. Bottom: Advance cover for *Steps in the Dark* by Mansell Black (Digit 1957), painting unrecorded.
(*A Study in Scarlet* image courtesy Jim Kealy. *Steps in the Dark* image from the author's collection.)

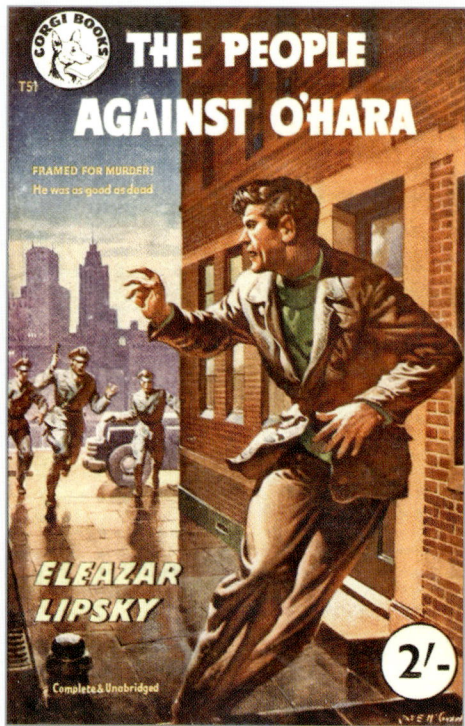

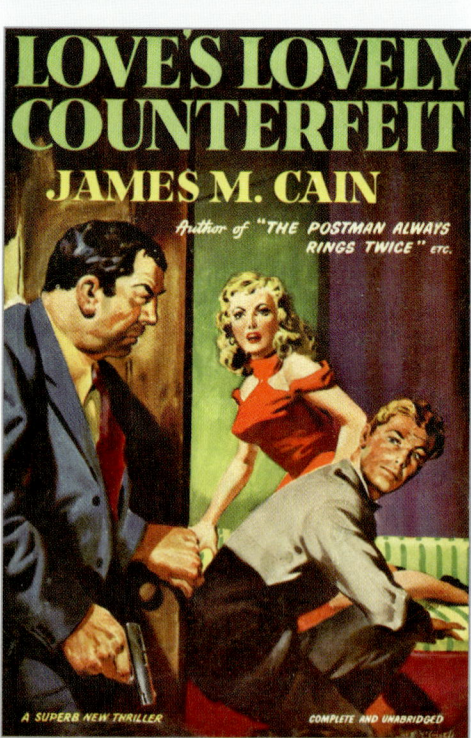

THE BEST OF THE REST: Top left: *The People Against O'Hara* by Eleazar Lipsky (Corgi T51, 1954); painted June 1954; but McConnell's workbook suggests that he painted an earlier version of this cover for a different publisher. Top right: *Agent of the Devil* by Hans Habe (Corgi GN754, 1959); painted May 1959. Again in the fashionable US paperback style. Bottom left: *A Hearse of Another Colour* by M E Chaber (Corgi SC972, 1961); painted September 1960. Bottom right: *Love's Lovely Counterfeit* by James M Cain (Robert Hale, 1954); painted April 1954.

THE BEST OF THE REST: *The House of Ruby Wogan* by Norman Gear (Digit R418, 1960); painted August 1960. One of McConnell's most demented covers.

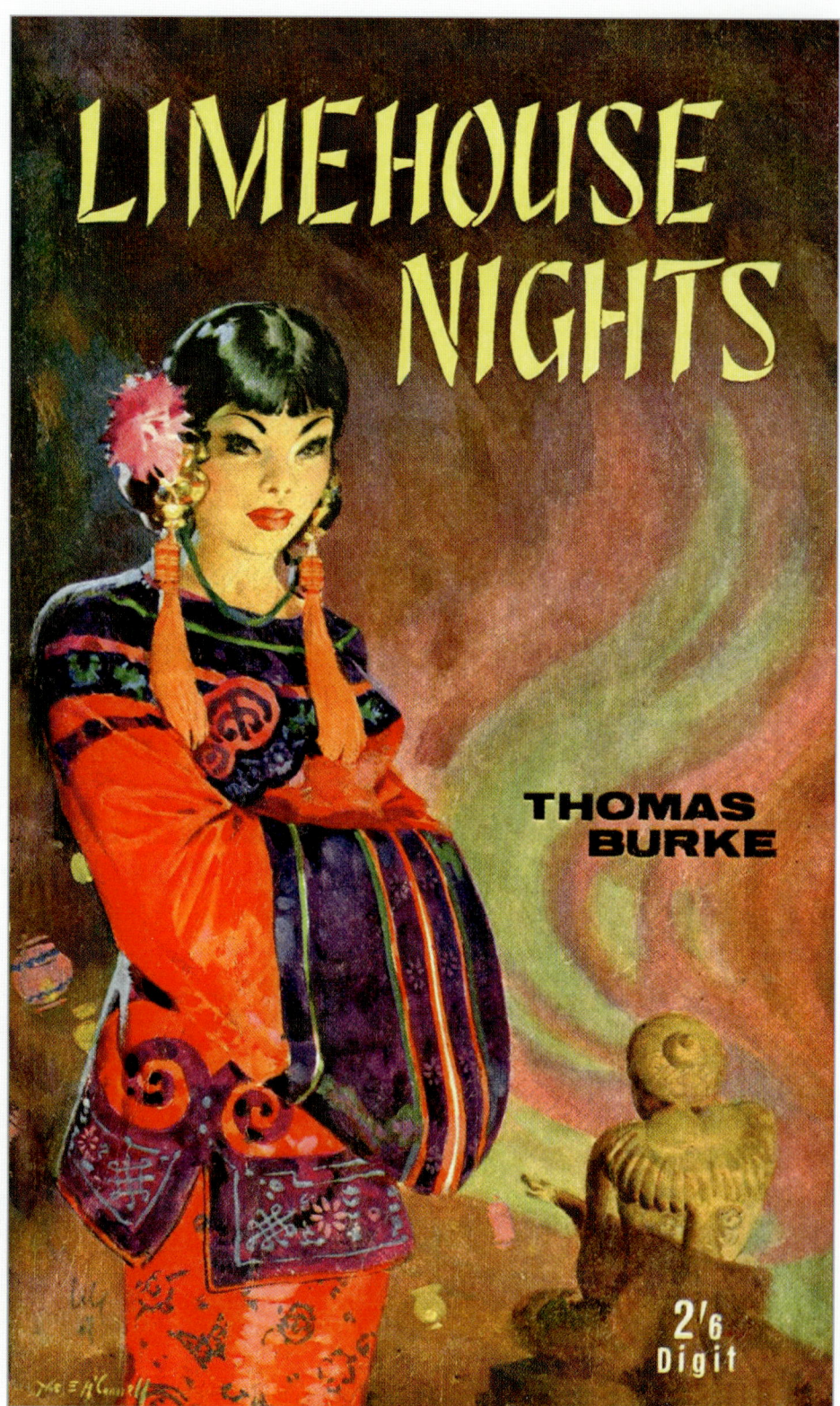

THE BEST OF THE REST: *Limehouse Nights* by Thomas Burke (Digit R486, 1961); painted January 1961. A 'Yellow Peril' cult classic, thick with opium and eroticism. (Image courtesy Jim Kealy.)

GALLERY

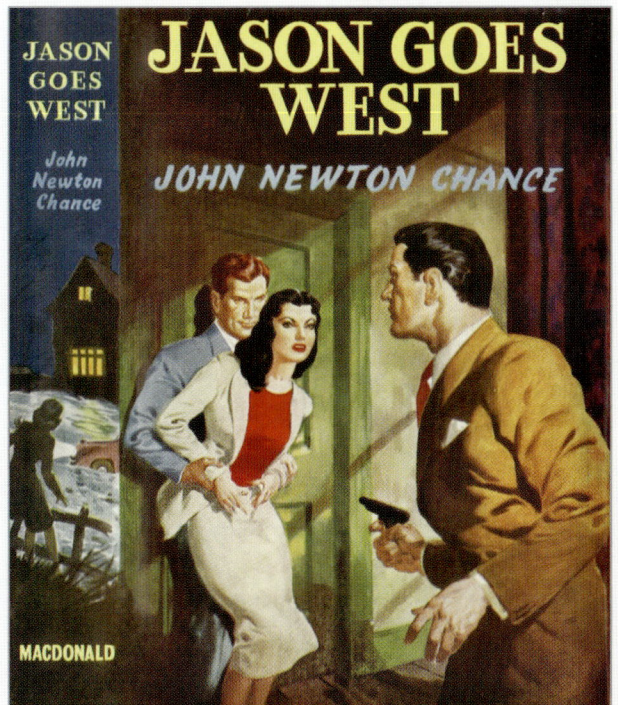
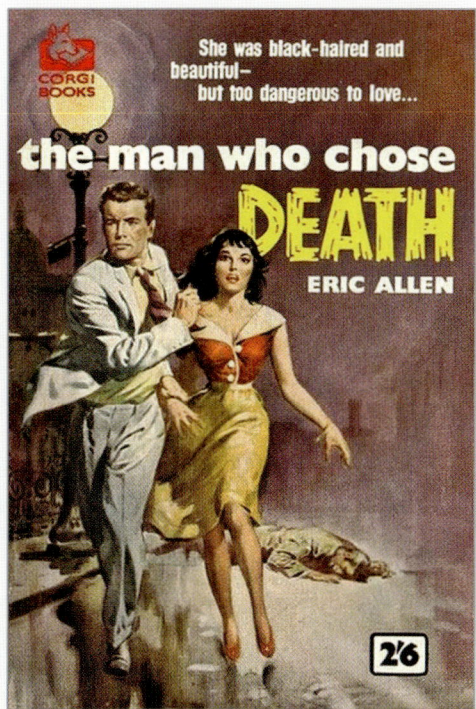
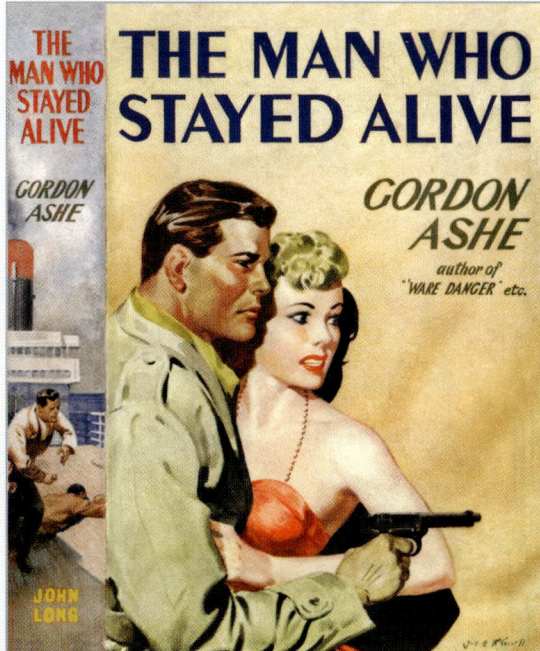

THE BEST OF THE REST: Top left: *Jason Goes West* by John Newton Chance (Macdonald, 1955); painted January 1955. Top right: *The Man who Chose Death* by Eric Allen (Corgi SC947, 1961); painted January 1961. Bottom left: *The Man who Stayed Alive* by Gordon Ashe (John Long, 1955); painted February 1955. A fortuitous juxtaposition of titles. Bottom right: *The Kidnapped Child* by Gordon Ashe (John Long, 1955); painted July 1954. (*The Man Who Chose Death* and *The Man Who Stayed Alive* images courtesy Jim Kealy.)

MINIATURE MARVELS

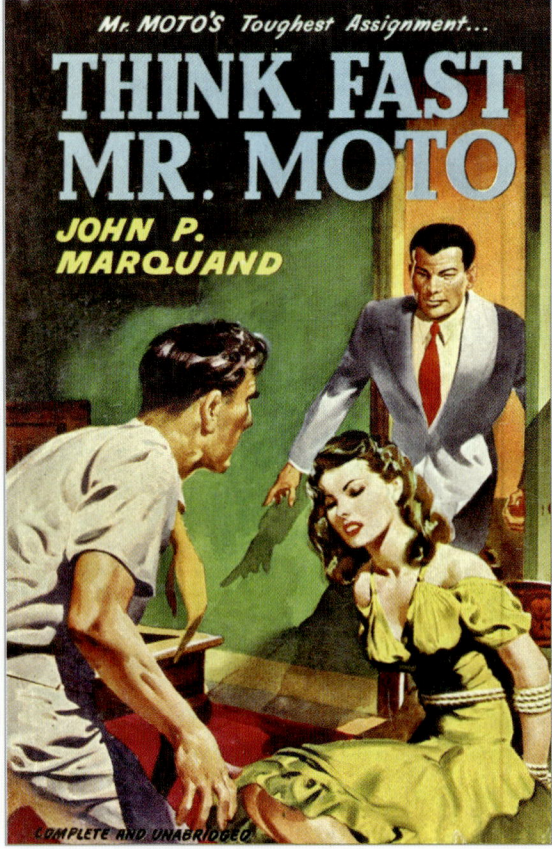

THE BEST OF THE REST: Top left: *Sing a Song of Cyanide* by Nigel Morland (Cassell, 1953); painted March 1952. Another Oriental menace. Top right: *Sin of Hong Kong* by Mark Corrigan (Consul Books, 1963); painted September 1962. More dark deeds in the Far East. Bottom left: *Think Fast Mr. Moto* by John P Marquand (Robert Hale, 1954); painted May 1954. An Oriental saviour rather than a menace. Bottom right: *Guilty – or Not Guilty?* by Horace Wyndham (Pinnacle Real Life Crime Stories No. 4, 1952); painted June 1952.

GALLERY

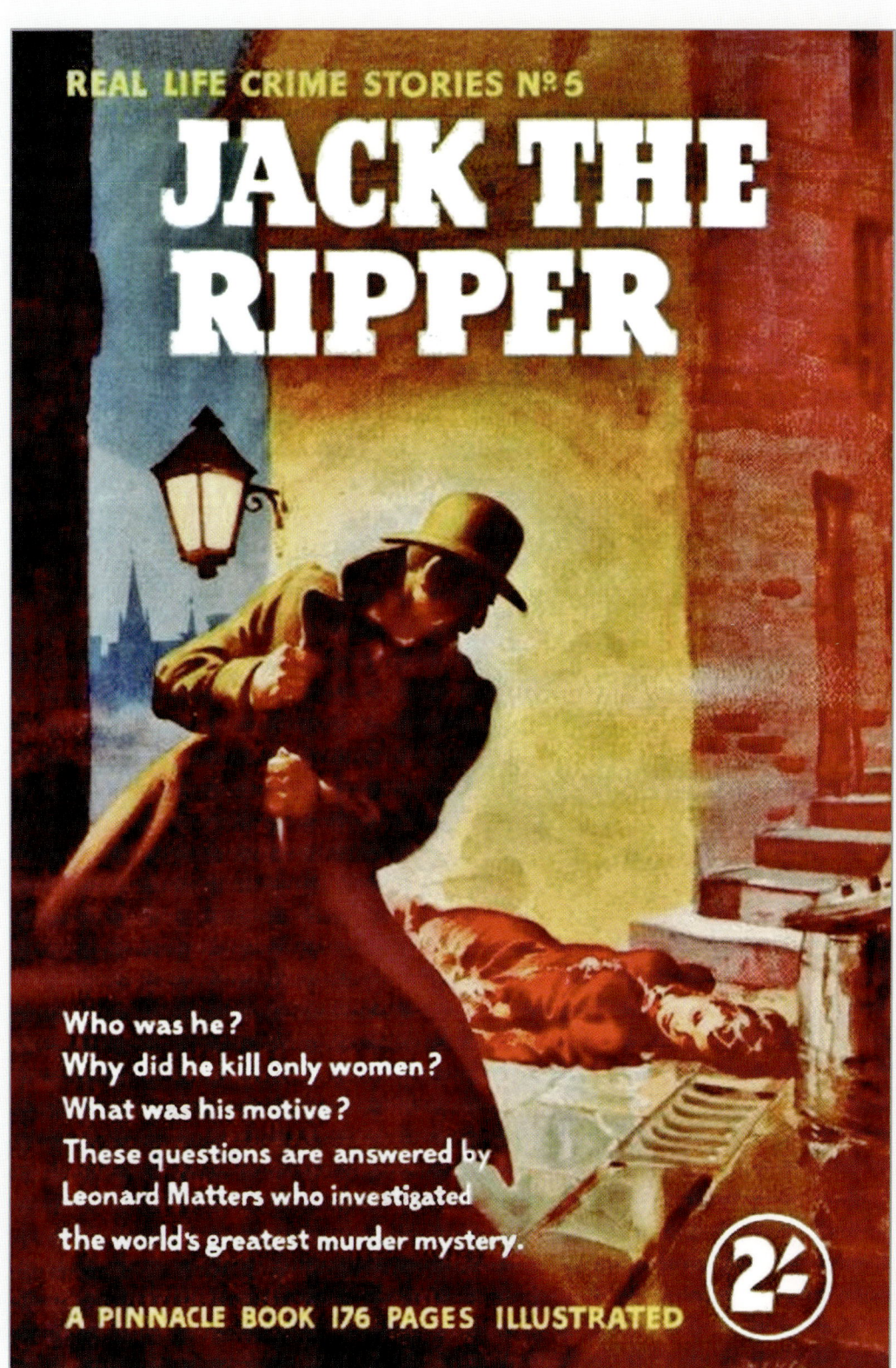

THE BEST OF THE REST: *Jack the Ripper* by Leonard Matters (Pinnacle Real Life Crime Stories No. 5, 1952); painted June 1952. (Image courtesy Jim Kealy.)

MINIATURE MARVELS

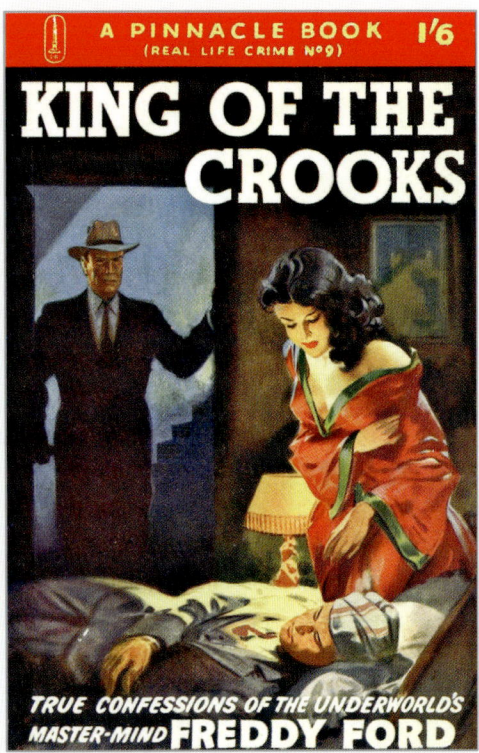
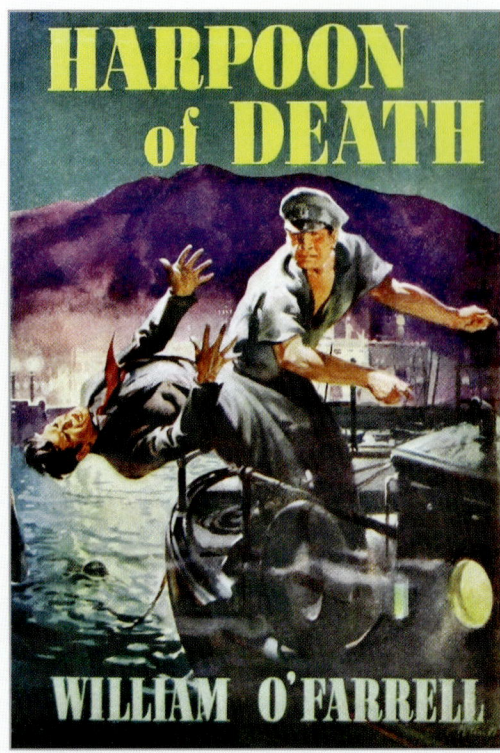
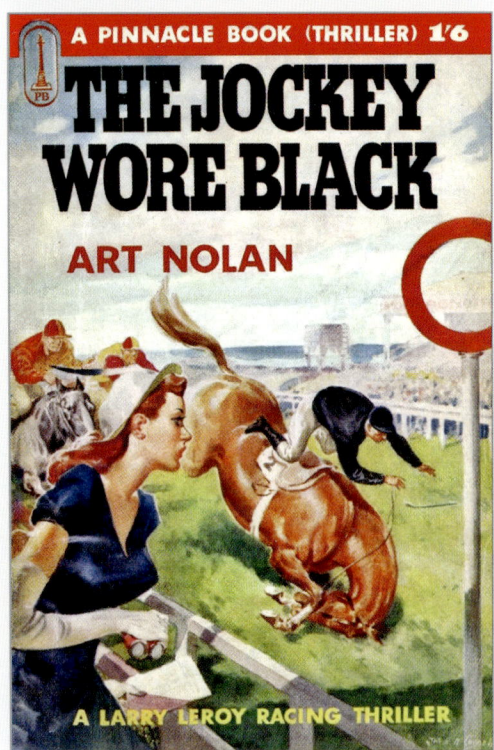
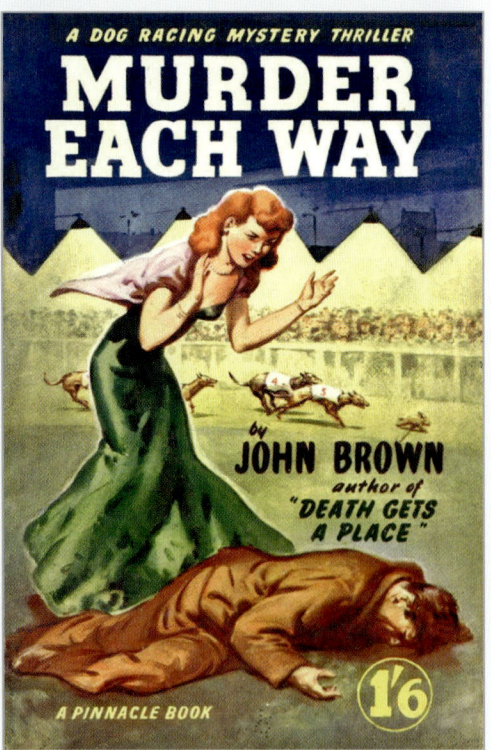

THE BEST OF THE REST: Top left: *King of the Crooks* by Freddie Ford (Pinnacle Real Life Crime Stories No.9, 1953); painted April 1953. Top right: *Harpoon of Death* by William O'Farrell (Dakers, 1953); painted October 1952. Bottom left: *The Jockey Wore Black* by Art Nolan (Pinnacle, 1953); painted January 1953. Bottom right: Murder Each Way by John Brown (Pinnacle, 1953); painted June 1952.

GALLERY

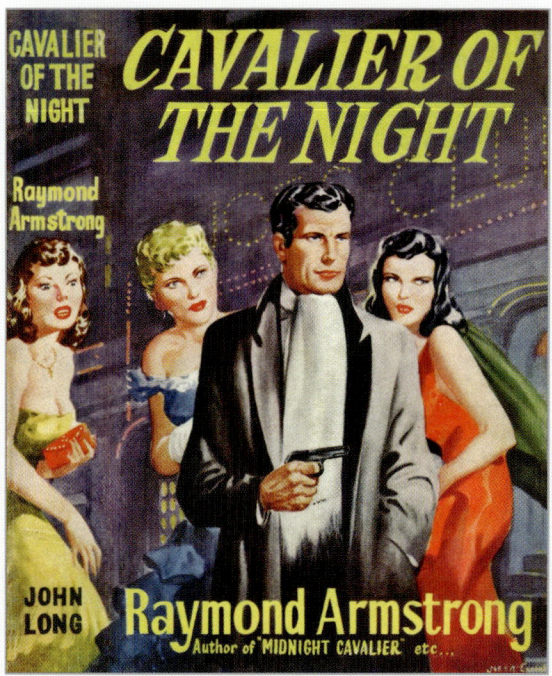

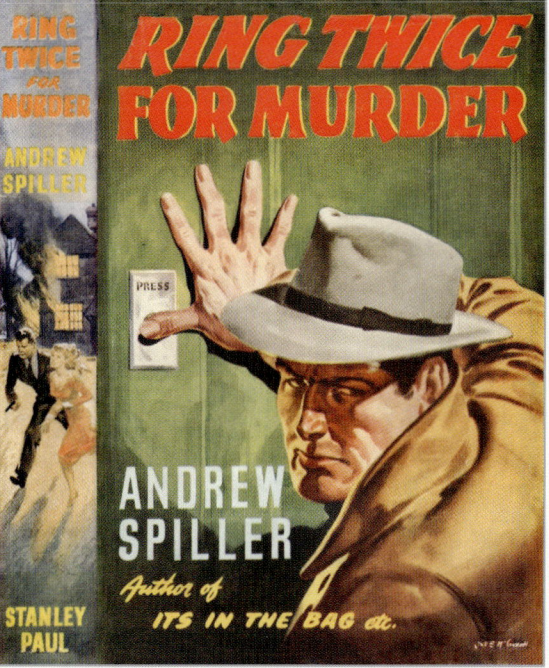

THE BEST OF THE REST: Top left: *Murder She Says!* By Reginald Campbell and Peter Motte (Cassell, 1952); painted January 1961. Top right: *Cavalier of the Night* by Raymond Armstrong (John Long, 1956); painted July 1955. Jason King, eat your heart out. Bottom left: *Black Cap for Murder* by Andrew Spiller (Stanley Paul, 1956); painted September 1955. Bottom right: *Ring Twice for Murder* by Andrew Spiller (Stanley Paul, 1955); painted February 1955. (*Ring Twice for Murder* image courtesy Jim Kealy.)

THE BEST OF THE REST: *Call Him Early for the Murder* by Nigel Morland (Cassell, 1952); painted January 1951. Naked bathers and a sinister discovery, all rendered in sombre greys and greens.

GALLERY

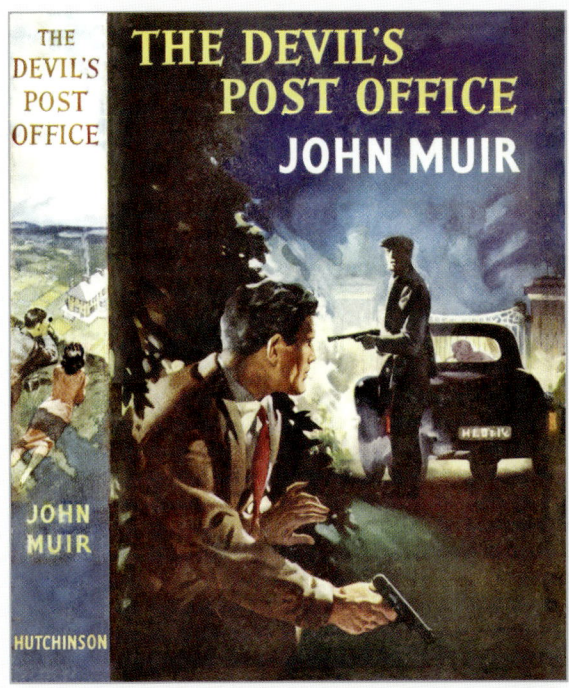

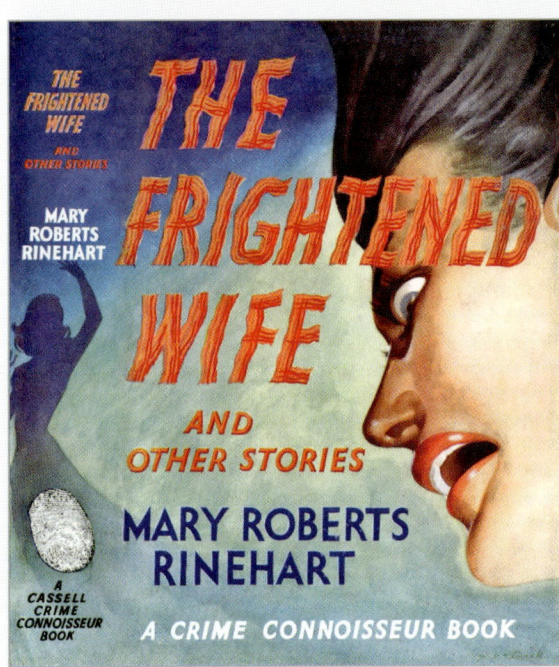

THE BEST OF THE REST: Top left: *The Devil's Post Office* by John Muir (Hutchinson, 1955); painted July 1954. Top right: *The Recoil* by K C Groom (Hutchinson, 1952); painted March 1952. Bottom left: *The Frightened Wife* by Mary Roberts Rinehart (Cassell, 1954); painted September 1953. Bottom right: *Death on my Shoulder* by Charles Franklin (Robert Hale, 1958); painted July 1957. (*The Frightened Wife* image courtesy Jim Kealy.)

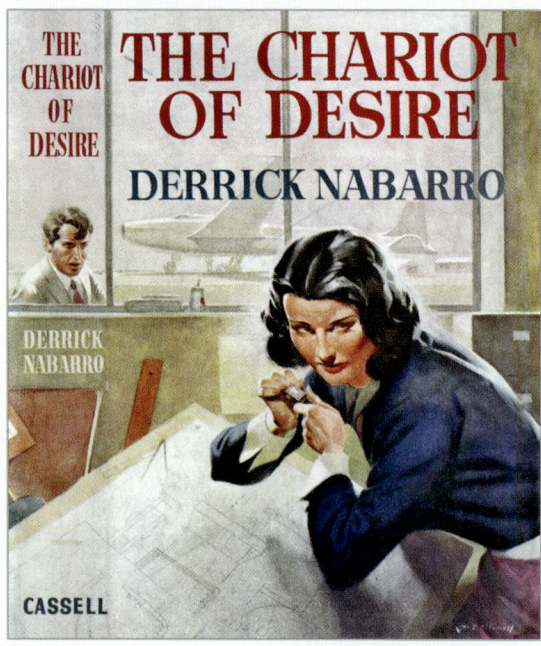
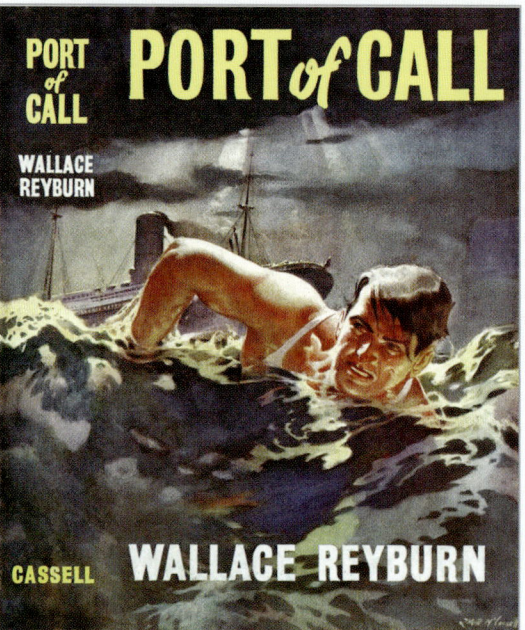

THE BEST OF THE REST: Top left: *Beat Back the Tide* by Dolores Hitchens (Macdonald, 1955); painted July 1954. Intimations of Hitchcock's *The Birds* (1963), although Daphne du Maurier's novella, on which the film was based, was published two years before McConnell painted this beauty. Top right: *Murder Looks Back* by Marjorie Alan (Robert Hale, 1955); painted September 1954. Bottom left: *The Chariot of Desire* by Derrick Nabarro (Cassell, 1956); painted July 1956. Miniaturising marvels. Bottom right: *Port of Call* by Wallace Reyburn (Cassell, 1957); painted July 1956. McConnell's technique enables him powerfully to suggest the jeopardy of rough-sea swimming. (*The Chariot of Desire* image courtesy Jim Kealy.)

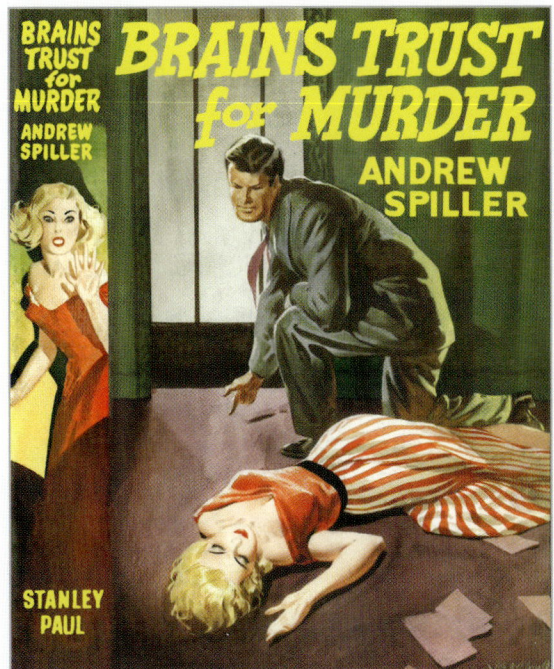

THE BEST OF THE REST: Top left: *Brains Trust for Murder* by Andrew Spiller (Stanley Paul, 1956); painted June 1956. Top right: *Murder in Mayfair* by Frederic Goldsmith (W H Allen, 1954); painted April 1954. Bottom left: *Death Among the Stars* by Jean Marsh (John Long, 1955); painted May 1955. Bottom right: *The Lady Had a Gun* by Nigel Morland (Cassell, 1951); painted June 1950.

Original artwork for *Trail Smoke* by Ernest Haycox, Western Library No. 4 (Amalgamated Press, 1950); painted March 1950.

5: A GUNMAN ON A HORSE: IMAGINING THE OLD WEST

> 'I particularly liked Westerns, because of the action.'
>
> James McConnell

If the Golden Age of crime fiction in Britain was the inter-war years, the 'Hi-ho Silver' Age of the Western was the first decade-and-a-half after World War Two. Although some of the legendary figures from the 19th Century American West had performed in successful stage shows in Britain before the First World War, inspiring publisher Cecil Aldine to issue the long-running Buffalo Bill Library series for children, tales of 'cowboys and Indians' achieved greater popularity during the 1920s and 1930s. Interest in the genre was driven by the Hollywood film, and quickly expanded to include books set in the old West. McConnell began painting covers for Westerns in the mid-1930s, but demand increased exponentially in the 1950s as the hundreds of American cowboy films – often 'B' movies made by specialist studios like Republic – were unloaded onto TV and supplemented by dedicated series such as *Wagon Train*, *Gunsmoke* and *The Lone Ranger*.

Publishers William Collins began issuing Westerns in the 1920s and, by the time McConnell began painting book jackets, had established their Wild West Club to exploit the burgeoning market. They would commission more than 70 cowboy covers from the artist over the next 20 years. It was the arrival in the early 1950s of paperback imprints dedicated to the genre that really propelled McConnell's output and challenged his ability to invent variations of the key iconography. Between 1951 and 1957, he painted almost 100 covers for Fiction House's Western series, which used yellow as its coded colour. However, this was comfortably (or perhaps uncomfortably for the illustrator's tired hand) eclipsed by the 182 covers he delivered for Amalgamated Press's digest-size Western and Cowboy Comics Library titles between 1950 and 1958. Nevertheless, this did not prevent McConnell from also being hired by most of the other publishing houses that had 'horse operas' on their lists, including Mills & Boon (46 covers), W H Allen (22), Scion (38), Hamiltons (31), Pearson (20), Robin Hood Press (16), R & L Locker (15), Foulsham (14), Ward Lock (12) and Cassell (10). Even T V Boardman, where Western fanatic

A 1938 advertisement for Collins' Wild West Club, as printed at the back of a number of the Western novels they published around that time. (Image courtesy Jim Kealy.)

JOIN THE WILD WEST CLUB
AND KEEP UP-TO-DATE WITH THE BEST NEW WILD WEST FICTION

THOUSANDS OF READERS, SICK OF SEX NOVELS, are turning to healthy yarns of life in the open spaces, where " men are men ! " To meet the demand for good, clean fiction, which is growing every day, the Wild West Club was inaugurated. A Panel of experts selects the best Wild West stories and three new books are published on the first Monday of every month. Doctors recommend Wild West books as the perfect antidote to depression, overwork and worry. If you want to be sure of hearing all about the best stories of love and adventure in the wild and woolly West, join the Wild West Club. You will receive at intervals a copy of the *Wild West Bulletin* which, sent you free of charge, tells you all about the new Wild West books.

Membership is Free

SEND A POSTCARD TO

THE WILD WEST CLUB
48 PALL MALL, LONDON, S.W.1

Dennis McLoughlin served as the art editor, commissioned him to paint most of its cowboy covers: 54 in all. Now it seems an almost impossible feat to be able to invent so many original compositions without any serious repetition. It was only a genuine love for stories of drama on the prairies that kept McConnell's imagination sufficiently fertile.

The effect of all this 'brush-slinging' was to typecast McConnell as a Wild West genre painter, albeit the premier one in Britain, by the time the more sophisticated and higher-paying paperback imprints began to expand their lists and print-runs. In September 1958, Stephen Mogridge used his regular paperback column in *Bookseller and Stationer* to comment on trends in Western fiction:

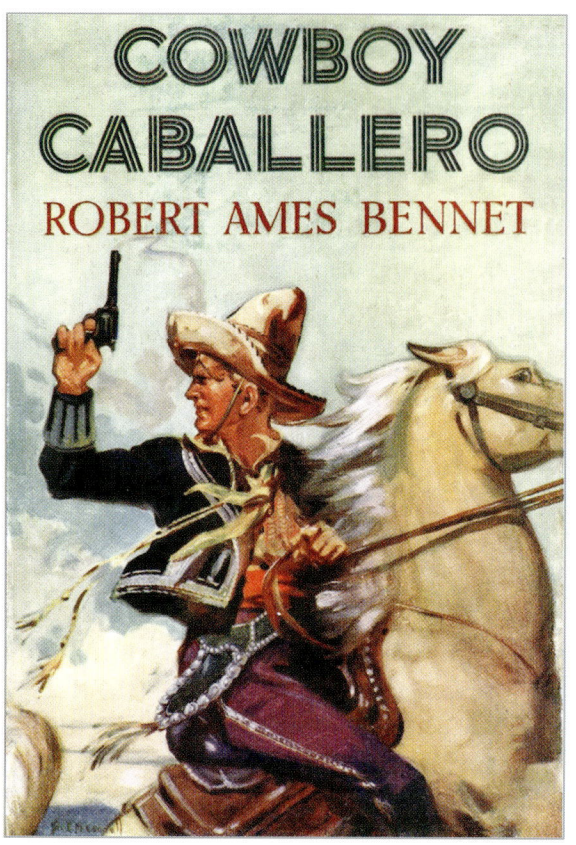

Cowboy Caballero by Robert Ames Bennet (Collins, 1938). (Image courtesy Jim Kealy.)

Arouse and Beware by MacKinlay Kantor (Corgi G563, 1958); painted October 1957. A paperback cover in the 'pulp' style. (Image courtesy Jim Kealy.)

'Latest trends in America, home of the Western, indicate that short stories and magazines of this kind are out. TV seems to have taken their place. But the market for paperback book-length Westerns has increased, despite TV. Run-of-the-mill Westerns are themselves being challenged by better plotted stories, particularly the historical Western. You might almost say that the non-fiction demand has hit the Western market … With Westerns pouring from so many paperback publishers here, this market trend is one to note when making selections for stock. Corgi Books seem to have had an eye on it for some time, for they publish many first-rate Westerns of the historical kind.'[52]

Original artwork for *Warbonnet* by Clay Fisher (Corgi SW1001, 1961); painted November 1960. (Image courtesy Jim Kealy.)

Original artwork for *South of Rio Grande* by Max Brand (Corgi T623, 1958); painted May 1958. (Image courtesy Jim Kealy.)

Above: American artist Frederic Remington's *The Lookout* (1887); a clear inspiration for McConnell, notably in the piece shown on the facing page.

Right: Original artwork for *Beyond the Pass* by Lee Leighton (Corgi TT540, 1958); painted December 1957. (Image courtesy Jim Kealy.)

Below: Advance cover for *Apache Ambush* by Will Cook (Corgi T519, 1958); painted September 1957. (Author's collection.)

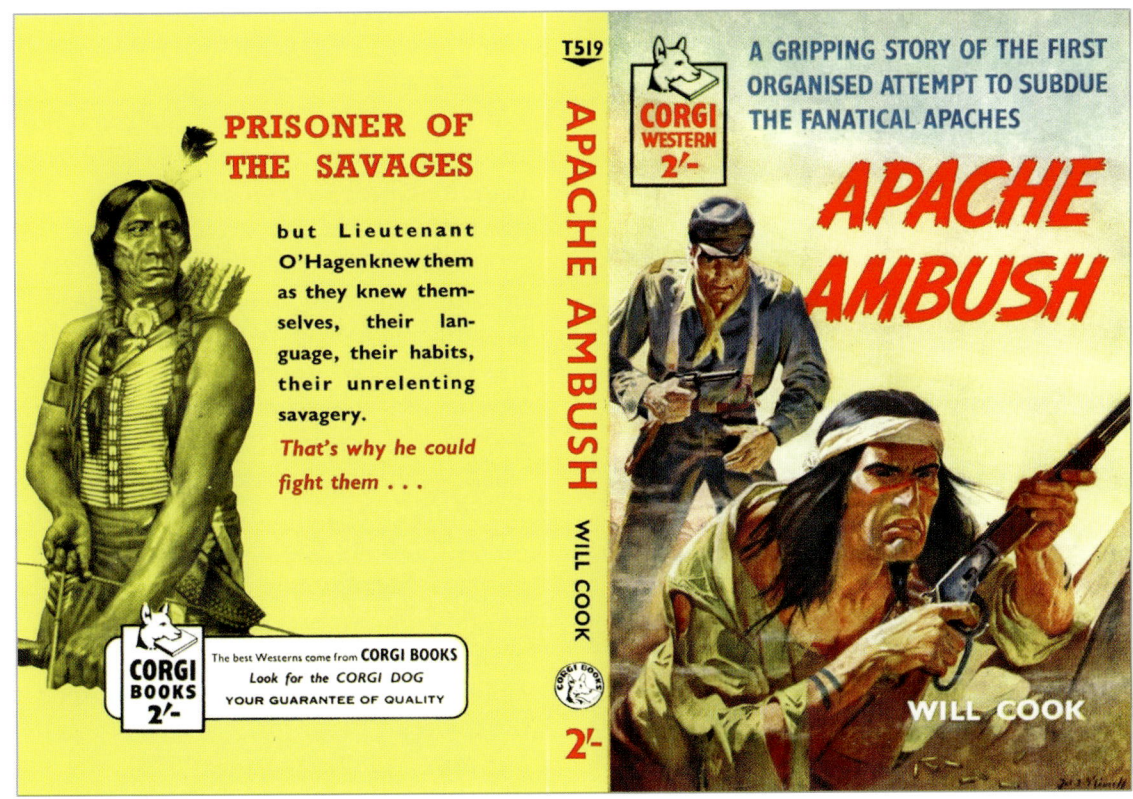

In the late 1950s, Corgi became the market leaders for the more sophisticated novels featuring cowboys, gun-slingers, horse soldiers and native American braves. McConnell was the imprint's illustrator of choice, and the work paid handsomely. It was fortunate that he was 'quick on the draw,' because the commissions came faster than Apaches on the warpath. 'I was a very fast worker,' he remembered proudly. 'I used to do two or three a week sometimes for Corgi. They used to pay £50 a jacket.' He painted the first, for E E Halleran's *Gunsmoke Valley*, in October 1952, just before the Great Smog brought London to a standstill, and the last, for Oliver Strange's *Sudden: Law of the Lariat*, nine years later, in November 1961, when United Artists announced that Sean Connery would play James Bond in *Dr. No* (1962) and Brian Epstein first saw the Beatles play at the Cavern Club. In

Bronco Apache by Paul I Wellman (Corgi SW1105, 1961); painted July 1961.

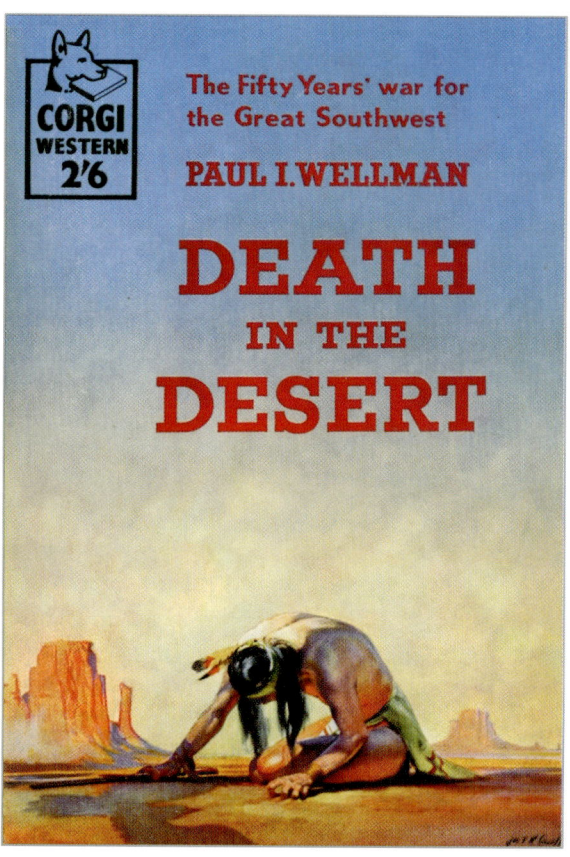

Death in the Desert by Paul I Wellman (Corgi S610, 1958); painted April 1958. (Image courtesy Jim Kealy.)

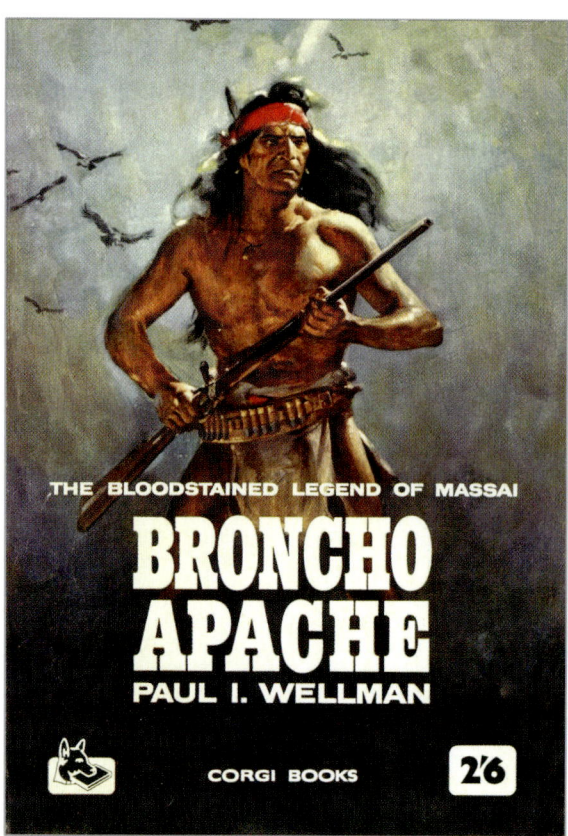

the end, there were one hundred Western paintings, including five for E E Halleran novels, eight for Oliver Strange, ten for Max Brand and eleven for Ernest Haycox.

Many of the earlier Corgi covers were in the American pulp style, images that breathlessly anticipated a moment of violence: the Confederate axeman awaiting the Yankee trooper on the cover of Mackinlay Kantor's *Arouse and Beware* (1958) (see page 172) is a classic example. The soldier creeping up behind the brave in the painting for Will Cook's *Apache Ambush* (1958) (see page 175) is another. But perhaps increasingly, McConnell's pictorial imagination embraced a more lonely and melancholic depiction of heroic American individualism: the lone bounty hunter among the towering peaks for Leigh Leighton's *Beyond the Pass* (1958) (see page 175); the warrior circled by buzzards for Paul I Wellman's *Broncho Apache* (1961); the slowly expiring fighters for the same author's *Death in the Desert* (1958) and *Death on the Prairie* (1958); the exhausted cowboy dwarfed by the stormy sky for the second volume of Jack Schaefer's *Out West* (1961); and most iconic of all, the mounted vigilante surveying the rocky landscape for Max Brand's *South of the Rio Grande* (1958) (see page 174) – these are paintings inspired less by the pulp magazines than by the great artists of the Western genre, such as Frederic Remington (1861-1909) and Charles Russell (1864-1926). In truth, McConnell owed much to Remington – not least the realistic depiction of horses in motion that the founding father of Wild West art had revolutionised. McConnell never had the advantage of observing cowboys, native Americans and their mounts first-hand, and had to rely on his daughter's pony as a model for equestrian subjects. To be able to imagine the American West so convincingly and movingly was a remarkable achievement for an English artist who had never crossed the Atlantic.

Above right: *Death on the Prairie* by Paul I Wellman (Corgi, 1958); painted January 1958. Below left: *The Gun* by Frank O'Rourke (Boardman, 1952); painted June 1952. Below right: *Out West: Volume Two* by Jack Schaefer (Corgi GW1038, 1961); painted February 1961.

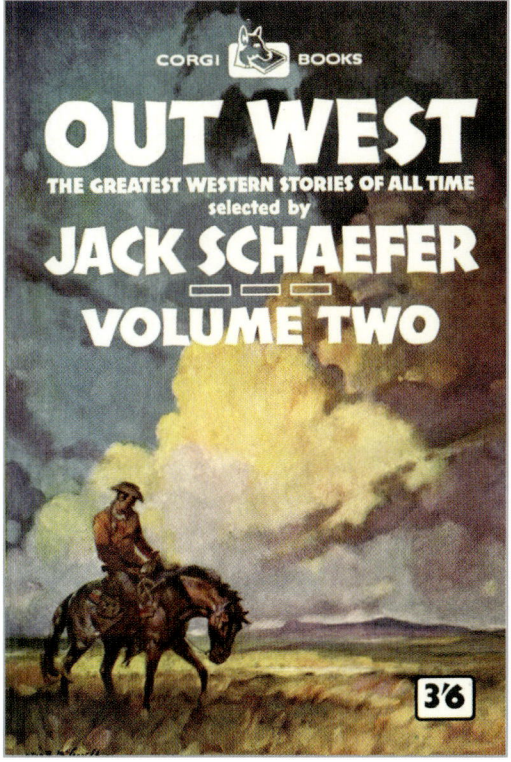

MINIATURE MARVELS

GALLERY

VARIATIONS ON A THEME: TWO-GUN HORSEMEN: *Foxfire Creek* by Calico Jones (Boardman, 1952); painted July 1951. (Image courtesy Jim Kealy.)

GALLERY

VARIATIONS ON A THEME: TWO-GUN HORSEMEN: Top left: *Double X Ranch* by Stetson Cody (W H Allen, 1958); painting not recorded. Top right: *Flaming Frontier* by Mike M'Cracken (Hamilton's, 1951); painted August 1950. Bottom left: *Injun Brand* by W R Hutton (Hamilton's, 1950); painted December 1949. Bottom right: *Feud Fury!* by Dean Kelly (Scion 1951), painted September 1950.

MINIATURE MARVELS

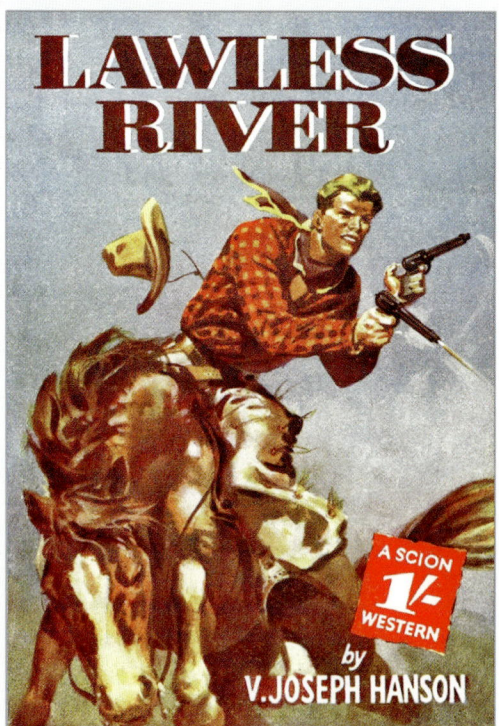

VARIATIONS ON A THEME: TWO-GUN HORSEMEN: Top left: *King Colt* by R L May (Hamilton's, 1951); painted October 1950. Top right: *Four Guns to Porcupine* by Shaun O'Hara (Hamilton's, 1952); painting not recorded. Bottom left: *Guns for the Valley* by Russell Storm (R & L Locker, 1948); painted August 1948. Bottom right: *Lawless River* by V Joseph Hanson (Scion, 1952); painted August 1951. (*King Colt* image courtesy Jim Kealy.)

GALLERY

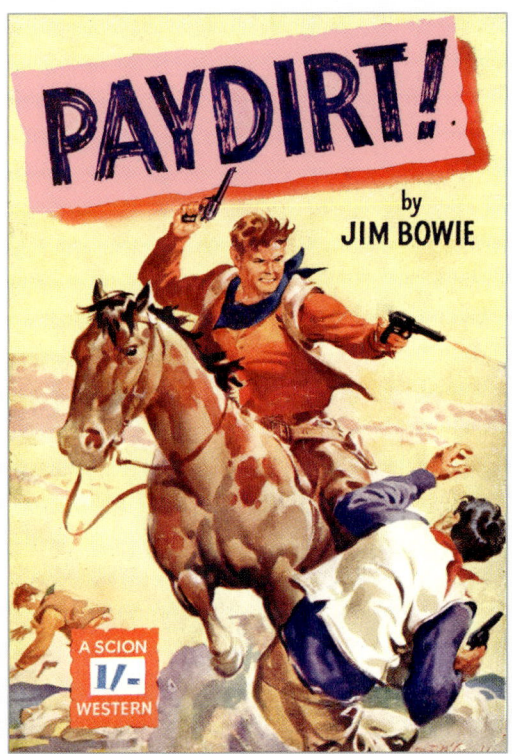

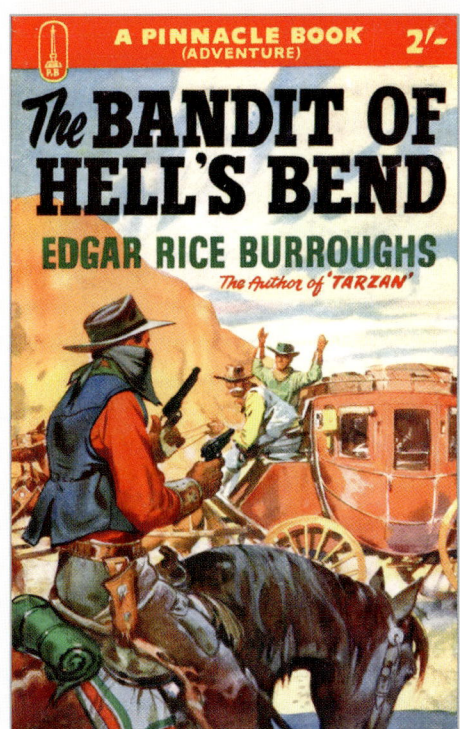

VARIATIONS ON A THEME: TWO-GUN HORSEMEN: Top left: *Paydirt!* by Jim Bowie (Scion, 1951); painted December 1950. Top right: *Rawhide Reckoning* by Webb Anders (Scion, 1953); painted January 1952. Bottom left: *The Bandit of Hell's Bend* by Edgar Rice Burroughs (Pinnacle, 1953); painted April 1953. Bottom right: *The Man from Thunder River* by Dave Waldo (Boardman, 1951); painted February 1951. (*Paydirt!* and *The Bandit of Hell's Bend* images courtesy Jim Kealy.)

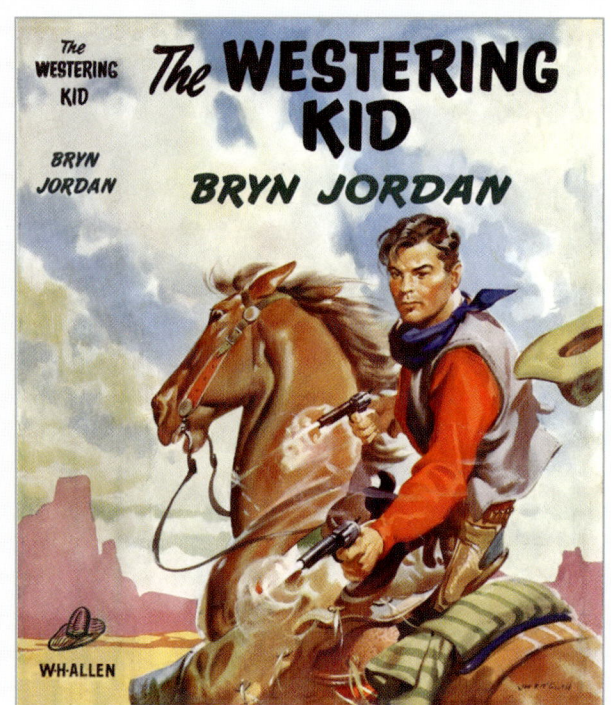
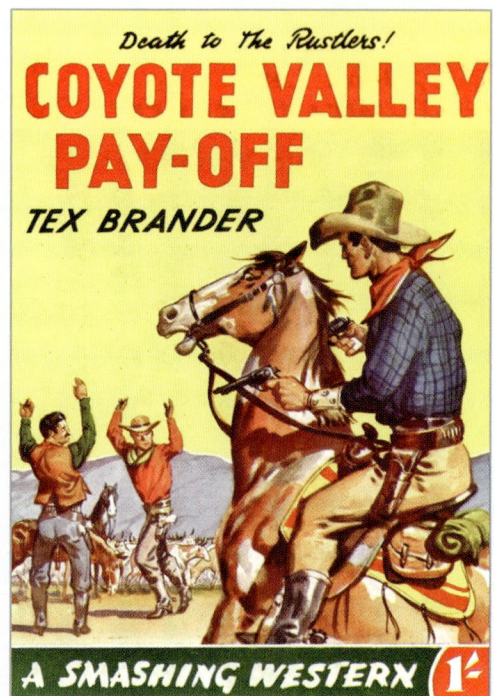

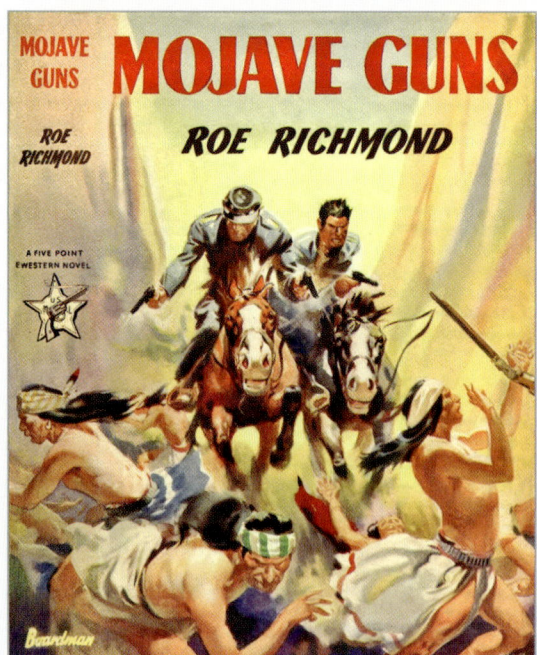

VARIATIONS ON A THEME: TWO-GUN HORSEMEN: Top left: *The Westering Kid* by Bryn Jordan (W H Allen, 1954); painted May 1954. Top right: *Coyote Valley Pay-Off* by Tex Brander (Fiction House No.166, 1954); painted October 1953. Bottom left: *The Bandit in Black* by Paul Evan Lehman (Hennel Locke, 1956); painted February 1956. Bottom right: *Mojave Guns* by Roe Richmond (Boardman, 1953); painted October 1952. (*The Westering Kid* and *The Bandit in Black* images courtesy Jim Kealy.)

VARIATIONS ON A THEME: THE REARING HORSE: *Riders in the Night* by Lee Floren (R & L Locker, 1948); painted April 1948.

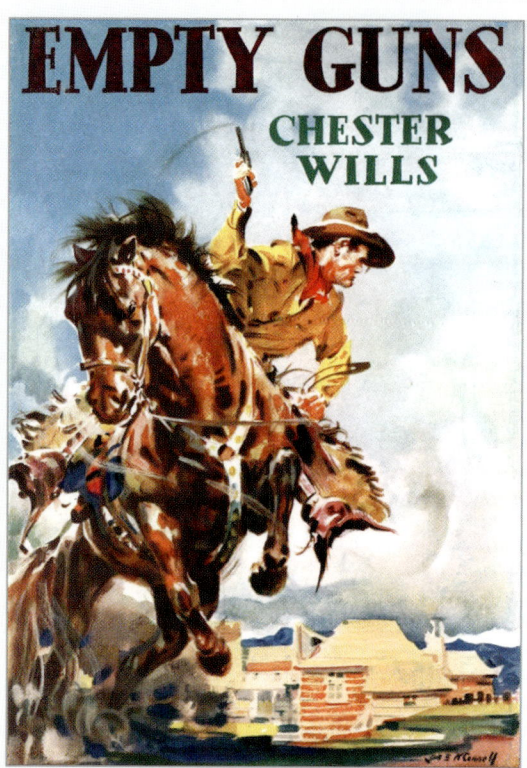
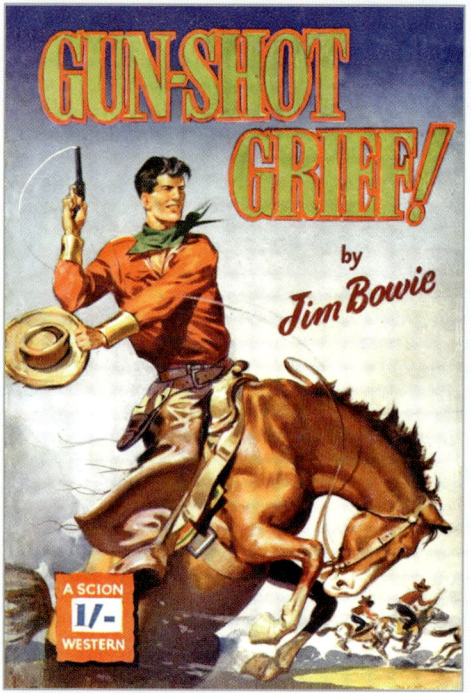
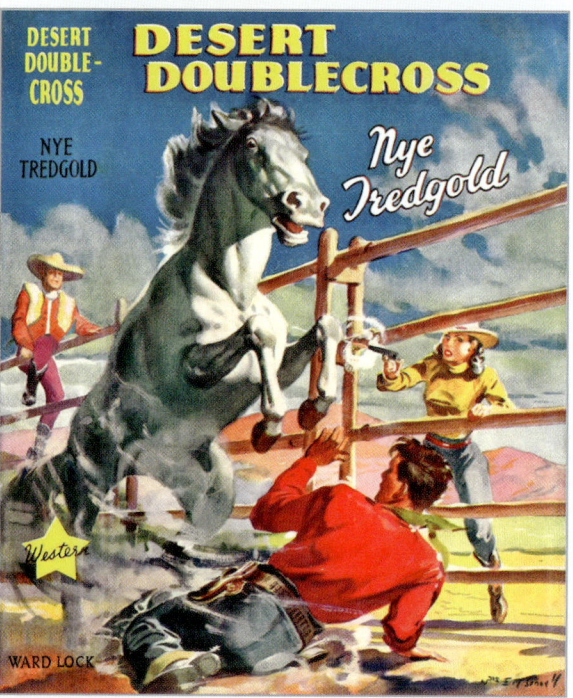

VARIATIONS ON A THEME: THE REARING HORSE: Top left: *Colt Law* by J Vincent Nolan (Hamilton's, 1950); painted July 1950. Top right: *Empty Guns* by Chester Wills (Collins, 1953); painted August 1952. Bottom left: *Gun-Shot Grief!* by Jim Bowie (Scion, 1951); painted December 1950. Bottom right: *Desert Doublecross* by Nye Tredgold (Ward Lock, 1953); painted October 1952. (*Empty Guns* image courtesy Jim Kealy.)

GALLERY

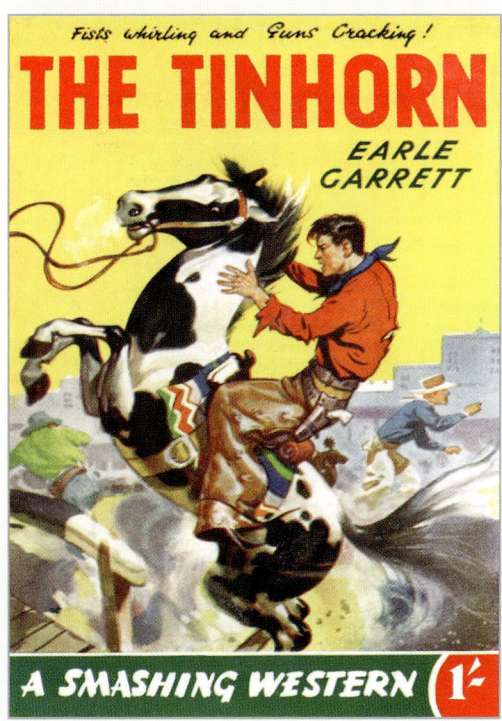

VARIATIONS ON A THEME: THE REARING HORSE: Top left: *Wild Summit* by Matt Stuart (Ward Lock, 1958); painted March 1958. Top right: *Owl-Hoot Trail* by Jamie Boyd (Fiction House, 1951); painted April 1951. Bottom left: Advance cover for *Rail-Road Rustlers* by Webb Anders (Fiction House No. 151, 1953); painted November 1952. Bottom right: Advance cover for *The Tinhorn* by Earle Garrett (Fiction House No. 189, 1955); painted November 1954. (Bottom two images from the author's collection.)

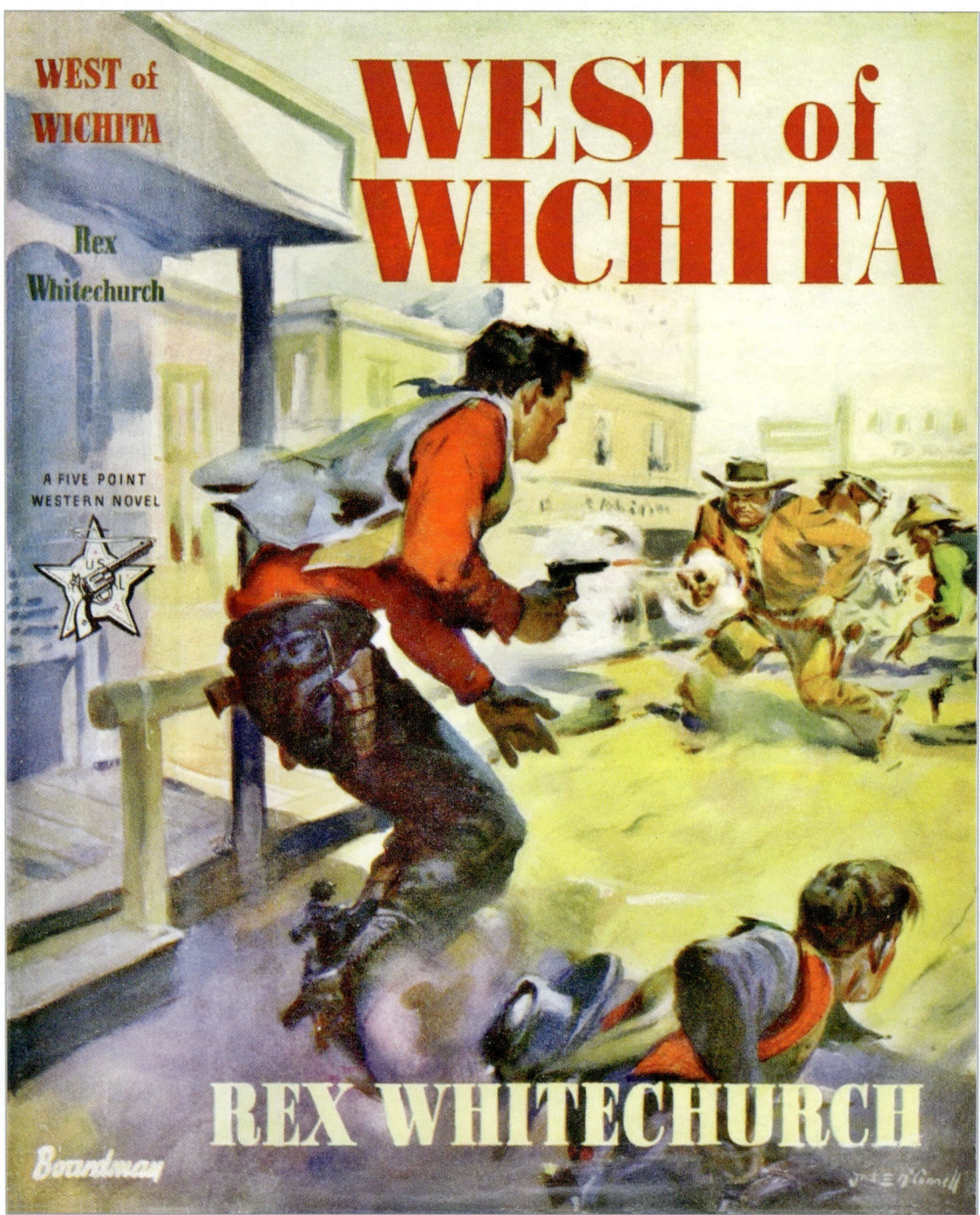

VARIATIONS ON A THEME: THE SHOOT-OUT: *West of Wichita* by Rex Whitechurch (Boardman, 1953); painted October 1952. As we see repeatedly, McConnell liked his cowboys dressed in a red shirt. Publishers and their art directors also approved of the colour red as it was eye-catching in a competitive sales field.

GALLERY

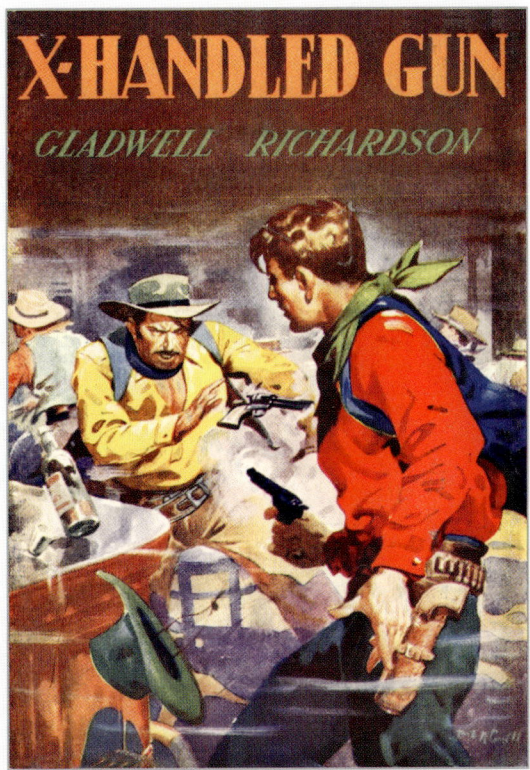

VARIATIONS ON A THEME: THE SHOOT-OUT: Top left: *X-Handled Gun* by Gladwell Richardson (Mills & Boon, 1954); painted May 1954. Top right: *When the Long Trail Calls* by Bryn Logan (Ward Lock, 1956); painted November 1954. Bottom left: *Trigger Music* by Jim Bowie (Scion, 1952); painted August 1951. Bottom right: *Showdown in Lead* by Jim Bowie (Scion, 1953); painted January 1952; McConnell's last cover for Scion. (*X-Handled Gun* image courtesy Jim Kealy.)

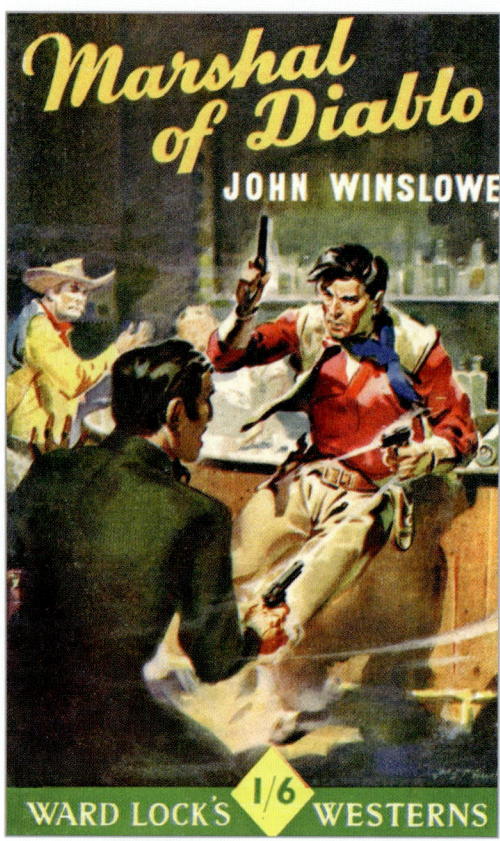

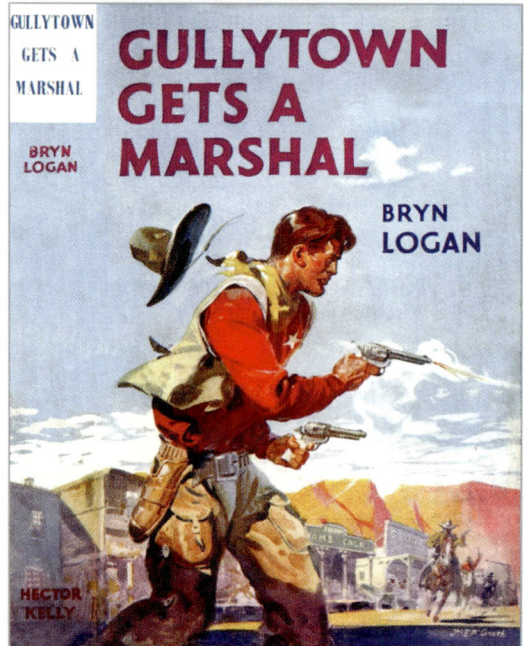
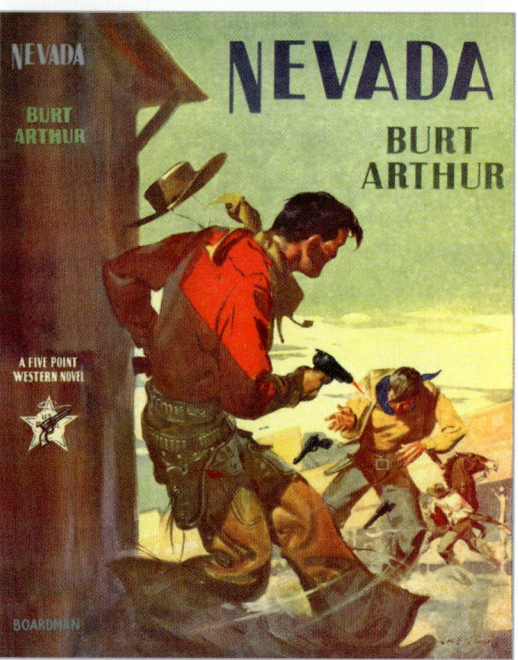

VARIATIONS ON A THEME: THE SHOOT-OUT: Top left: *Marshal of Diablo* by John Winslowe (Ward Lock, 1953); painted December 1951. Top right: *End of a Feud* by Clinton Wayne (Hector Kelly, 1952); painted July 1951. Bottom left: *Gullytown Gets a Marshal* by Bryn Logan (Hector Kelly, 1951); painted February 1949. Bottom right: *Nevada* by Burt Arthur (Boardman, 1951); painted March 1951. (*Gullytown Gets a Marshal* image courtesy Jim Kealy.)

VARIATIONS ON A THEME: THE SHOOT-OUT: *Roaring* Guns by Charles H Snow (R & L Locker, 1949); painted November 1948. (Image courtesy Jim Kealy.)

VARIATIONS ON A THEME: THE SHOOT-OUT: Advance cover for *Guns Up* by Charles Neider (Pan G228, 1958); painted December 1957. (Author's collection.)

GALLERY

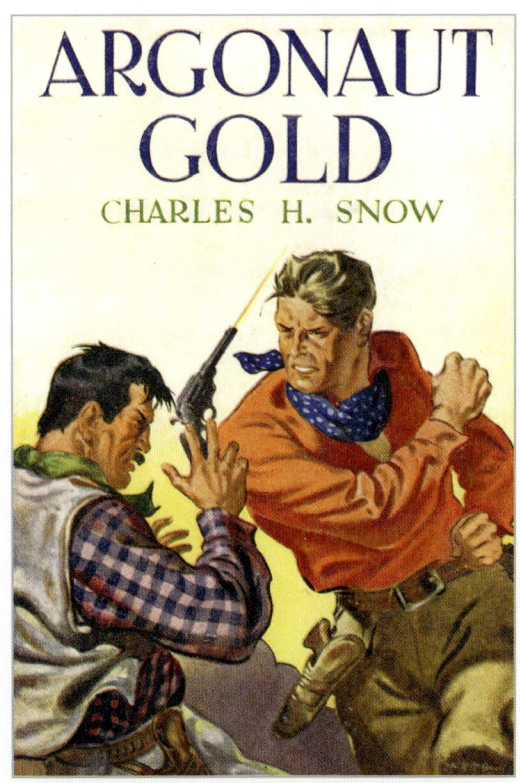
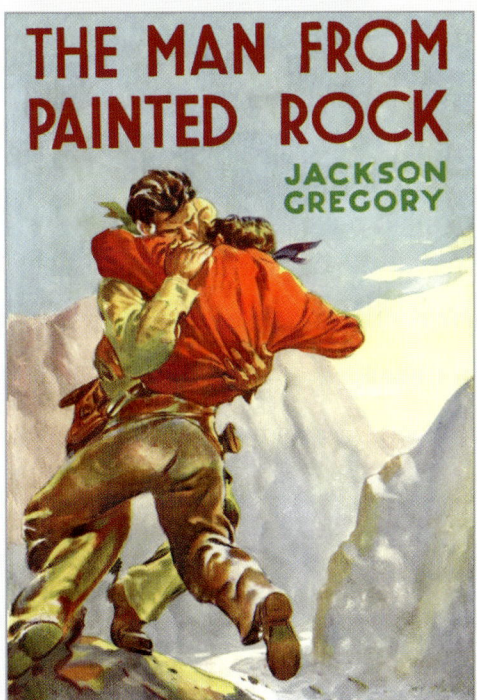
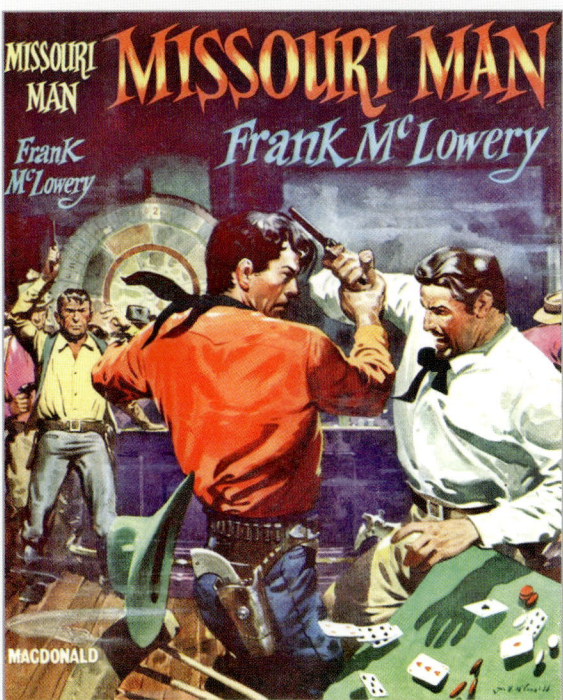

VARIATIONS ON A THEME: HAND-TO-HAND COMBAT: Top left: *Guns of Wyoming* by Lee Floren (Partridge, 1950); painted May 1950. Top right: *Argonaut Gold* by Charles H Snow (R & L Locker, 1949); painted November 1948. Bottom left: *The Man from Painted Rock* by Jackson Gregory (Collins, 1949); painted October 1948. Bottom right: *Missouri Man* by Frank McLowery (Macdonald, 1955); painted November 1954. (*The Man From Painted Rock* image courtesy Jim Kealy.)

VARIATIONS ON A THEME: HAND-TO-HAND COMBAT: *Range Justice* by Paul Evan Lehman (W H Allen, 1953); painted December 1952. (Image courtesy Jim Kealy.)

GALLERY

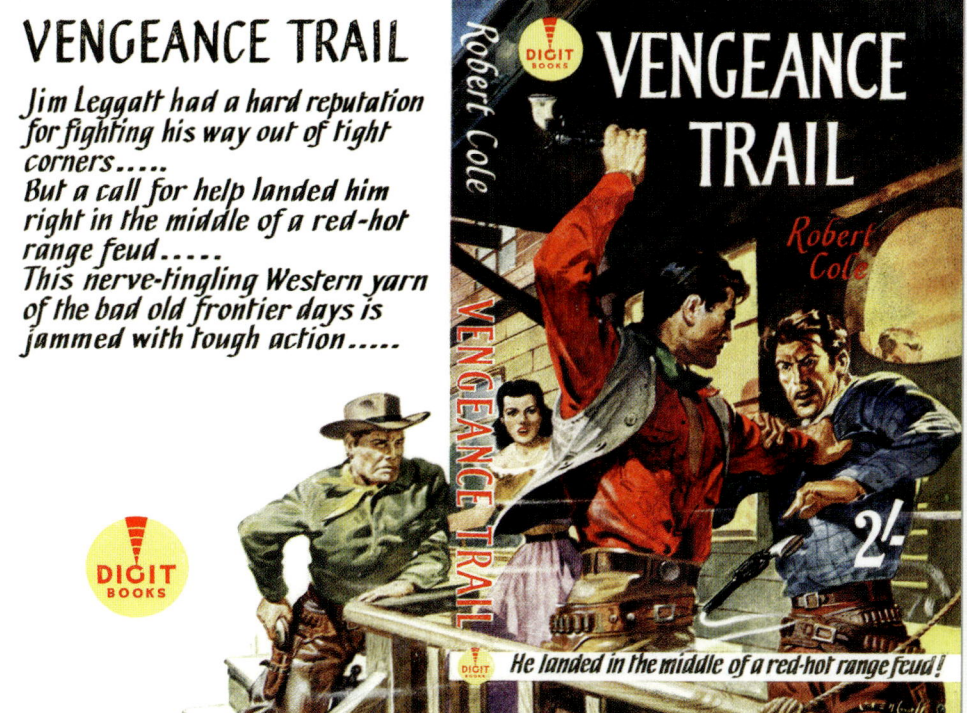

VARIATIONS ON A THEME: HAND-TO-HAND COMBAT: Top left: *The Devil's Doorstep* by Paul Evan Lehman (Hennel Locke, 1953); painted March 1953. Top right: *Wild Bunch* by Webb Anders (Scion, 1951); painted March 1951. Almost the same scene from a different angle. Bottom: Advance cover for *Vengeance Trail* by Robert Cole (Digit, 1957); painting not recorded. This was the last of three covers that McConnell painted in six years for books titled *Vengeance Trail*, all by different authors and for different publishers. So many Westerns were published in the 1950s that suitable genre titles had to be recycled. (*The Devil's Doorstep* image courtesy Jim Kealy. *Vengeance Trail* image from the author's collection.)

VARIATIONS ON A THEME: HAND-TO-HAND COMBAT: *Red Silver!* by V Joseph Hanson (Scion, 1951); painted October 1950.

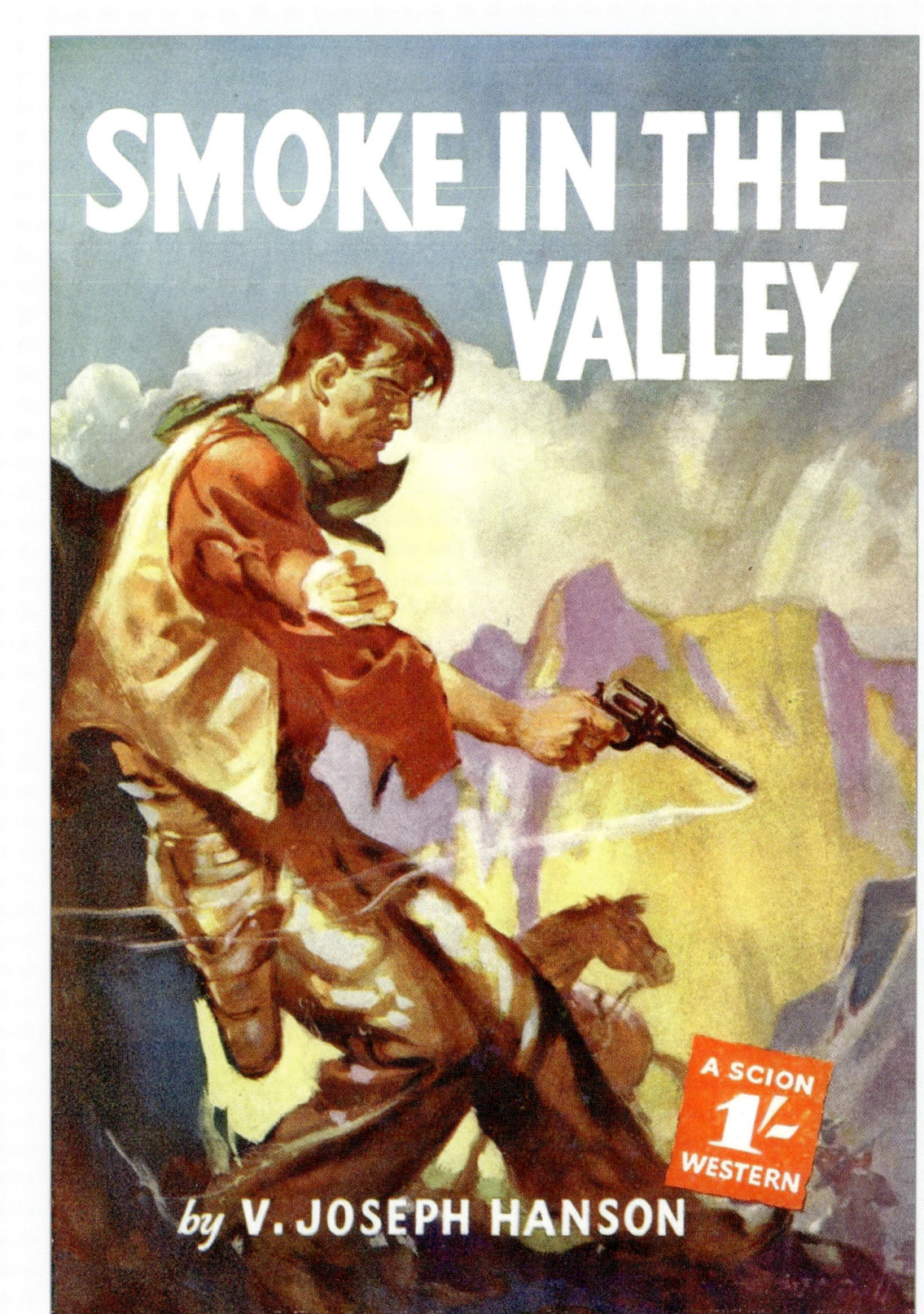

VARIATIONS ON A THEME: THE WOUNDED COWBOY: *Smoke in the Valley* by V Joseph Hanson (Scion, 1951); painted November 1950.

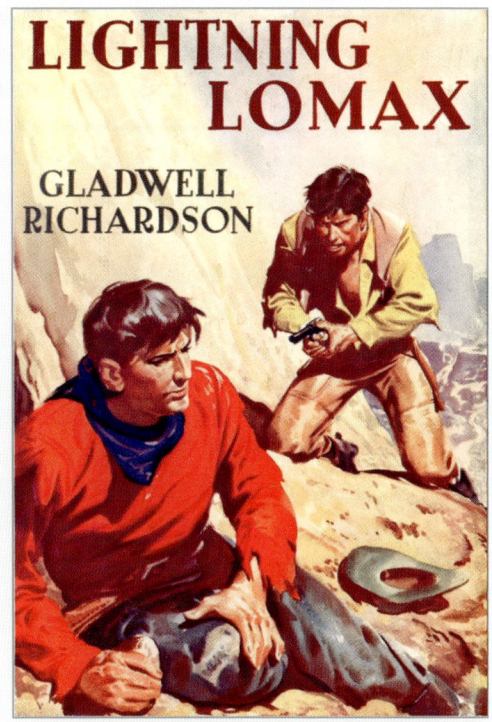
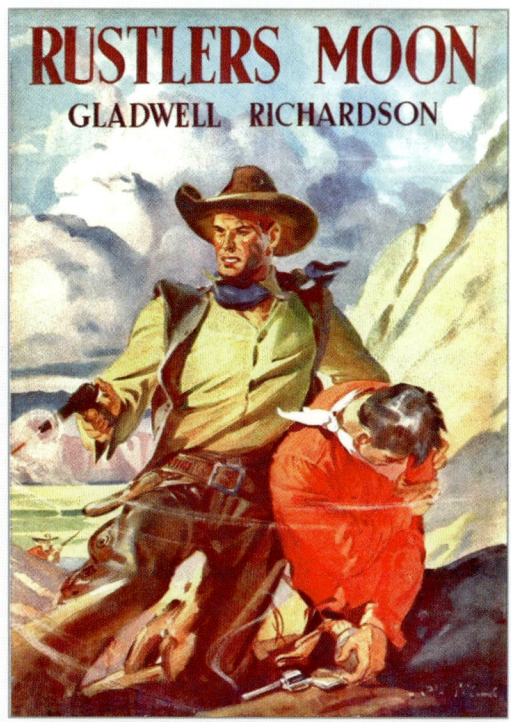
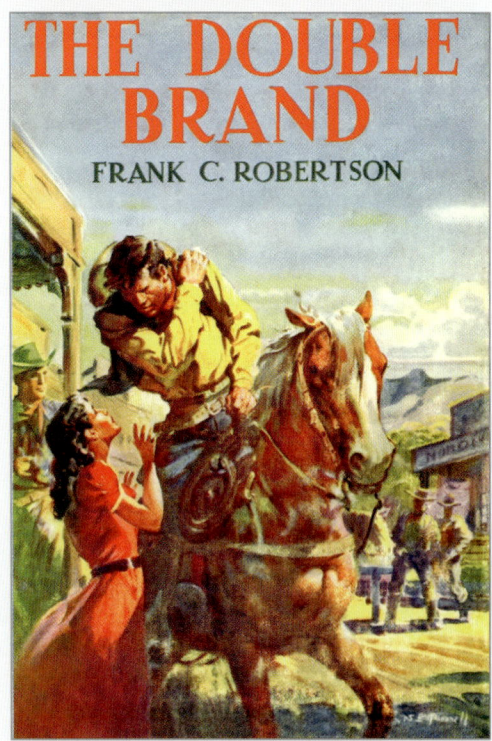
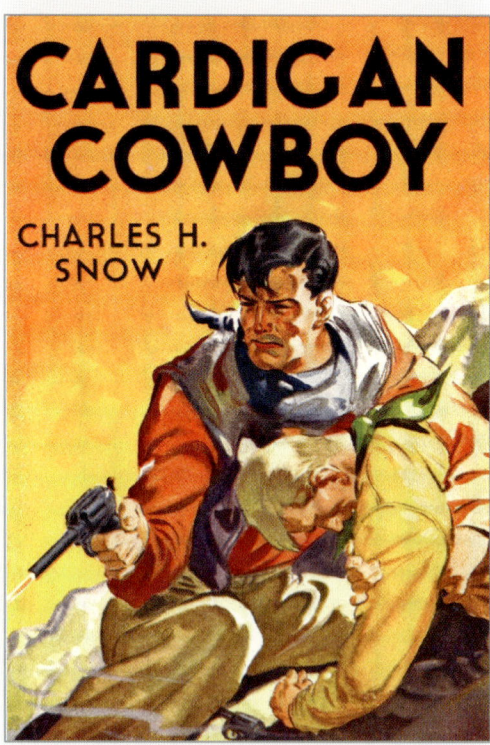

VARIATIONS ON A THEME: THE WOUNDED COWBOY: Top left: *Lightning Lomax* by Gladwell Richardson (Mills & Boon, 1955); painted October 1954. Top right: *Rustlers Moon* by Gladwell Richardson (Boardman, 1950); painted June 1950. Bottom left: *The Double Brand* by Frank C Robertson (Collins, 1954); painted August 1953. Bottom right: *Cardigan Cowboy* by Charles H Snow (R & L Locker, 1949); painted November 1948. Perhaps a sleeveless cardigan worn with the ubiquitous red shirt. (All images except *Cardigan Cowboy* courtesy Jim Kealy.)

GALLERY

BOARDMAN WESTERNS: Top left: *Ride on Stranger* by Dave Waldo (Boardman, 1953); painted January 1953. Top right: *The Killer* by Burt Arthur (Boardman, 1953); painted October 1952. Bottom left: *Bar-M Boss* by Weston Clay (Boardman, 1951); painted July 1951. Bottom right: *This is My Range* by Paul Evan Lehman (Boardman, 1953); painted November 1952.

MINIATURE MARVELS

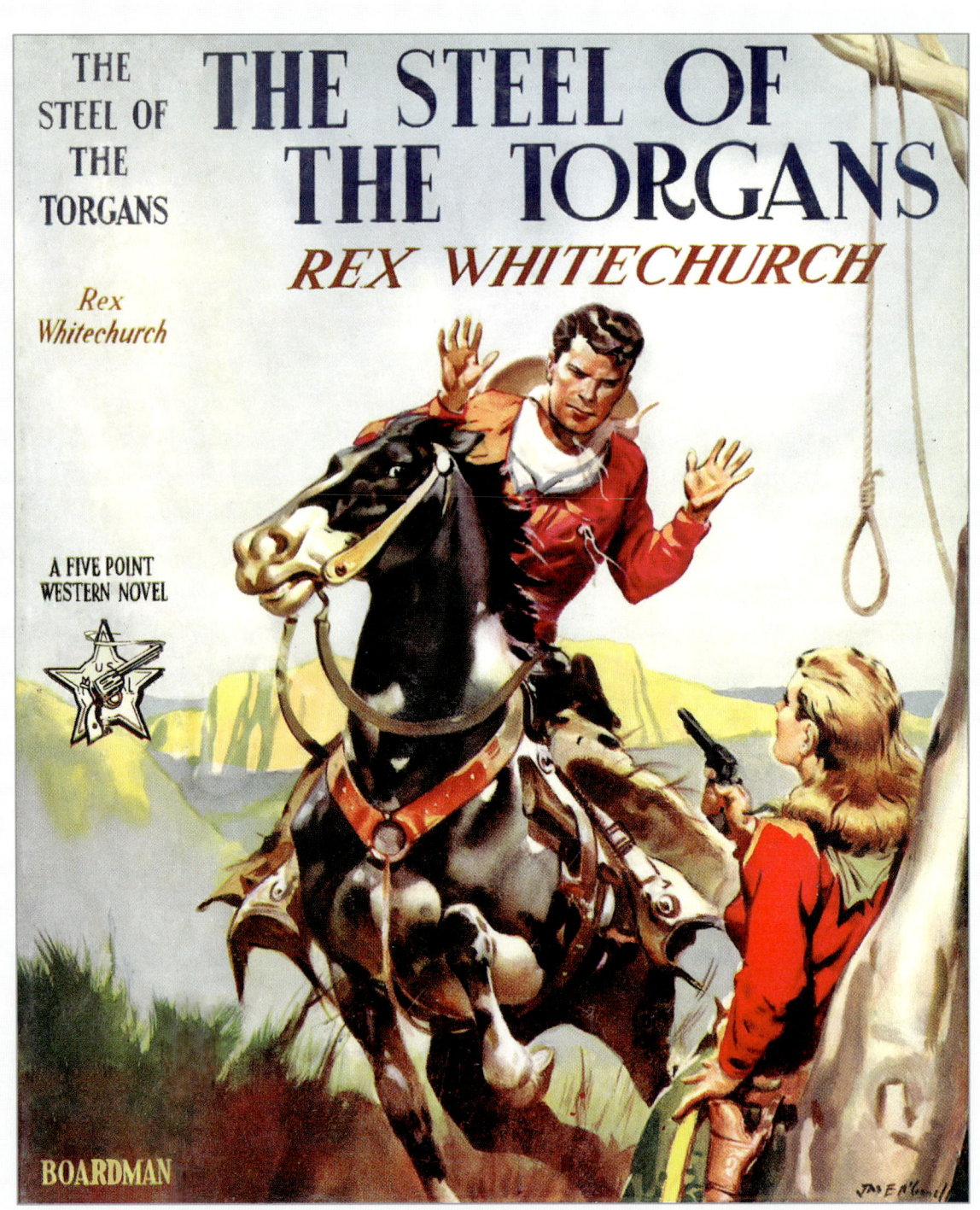

BOARDMAN WESTERNS: *The Steel of the Torgans* by Rex Whitechurch (Boardman, 1952); painted December 1951.

GALLERY

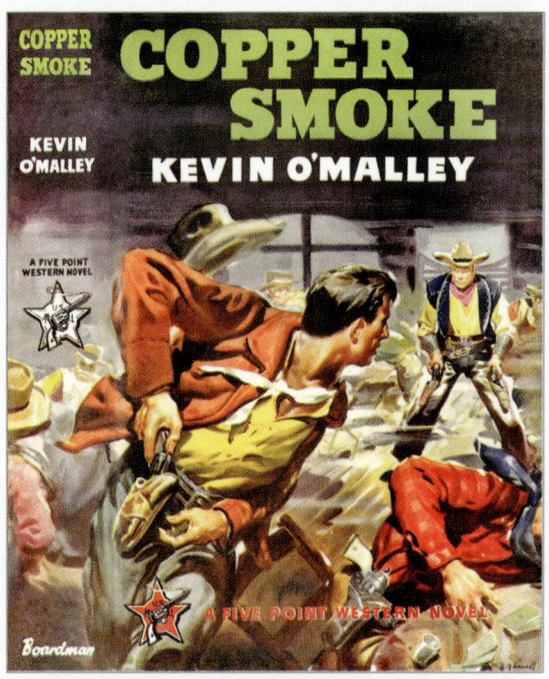

BOARDMAN WESTERNS: Top left: *Two-Gun Law* by Robert J Hogan (Boardman, 1952); painted January 1952. Top right: *Copper Smoke* by Kevin O'Malley (Boardman, 1953); painted May 1953. Bottom left: *Ticket to Remington* by Mark Donovan (Boardman, 1953); painted January 1953. Bottom right: *Quick Trigger* by Gladwell Richardson (Boardman, 1953); painted April 1953.

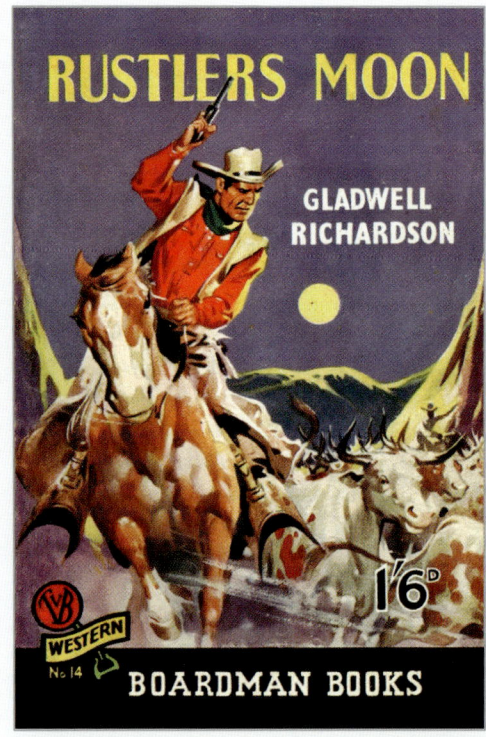

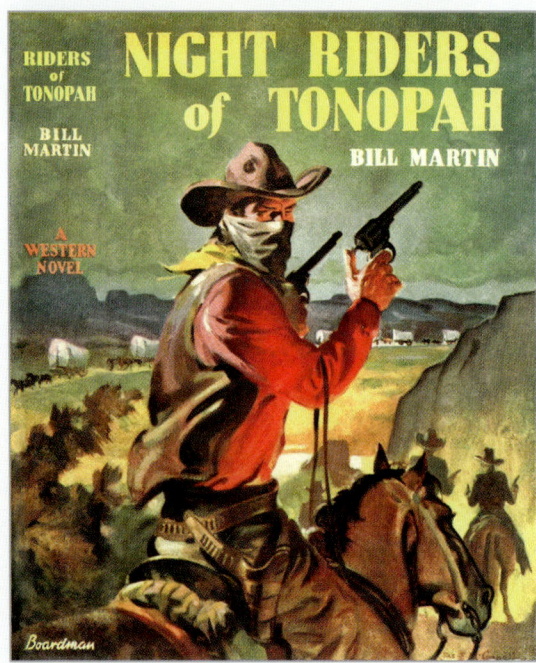

BOARDMAN WESTERNS: Top left: *Rustlers Moon* by Gladwell Richardson (Boardman paperback, 1952); painted June 1950. Top right: *The Long Noose* by Lee E Wells (Boardman, 1953); painted July 1953, and McConnell's last cover for Boardman. Bottom left: *Night Riders of Tonopah* by Bill Martin (Boardman, 1951); painted October 1950. Bottom right: *Block Diamond Round-Up* by Duke Patterson (Boardman, 1952); painted May 1952.

COLLINS WESTERNS: *A Starry Night* by B M Bower (Collins, 1939); this image is taken from a 1940s reprint.

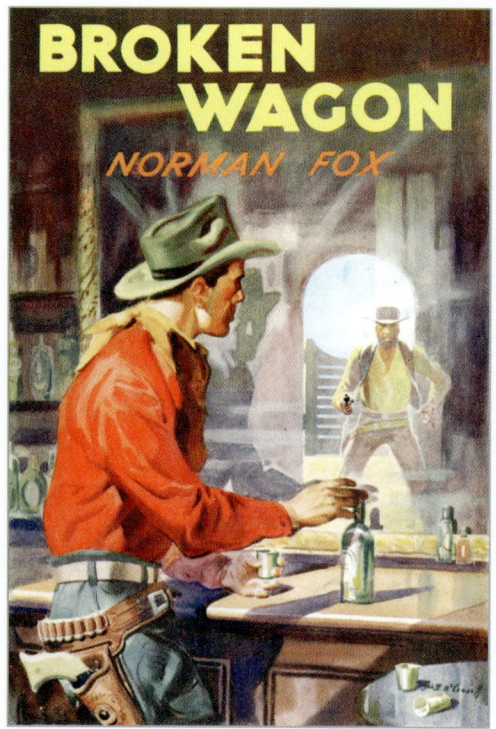
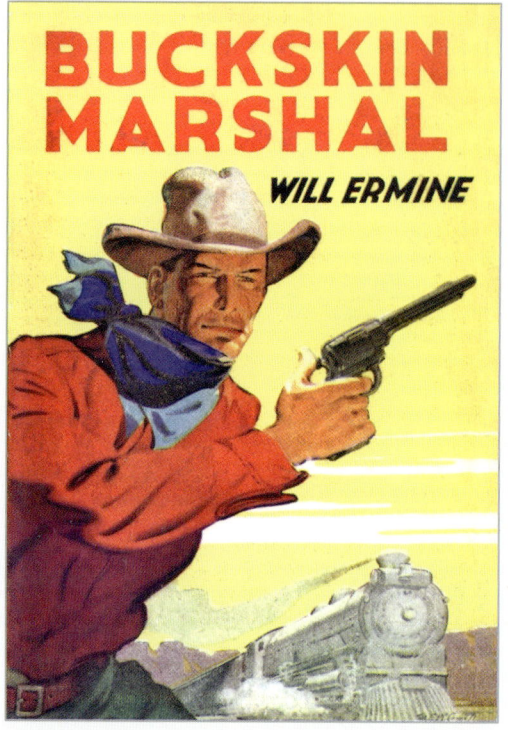
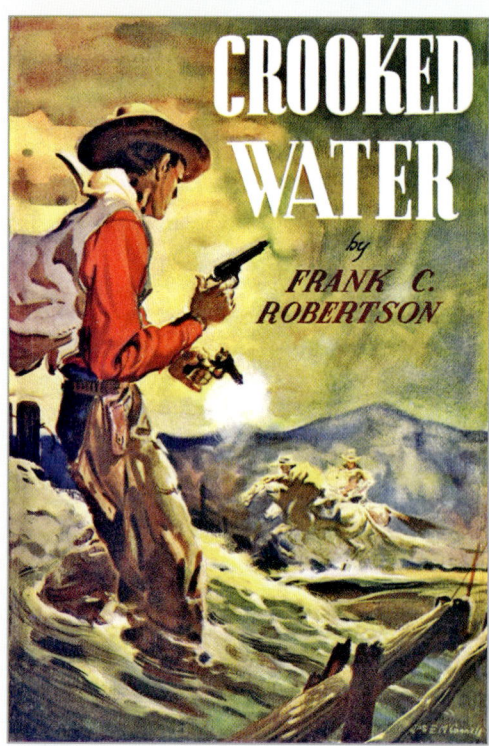

COLLINS WESTERNS: Top left: *Broken Wagon* by Norman Fox (Collins, 1954); painted April 1954. Top right: *Buckskin Marshal* by Will Ermine (Collins, 1946); painted September 1945. Bottom left: *Crooked Water* by Frank C Robertson (Collins, 1953); painted July 1952. Bottom right: *High Vermilion* by Luke Short (Collins, 1949); painted June 1948. (*Broken Wagon* and *High Vermillion* images courtesy Jim Kealy.)

GALLERY

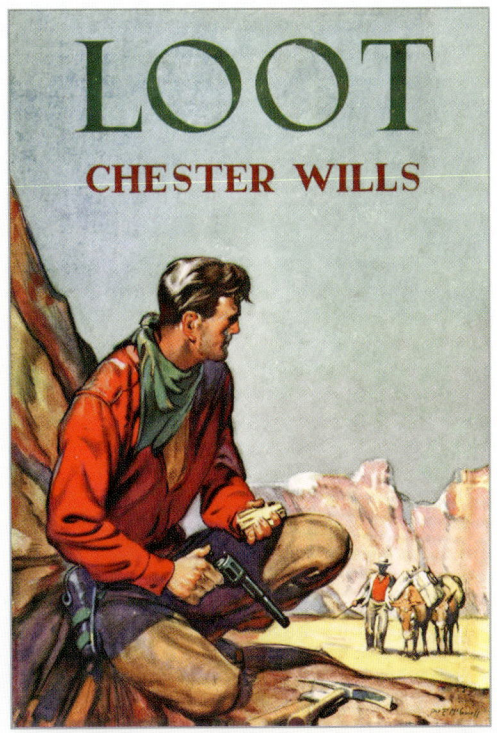
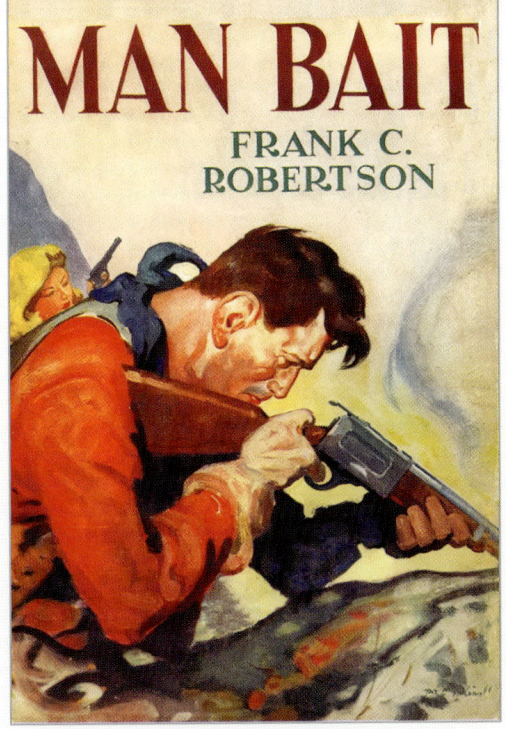

COLLINS WESTERNS: Top left: *Lonely Trail* by Jackson Gregory (Collins, 1947); painted December 1946. Top right: *Loot* by Chester Wills (Collins, 1947); painted March 1947. Bottom left: *Man Bait* by Frank C Robertson (Collins, 1948); painted April 1947. Bottom right: *Mountain Money* by Ranger Lee (Collins, 1947); painted May 1946. (*Lonely Trail* and *Man Bait* images courtesy Jim Kealy.)

COLLINS WESTERNS: *Ride Out and Die* by Frank C Robertson (Collins, 1952); painted January 1952. (Image courtesy Jim Kealy.)

GALLERY

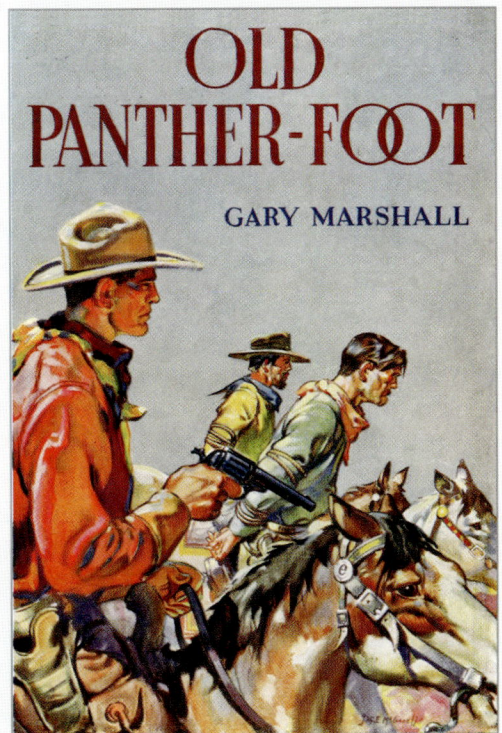

COLLINS WESTERNS: Top left: *Reach for the Skies* by Frank C Robertson (Collins, 1951); painted April 1951. Top right: *Renegade Canyon* by Peter Dawson (Collins, 1950); painted April 1950. Bottom left: *Old Panther-Foot* by Gary Marshall (Collins, 1950); painting not recorded. Bottom right: *Rattlesnake* by Wade Smith (Collins, 1946); painted December 1945. (All images courtesy Jim Kealy.)

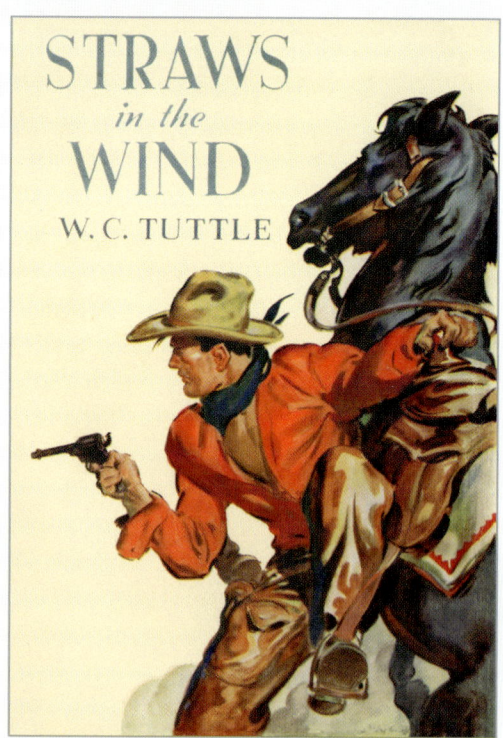

COLLINS WESTERNS: Top left: *Riders Against the Sky* by Frank C Robertson (Collins, 1951); painted January 1951. Top right: *Rope Crazy* by Frank C Robertson (Collins, 1948); painted March 1948. Bottom left: *Roughshod* by Norman Fox (Collins, 1952); painted November 1951. Bottom right: *Straws in the Wind* by W C Tuttle (Collins, 1948); painted December 1947. (All images except *Riders Against the Sky* courtesy Jim Kealy.)

GALLERY

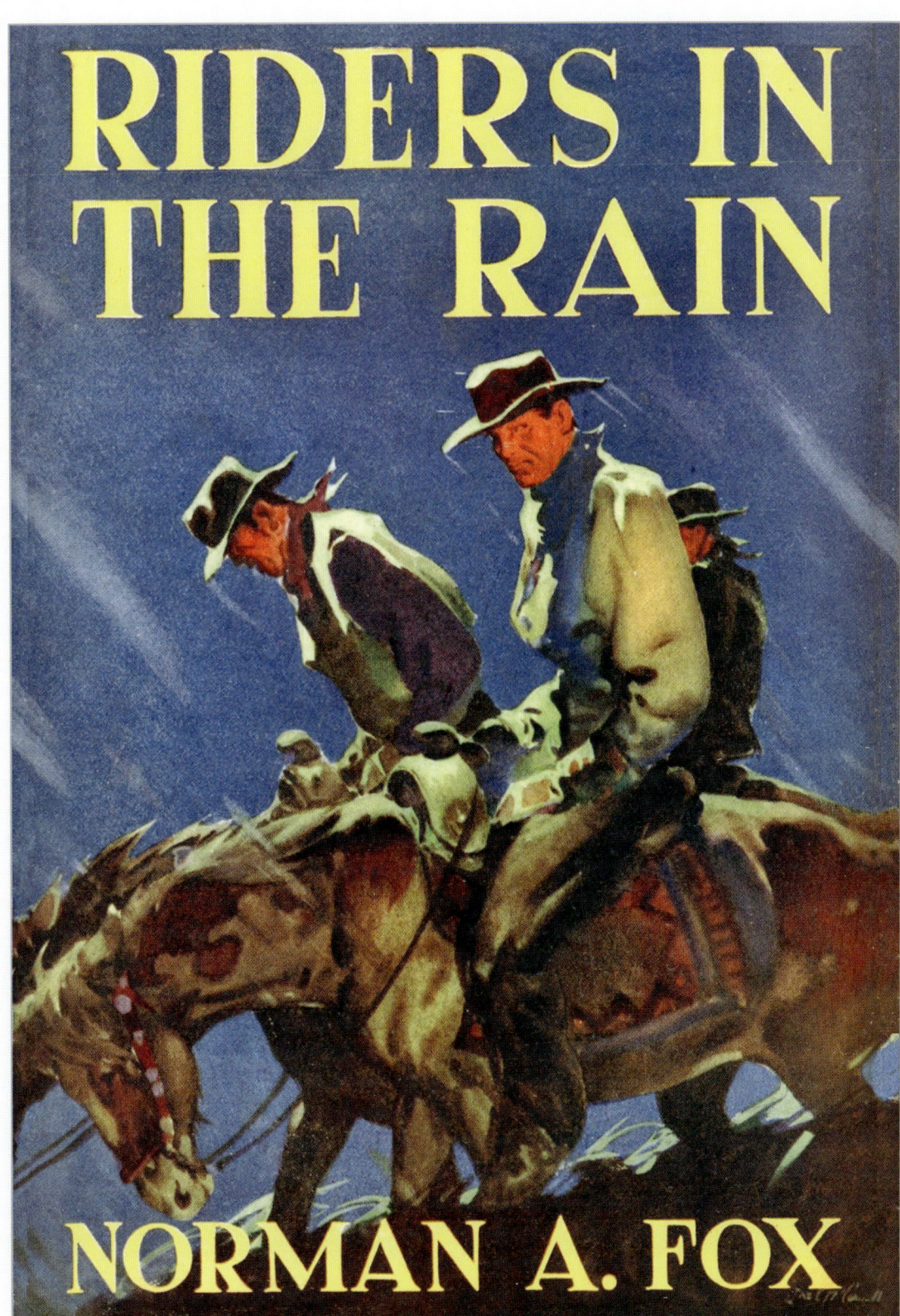

COLLINS WESTERNS: *Riders in the Rain* by Norman A Fox (Collins, 1947); painting not recorded. (Image courtesy Jim Kealy.)

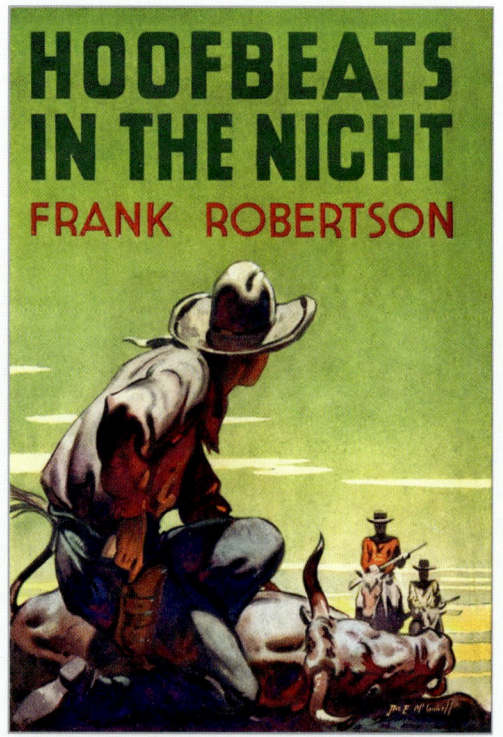

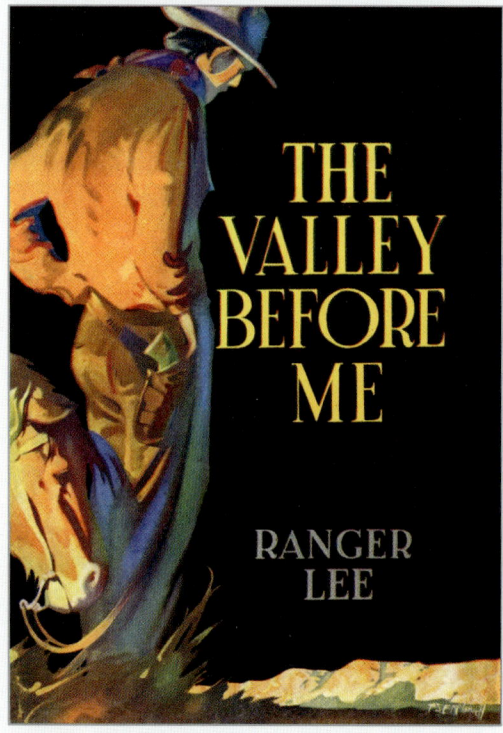
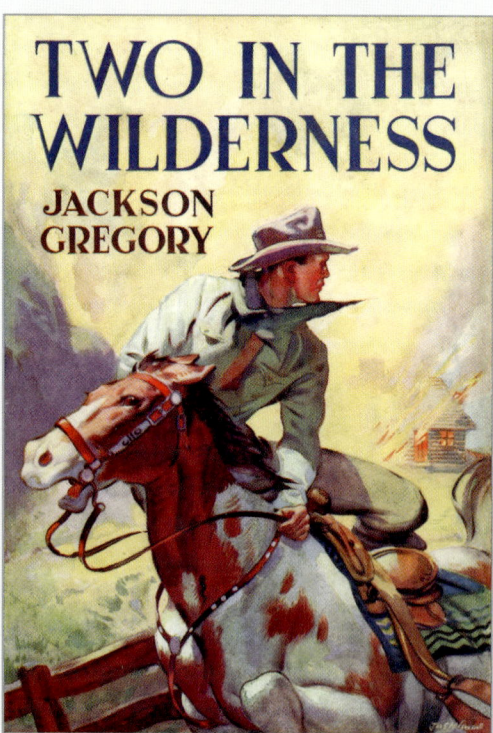

COLLINS WESTERNS: Top left: *Hoofbeats in the Night* by Frank Robertson (Collins, 1946); painted October 1945. Top right: *The Road to Paint Rock* by Frank C Robertson (Collins, 1950); painted June 1949. Bottom left: *The Valley Before Me* by Ranger Lee (Collins, 1946); painted December 1945. Bottom right: *Two in the Wilderness* by Jackson Gregory (Collins, 1947); painted April 1947. (All images except *The Road to Paint Rock* courtesy Jim Kealy.)

GALLERY

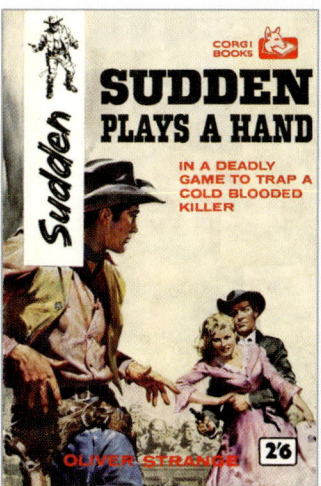

CORGI WESTERNS: THE EVOLVING IMAGE: Above left: McConnell's original cover artwork for *Sudden Plays a Hand* by Oliver Strange, painted November 1960. Above right: the first Corgi edition (Corgi SW991, 1961) (top) and the seventh edition (Corgi 552 07275 3, 1968) (bottom). (Original artwork image courtesy Jim Kealy.)

Sudden Plays a Hand was one of 32 covers that McConnell painted for Corgi in 1960. All but four of them were for Westerns. Oliver Strange (1871-1952), who wrote a series of ten books featuring a Robin-Hood-style gunfighter nicknamed Sudden because he was so quick on the draw, was a British author who probably had minimal direct experience of the American West. The books were originally published by Newnes between 1930 and 1950, but were popular enough for Corgi to republish the entire series in paperback, and even to encourage one of its editors to write a second series of rather repetitive adventures. McConnell, who had no more experience of the Old West than Strange, painted covers for nine of the books in the original series, the tenth (*Sudden Outlawed*) being the work of his friend, Corgi's Art Director John Richards, presumably because McConnell was unable to take on any more work. *Sudden Plays a Hand* was the last of the original series to be written, but the third cover commissioned. The book was a steady seller and went through multiple editions during the 1960s. McConnell's painting was adapted to fresh typographical treatments for each edition.

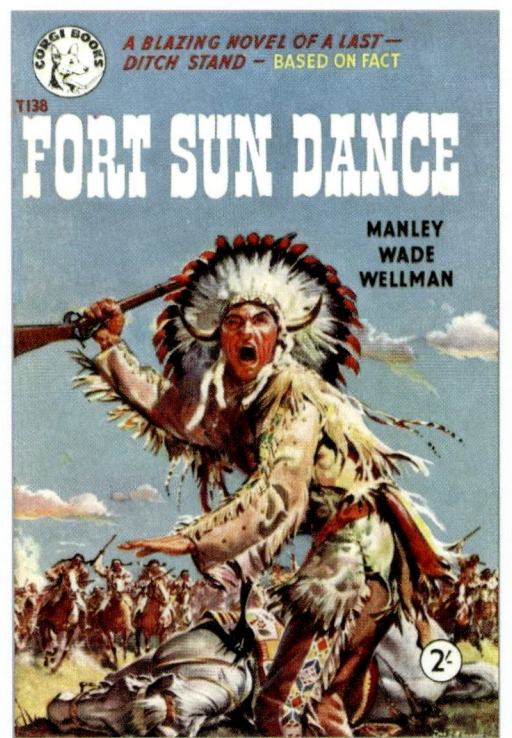

Like that of many of the authors selected by Corgi, McConnell's work was largely sympathetic to Native Americans and their struggle to resist the expansionist settler state and its professional army. His braves and their leaders are proud and fearless, and are strongly individuated within their war-like 'type'. Remarkably for someone who had probably never met a North American aboriginal, his 'Indians' seem closely observed and finely detailed.

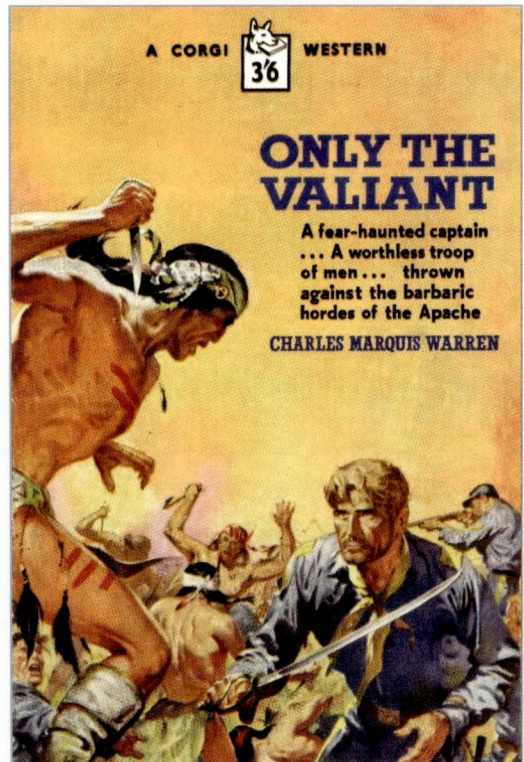
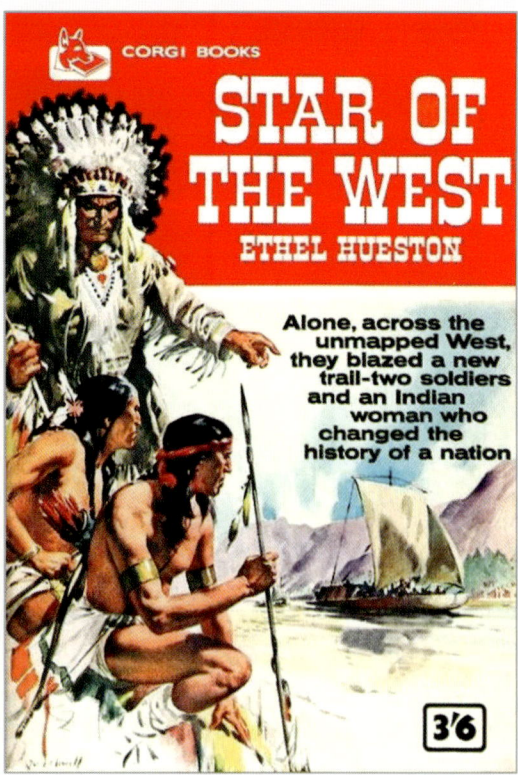

CORGI WESTERNS: NATIVE AMERICAN RESISTANCE: Top left: *Fort Sun Dance* by Manley Wade Wellman (Corgi T138, 1955); painted July 1955. Bottom left: Only the Valiant by Charles Marquis Warren (Corgi GW750, 1959); painted February 1959. Bottom right: *Star of the West* by Ethel Hueston (Corgi GW915, 1960); painted June 1960.

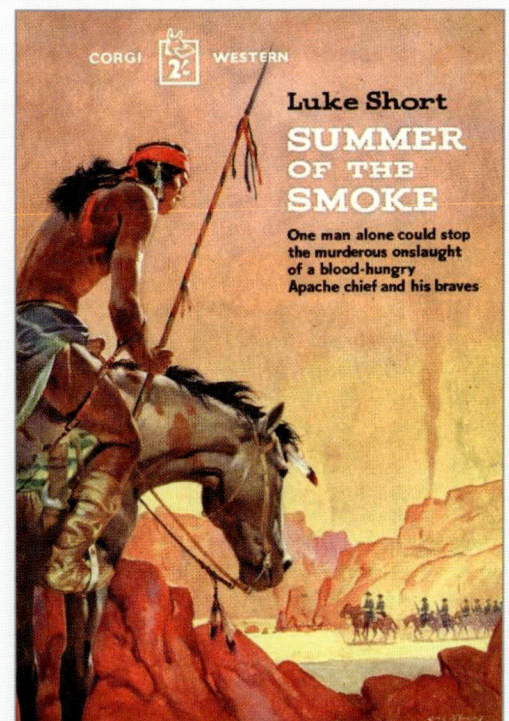
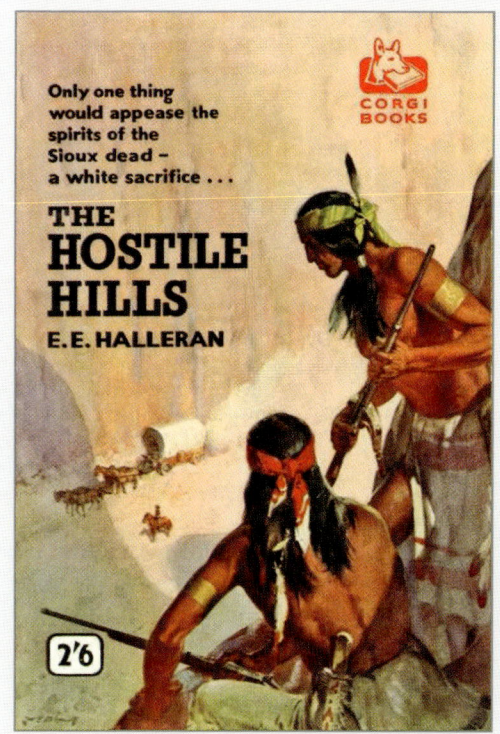

CORGI WESTERNS: NATIVE AMERICAN RESISTANCE: Top left: Advance cover for *Summer of the Smoke* by Luke Short (Corgi T696, 1959); painted November 1958. Top right: *The Hostile Hills* by E E Halleran (Corgi SW814, 1960); painted September 1969. Bottom left: Advance cover for *The Light in the Forest* by Conrad Richter (Corgi T672, 1959); painted September 1958. Bottom right: *Valley of the Shadow* by Charles Marquis Warren (Corgi SW749, 1959); painted February 1959. (Advance cover images from the author's collection.)

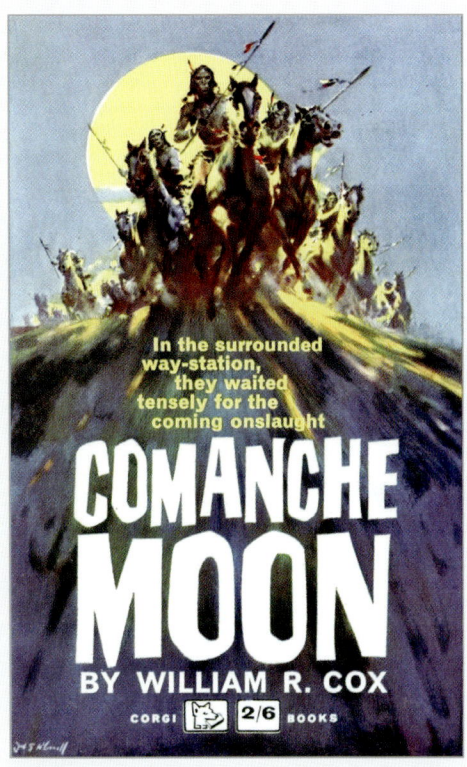

CORGI WESTERNS: NATIVE AMERICAN RESISTANCE: Top left: *Comanche Moon* by William R Cox (Corgi SW1106, 1961); painted August 1961. Top right: *The Great Betrayal* by Dorothy Gardiner (Corgi G483, 1957); painted June 1957. Bottom left: *Sun Dance* by Fred Grove (Corgi SW803, 1960); painted July 1959. Bottom right: *Proud Land* by Logan A Forester (Corgi GW974, 1961); painted September 1960. (*Proud Land* image courtesy Jim Kealy.)

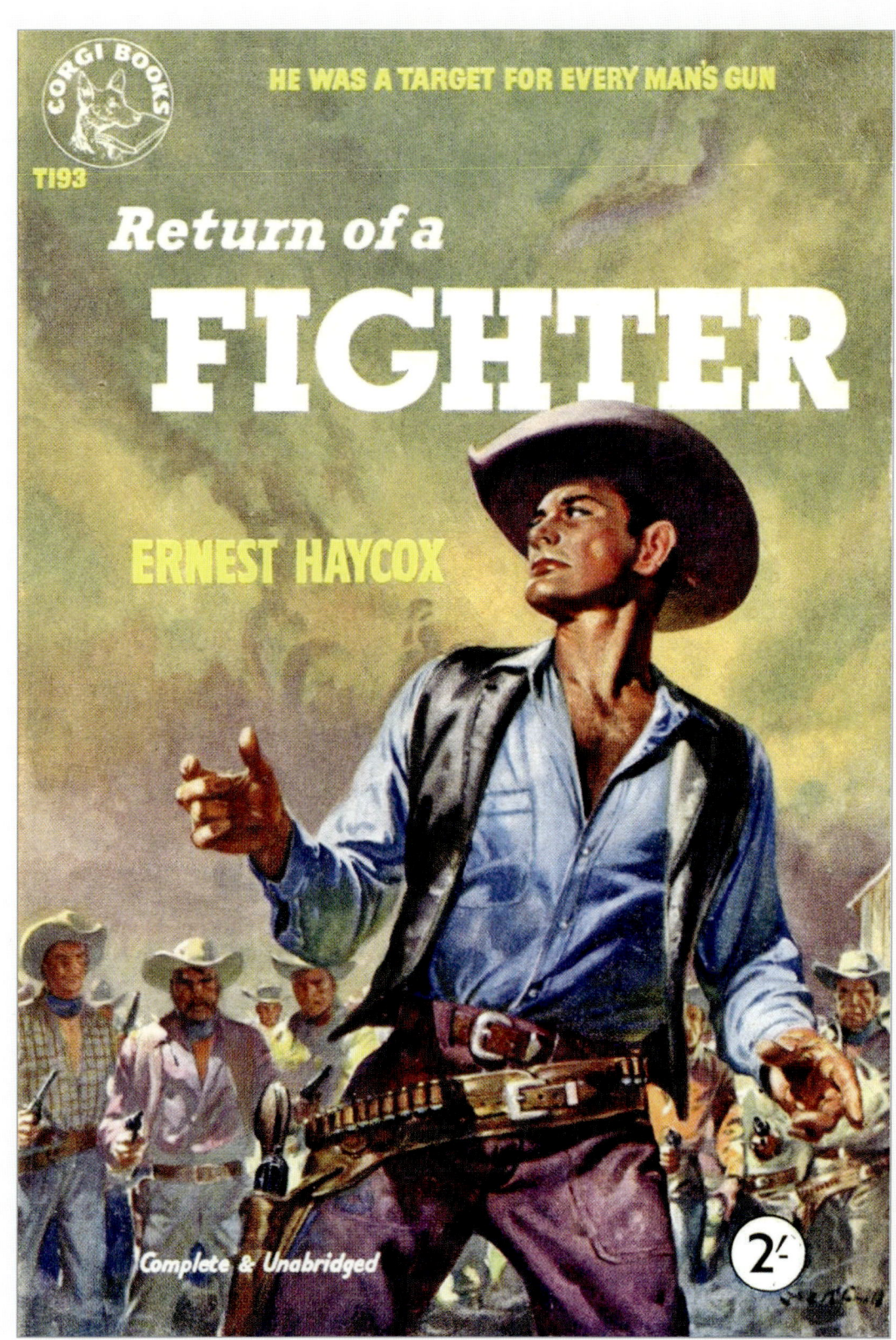

CORGI WESTERNS: LAWMEN AND OUTLAWS: *Return of a Fighter* by Ernest Haycox (Corgi T193, 1956); painted March 1956.

MINIATURE MARVELS

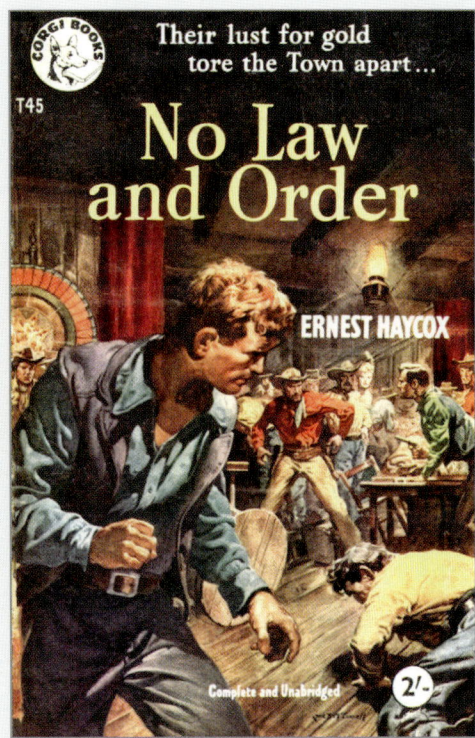

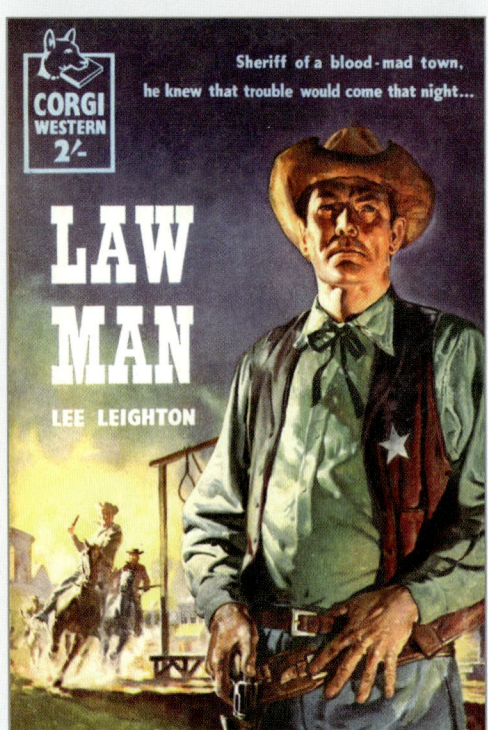

CORGI WESTERNS: LAWMEN AND OUTLAWS: Top left: *No Law and Order* by Ernest Haycox (Corgi T45, 1954); painted November 1953. McConnell's third cover for Corgi. Top right: *The Saga of Billy the Kid* by Walter Noble Burns (Corgi T88, 1955); painted August 1954. Bottom left: *Law Man* by Lee Leighton (Corgi T573, 1958); painted December 1957. Bottom right: *Blood on the Trail* by Max Brand (Corgi SW1012, 1961); painted December 1960. (*No Law and Order* and *The Saga of Billy the Kid* images courtesy Jim Kealy.)

GALLERY

CORGI WESTERNS: LAWMEN AND OUTLAWS: Top left: *Canyon Passage* by Ernest Haycox (Corgi T215, 1956); painting not recorded. Top right: Advance cover for *Riders West* by Ernest Haycox (Corgi S685, 1959); painted September 1958. Bottom left: *Sudden ... Gold Seeker* by Oliver Strange (Corgi SW1026, 1961); painted January 1961. Bottom right: *Holsters and Heroes* by the Western Writers of America (Corgi SW830, 1960); painted September 1959. (*Canyon Passage* image courtesy Jim Kealy. *Riders West* image from the author's collection.)

CORGI WESTERNS: LAWMEN AND OUTLAWS: *Sudden Takes the Trail* by Oliver Strange (Corgi SW1116, 1961), painted August 1961.

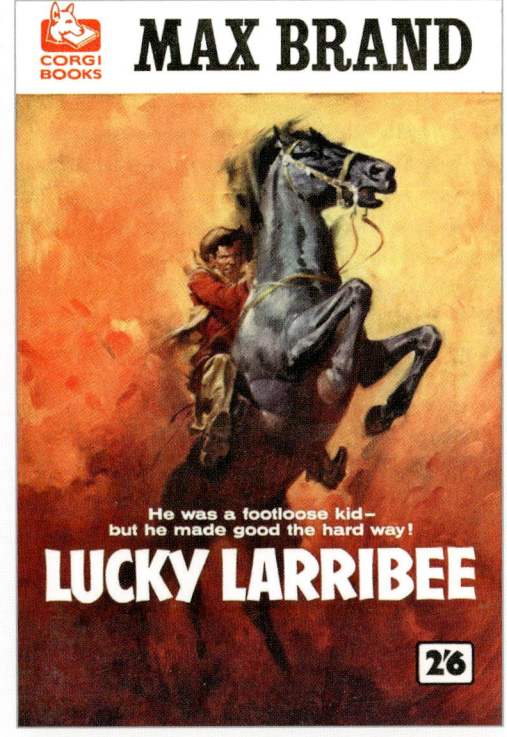

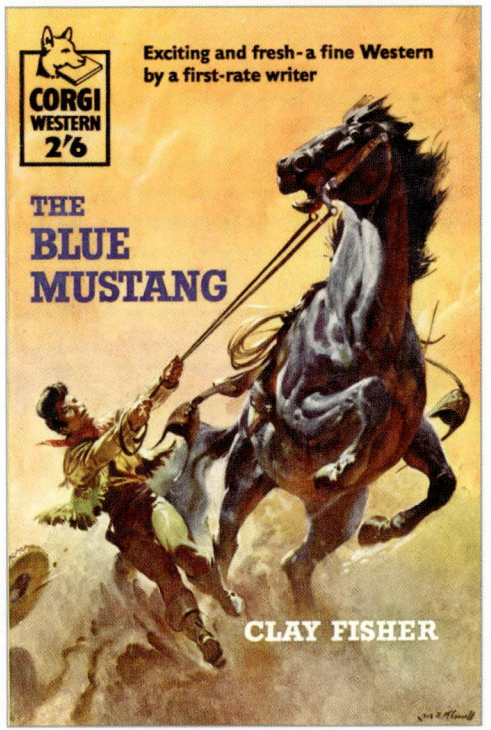

CORGI WESTERNS: COWBOYS: Top left: Advance cover for *Dust of the Trail* by Bennett Foster (Corgi SW694, 1959); painted September 1958. Top right: *Lucky Larribee* by Max Brand (Corgi SW1094, 1961); painted June 1961. Bottom left: *Stampede* by Chad Merriman (Corgi SW999, 1961); painted November 1960. Bottom right: *The Blue Mustang* by Clay Fisher (Corgi SW562, 1958); painted December 1957. (*Dust of the Trail* image from the author's collection.)

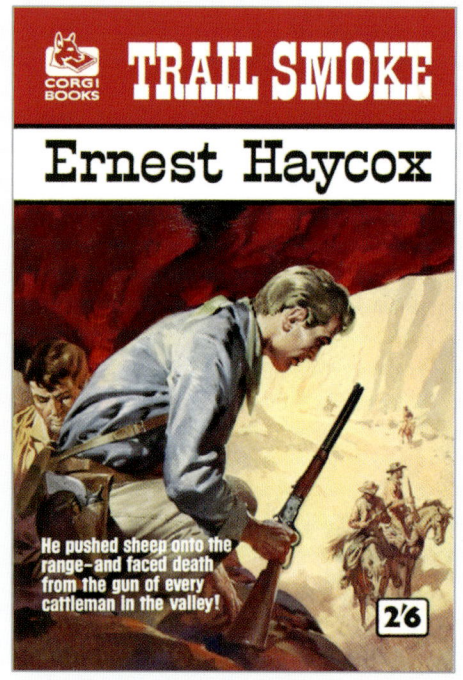 

CORGI WESTERNS: COWBOYS: Above: *Trail Smoke* by Ernest Haycox (Corgi SW876, 1960) (left); and McConnell's original artwork for this cover, painted February 1960 (right). Below: *The Seven Men at Mimbres Springs* by Will Henry (Corgi SW849, 1960) (left); and McConnell's original artwork for this, painted March 1960 (right). (*Trail Smoke* published cover image courtesy Jim Kealy.)

GALLERY

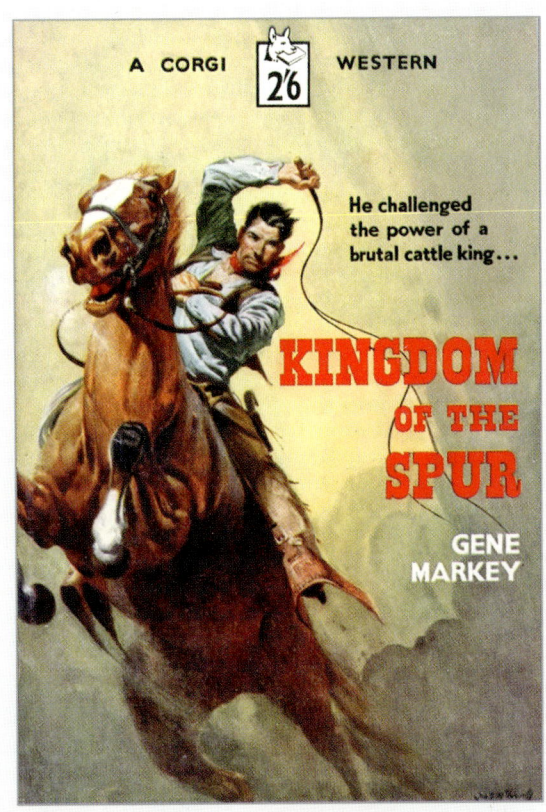

CORGI WESTERNS: COWBOYS:

Top left: *The Raw Country* (aka *The Big Die*) by Lee Wells (Corgi T469, 1957); painted May 1957.

Top right: *Kingdom of the Spur* by Gene Markey (Corgi S621, 1958); painted June 1958.

Right: In November 1976 – fittingly, the year McConnell was made an honorary member of the Society of Illustrators – his outstanding, dynamic painting for *Kingdom of the Spur* was reused on the cover of an issue of the American visual arts journal *Art Direction*. The following year, the same image was reused once more, along with two other McConnell book cover pieces for Corgi Westerns – those for Chad Merriman's *Stampede* (see page 217) and E E Halleran's *The Hostile Hills* (see page 211) – for a set of three large posters advertising the Gags jeans brand. (All four images courtesy Jim Kealy.)

Pride of the South by Elizabeth Seifert (Collins, 1950); painted May 1949.

6: A LASS, A LAD AND A LANDSCAPE: PICTURING THE PERFECT ROMANCE

'The coloured illustration on the front usually shows two people, one of each sex, who, by their expressions of pensive intensity and their desperate gestures, are seen to be having an Important Human Relationship.'

> Rachel Anderson, *The Purple Heart Throbs*, 1974.[53]

Love stories for a largely female readership developed as a popular literary genre in the 19th Century. Early examples of such novels often incorporated lofty moralising and strong Christian convictions. But by the 1930s, when McConnell was first asked to illustrate covers in the genre, it was beginning to become more focused on the early stages of a heterosexual romance that would lead to the idyll of a lasting marriage. Specialist writers such as Ruby Ayres, Denise Robins and Barbara Cartland produced novels by the hundreds; and, despite critical neglect and scorn for their naïve idealism and emotional register, the love story established itself as perhaps the most sought-after reading matter in the circulating libraries boom of the inter-war years. A specialist training academy, the Femina School of Writing in London's Mitre Court (practically on the doorstep of McConnell's studio), offered a course for budding authors: 'The big demand to-day is for articles and stories appealing particularly to WOMEN,' ran its advertising copy. 'Women writers have a bigger chance than ever before. Editors want THE WOMAN'S POINT OF VIEW.' The Femina School was run by women writers for others of their sex who wanted 'to express themselves by writing.'[54]

If anything, the war only intensified the appeal of a good story of successful romance, either in a contemporary setting or as the centre of a wider historical reverie. In her advice to budding fiction writers, Christine Campbell Thomson wrote:

> 'I am not suggesting for one moment that the romance novel always becomes a best-seller .... But it is probably the most steady bet in the novel market through good times and bad. "It's love that makes the world go round," and it certainly makes the book circulate round and round the library subscribers who, in normal times, are the biggest public an author is likely to have.'[55]

The Altar of Honour by Ethel M Dell (Hutchinson, 1954); painted March 1954.

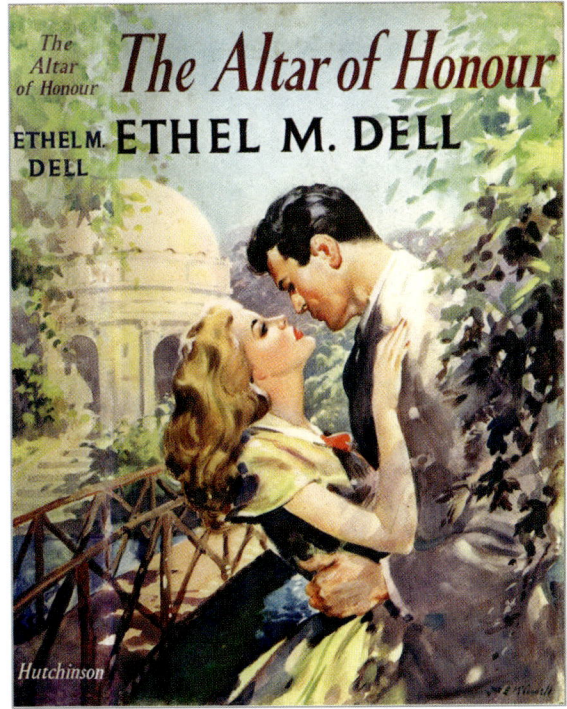

Because the popularity of many romance writers endured, sometimes for half a century or more, the dust jacket illustrations became a way of updating the stories when their novels were given new reissues. Sometimes these reissues were 'revised editions' with some of the worst anachronisms edited out, but more often the jacket artwork disguised a narrative and setting from the era of the reader's mother or even her grandmother. In more extreme cases, the demurely-clad Victorian or Edwardian heroine of Annie S Swan and her sister writers would be given a modern makeover, with rouged lips, backless satin bias-cut dress, cigarette-holder and languid pose. Unless the story was an 'historical' romance, rendering a contemporary cover would be part of McConnell's job. He would have relied on a synopsis supplied by the publisher and some guidelines from the art director, alleviating the need for him actually to read the book. In fact, though, he received relatively few of these contemporising-type commissions, and those he did receive – from

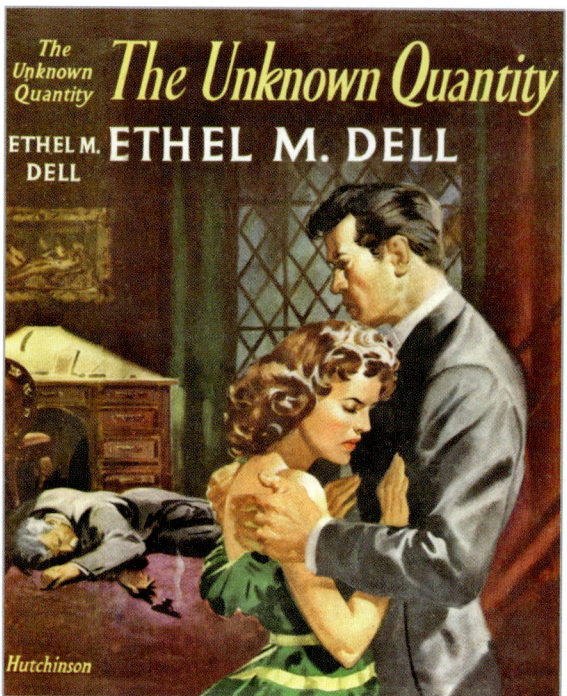

The Unknown Quantity by Ethel M Dell (Hutchinson, 1954); painted February 1954. This and other Hutchinson and Cassell editions of Ethel M Dell's titles were reissues of novels originally published between 1920 and 1930.

The Obstacle Race by Ethel M Dell (Cassell, 1955); painted April 1955. The female subject is a contemporary look-a-like of film star Jean Simmons.

publishers Cassell and Hutchinson for updating Ethel M Dell's religious-romantic novels, for instance – he met with considerable subtlety. Much more frequently, he worked on first editions, including a considerable number of period-costume romances.

The most frequent commissioners of McConnell's romance dust jackets were publishers Robert Hale, Ward Lock and the Hutchinson group. Robert Hale, a romantic fiction specialist, had engaged him almost exclusively for this genre between 1936 and 1943, but allowed him to diversify when he resumed illustrating for them in 1952. Nonetheless, he supplied them with covers for post-war romances by Kathleen Picken, Claire Richie, Theresa Charles, Evadne Price, Christine Jope-Slade, Henrietta Mason, Vicky Lancaster (Dorothy Phoebe Ansle), Catherine Page, Helen Eastwood and American authors Faith Baldwin and Josephine Lawrence, and also a couple in the fast-disappearing desert-romance sub-genre for Hermina Black and Elizabeth Fenton (Kathleen Lindsay). McConnell was also responsible for the cover of the first British edition of one of the early books by the future blockbuster author Harold Robbins: *Never Leave Me* (1956) was a spicier-than-usual work in the genre. However, the author with whom McConnell was most closely associated was Ursula Bloom, the world's most prolific woman writer. For a decade, he was the painter-of-choice for the jackets of Bloom's long series of mostly Tudor historical romances written under the exotic pseudonym Lozania Prole. Between 1954 and 1963, he painted eighteen covers for Lozania Prole stories, and from 1959 these became his sole commissions from Robert Hale.

James McConnell's post-war romantic fiction work for Ward Lock began in 1950 with

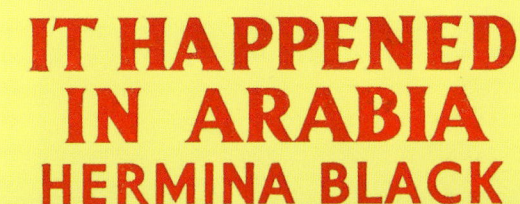

It Happened in Arabia by Hermina Black (Robert Hale, 1955); painted November 1954.

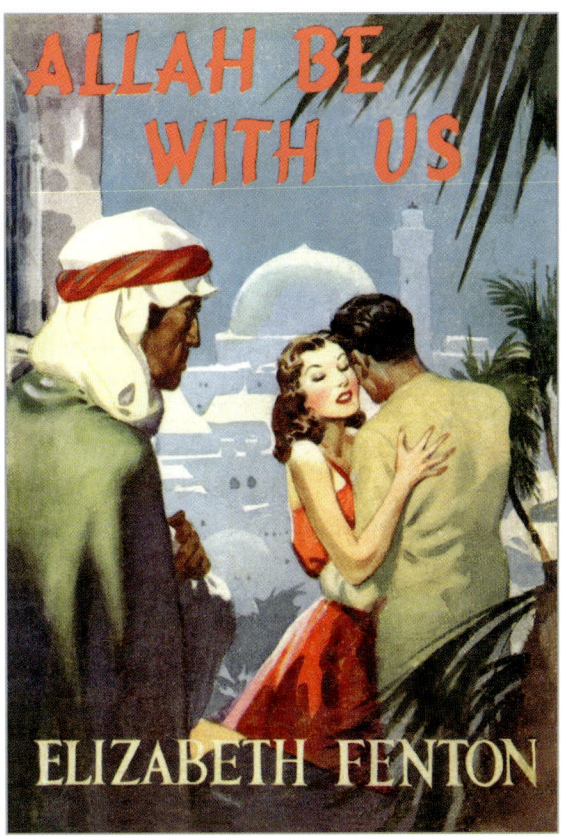

Allah be with Us by Elizabeth Fenton (Robert Hale, 1956); painted February 1956.

covers for novels by Isabel Peacocke and Dorothy Quentin, and although he gave them the occasional cowboy cover, the romance genre dominated his commissions from this publishing house. Over a seven year period, he produced five covers for books by Kathleen Treves, four for Quentin and Kay Winchester, two for Peacocke and Laura Whetter, and one each for Diana Ridley, Mabel Esther Allan, Doris Howe, the veteran Australian storyteller Effie Adelaide Rowlands and the appropriately pseudonymed Valentine (Archibald Thomas Pechey).

This work for Ward Lock was exclusively for dust wrappers, but the Hutchinson group wanted not only jacket paintings but also covers for its Arrow paperback imprint. For the most part, McConnell was asked to imagine the heroines created by his fellow Northumbrian Anne Hepple (Anne Hepple

Never Leave Me by Harold Robbins (Robert Hale, 1956); painted February 1956.

Dickinson) and by Naomi Jacob. To give Jacob's books the feeling of a distinctive series, he often placed her contemplative heroine on the left of the composition, filling the rest of the space with a rural landscape. For *Antonia*, the first of the Arrow series, he even included a landscape painter — a prediction of what he himself would eventually become, perhaps. There was no shortage of wild country, too, in his covers for the Northern romances of Anne Hepple, but rather more action. In these images, capable Celtic heroes do their best to keep their sweethearts safe amongst the wind-blown heather and bracken.

McConnell dust jacket paintings were scattered

Below: *Antonia* by Naomi Jacob (Arrow, 1956); painted April 1956. Top right: *Sally Cockenzie* by Anne Hepple (Arrow, 1963); painted October 1962. Bottom right: *Sigh No More* by Anne Hepple (Arrow, 1963); painted February 1963.

across the Hutchinson group's publishers, with the lion's share going to Hurst & Blackett. Typically, they were for historical romances, and the dominant author by far was the ultra-prolific Kathleen Lindsay (1903-1973), sometimes using the pen-name Margaret Cameron. Surprisingly, McConnell continued to paint jackets for her novels until January 1968, five years after he stopped producing cover art for all the other Hutchinson group authors. *My Dearest Dear* (Cameron) and *She was my Beloved* (Lindsay), both painted in January 1968, appear to have been his last dust jackets for any publisher.

For Cassell, McConnell painted about eighteen post-war covers for books primarily targeted at women readers. The most favoured authors were American novelist Anne Duffield (with 8); composer Frederick Delius's niece Dorothy Black (4); and Catholic writer of rural novels Sheila Kaye-Smith (3). But the stand-outs were arguably the wistful female figure in a landscape for Teresa Charles' *The Burning Beacon* (1956) and the spectacular wrap-around Spanish procession for Rowland Winn's *Carmela* (1954).

On the other hand, Collins, a publisher with a strong reputation for women's fiction, still preferred to direct McConnell toward Western and crime subjects. He painted only half-a-dozen post-war romance covers for them, most notably for novels by Elizabeth Seifert; an author who, after working as a clinical secretary in an American hospital, became a significant pioneer in the doctor-nurse romance sub-genre.

Although McConnell delivered more than 100 cover paintings for women's fiction to a variety of publishers in the twenty years after World War Two, his most well-known remain those for Pan's best-selling reprints of works by Georgette Heyer. The run of eight paintings (one of them unused) began in May 1959 with *The Talisman Ring* and ended in October 1962 with *The Foundling*. The stories, set in the early 19th Century, were said in the copy added to one cover (*The Corinthian*) to be 'Bewitching romance, dashing adventure – in the glittering days of Regency England.' These Heyer covers are typified by *An Infamous Army*, featuring a self-confident heroine straight out of *Vanity Fair*, placed in the left foreground, like so many of McConnell's Pan compositions, and rendered in Headean green and purple, while behind her Wellington's army prepares for battle. Through the woman's enigmatic smile and the soldier's anxious glance, the artist brilliantly conveys that something interesting has passed between his characters. It is a cover that arouses the reader's curiosity, as does that for *These Old Shades*, a tale of 'Romance, Intrigue, Adventure,' for which McConnell conjures a powerful steed as a catalyst of love between a handsome Regency buck and a beautiful cross-dressed woman. He may be rarely thought of as a painter of romantic scenes, but McConnell's work in the genre is both more prolific and of higher quality than most imagine. The work, however, crosses over into a genre for which he is more widely recognised: historical subjects.

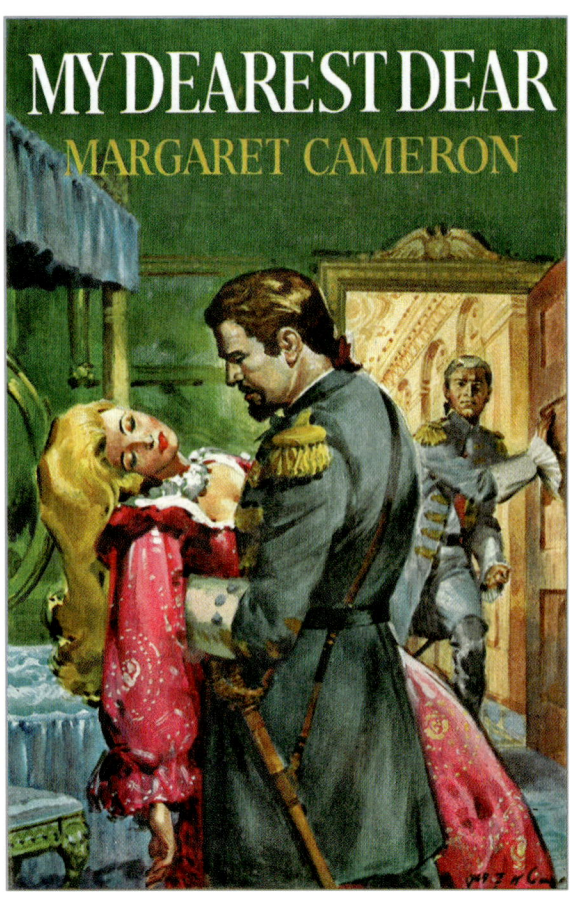

My Dearest Dear by Margaret Cameron (Hurst & Blackett, 1968); painted January 1968.

Left: *The Burning Beacon* by Theresa Charles (Cassell, 1956); painted February 1956. (Image courtesy Jim Kealy.)

Above: Cupid, painted in February 1953 as a standard cover image for a range of cheap reprints of Cassell romance novels. It hovers playfully somewhere between a chocolate box lid and an old-master altarpiece.

Below: *Carmela* by Rowland Winn (Cassell, 1954); painted February 1954.

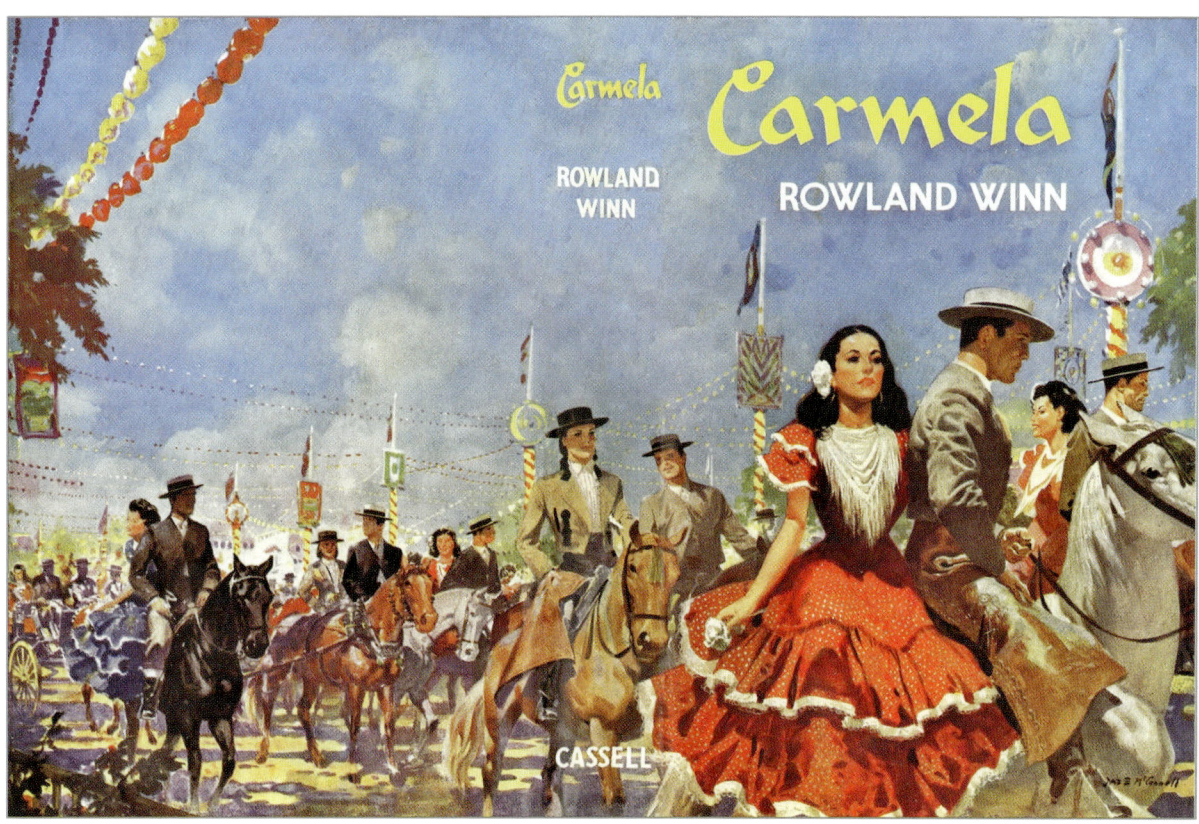

GALLERY

No Time for Romance by Kathleen Treves (Ward Lock, 1954); painted May 1953. Time enough to paint a couple of hundred covers! (Image courtesy Jim Kealy.)

THE GEORGETTE HEYERS: Original artwork for *Friday's Child* by Georgette Heyer (Pan X70, 1960); painted December 1959.

MINIATURE MARVELS

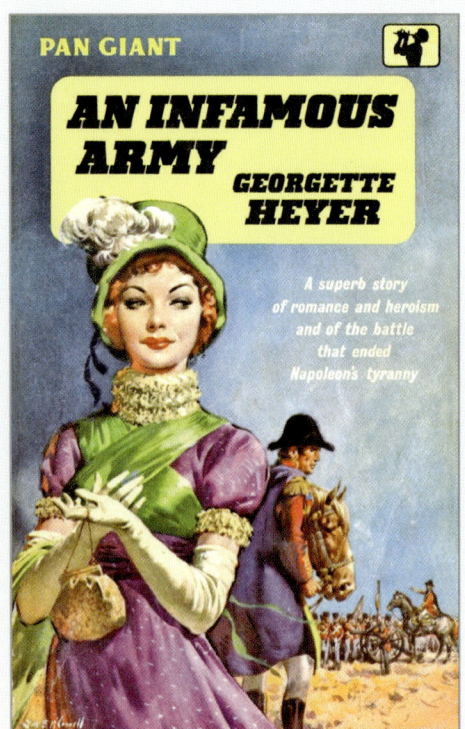
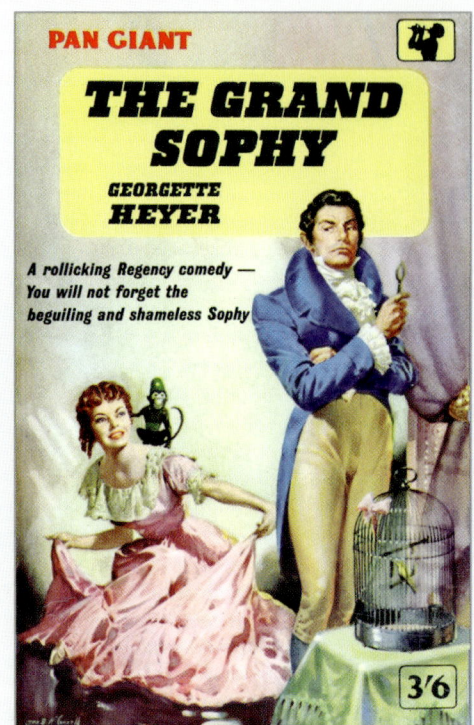
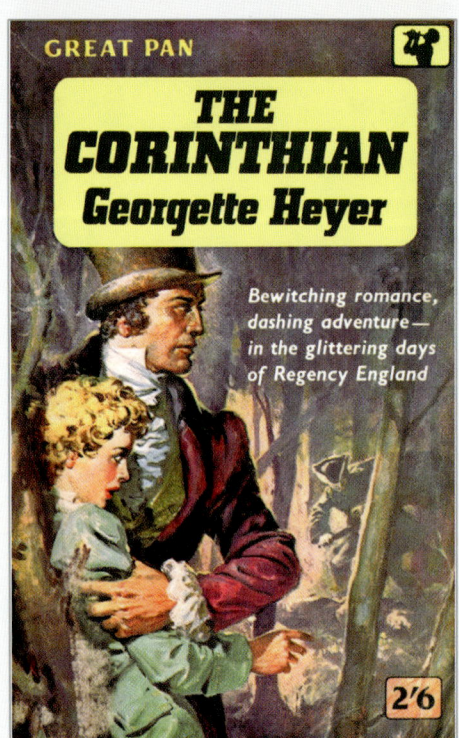
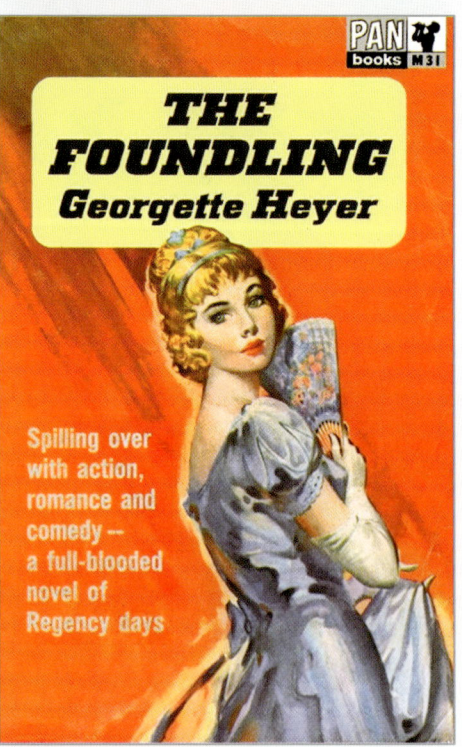

THE GEORGETTE HEYERS: Top left: *An Infamous Army* by Georgette Heyer (Pan X88, 1961); painted October 1960. Top right: *The Grand Sophy* by Georgette Heyer (Pan X64, 1960); painted December 1959. Bottom left: *The Corinthian* by Georgette Heyer (Pan X285, 1962); painted October 1961. Bottom right: *The Foundling* by Georgette Heyer (Pan M31, 1963); painted October 1962. McConnell's last cover for Pan. (*The Grand Sophy* and *The Corinthian* Images courtesy Jim Kealy.)

THE GEORGETTE HEYERS: *The Talisman Ring* by Georgette Heyer (Pan G311, 1959); painted May 1959. (Image courtesy Jim Kealy.)

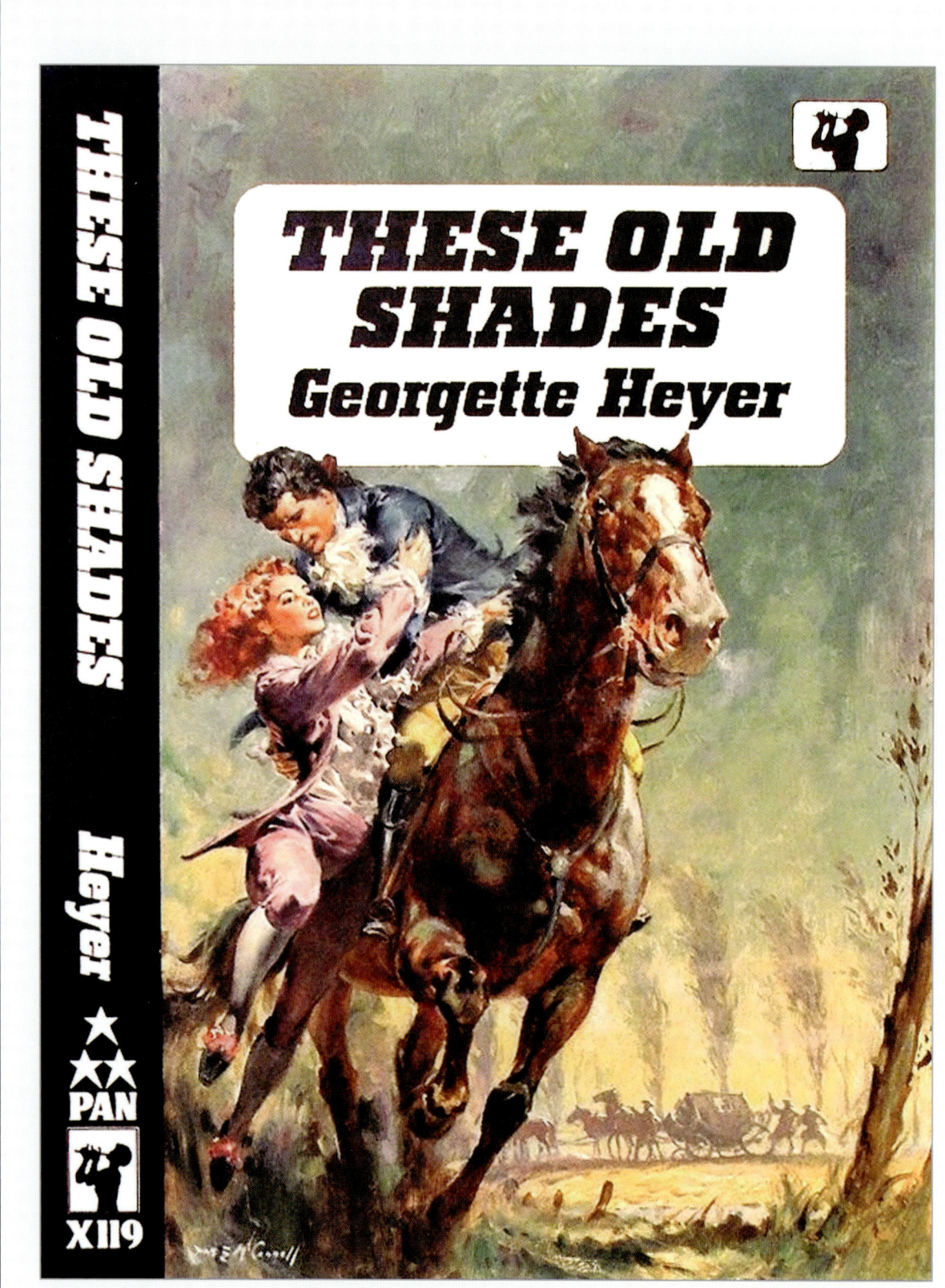

THE GEORGETTE HEYERS: Original artwork for *These Old Shades* by Georgette Heyer (Pan X119, 1962); painted September 1961.

GALLERY

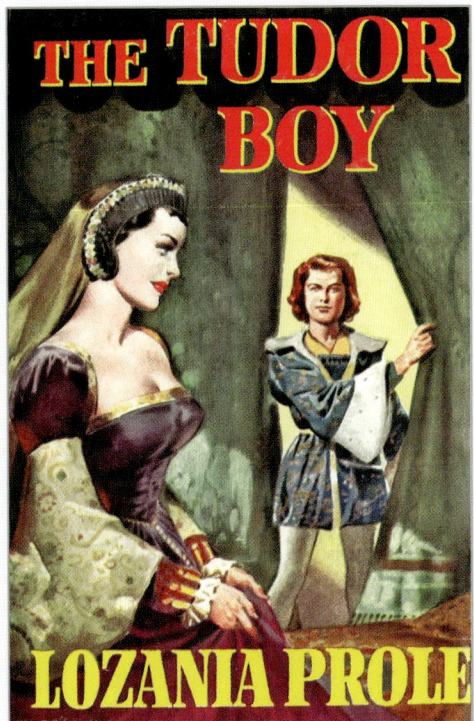

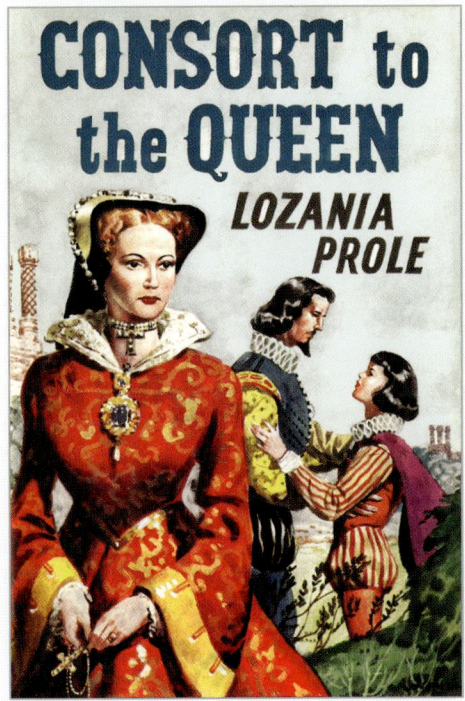

THE LOZANIA PROLES: Top left: *The Tudor Boy* by Lozania Prole (Robert Hale, 1960); painted November 1959. Top right: *The King's Pleasure* by Lozania Prole (Digit, 1957). This was the first in the Prole series; originally painted in January 1954 for the Robert Hale first edition, it was adapted in April 1957 for this paperback. Joan Collins to a tee. Bottom left: *Consort to the Queen* by Lozania Prole (Robert Hale, 1959); painted January 1959. Bottom right: *Henry's Last Love* by Lozania Prole (Robert Hale, 1958); painted October 1957.

233

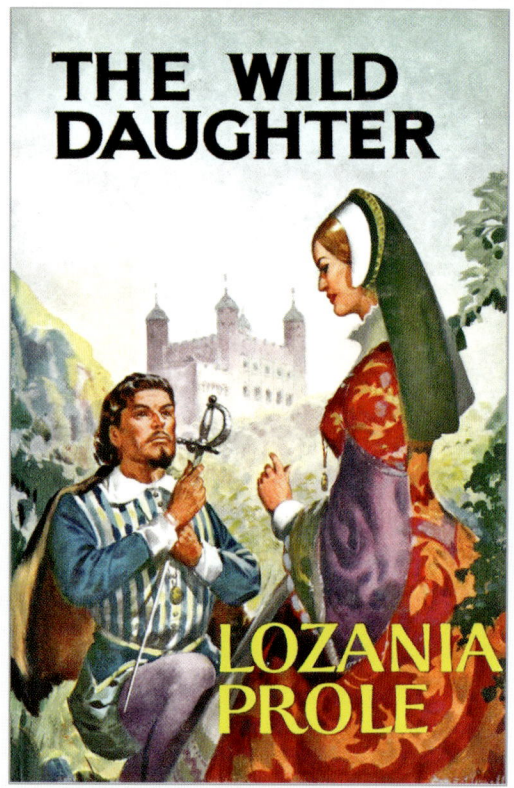
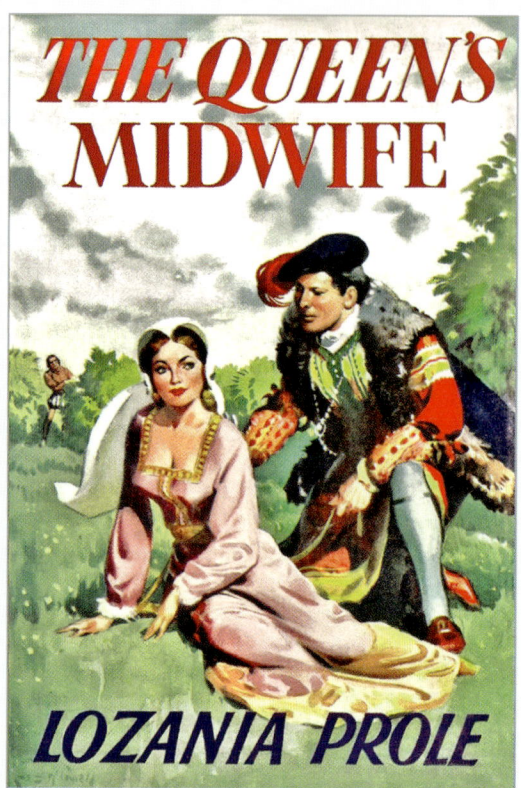

THE LOZANIA PROLES: Top left: *The Wild Daughter* by Lozania Prole (Robert Hale, 1963); painted March 1963. Top right: *The Queen's Midwife* by Lozania Prole (Robert Hale, 1961); painted July 1960. Bottom left: *My Wanton Tudor Rose* by Lozania Prole (Robert Hale, 1956); painted October 1955. Bottom right: *Henry's Golden Queen* by Lozania Prole (Robert Hale, 1964); painted August 1963. McConnell's final painting for this publisher.

GALLERY

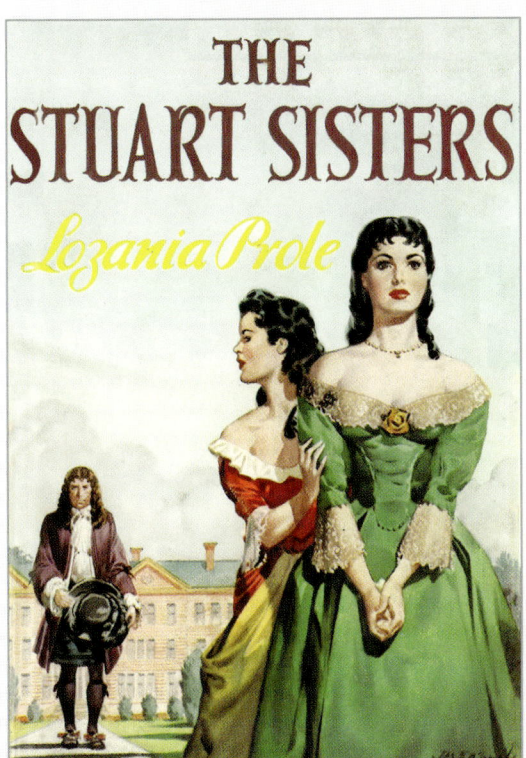
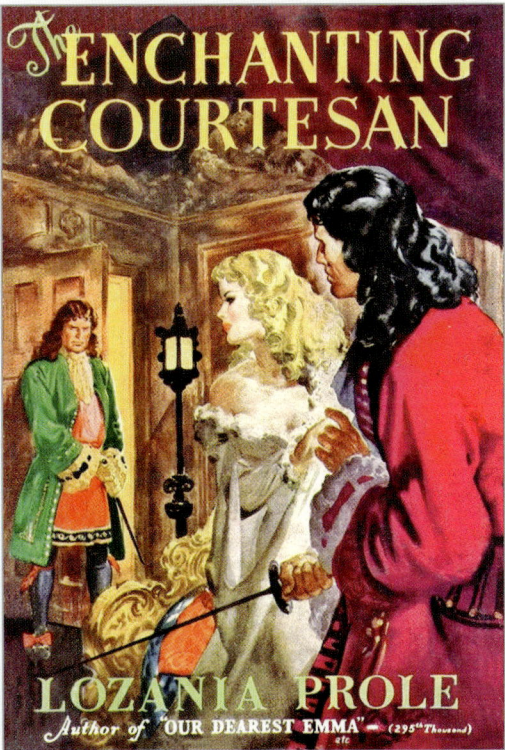

THE LOZANIA PROLES: Top left: *My Love! My Little Queen!* by Lozania Prole (Robert Hale, 1961); painted June 1960. Top right: *A King's Plaything* by Lozania Prole (Robert Hale, 1962); painted August 1961. Bottom left: *The Stuart Sisters* by Lozania Prole (Robert Hale, 1958); painted February 1957. Bottom right: *The Enchanting Courtesan* by Lozania Prole (Robert Hale, 1955); painted September 1954. (*The Enchanting Courtesan* image courtesy Jim Kealy.)

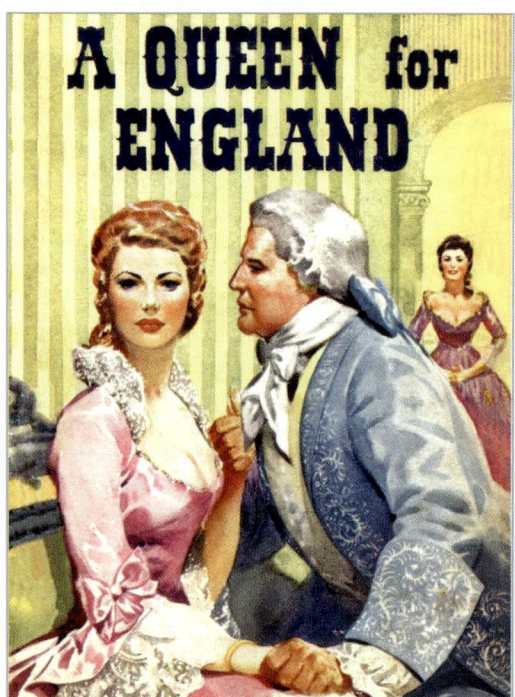

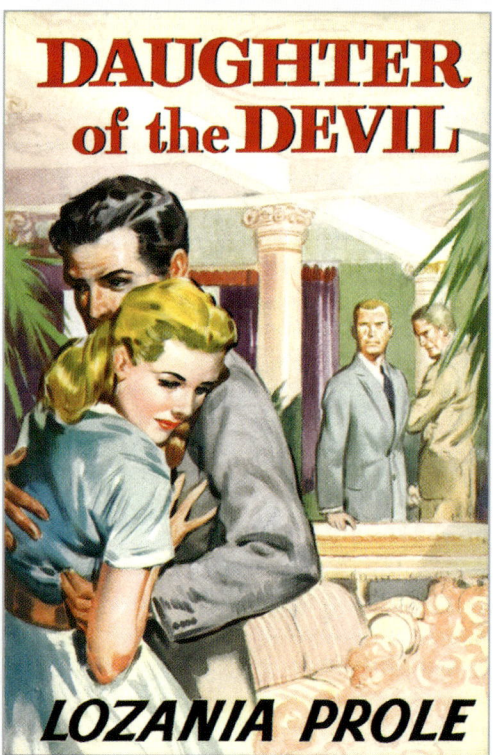

THE LOZANIA PROLES: Top left: *A Queen for England* by Lozania Prole (Robert Hale, 1957); painted March 1956. Top right: *Queen Guillotine* by Lozania Prole (Robert Hale, 1962); painted June 1961. Bottom left: *The Little Victoria* by Lozania Prole (Robert Hale, 1957); painted October 1956. Perhaps more than anything else, the Lozania Prole covers demonstrate McConnell's ability to research historical costumes and make the characters look comfortable in them. Bottom right: *Daughter of the Devil* by Lozania Prole (Robert Hale, 1962); painted January 1962. A rare excursion into modern dress.

THE KATHLEEN LINDSAYS: *Madonna of Hell* by Kathleen Lindsay (Hutchinson, 1954); painted January 1954. This book, which was later reprinted with McConnell's cover for the Valentine Romance Club, bore the first of the artist's paintings for the author. It set a tone for the series, which was a notch darker and more erotic than many of the other romances he illustrated, at least in the 1950s.

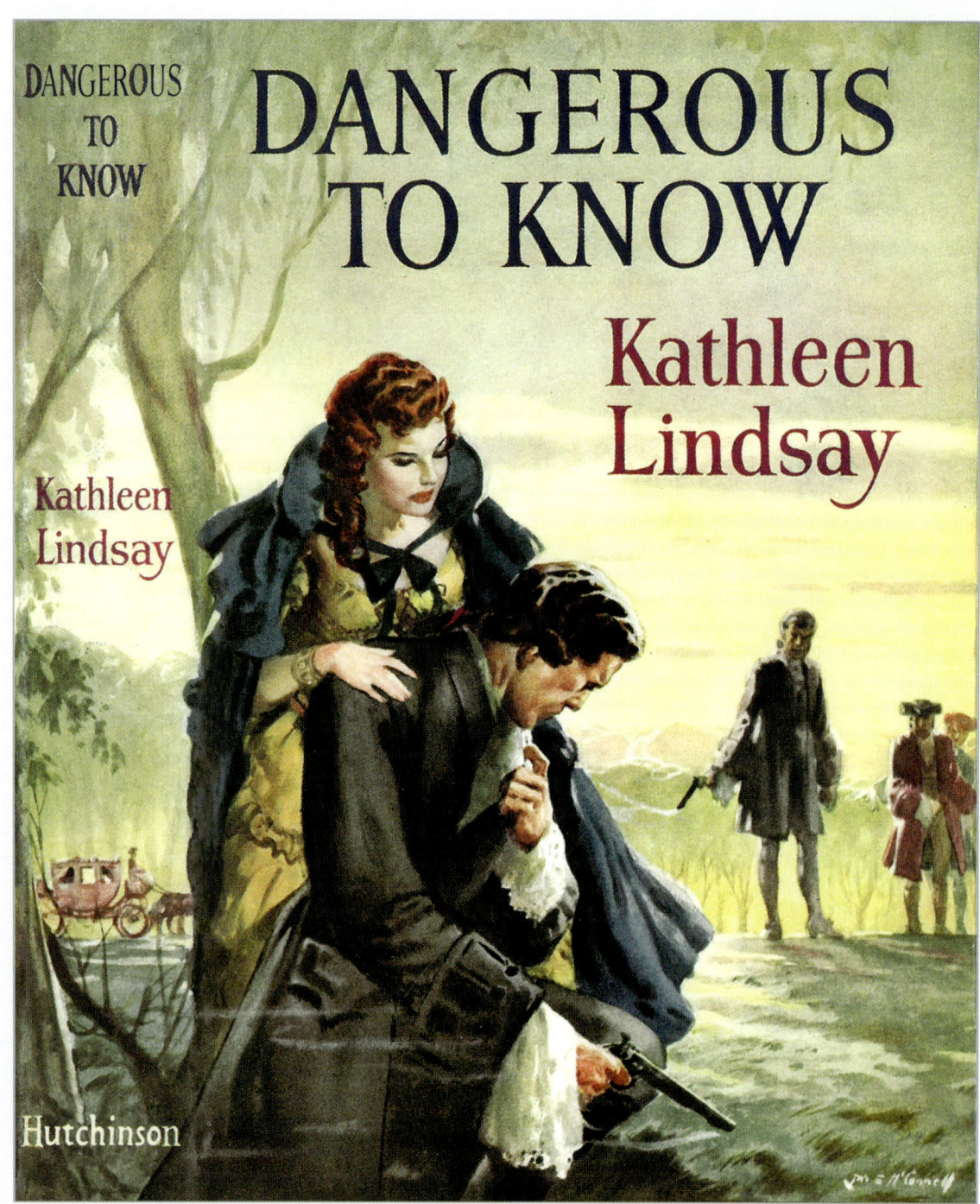

THE KATHLEEN LINDSAYS: *Dangerous to Know* by Kathleen Lindsay (Hutchinson, 1956); painted October 1955.

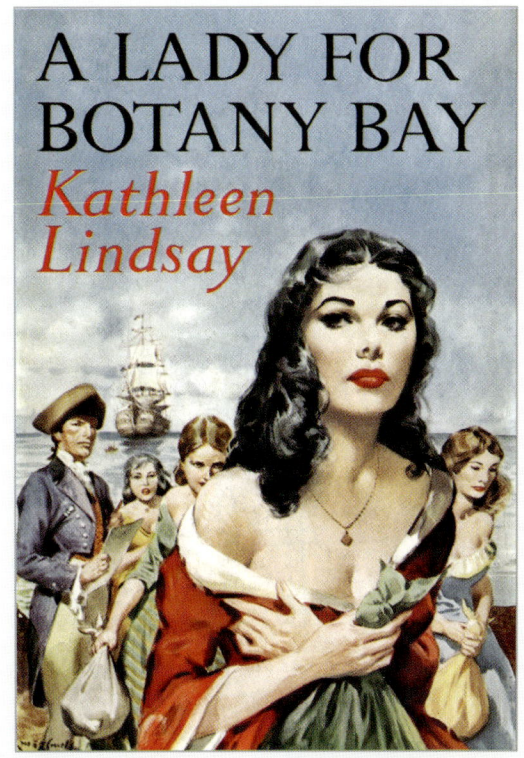

THE KATHLEEN LINDSAYS: Top left: *Dark Destiny* by Kathleen Lindsay (Hutchinson, 1955); painted May 1954. Top right: *A Lady for Botany Bay* by Kathleen Lindsay (Hutchinson's Valentine Romance Club, 1961); painted December 1960. These Australian settings were probably the consequence of Lindsay's residence there during one of her three marriages. Bottom left: *Tomorrow We Die* by Kathleen Lindsay (Hutchinson, 1955); painted February 1955. Bottom right: *There is no Yesterday* by Kathleen Lindsay (Hurst & Blackett, 1962); painted April 1962.

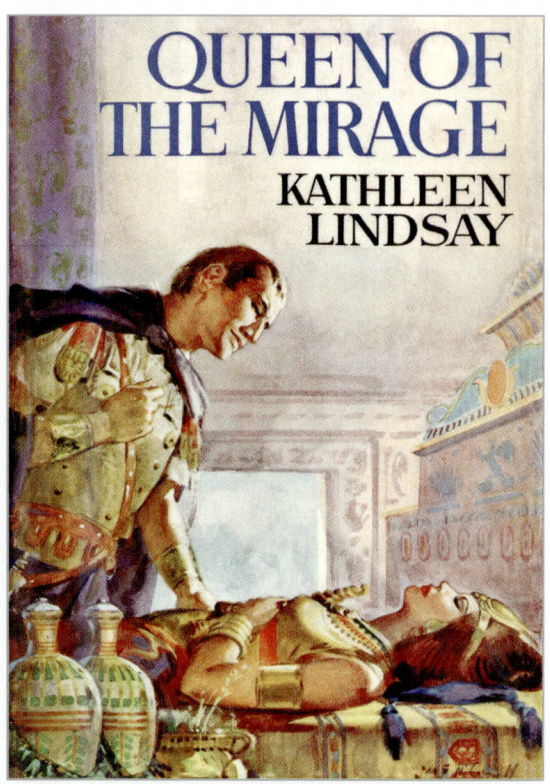
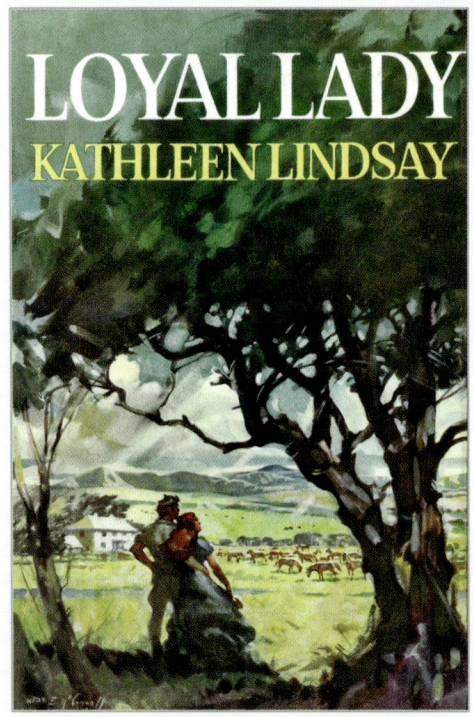

THE KATHLEEN LINDSAYS: Top left: *Theodora* by Kathleen Lindsay (Hurst & Blackett, 1964); painted August 1963. Top right: *Queen of the Mirage* by Kathleen Lindsay (Hurst & Blackett, 1966); painted February 1966. Bottom left: *Loyal Lady* by Kathleen Lindsay (Hurst & Blackett, 1965); painted August 1964. Bottom right: *The Devil's Dominion* by Kathleen Lindsay (Hutchinson, 1956); painted May 1956.

GALLERY

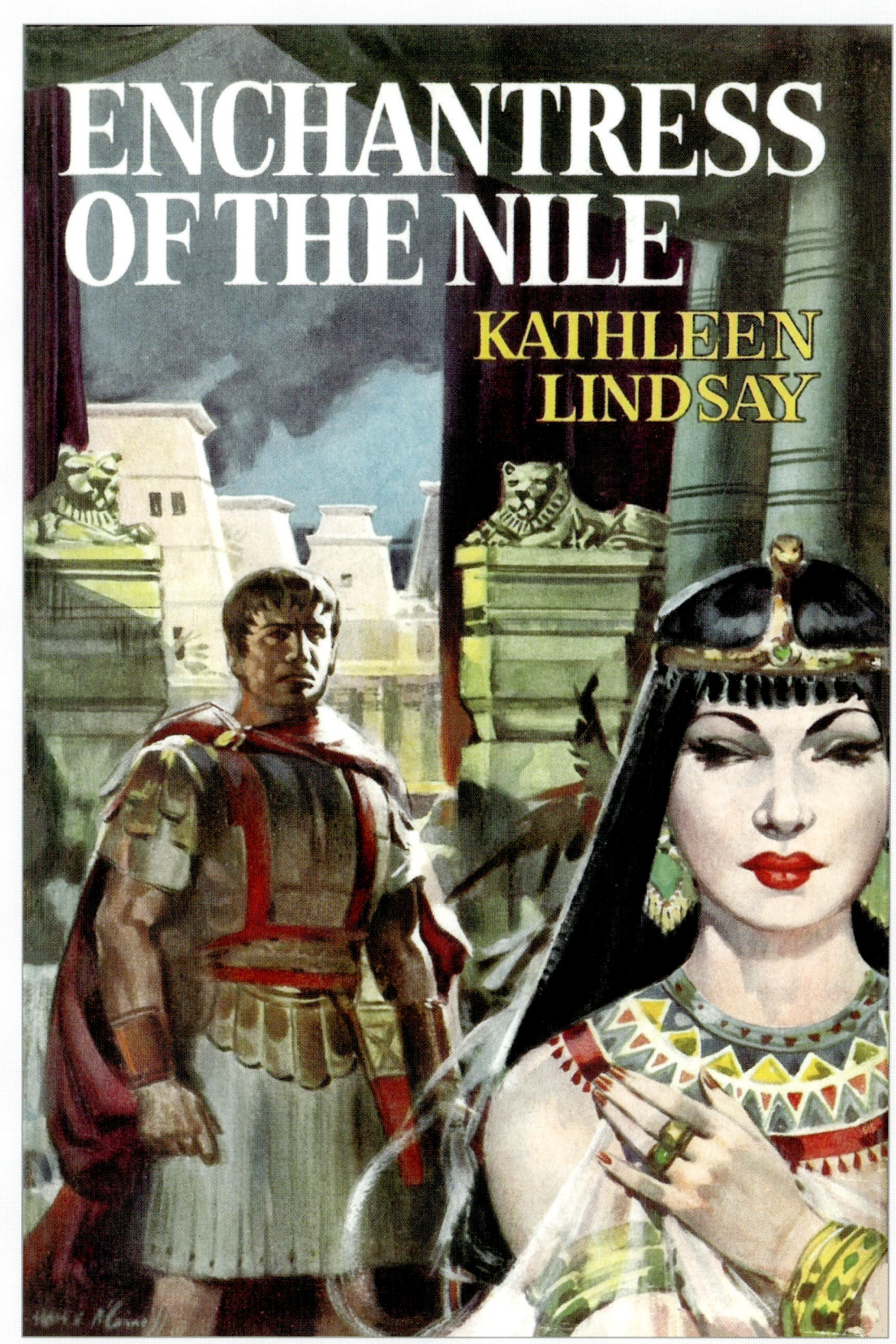

THE KATHLEEN LINDSAYS: *Enchantress of the Nile* by Kathleen Lindsay (Hurst & Blackett, 1965); painted January 1965.

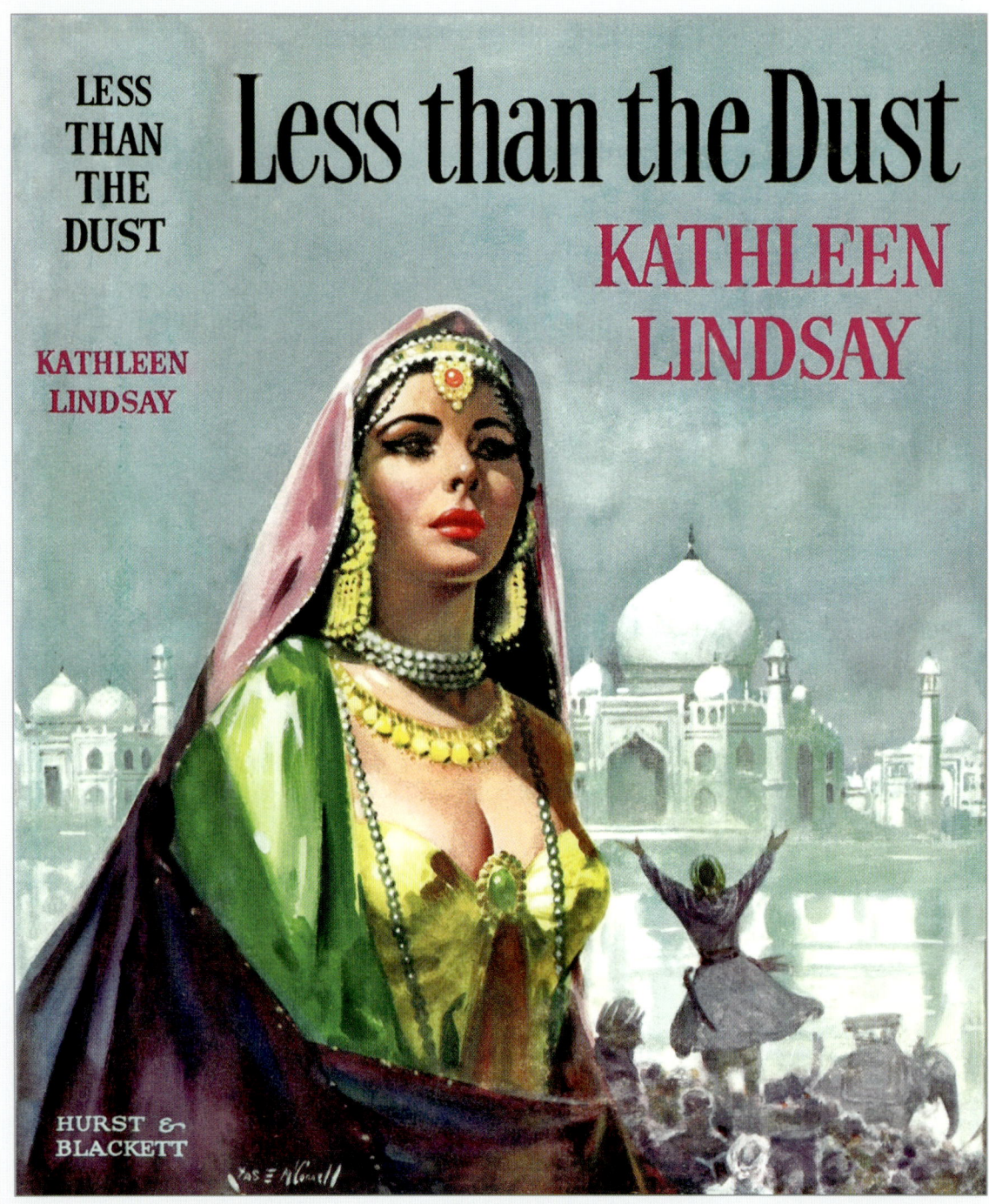

THE KATHLEEN LINDSAYS: *Less than the Dust* by Kathleen Lindsay (Hurst & Blackett, 1963); painted March 1963. Lindsay used at least eleven pen names, including Margaret Cameron (see examples on the facing page and page 244), and is said to have written some 900 books during a fifty-year career. That would mean a book every twenty days – a sustained work-rate that is barely credible. In all, McConnell painted at least 29 covers for her novels. In the early 1960s he was also illustrating for Georgette Heyer when she accused Lindsay of plagiarising her work.

GALLERY

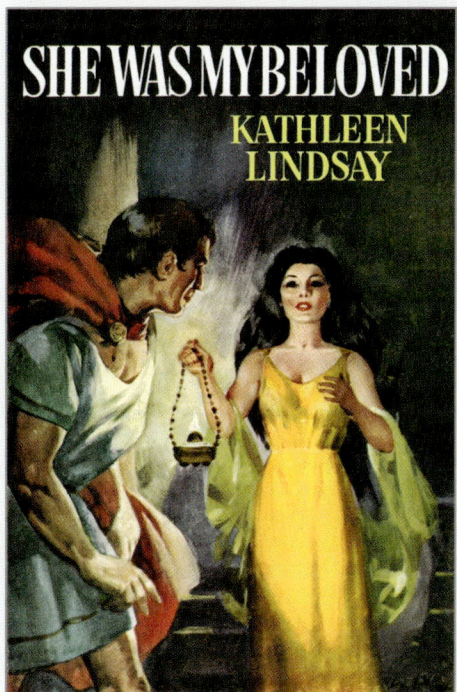

THE KATHLEEN LINDSAYS: Top left: *Katoushka* by Margaret Cameron (Hutchinson, 1966); painted November 1965. Top right: *Fanfare for Margaret* by Margaret Cameron (Hurst & Blackett, 1967); painted July 1966. Bottom left: *She was my Beloved* by Kathleen Lindsay (Hurst & Blackett, 1968); painted January 1968. Bottom right: *Paulette* by Kathleen Lindsay (Hurst & Blackett, 1962); painted August 1961.

THE KATHLEEN LINDSAYS: *Anastasia* by Margaret Cameron (Hurst & Blackett, 1967); painted February 1967.

GALLERY

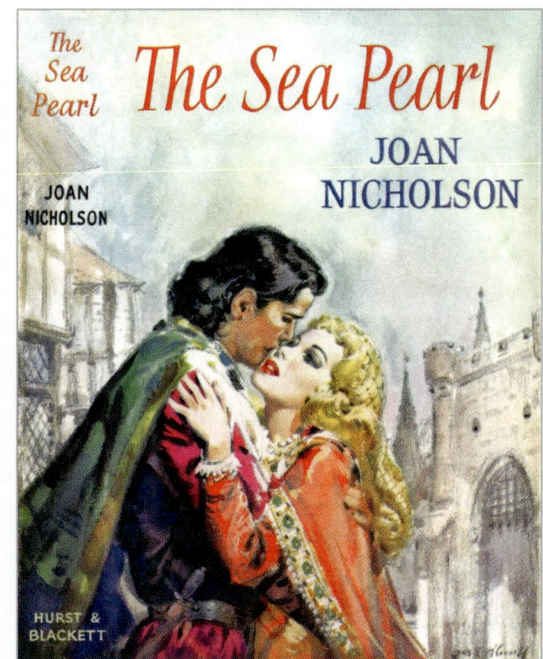

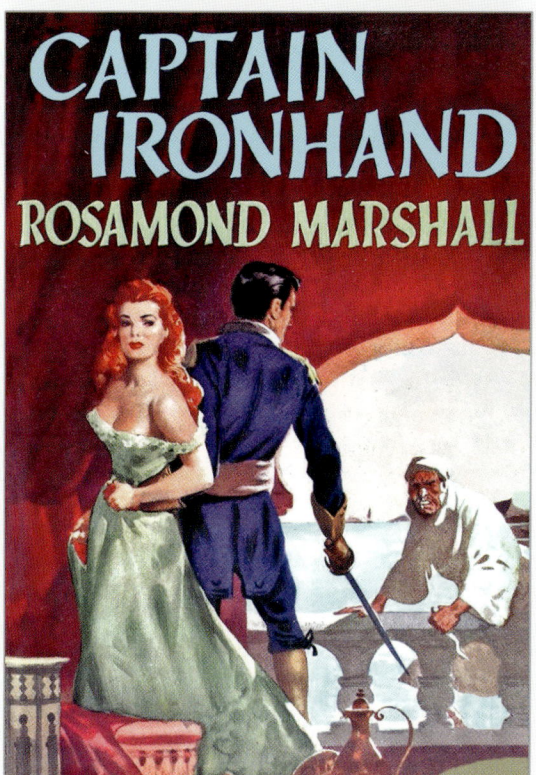

MORE HISTORICAL ROMANCES: Top left: *The Sea Pearl* by Joan Nicholson (Hurst & Blackett, 1961); painted May 1961. Top right: *The Silver Leopard* by F van Wyck Mason (Jarrolds, 1954); painting not recorded. Bottom left: *Kitty* by Rosamond Marshall (Alvin Redman, 1956); painted January 1956. Bottom right: *Captain Ironhand* by Rosamond Marshall (Alvin Redman, 1957); painted May 1957.

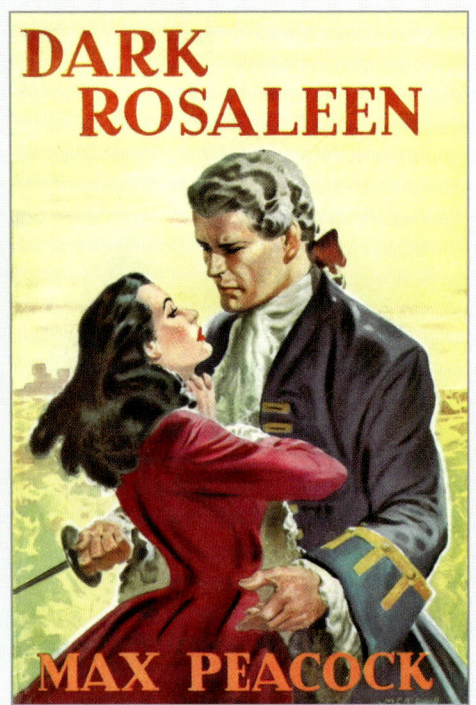

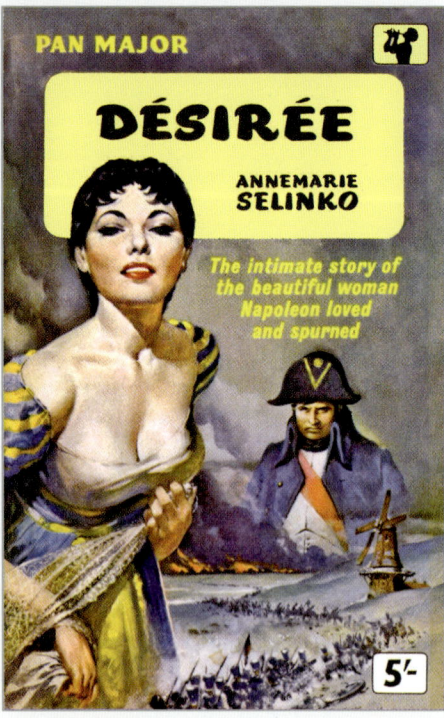

MORE HISTORICAL ROMANCES: Top left: *Dark Rosaleen* by Max Peacock (Robert Hale, 1955); painted September 1954. Top right: *The Shepherd's Crook* by Paul Frischauer (Cassell, 1953); painted April 1953. Bottom left: *The Spanish Bride* by Walter O'Meara (Alvin Redman, 1956); painted September 1955. Bottom right: *Désirée* by Annemarie Selinko (Pan M6, 1959); painted November 1958. (*Désirée* image courtesy Jim Kealy.)

GALLERY

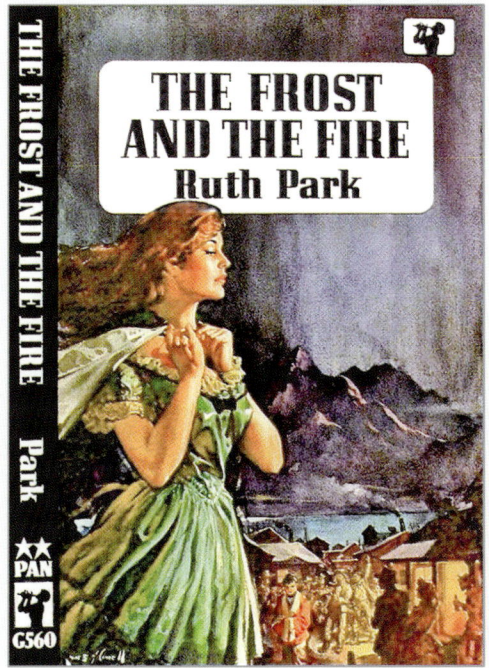

MORE HISTORICAL ROMANCES: Top left: Original artwork for *The Frost and the Fire* by Ruth Park (Pan G560, 1962); painted October 1961. Top right: *Cassy Scandal* by Zola Ross (Alvin Redman, 1956); painted December 1955. Bottom left: *Wings of the Morning* by Frederic F van de Water (Jarrolds, 1957); painted October 1956. Bottom right: *Love and Julian Farne* by Neil Bell (Alvin Redman, 1964); painted February 1964. (*The Frost and the Fire* and *Cassy Scandal* images courtesy Jim Kealy.)

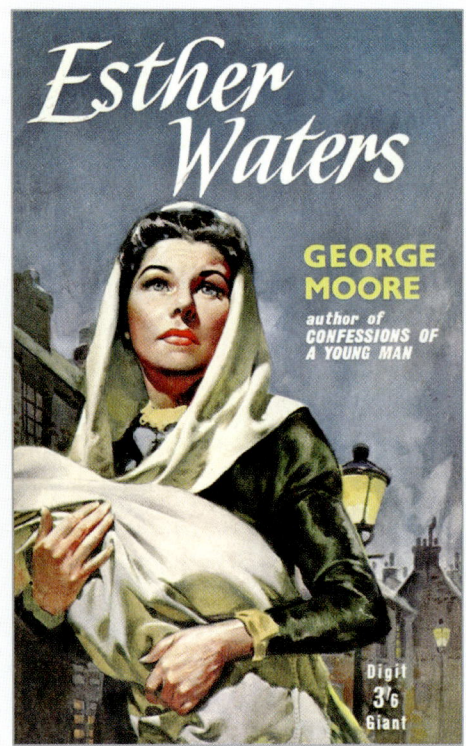

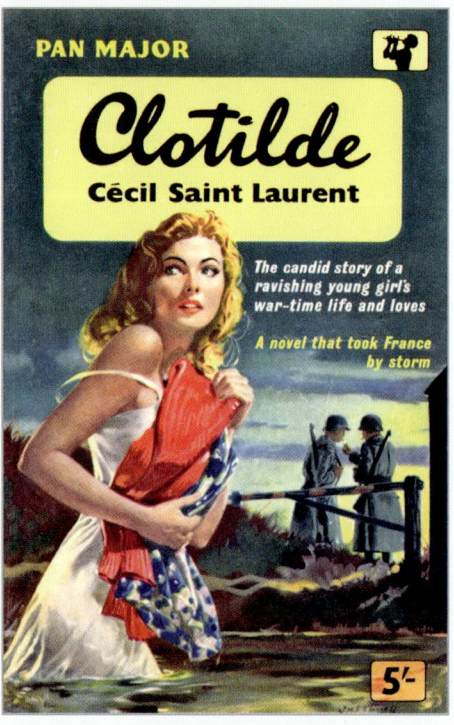

MORE HISTORICAL ROMANCES: Top left: *Esther Waters* by George Moore (Digit G500, 1961); painted February 1961. Top right: *The Idol of Paris* by Barbara Levy (Alvin Redman, 1962); painted December 1961. Bottom left: *Blue Hurricane* by F van Wyck Mason (Jarrolds, 1955); painted October 1954. Bottom right: *Clotilde* by Cécil Saint Laurent (Pan M7, 1959); painted May 1959; 'historical' in the sense that it was painted 15 years after the period it depicts. (All images except *The Idol of Paris* courtesy Jim Kealy.)

MODERN LOVE: *Good and Evil* by Wallace Reyburn (Cassell, 1962); painted February 1962. Love comes in many forms.

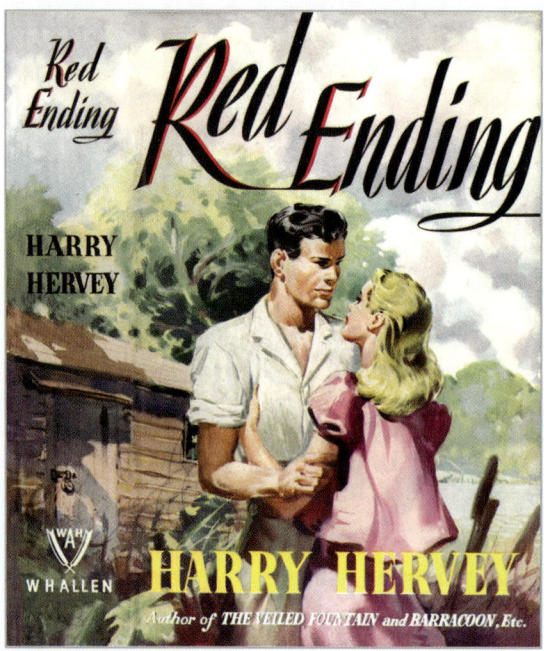

MODERN LOVE: THE ROMANTIC COUNTRYSIDE: Top left: *The Ploughman's Progress* by Sheila Kaye-Smith (Cassell, 1952); painted December 1951. Love doesn't get more bucolic than this. Top right: *Arnella* by Kay Winchester (Ward Lock, 1957); painted September 1956. Bottom left: *Red Ending* by Harry Hervey (W H Allen, 1952); painted April 1952. Bottom right: *Enchantment* by Laura Conway (Collins, 1956); painted June 1955.

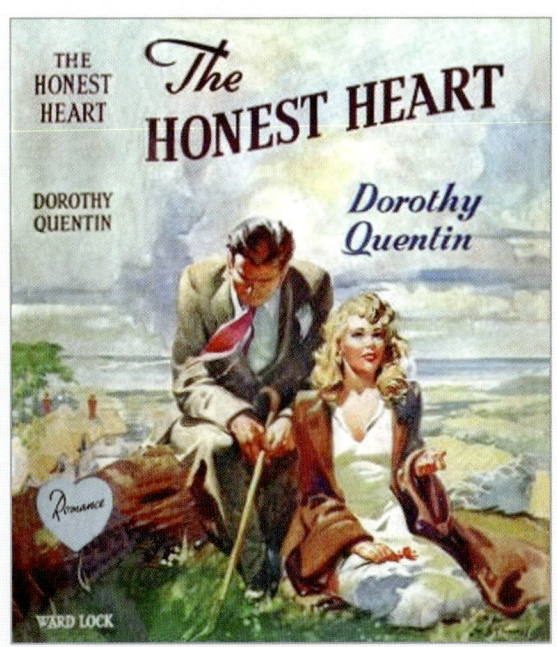

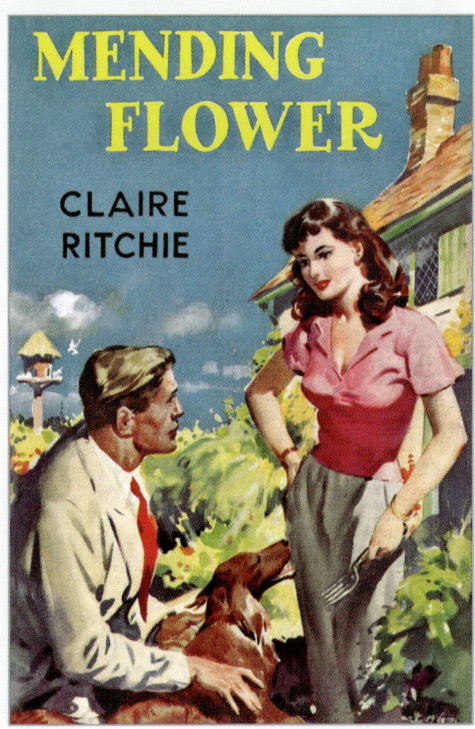

MODERN LOVE: THE ROMANTIC COUNTRYSIDE: Top left: *Flash of Youth* by Laura Whetter (Ward Lock, 1953); painted June 1952. Top right: *The Honest Heart* by Dorothy Quentin (Ward Lock, 1952); painted June 1951. A painting with exceptional social and emotional complexity. Bottom left: *Joanna Linden* by Diana Raymond (Cassell, 1952); painted November 1951. A delicate, windswept watercolour. Bottom right: *Mending Flower* by Claire Ritchie (Robert Hale, 1955); painted June 1954.

MINIATURE MARVELS

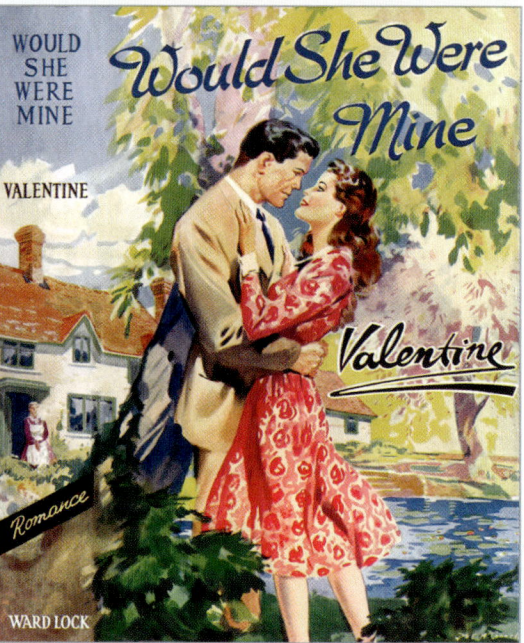

MODERN LOVE: THE ROMANTIC COUNTRYSIDE: Top left: *The Heart Line* by Effie A Rowlands (Ward Lock, 1953); painting not recorded. Top right: *The Invisible Cord* by Viola Castang (W H Allen, 1958); painted April 1958. Bottom left: *The Wild Olive* by May Sutherland (Hutchinson, 1954); painted May 1954. Bottom right: *Would She Were Mine* by Valentine (Ward Lock, 1954); painted March 1954.

LOVE TENDER AND VIOLENT: *Love Rules the World* by F E Baily (W H Allen, 1954); painted November 1953.

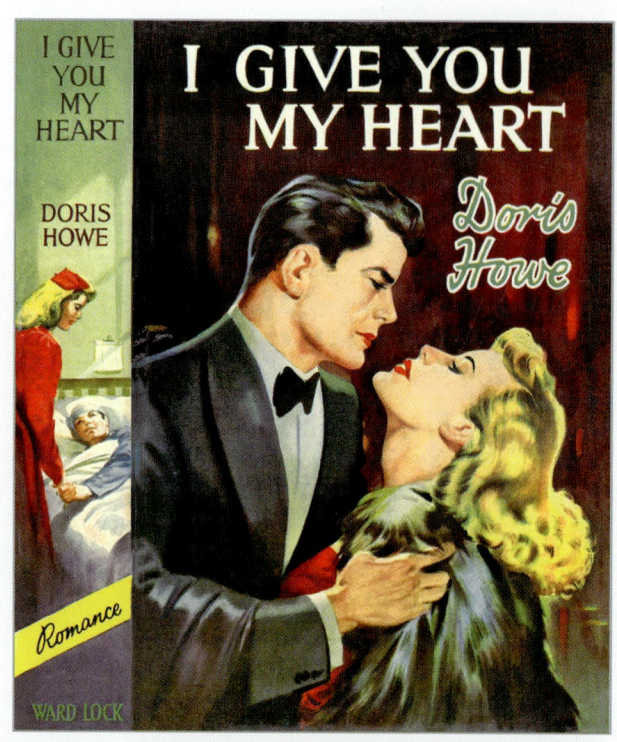
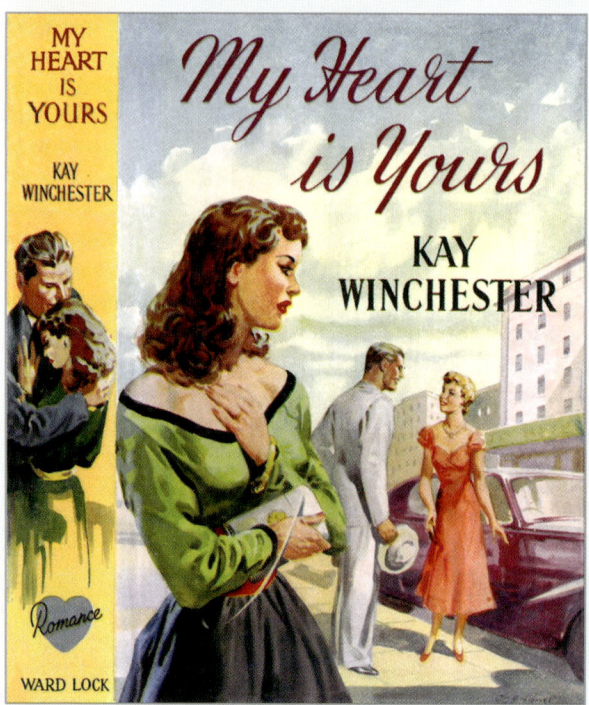
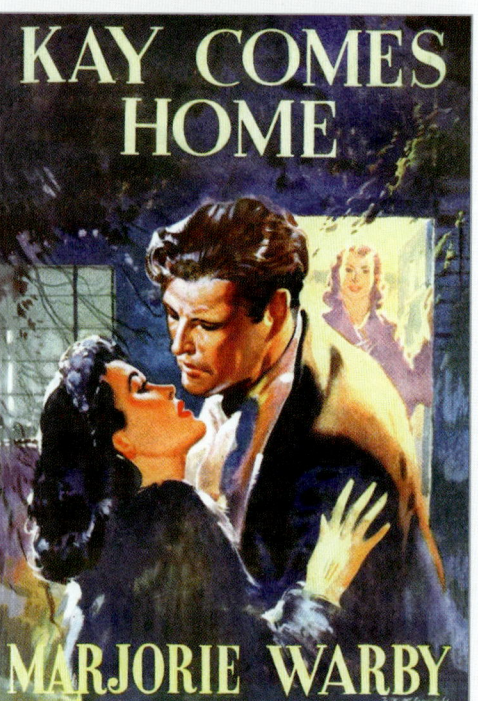

LOVE TENDER AND VIOLENT: Top left: *I Take What I Want* by Marjorie Price (Collins, 1946); painted January 1946 in the stripped-down, block-colour style popular for romantic fiction in the early post-war years. Top right: *I Give You my Heart* by Doris Howe (Ward Lock, 1955); painted July 1954. Bottom left: *My Heart is Yours* by Kay Winchester (Ward Lock, 1954); painted September 1953. Bottom right: *Kay Comes Home* by Marjorie Warby (Collins, 1954); painted August 1953.

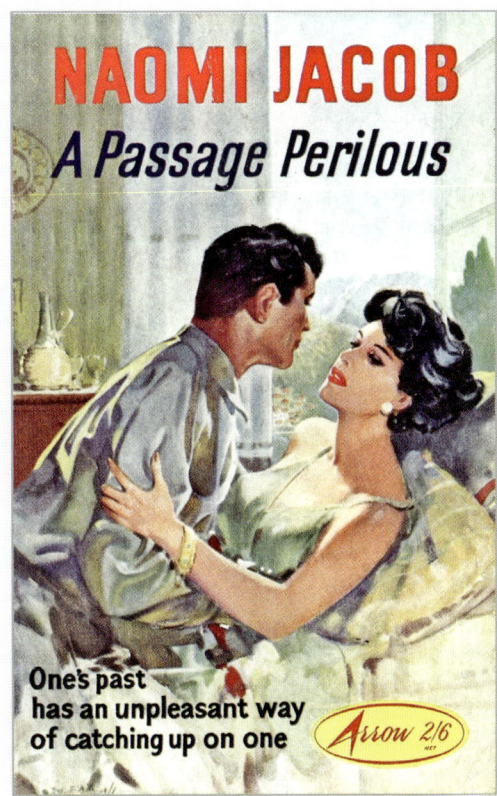
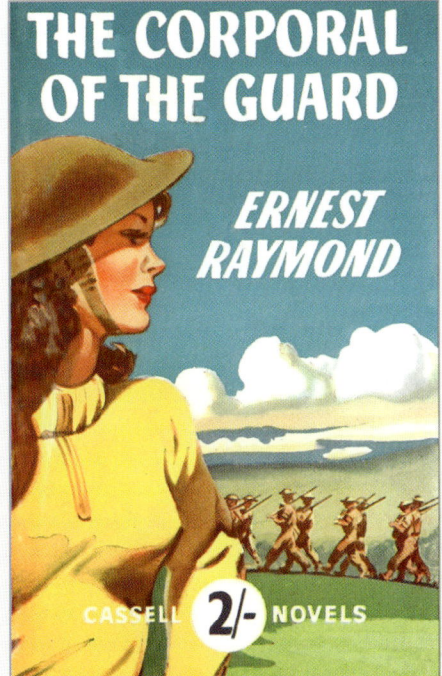
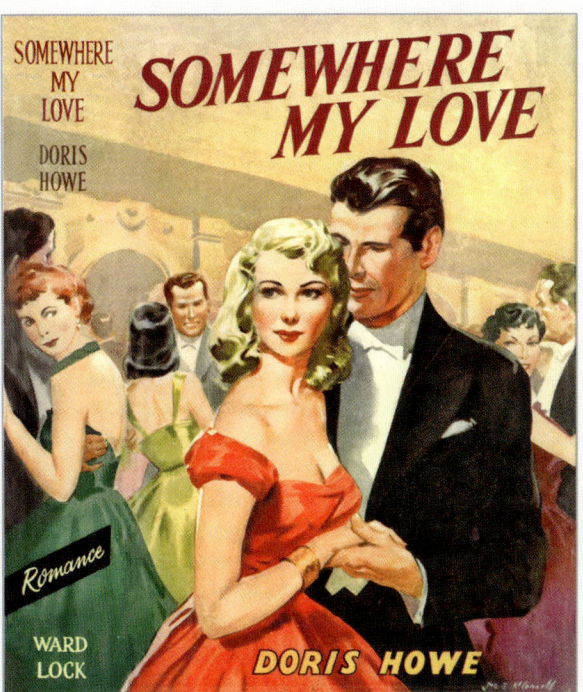

LOVE TENDER AND VIOLENT: Top left: *One Master Passion* by N Cosette Keeling (Stanley Paul, 1955); painted May 1954. Top right: *A Passage Perilous* by Naomi Jacob (Arrow, 1962); painted May 1962. Bottom left*: The Corporal of the Guard* by Ernest Raymond (Cassell, 1952); painted February 1952. Bottom right: *Somewhere My Love* by Doris Howe (Ward Lock, 1955); painted December 1954.

MINIATURE MARVELS

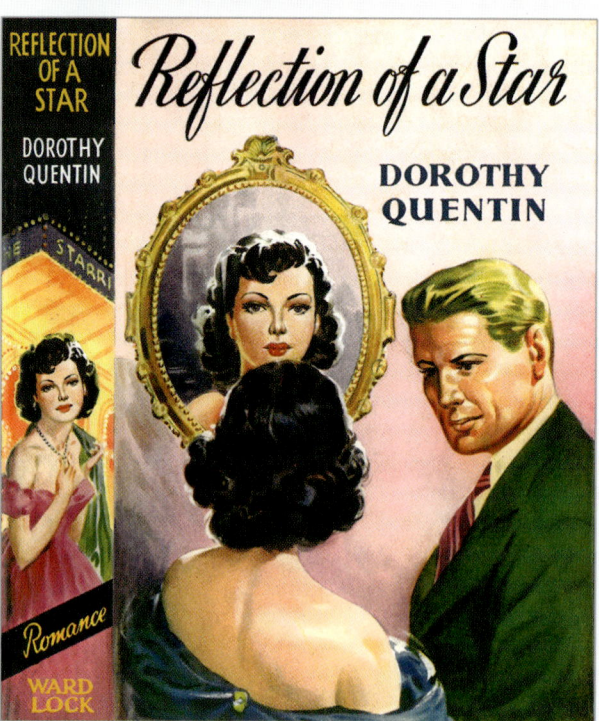

LOVE TENDER AND VIOLENT: Top left: *In Search of Love* by Vicky Lancaster (Robert Hale, 1955); painted May 1955. Unusually action-packed for a romance cover. Top right: *The Golden Shoestring* by Faith Baldwin (Robert Hale, 1955); painted December 1954. Bottom left: *The Enchanted Swan* by Christine Jope-Slade (Robert Hale, 1952); painting not recorded. Bottom right: *Reflection of a Star* by Dorothy Quentin (Ward Lock, 1956); painted June 1955.

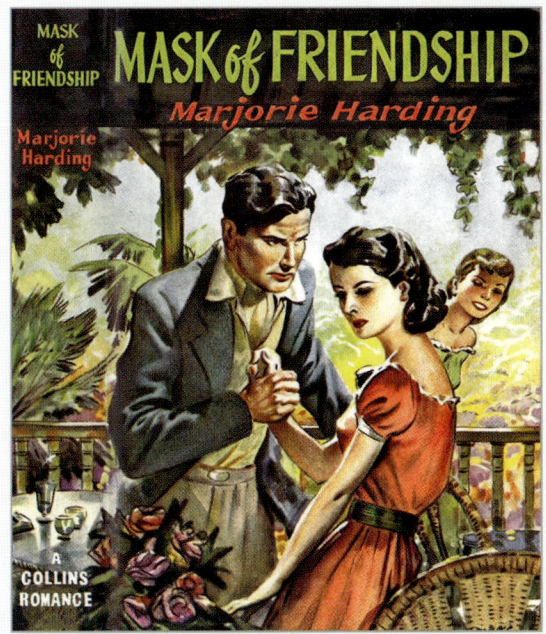
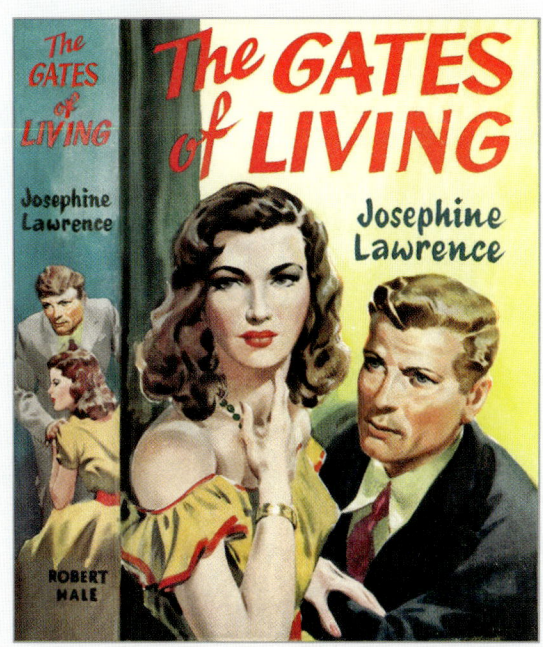

LOVE TENDER AND VIOLENT: Top left: *Mask of Friendship* by Marjorie Harding (Collins, 1956); painted August 1955. Top right: *The Gates of Living* by Josephine Lawrence (Robert Hale, 1956); painted June 1955. Bottom left: *The Golden Slipper* by Helen Eastwood (Robert Hale, 1956); painted July 1955. Bottom right: *The Image of Kate* by Mary Astor (Alvin Redman, 1962); painted May 1962 in the freer, sketchier style of the 1960s. (*The Golden Slipper* image courtesy Jim Kealy.)

LOVE TENDER AND VIOLENT: *The Doctor Dares* by Elizabeth Seifert (Collins, 1950); painted March 1950. The beginning of the hospital romance sub-genre, which would become enormously popular after the founding of Britain's National Health Service.

GALLERY

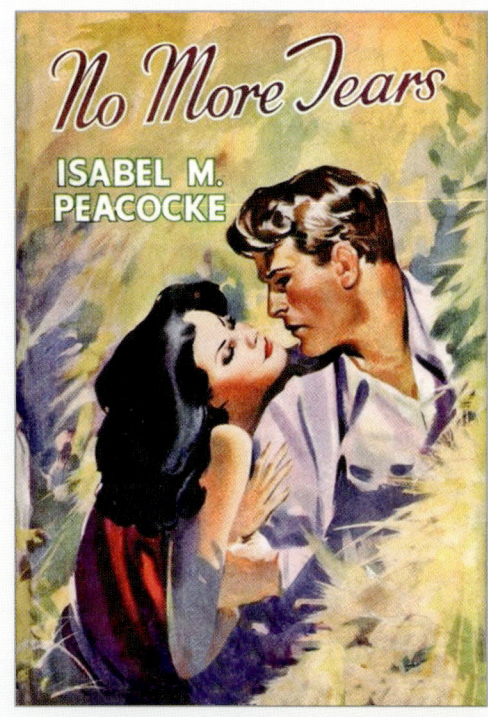

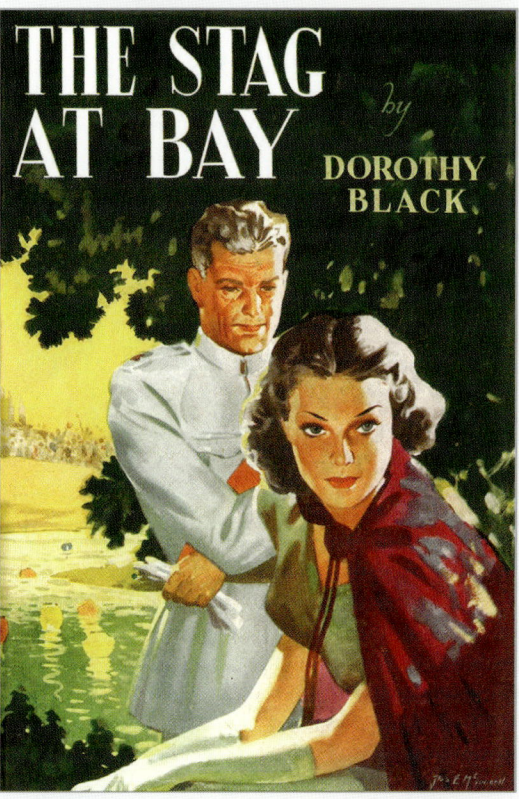

LOVE TENDER AND VIOLENT: Top left: *The Glowing Heart* by Kathleen Treves (Ward Lock, 1953); painted December 1952. Top right: *No More Tears* by Isabel M Peacocke (Ward Lock, 1951); painted September 1950. Bottom left: *The New Doctor* by Elizabeth Seifert (Collins, 1951); painted November 1950. Love amidst the falling leaves. Bottom right: *The Stag at Bay* by Dorothy Black (Cassell, 1950); painted August 1949.

MINIATURE MARVELS

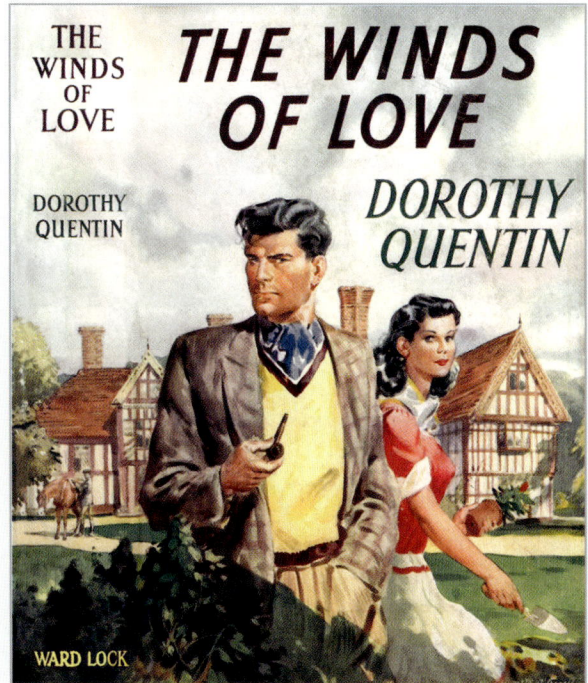
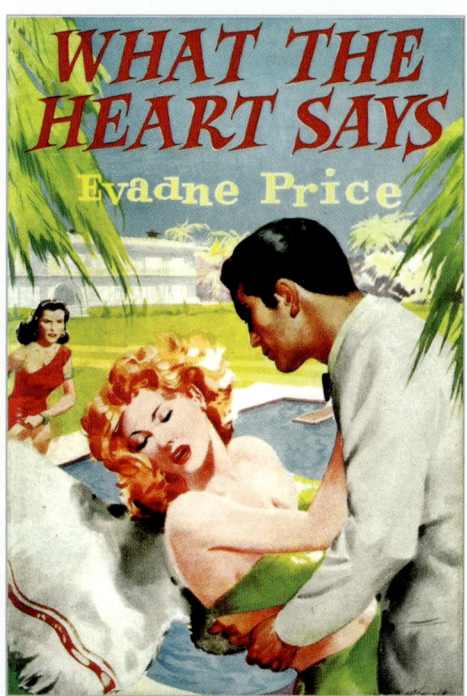
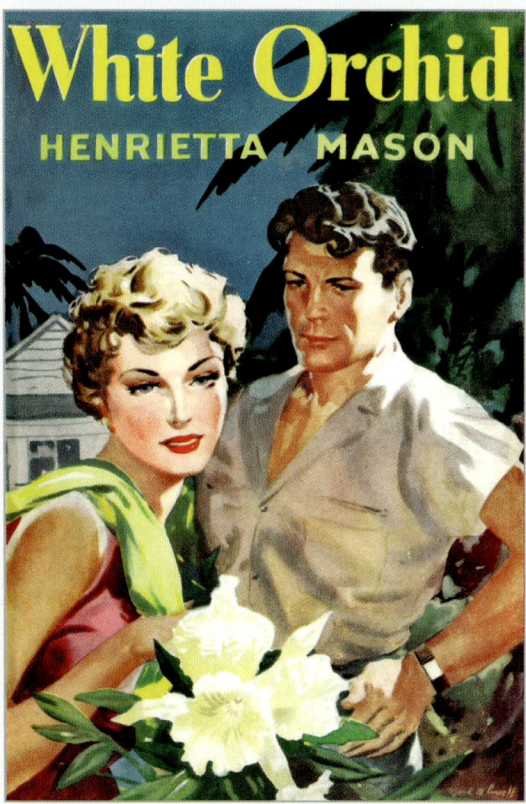

LOVE TENDER AND VIOLENT: Top left: *The Winds of Love* by Dorothy Quentin (Ward Lock, 1951); painted December 1950. Top right: *What the Heart Says* by Evadne Price (Robert Hale, 1956); painted July 1955. Bottom left: *White Orchid* by Henrietta Mason (Robert Hale, 1955); painted July 1954. Bottom right: *Poor Man's Darling* by Helena Grose (Collins, 1950); painted April 1950.

LOVE TENDER AND VIOLENT: *The Winds of March* by Robert Woollcombe (Cassell, 1962); painted February 1962.

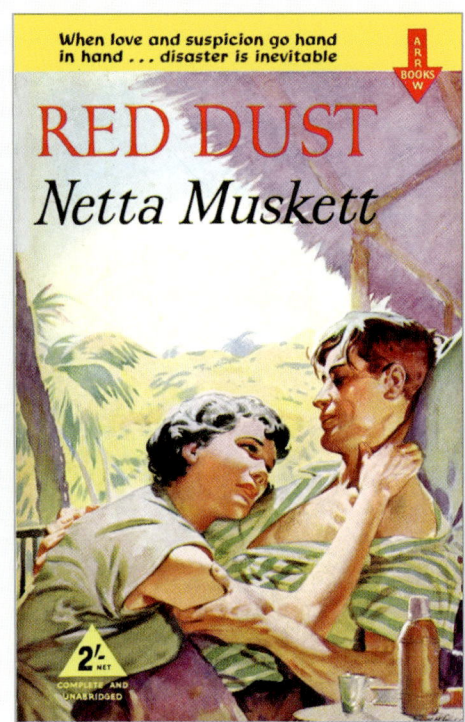

LOVE IN FOREIGN PARTS: Top left: *Red Dust* by Netta Muskett (Arrow, 1957); painted October 1956. Top right: *Violetta* by Anne Duffield (Cassell, 1960); painted November 1959. Bottom left: *Castle in Spain* by Anne Duffield (Cassell, 1958); painted October 1957. Bottom right: *The Grand Duchess* by Anne Duffield (Cassell, 1953); painted September 1952. (*The Grand Duchess* image courtesy Jim Kealy.)

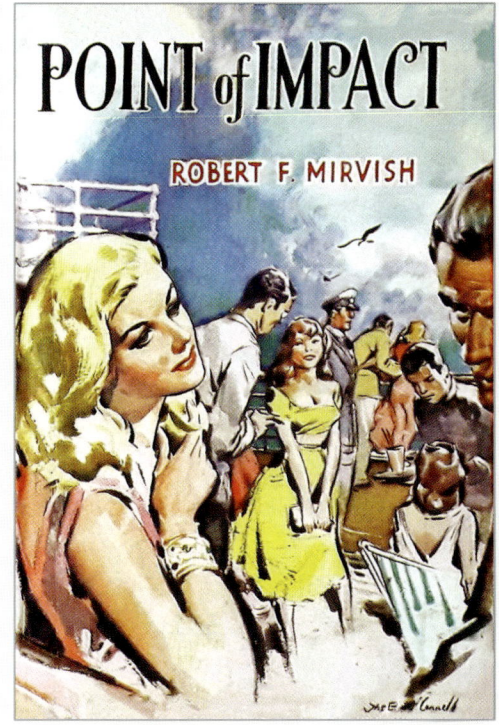

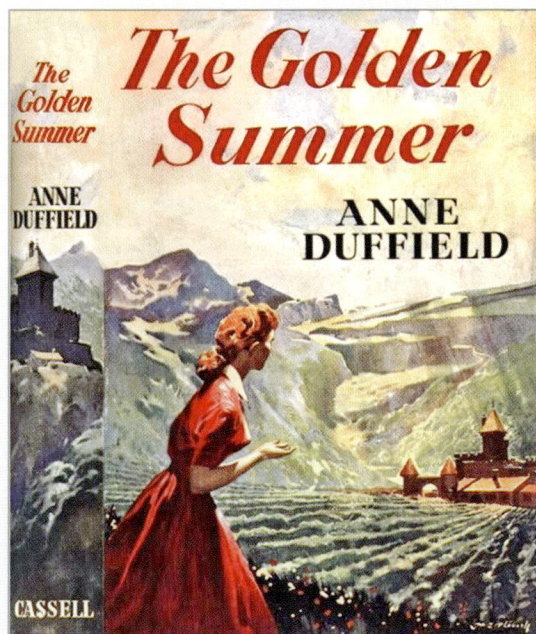
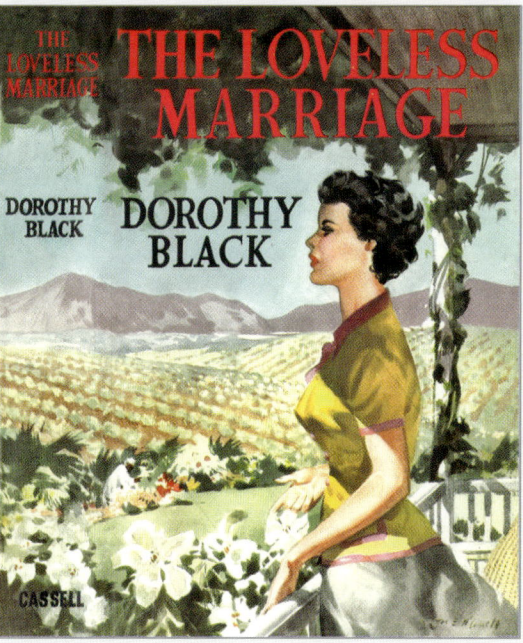

LOVE IN FOREIGN PARTS: Top left: *Point of Impact* by Robert F Mirvish (Alvin Redman, 1962); painted November 1961. Top right: *Glittering Heights* by Anne Duffield (Cassell, 1956); painted October 1955. Bottom left: *The Golden Summer* by Anne Duffield (Cassell, 1954); painted September 1953. A further excursion to the rural idyll. Bottom right: *The Loveless Marriage* by Dorothy Black (Cassell, 1958); painted April 1957.

LOVE IN FOREIGN PARTS: *Gentle Stranger* by Dorothy Black (Cassell, 1956); painted August 1955.

GALLERY

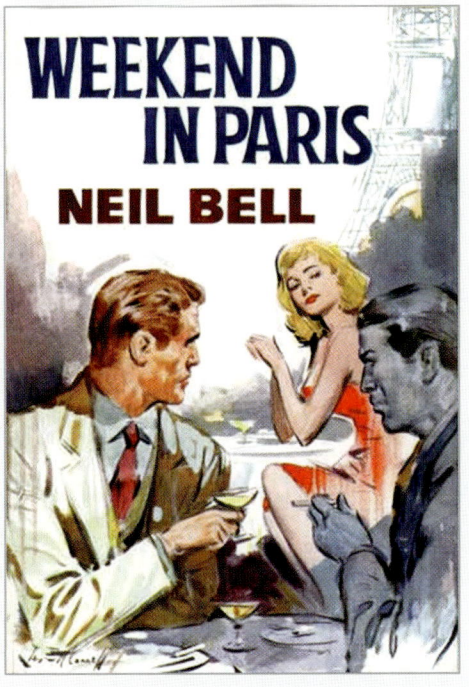

LOVE IN FOREIGN PARTS: Top left: *The Cub* by Ethel Turner (Ward Lock, July 1954); painted July 1953. Australian love. Top right: *The Witch-Doctor* by S C George (Museum Press, 1955); painted August 1954. Putting a spell on you. Bottom left: *Weekend in Paris* by Neil Bell (Alvin Redman, 1962); painted January 1962. McConnell had painted his first cover for a Neil Bell book in the late 1930s. Bottom right: *Light the Bright Candles* by Ray Dorien (W H Allen 1954); painted April 1954.

The Miracle Man by Douglas V Duff (Cassell, 1953); painted March 1953.

7: THRILLS A-PLENTY: FANTASY, WAR AND ADVENTURE

'The old idea that a historical novel was composed of a set of characters who spoke "olde" English ... and behaved in an incredibly romantic manner has passed away with the passing of a period. Now the reader usually demands accuracy and plausibility.'

Christine Campbell Thomson, 1946.[56]

Before the 1914-18 Flanders slaughterhouse drained most of the red-blooded heroism from the romantic myths of armed conflict, the historical novel had been a popular masculine genre. It fostered martial emotions and manly pride – particularly among schoolboys and young men. When the trenches decimated a whole generation of those readers, the genre declined in popularity and shifted closer to romantic fiction, transforming the gender composition of its readership in the process. By the 1950s, the romantic ages of the Tudors and the Regency began to dominate British historical fiction, delicately shimmying their way past the swashbuckling adventures of Rafael Sabatini, the Empire epics of G A Henty and the picaresque yarns of Jeffrey Farnol.

Cutlass Empire by F van Wyck Mason (Arrow 416J, 1956); painted November 1955.

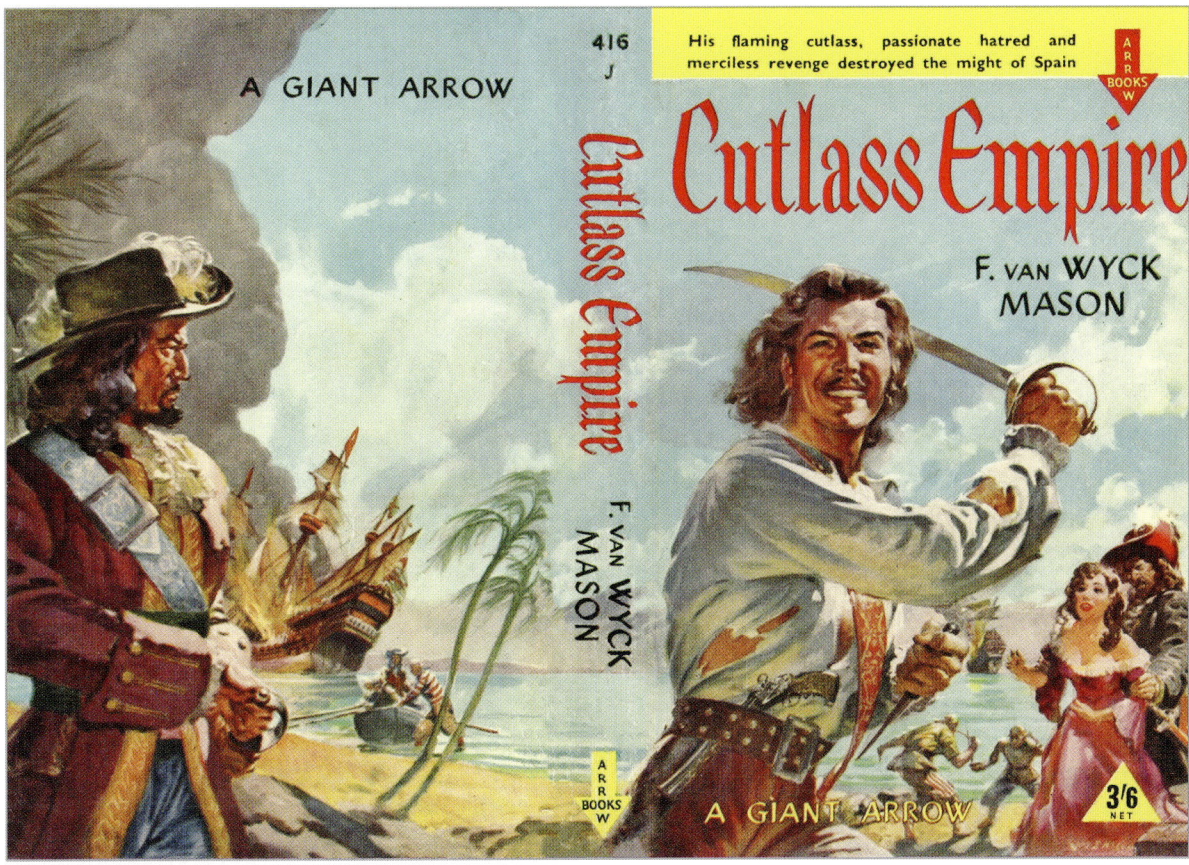

Above: *Fortune's Fool* by Rafael Sabatini (Pan X120, 1962); painted July 1961. (Image courtesy Jim Kealy.)

Below: *The Mercenary* by Jan Westcott (Alvin Redman, 1963); painted April 1963.

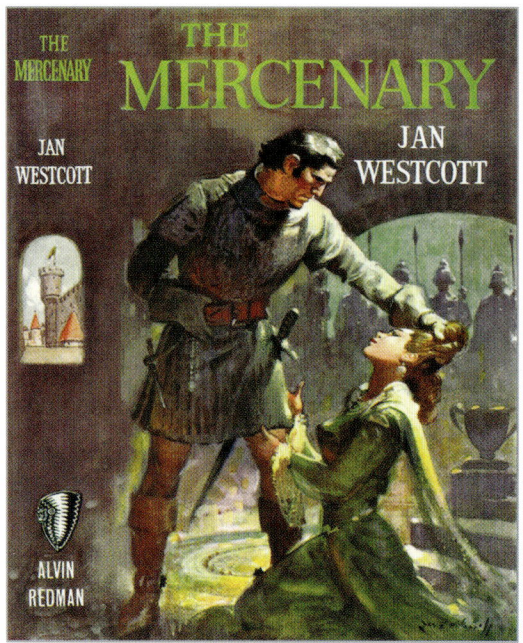

Testosterone-fuelled action could be more easily found in the fantasy genre, and pre-eminently in the works of Edgar Rice Burroughs. Jungles and other planets, it seemed, were the place for adventure.

If you were a publisher's art director in the three decades after World War Two, and you were looking for cover illustrations that would inspire readers seeking an exciting and perhaps escapist story, James McConnell offered a one-stop shop. Few competitors could summon up a sense of action quite so convincingly as McConnell, who could also offer flawless authenticity for historical settings. One has only to gaze upon the impressive swashbuckling panorama created for the wrap-around cover of F van Wyck Mason's piratical *Cutlass Empire* (see previous page). By the time it was painted in November 1955, McConnell had developed the ability to depict action in any historical period; something that would ultimately sustain his career as an illustrator for children's educational magazines. In paintings like those for Helga Moray's *Dark Fury* (Corgi, 1959) and Jan Westcott's *The Mercenary* (Alvin Redman, 1963), with their strong suggestions of sexual violence, he was also capable of giving his swashbucklers a more noir treatment that might not have been so suitable for children.

His depictions of the historical past usually avoid chocolate-box whimsey in favour of a vision that understands the nasty and brutish backdrop to chivalric derring-do. The cover for Rafael Sabatini's *Fortune's Fool* (Pan, 1962) is a particularly fine example from later in his career, but there are darker and more brooding covers that he produced earlier on. These paintings, with their muted colour palate of greys and browns, date from the beginning of World War Two and seem to be imbued with the anxiety of the time. There is a bleakness to the mood of his piece for Frederick Niven's *Mine Inheritance* (see page 86), despite the heroic quality of the man defiantly defending his family and homestead by force of arms. The symbolism of the darkening clouds would not have been lost on readers in 1940. Nor would the

Dark Fury by Helga Moray (Corgi G640, 1959); painting not recorded.

contemporary relevance of the painting he provided for S Fowler Wright's *The Siege of Malta* (Frederick Muller, 1942), depicting the shadowy figures of a soldier and a civilian moving fearfully through the night. It was a scenario all too familiar to an ARP worker like McConnell.

McConnell could be relied on to produce striking and convincing covers for historical stories, but he was a little less at home with the fantasy genre. That did not deter publishers W H Allen from commissioning him as their Tarzan illustrator when they began to republish the novels of Edgar Rice Burroughs in their Pinnacle paperback range in 1952. Over the following five years, McConnell painted eight Tarzan and twelve other covers for Burroughs' fantasies. In truth, although never less than highly competent, the paintings are a mixed

Below: *The Jungle Tales of Tarzan* by Edgar Rice Burroughs (Pinnacle, 1954); painted November 1953.

Above: *The Siege of Malta* by S Fowler Wright (Frederick Muller, 1942); painting unrecorded.

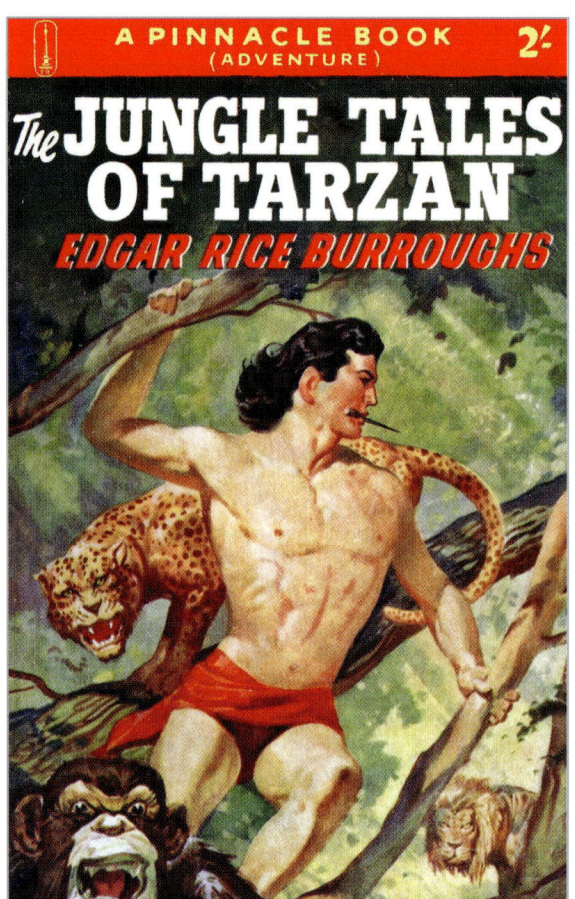

bag. The first batch of Tarzans feature rather more vigorous compositions and accomplished brushwork than the ones from December 1957; the latter were probably completed in a hurry as he did not take time to sign them – usually an indication of dissatisfaction with the results. Indeed, when asked about his paintings of the Lord of the Jungle some forty years later, McConnell had no memory of them at all. They are, nonetheless, listed in his workbook.

His covers for Burroughs' sci-fi novels are generally more memorable, despite occasional reliance on pre-war American artwork for inspiration and even, in the case of *The Master Mind of Mars* (painted May 1954), on the Methuen first edition jacket by George Micklewright. Similarly, McConnell's cover for L Sprague de Camp's *Rogue Queen*, completed the previous month, relied quite heavily on Ed Emshwiller's suggestive painting for the 1951 Dell Books edition. These borrowings and homages may have been carried out with the

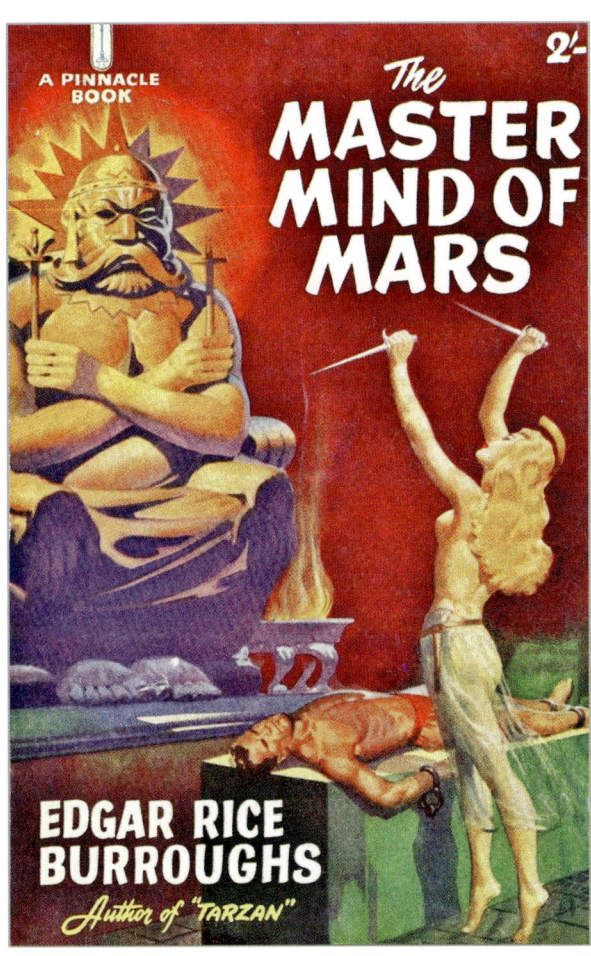
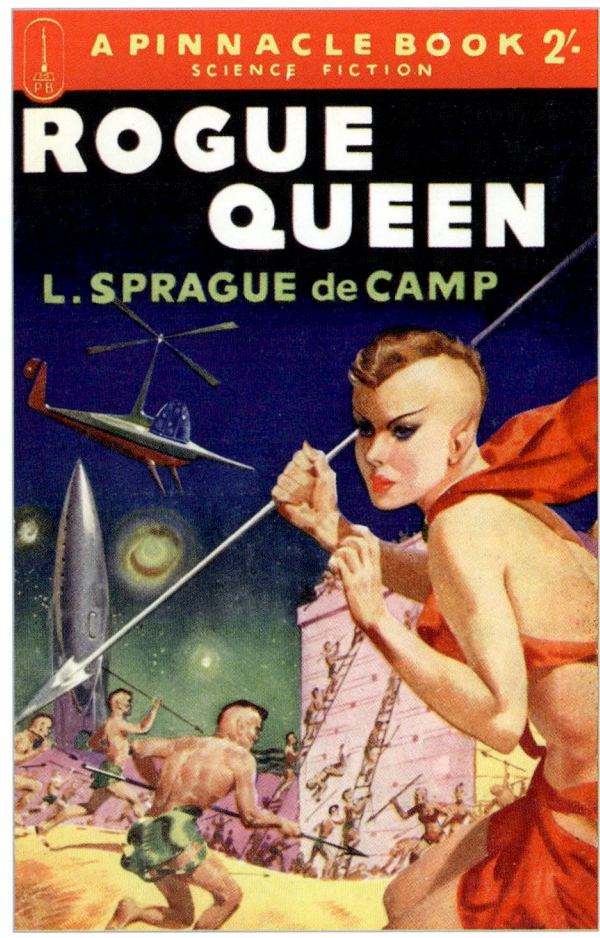
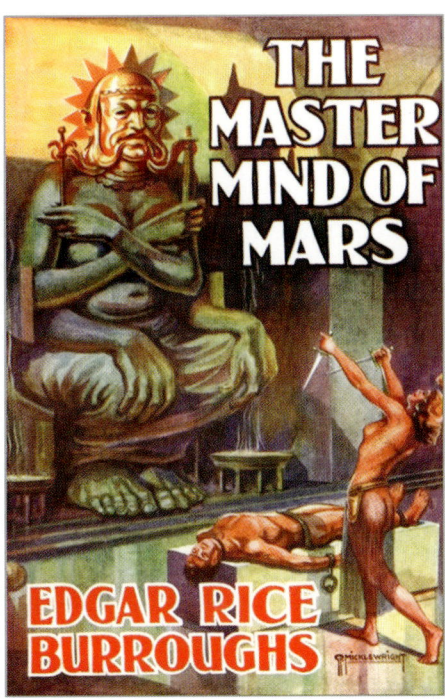

Above left: McConnell's cover for the Edgar Rice Burroughs fantasy novel *The Master Mind of Mars* (Pinnacle, 1954); painted May 1954.

Above right: McConnell's cover for *Rogue Queen* by L Sprague de Camp (Pinnacle, 1954); painted April 1954.

Left: obvious inspirations: the George Micklewright cover of *The Master Mind of Mars* (Methuen, 1939) and the Ed Emshwiller one for *Rogue Queen* (Dell, 1951).

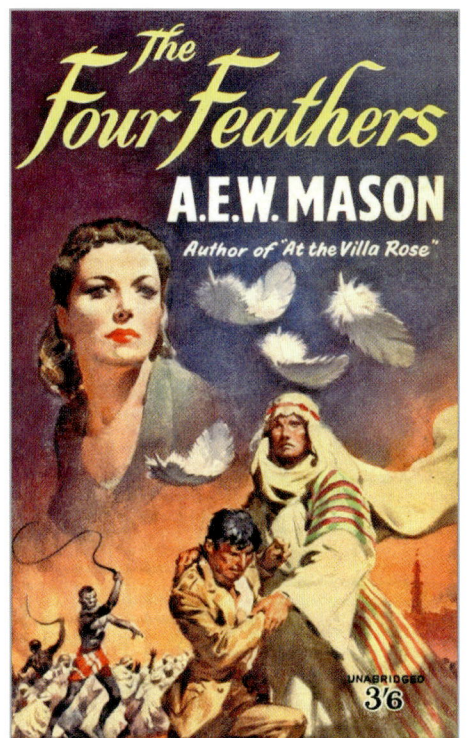

Four of McConnell's relatively few war-themed covers. Top left: *The Four Feathers* by A E W Mason (John Murray, 1960); painted March 1960. Top right: *Or By Default* by George Vaizey (Harrap, 1957); painted January 1957. Bottom left: *Johnny Kinsman* by John Watson (Cassell, 1955); painted April 1955. Bottom right: *Stalingrad* by Heinz Schröter (Pan X58, 1960); painted September 1959.

THRILLS A-PLENTY: FANTASY, WAR AND ADVENTURE

encouragement of W H Allen's art director, or may have been indicative of McConnell's own lack of confidence in depicting fantasy scenarios, or perhaps simply his ever-increasing mid-1950s workload. His work in the fantasy genre was limited, though, and so too was that in illustrating war scenes. The cover for 'The most controversial book of the year,' Alex Weissberg's *Advocate for the Dead* (Four Square, 1958), is one of his most impactful: a dramatic wrap-around piece, executed in the film-poster style, as is the complex composition for A E W Mason's *The Four Feathers* (John Murray, 1960). But perhaps his most interesting and unusual is that for Heinz Schröter's *Stalingrad* (Pan, 1960), a subject previously tackled by Heade. The dead hand protruding from the snowy grave is a chilling reference back to a similar trope McConnell used for his November 1953 jacket painting for Charles Franklin's crime novel *Perchance to Kill* (see page 152), but here it carries greater symbolic weight. Novels and memoirs of World War Two were a major feature of the paperback publishing industry in the 1950s, but McConnell was largely bypassed for them by commissioning art directors.

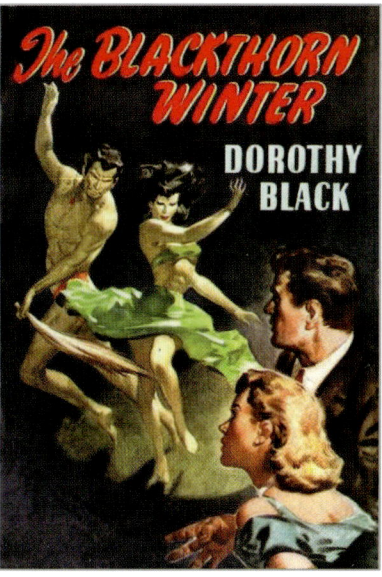

Above: a fantasy-style jacket piece for Dorothy Black's *The Blackthorn Winter* (Cassell, 1953); painted January 1953.

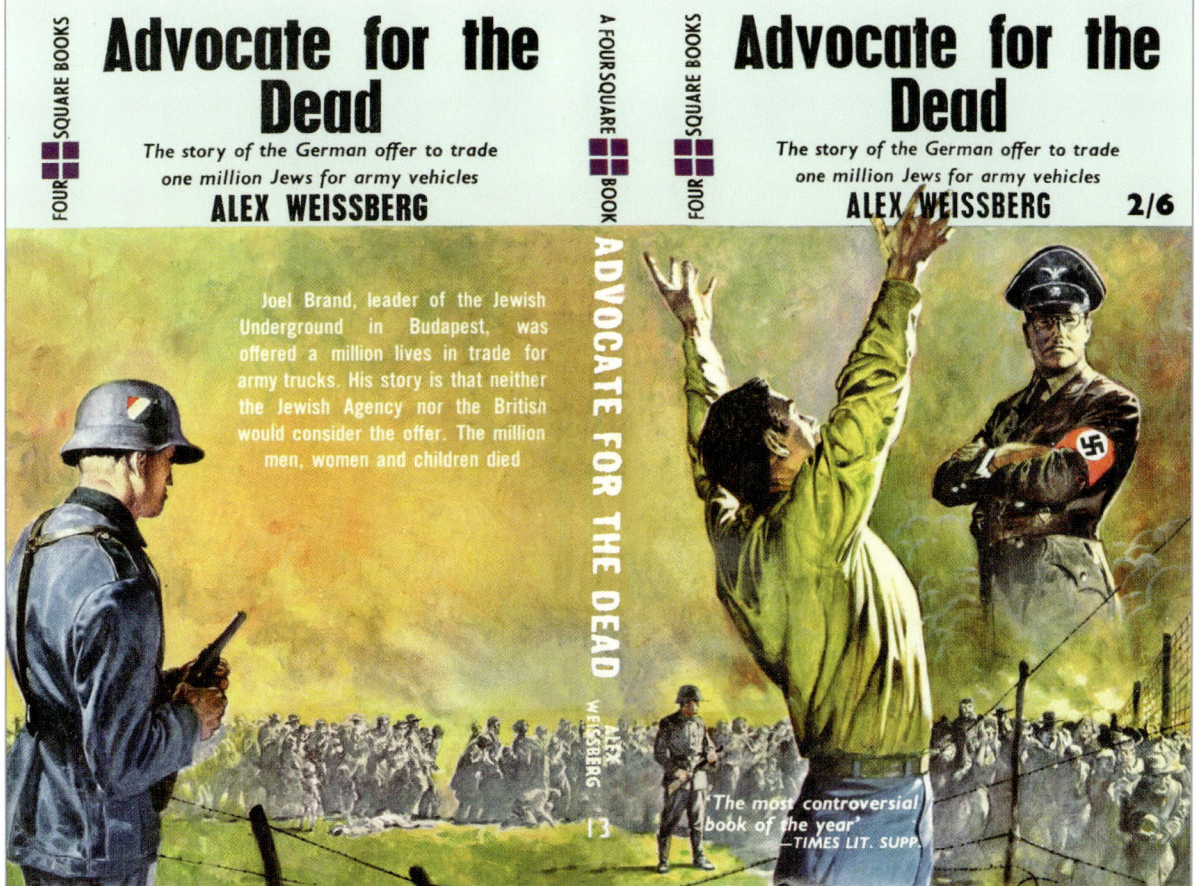

McConnell's wrap-around cover for Alex Weissberg's *Advocate for the Dead* (Four Square, 1958); painted December 1957.

GALLERY

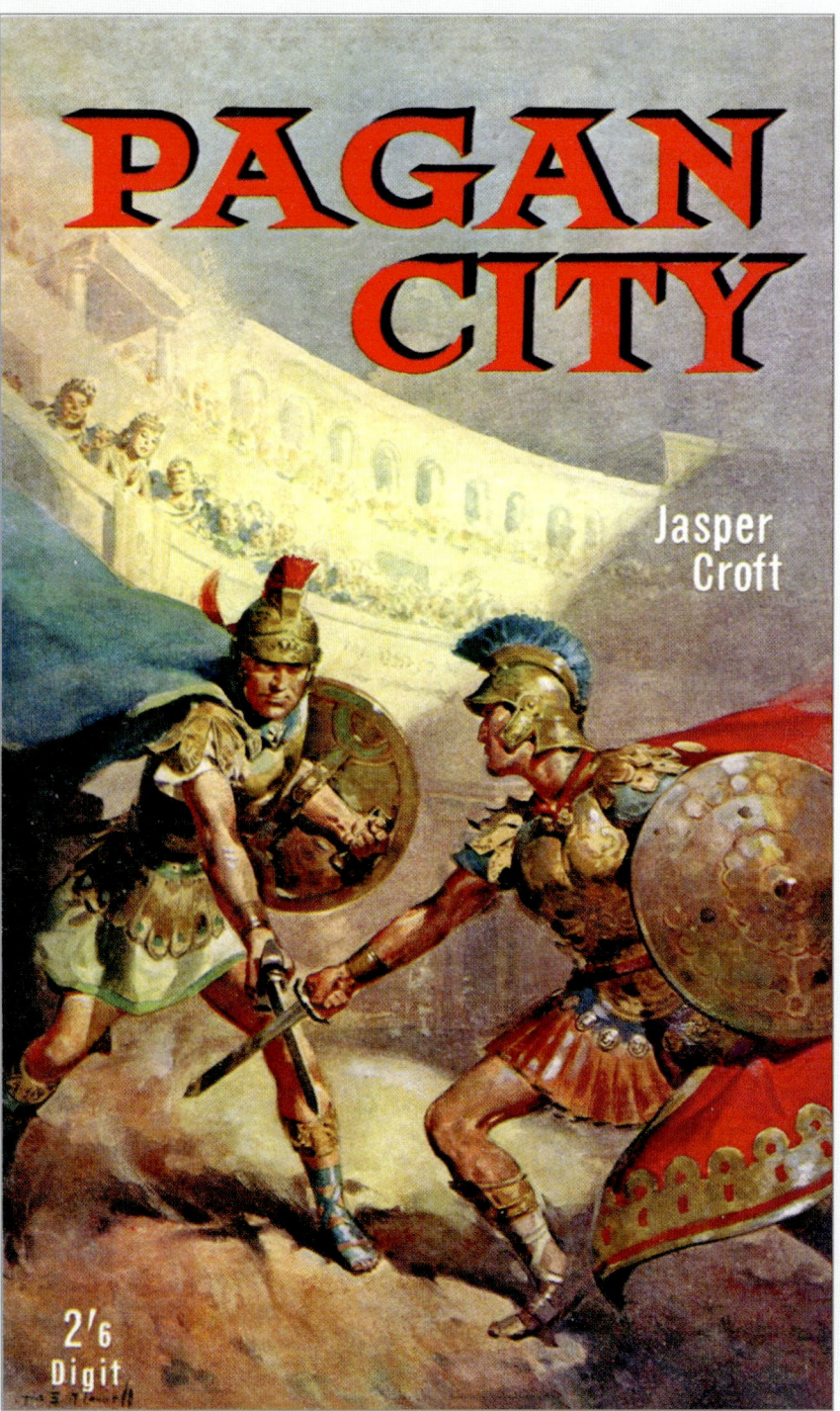

HISTORICAL ACTION: *Pagan City* by Jasper Croft (Digit G483, 1961); painted January 1961.

GALLERY

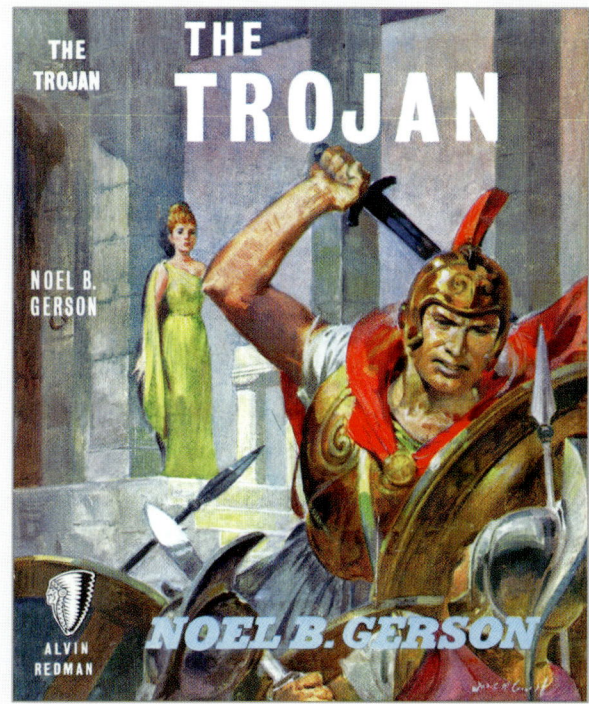

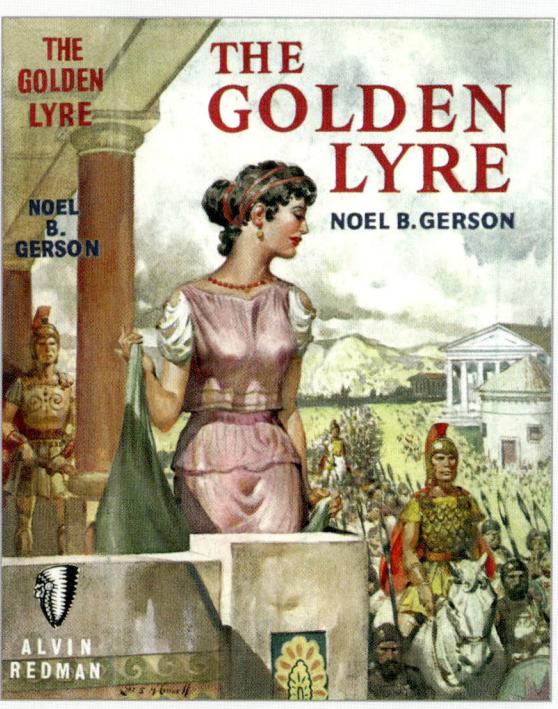

HISTORICAL ACTION: Top left: *The Trojan* by Noel B Gerson (Alvin Redman, 1963); painted July 1962. Top right: *Baton Sinister* by Carl J Spinatelli (Alvin Redman, 1960); painted December 1959. Bottom left: *The Wolf from the West* by Eliot Crawshay-Williams (John Long, 1947); painted August 1946. Bottom right: *The Golden Lyre* by Noel B Gerson (Alvin Redman, 1963); painted May 1963. (*The Trojan* image courtesy Jim Kealy.)

MINIATURE MARVELS

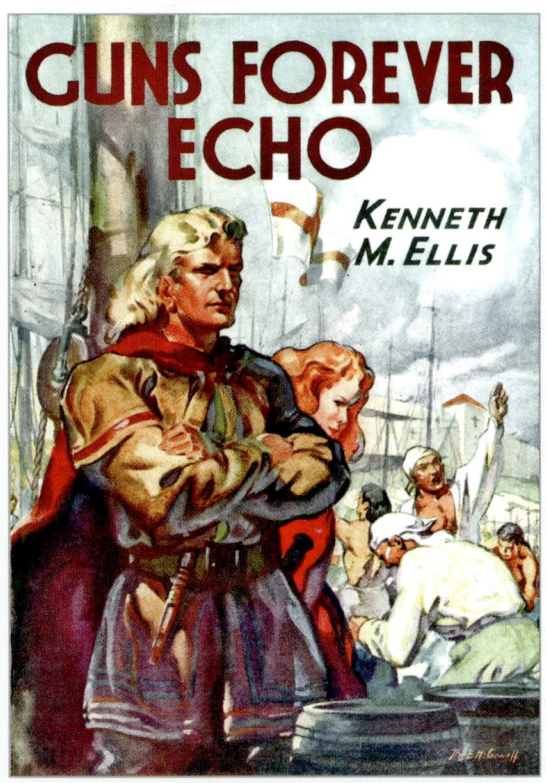
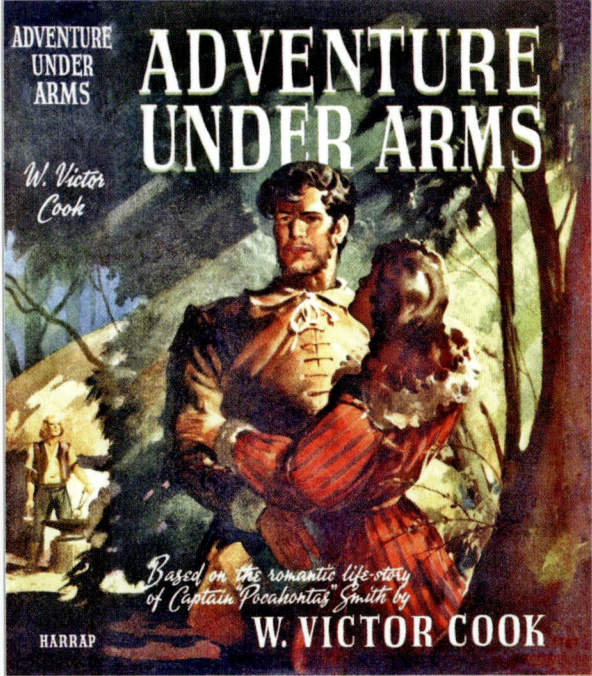

HISTORICAL ACTION: Top left: *Death to the Orange* by Max Peacock (Robert Hale, 1956); painted June 1955. Top right: *Guns Forever Echo* by Kenneth M Ellis (Cassell, 1949); painted September 1947. Bottom left: *Adventure Under Arms* by W Victor Cook (Harrap, 1951); painted August 1950. Bottom right: *The Hounds of God* by Rafael Sabatini (Consul, N1033, 1961); painted July 1961.

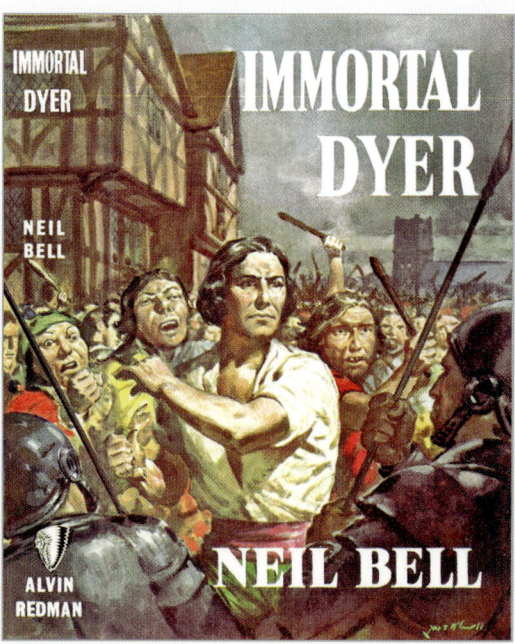
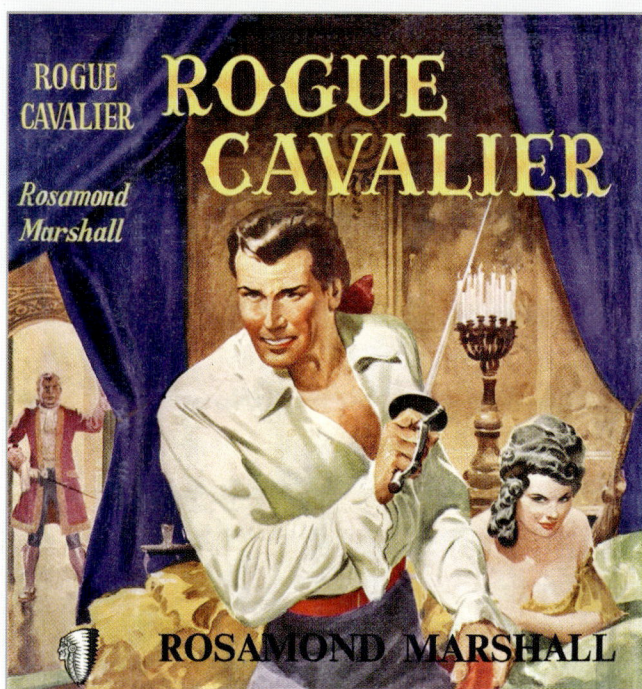

HISTORICAL ACTION: Top left: *Sword of Vengeance* by Sylvia Thorpe (Rich & Cowan, 1957); painted February 1956. Top right: *Immortal Dyer* by Neil Bell (Alvin Redman, 1964); painted January 1964. Bottom left: *Rogue Cavalier* by Rosamond Marshall (Alvin Redman, 1956); painted July 1955 and McConnell's first jacket for the publisher. Bottom right: *Hangman's Cliff* by Robert Neill (Arrow, 518 1958); painted April 1958.

MINIATURE MARVELS

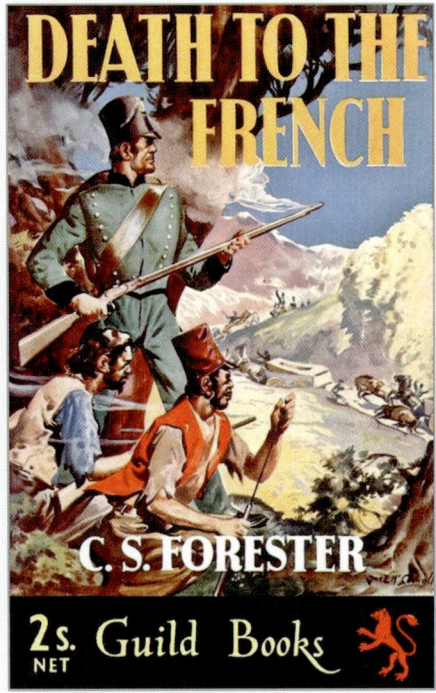
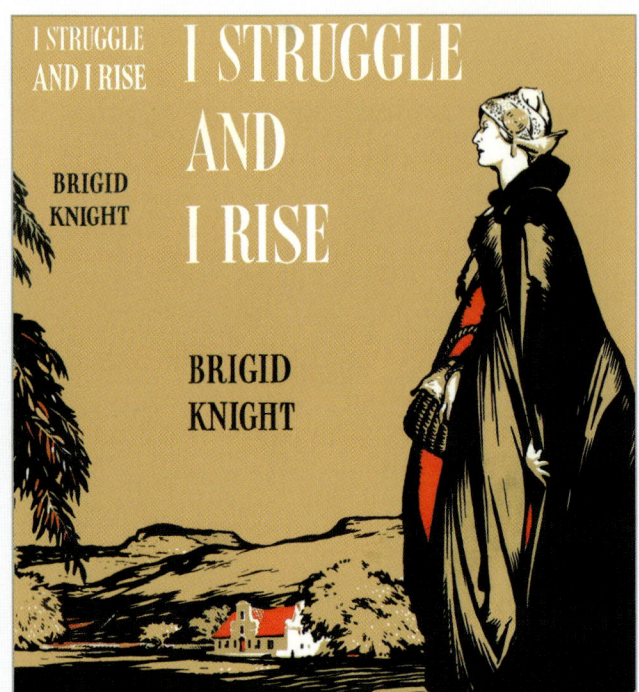

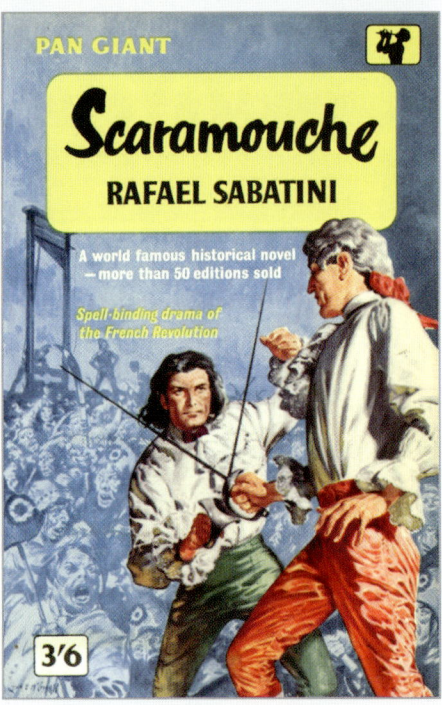

HISTORICAL ACTION: Top left: *Death to the French* by C S Forester (Guild, 1953); painted March 1953. Top right: *I Struggle and I Rise* by Brigid Knight (Cassell, 1947); painted December 1946. A cover of clean lines and quiet dignity for this novel set during a 16th Century Spanish attack on the Netherlands. Bottom left: *Angel With Spurs* by Paul I Wellman (Cassell, 1948); painted February 1947. An image from Spanish history. Bottom right: Advance cover for *Scaramouche* by Rafael Sabatini (Pan X75, 1960); painted September 1959. McConnell had already painted a cover for an earlier Arrow edition of this title. (*Death to the French* image courtesy Jim Kealy. *Scaramouche* image from the author's collection.)

GALLERY

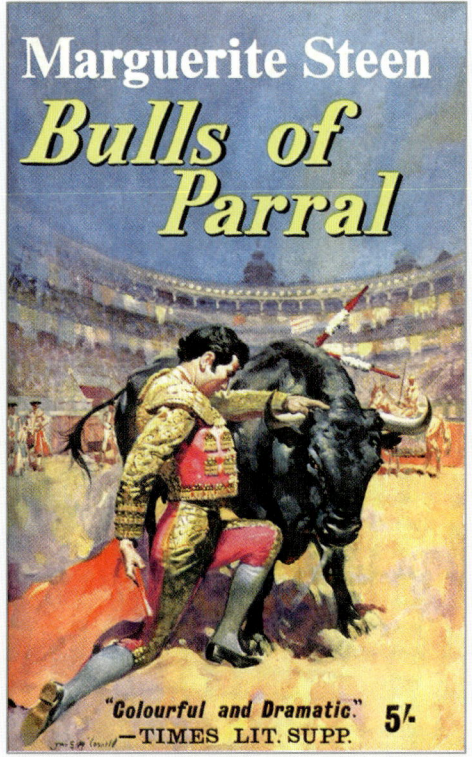

HISTORICAL ACTION: Above left: *Montes the Matador* by Frank Harris (Guild, 1952); painted November 1952. Above right: *Bulls of Parral* by Marguerite Steen (Digit G453, 1961); painted November 1960. These two images of *toreros* at the *corrida de toros*, separated by eight years, capture something of the colour, spectacle and brutality of the event at a time when Franco's Spain was slowly growing as a tourist destination for British holidaymakers. McConnell also executed for jigsaw manufacturer Philmar a depiction of the grand parade that opens the *corrida*; the original painting for this is pictured below.

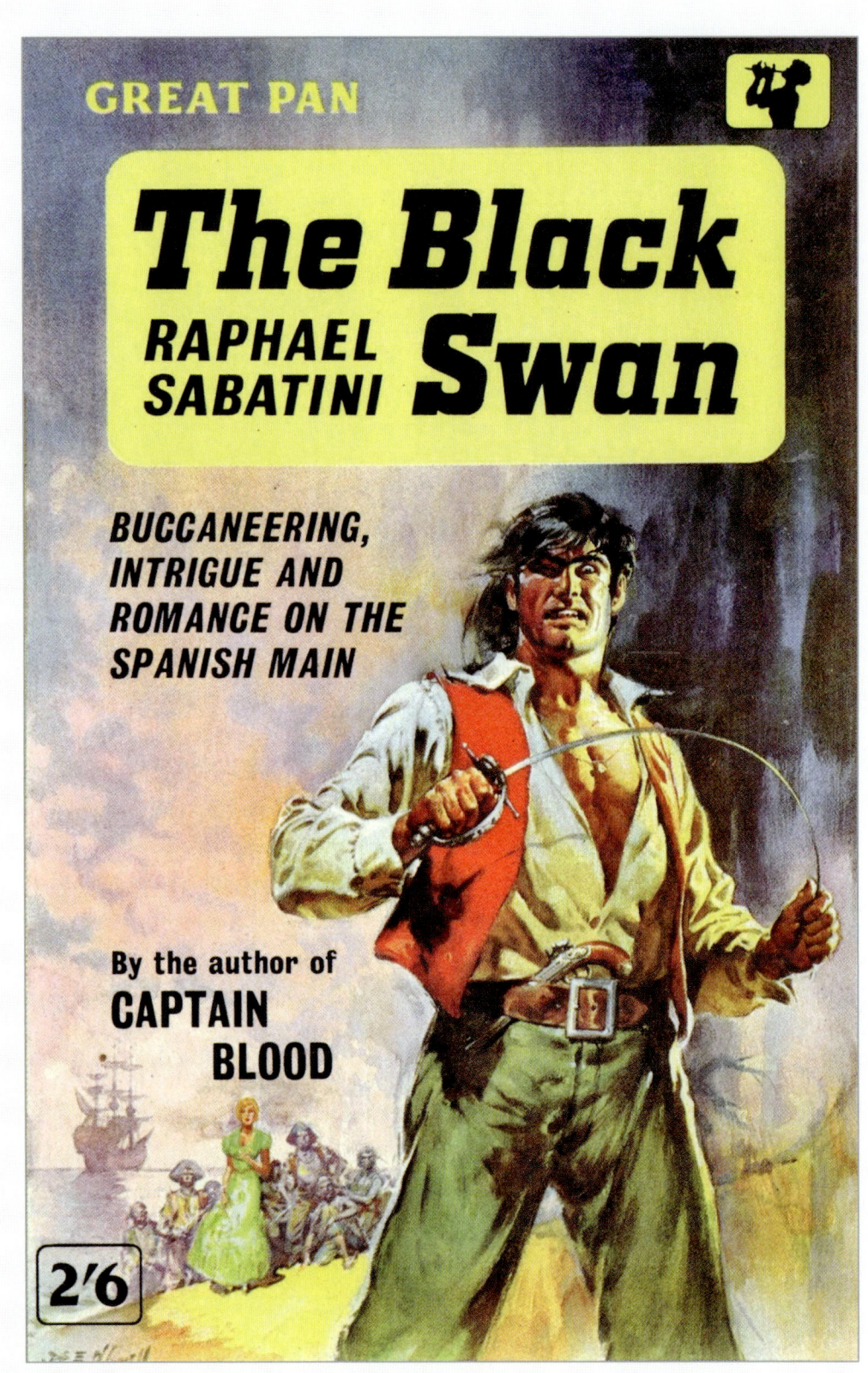

HEROES OF THE HIGH SEAS AND SNOWY WASTELANDS: Advance cover for *The Black Swan* by Rafael Sabatini (Pan G591, 1962); painted February 1962. Note the misspelling of the author's first name, which remained uncorrected on the published cover. (Image from the author's collection.)

GALLERY

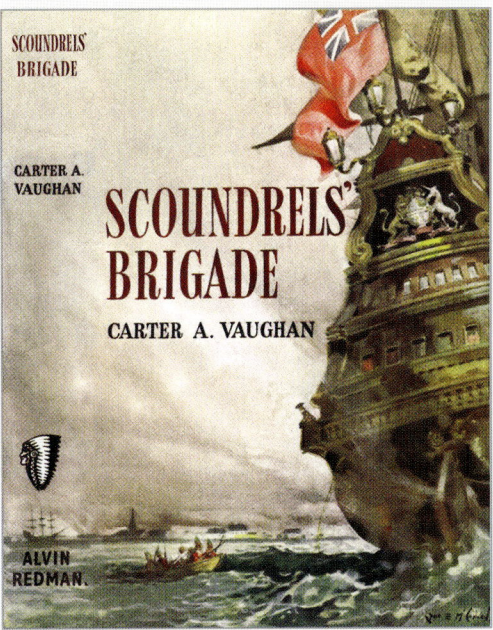

HEROES OF THE HIGH SEAS AND SNOWY WASTELANDS: Top left: *The Land is Bright* by Noel B Gerson (Alvin Redman, 1962); painted March 1962. Top right: *Edge of Piracy* by Donald Barr Chidsey (Alvin Redman, 1965); painted March 1965. Bottom left: *The Haunted Journey* by Robert Murphy (Cassell, 1962); painted April 1962. Bottom right: *Scoundrels' Brigade* by Carter A Vaughan (Alvin Redman, 1963); painted March 1962. (*The Haunted Journey* image courtesy Jim Kealy.)

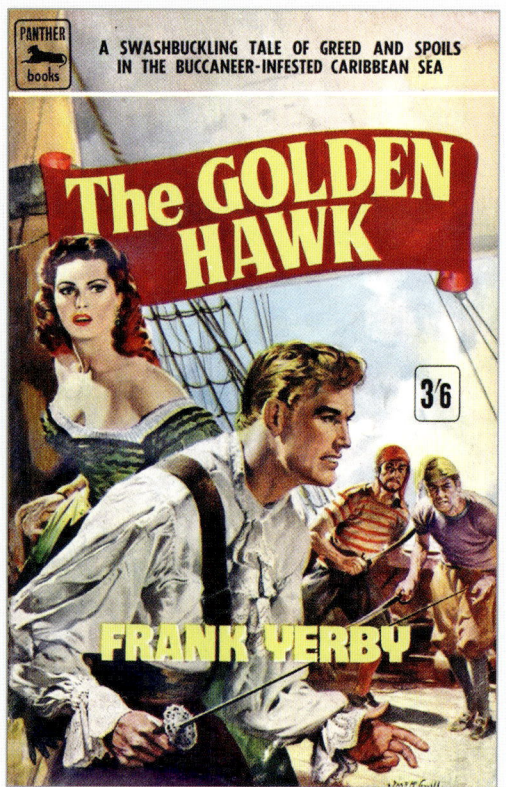
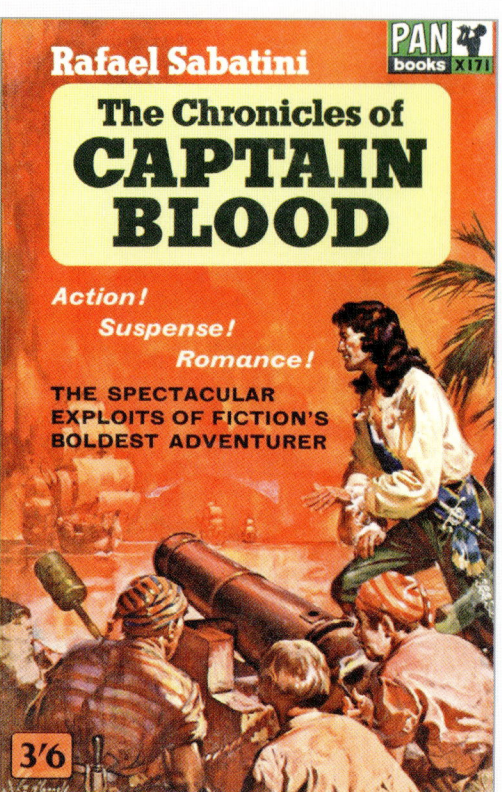

HEROES OF THE HIGH SEAS AND SNOWY WASTELANDS: Top left: *The Golden Hawk* by Frank Yerby (Panther 825, 1958); painted November 1957. Top right: *The Chronicles of Captain Blood* by Rafael Sabatini (Pan X171, 1962); painted April 1962. Bottom left: *The Sea Hawk* by Rafael Sabatini (Arrow 488, 1958); painting not recorded. Bottom right: *Dragon Cove* by Carter A Vaughan (Alvin Redman, 1964); painted July 1964. (*The Chronicles of Captain Blood* image courtesy Jim Kealy.)

GALLERY

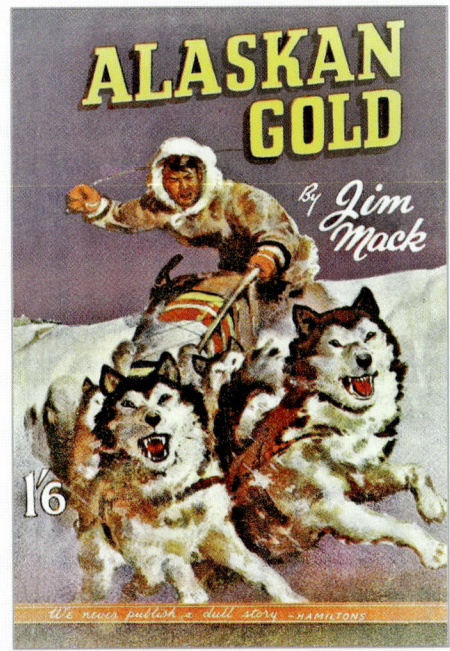
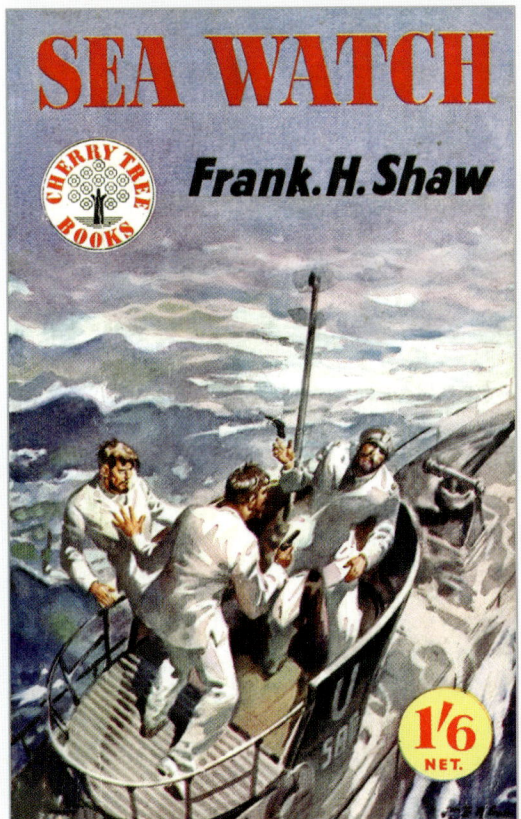

HEROES OF THE HIGH SEAS AND SNOWY WASTELANDS: Top left: *Nor on What Seas* by Ewart Brookes (Jarrolds, 1956); painted December 1955. Top right: *Alaskan Gold* by Jim Mack (Hamilton's, 1951); painted December 1950. Bottom left: *Sea Watch* by Frank H Shaw (Cherry Tree, 1953); painted July 1952. Bottom right: *Atlantic Gold!* by Frank H Shaw (Cherry Tree, 1953); painted March 1952.

HEROES OF THE HIGH SEAS AND SNOWY WASTELANDS: *The Golden Lode* by Andrew Davidson (Hutchinson, 1956); painted February 1956. McConnell painted no fewer than eighteen covers with 'Golden' in the title.

LOVERS AND LIBERTINES: *The Devil's Bride* by Carter A Vaughan (Alvin Redman, 1960); painted March 1959.

MINIATURE MARVELS

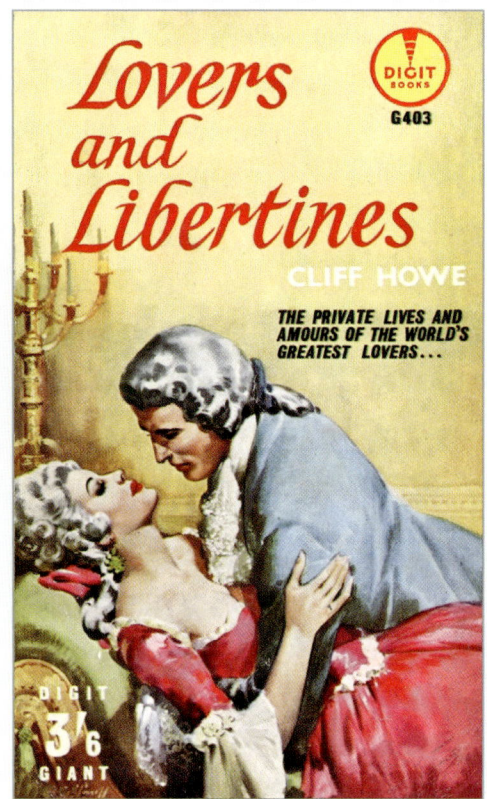

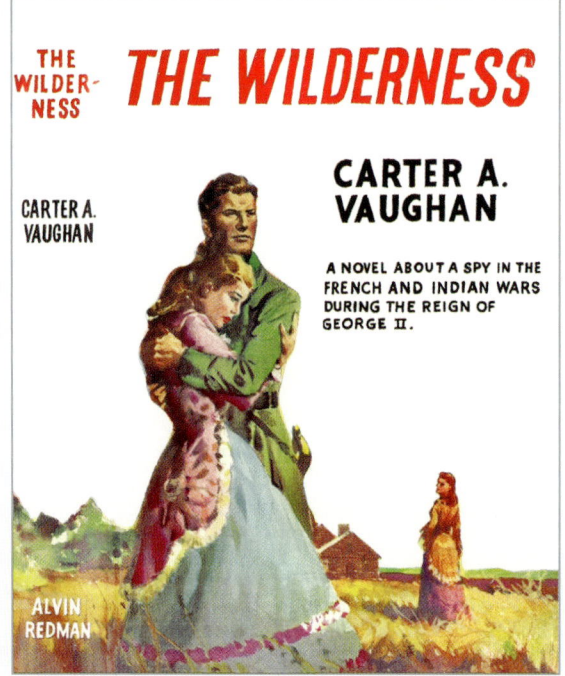

LOVERS AND LIBERTINES: Top left: *Lovers and Libertines* by Cliff Howe (Digit G403, 1960); painted July 1960. Top right: Original artwork for *Gino* by Lorenzo Madalena (Corgi GN920, 1960); painted May 1960. Bottom left*: The Wilderness* by Carter A Vaughan (Alvin Redman, 1960); painted July 1959. Bottom right: *Jew Süss* by Lion Feuchtwanger (Arrow 517, 1959); painted October 1958.

GALLERY

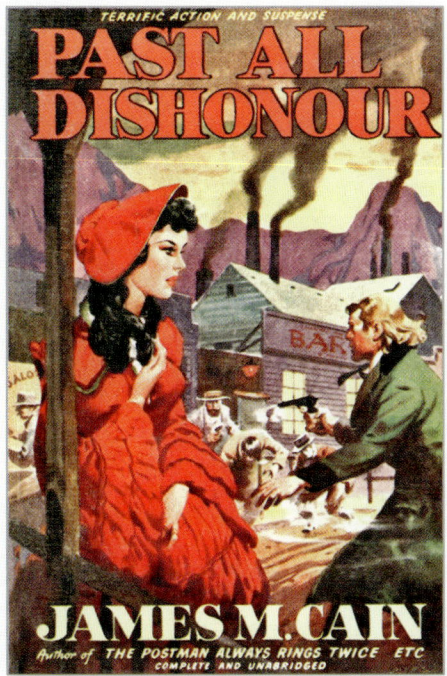

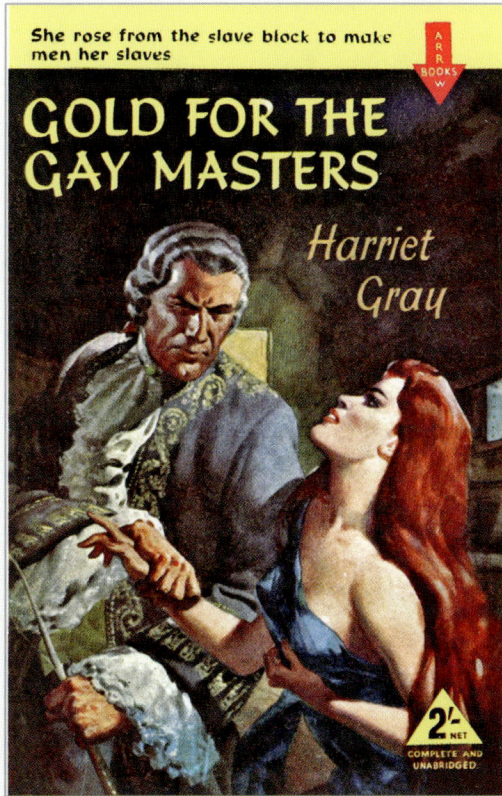

LOVERS AND LIBERTINES: Top left: *Past All Dishonour* by James M Cain (Robert Hale, 1954); painted April 1954. Top right: *The Strongest Enemy* by Henry Gaston (Alvin Redman, 1964); painted June 1964. Bottom left*: Nell* by Olivia Leigh (Digit R537, 1961); painted July 1961. Bottom right: *Gold for the Gay Masters* by Harriet Gray (Arrow 469, 1957); painted February 1957. (*The Strongest Enemy* image courtesy Jim Kealy.)

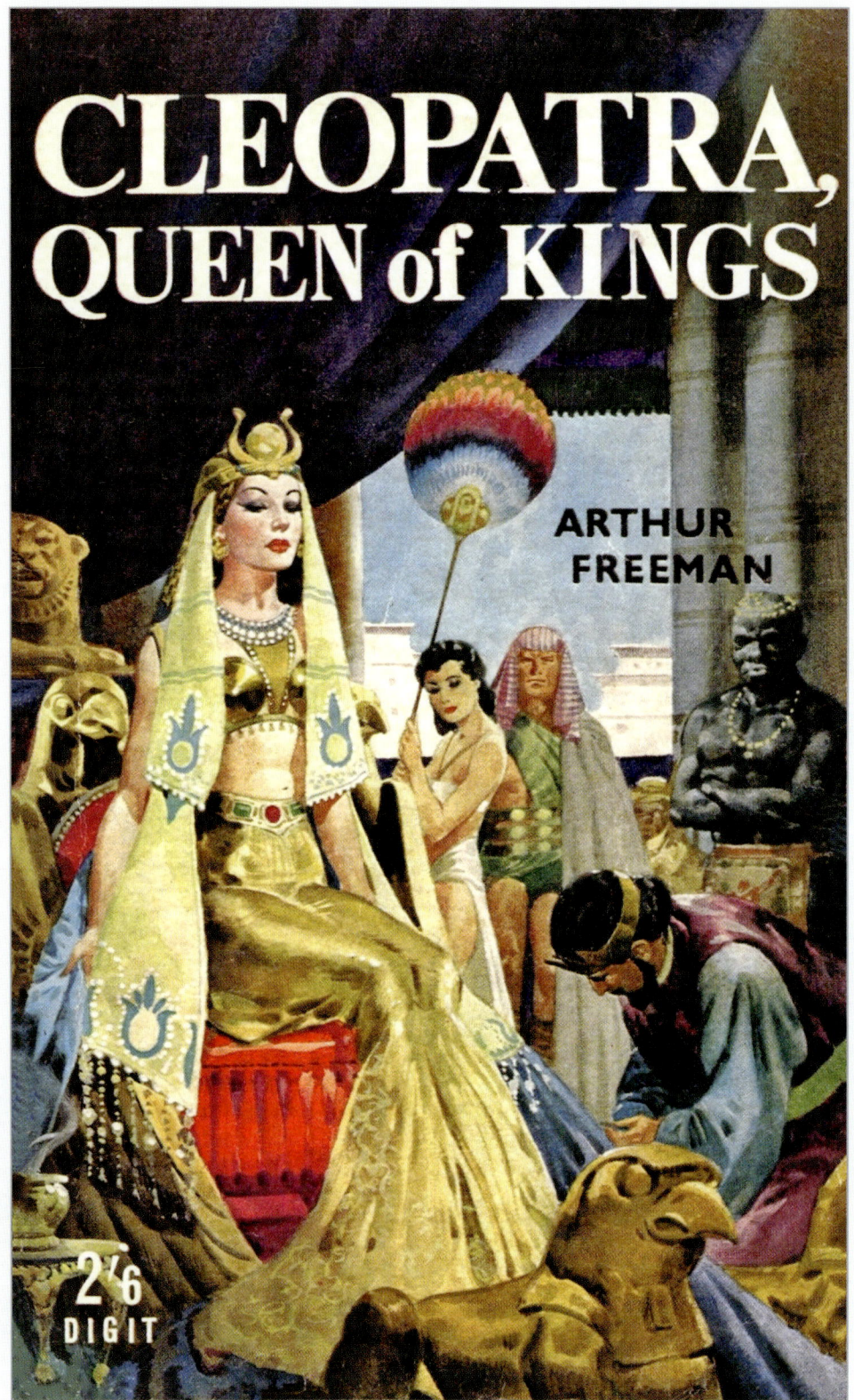

LOVERS AND LIBERTINES: *Cleopatra, Queen of Kings* by Arthur Freeman (Digit R496, 1961); painted February 1961.

GALLERY

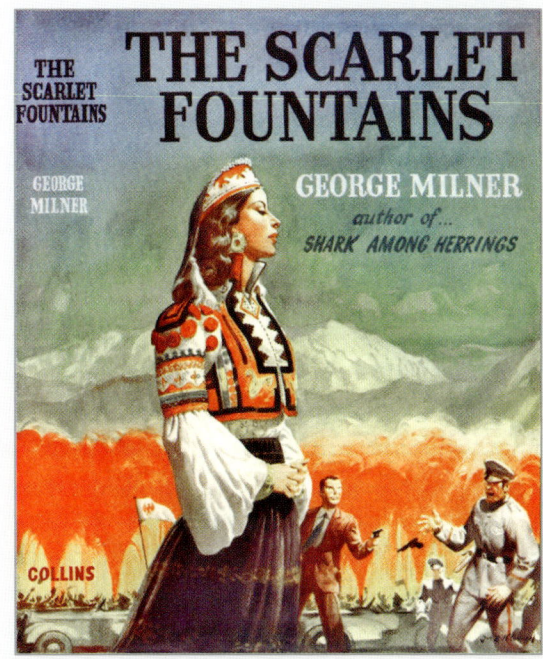
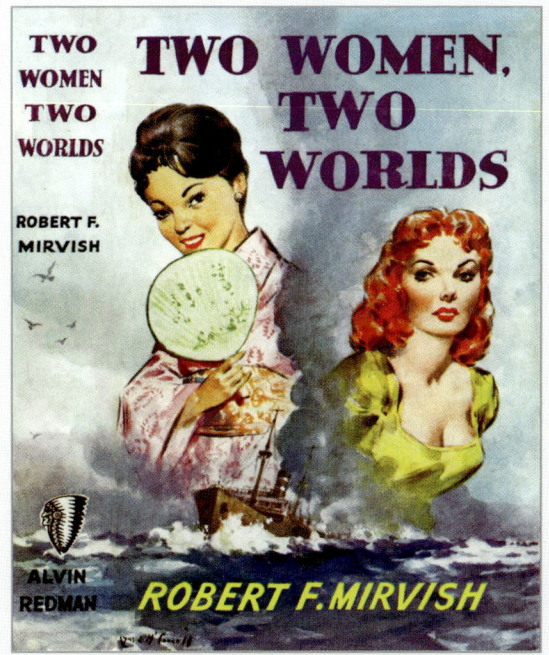

LOVERS AND LIBERTINES: Top left: *The Scarlet Fountains* by George Milner (Collins, 1956); painted June 1955. Top right: *Two Women, Two Worlds* by Robert F Mirvish (Alvin Redman, 1961); painted December 1960. Bottom left: Original artwork for *The Treasure of Pleasant Valley* by Frank Yerby (Four Square 160, 1959); painted February 1959. Bottom right: *The Memoirs of Casanova* translated by Lowell Bair (Corgi GG1071, 1961); painted May 1961. (*Two Women, Two Worlds* image courtesy Jim Kealy.)

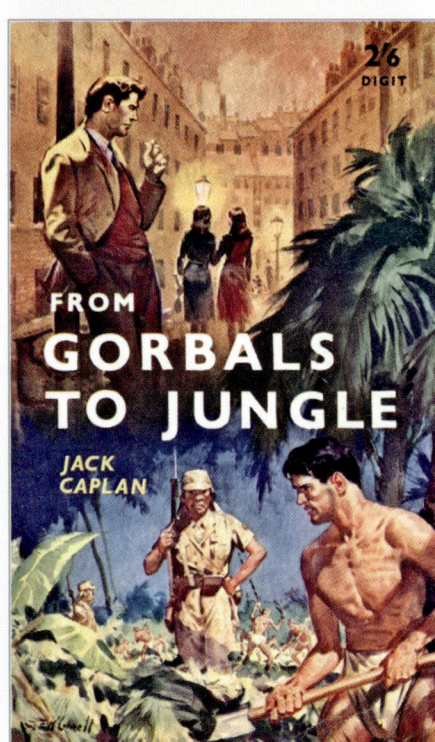

WAR AND REBELLION: Top left: *Bengal Lancer* by F Yeats-Brown (Digit R409, 1960); painted July 1950. Top right: *Banner Over Pusan* by Ellery Anderson MBE MC (Digit R534, 1960); painted June 1961. Bottom left: *From Gorbals to Jungle* by Jack Caplan (Digit R530, 1961); painted June 1961. Bottom right: *Resistance Fighter* by Francis Reid (Digit R541, 1961); painted July 1961.
(*Banner Over Pusan* and *From Gorbals to Jungle* images courtesy Jim Kealy.)

GALLERY

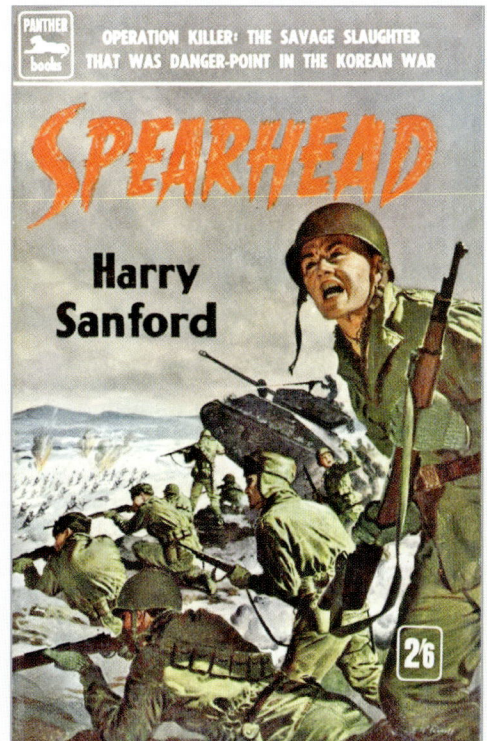

WAR AND REBELLION: Top left: *Spearhead* by Harry Sanford (Panther 833, 1958); painted December 1957. Top right: *Zig-Zag* by John Gilbert (Four Square 272, 1961); painted December 1959. Bottom left: *Twilight of the Dragon* by Peter Bourne (Arrow Books 478, 1957); painting not recorded. Bottom right: *The Patriot* by Pearl S Buck (Four Square 98, 1959); painted December 1957.

WAR AND REBELLION: *Cleared Narvik 2000* by Robert F Mirvish (Alvin Redman, 1962); painted August 1961. (Image courtesy Jim Kealy.)

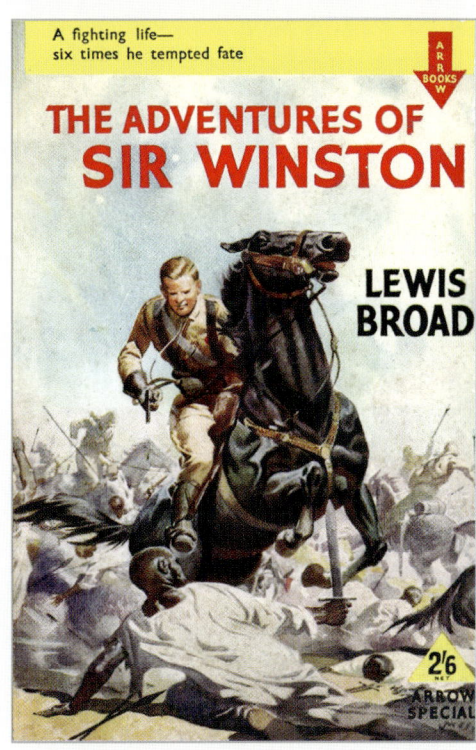
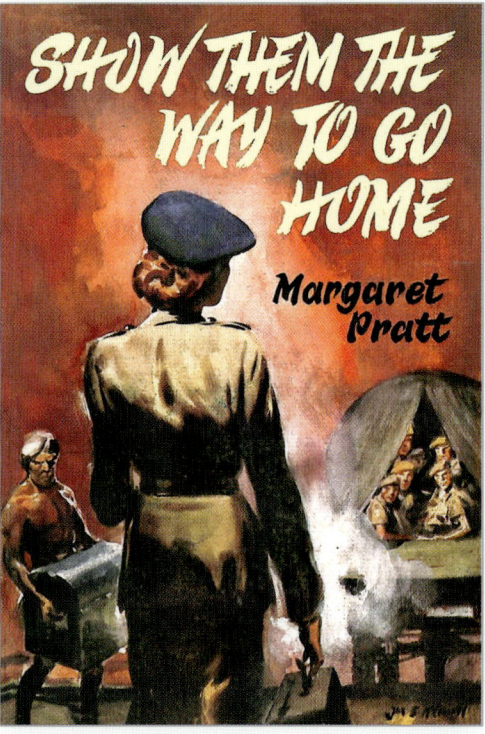

WAR AND REBELLION: Top left: *Down* by Walt Grove (Consul N1026, 1961); painted July 1961. Top right: *The Morning Will Come* by Naomi Jacob (Arrow 686, 1962); painted May 1962. Bottom left: *The Adventures of Sir Winston* by Lewis Broad (Arrow 436H, 1957); painted May 1956. Bottom right: *Show Them the Way to Go Home* by Margaret Pratt (Cassell, 1955); painted February 1955.

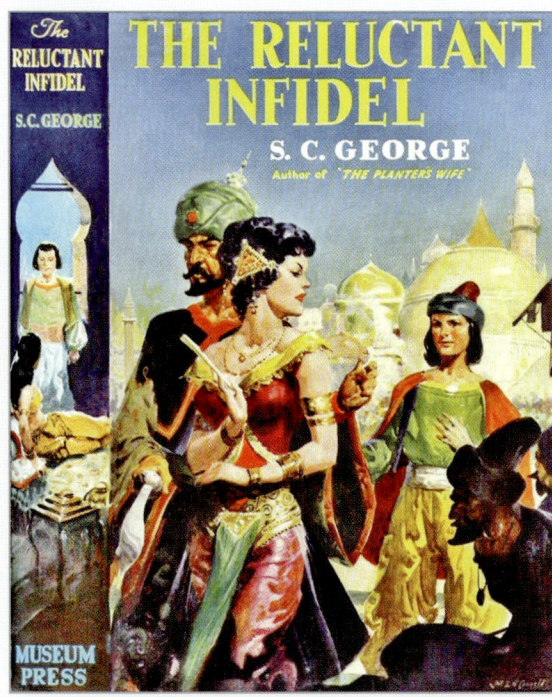
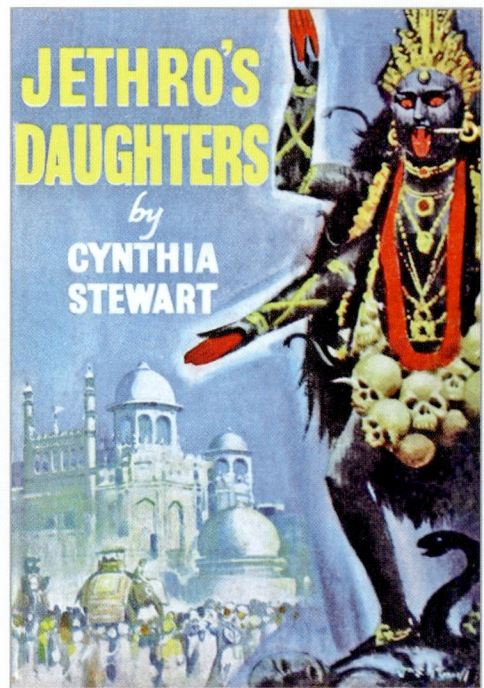
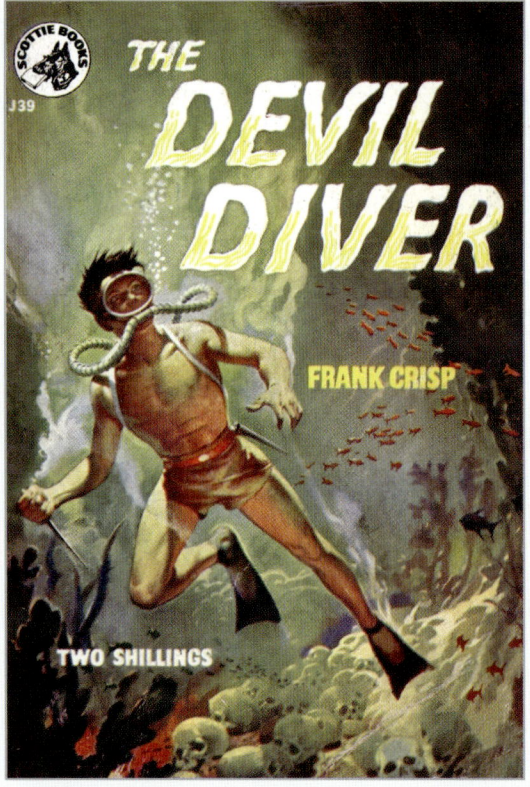

FANTASY AND EXOTICISM: Top left: *The Reluctant Infidel* by S C George (Museum Press, 1954); painted March 1953. Top right: *Jethro's Daughters* by Cynthia Stewart (Alvin Redman, 1964); painting not recorded. Bottom left: *The Devil Diver* by Frank Crisp (Scottie J39, 1956); painted March 1956. Bottom right: *The Quest of Julian Day* by Dennis Wheatley (Arrow 632, 1962); painting not recorded.

FANTASY AND EXOTICISM: *The Golden Amazon Returns* by John Russell Fearn (World's Work, 1948); painting not recorded.

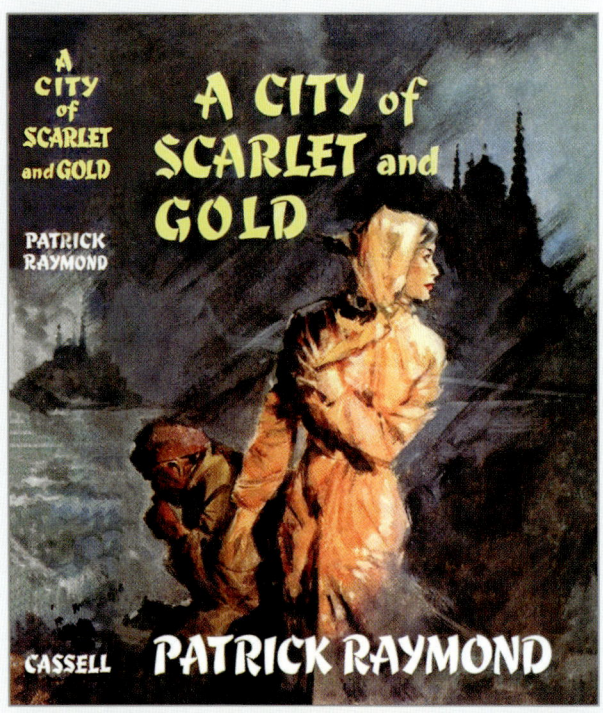
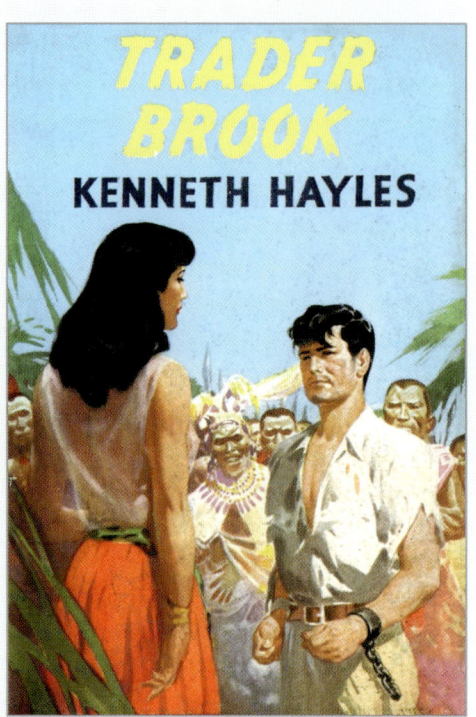
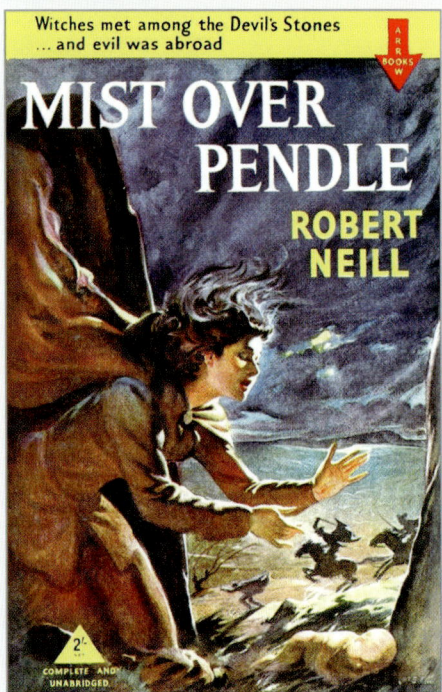

FANTASY AND EXOTICISM: Top left: *A City of Scarlet and Gold* by Patrick Raymond (Cassell, 1963); painted September 1962. Top right: *Trader Brook* by Kenneth Hayles (Robert Hale, 1957); painted November 1956. Bottom left: *Mist Over Pendle* by Robert Neill (Arrow, 1955); painted October 1954. Bottom right: *The Witch of Manga Reva* by Garland Roark (Alvin Redman, 1964); painted December 1963. (*A City of Scarlet and Gold* image courtesy Jim Kealy.)

GALLERY

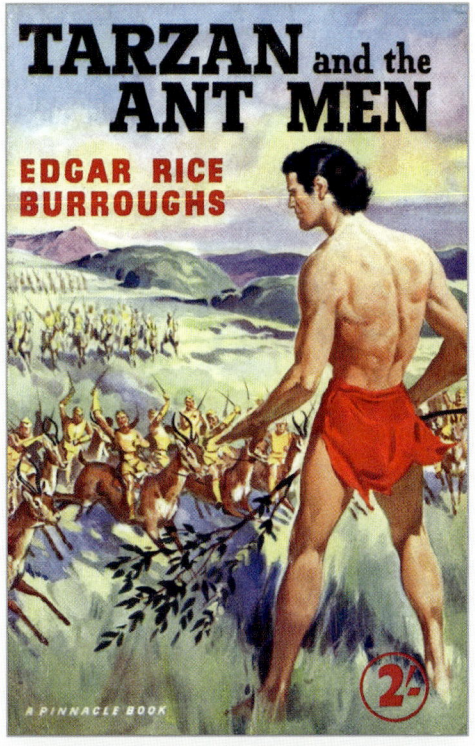
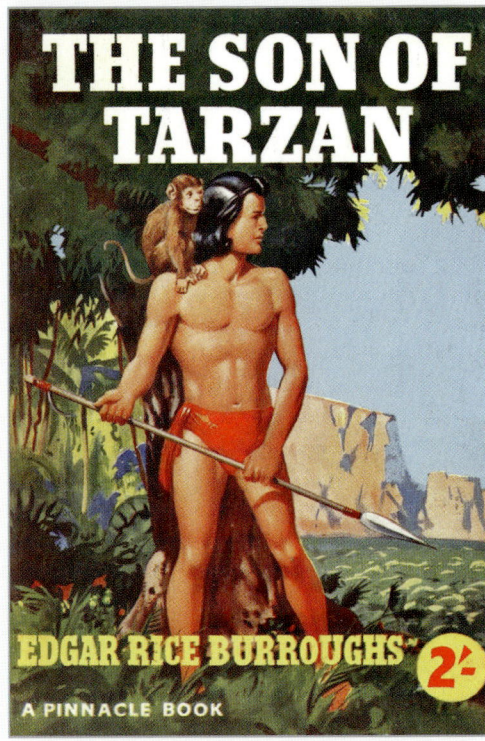
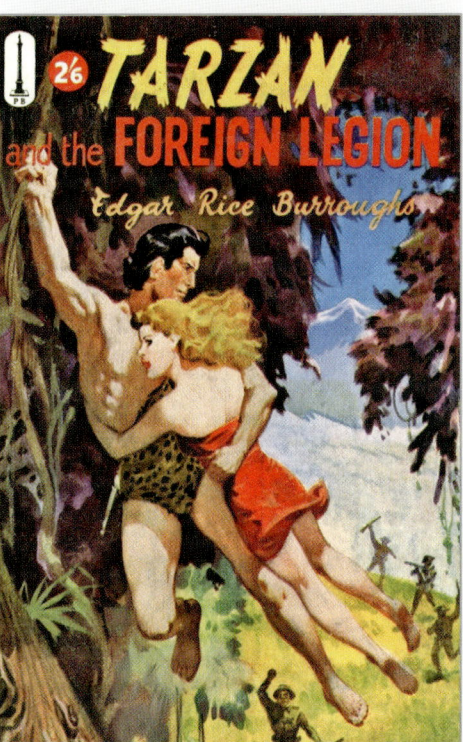

FANTASY AND EXOTICISM: Top left: *Tarzan and the Golden Lion* by Edgar Rice Burroughs (Pinnacle, 1952); painted July 1952. Top right: *Tarzan and the Ant Men* by Edgar Rice Burroughs (Pinnacle, 1953); painted November 1952. Bottom left: *The Son of Tarzan* by Edgar Rice Burroughs (Pinnacle, 1952); painted July 1952. Bottom right: *Tarzan and the Foreign Legion* by Edgar Rice Burroughs (Pinnacle, 1958); painted December 1957. (*Tarzan and the Golden Lion* and *Tarzan and the Foreign Legion* images courtesy Jim Kealy.)

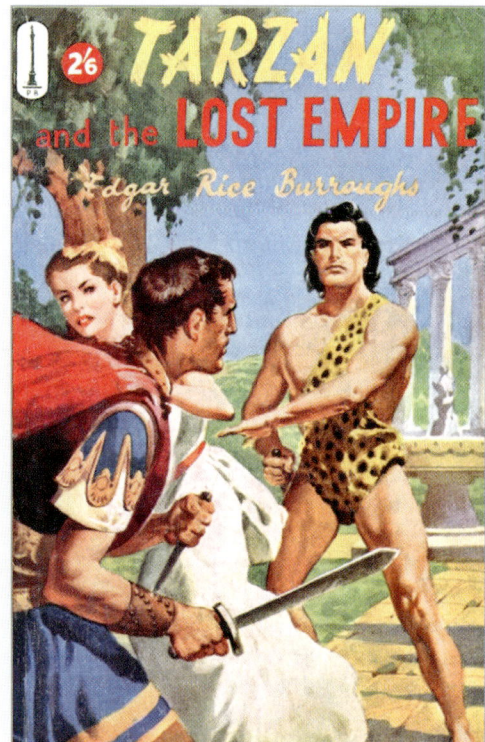

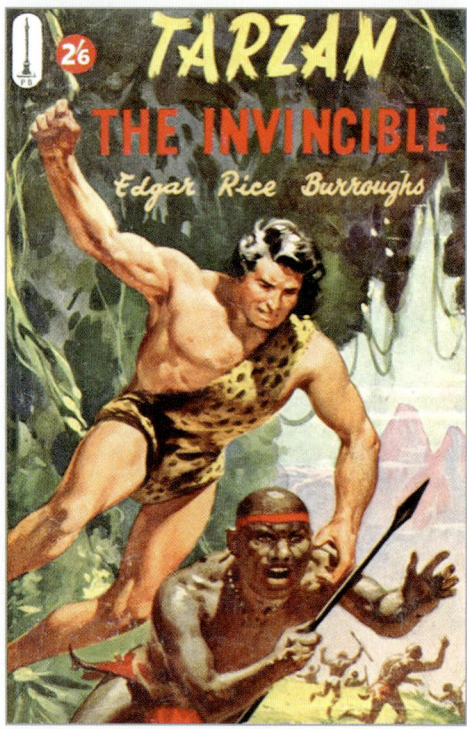
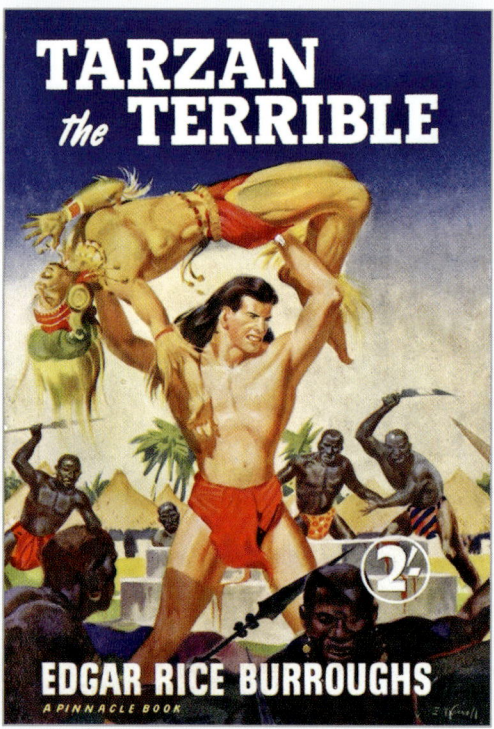

FANTASY AND EXOTICISM: Top left: *Tarzan and the Lost Empire* by Edgar Rice Burroughs (Pinnacle, 1958); painted December 1957. Top right: *Tarzan Lord of the Jungle* by Edgar Rice Burroughs (Pinnacle, 1958), painted December 1957. Bottom left*: Tarzan the Invincible* by Edgar Rice Burroughs (Pinnacle, 1958), painted December 1957. Bottom right: *Tarzan the Terrible* by Edgar Rice Burroughs (Pinnacle, 1953), painted September 1952. (All images except *Tarzan the Terrible* courtesy Jim Kealy.)

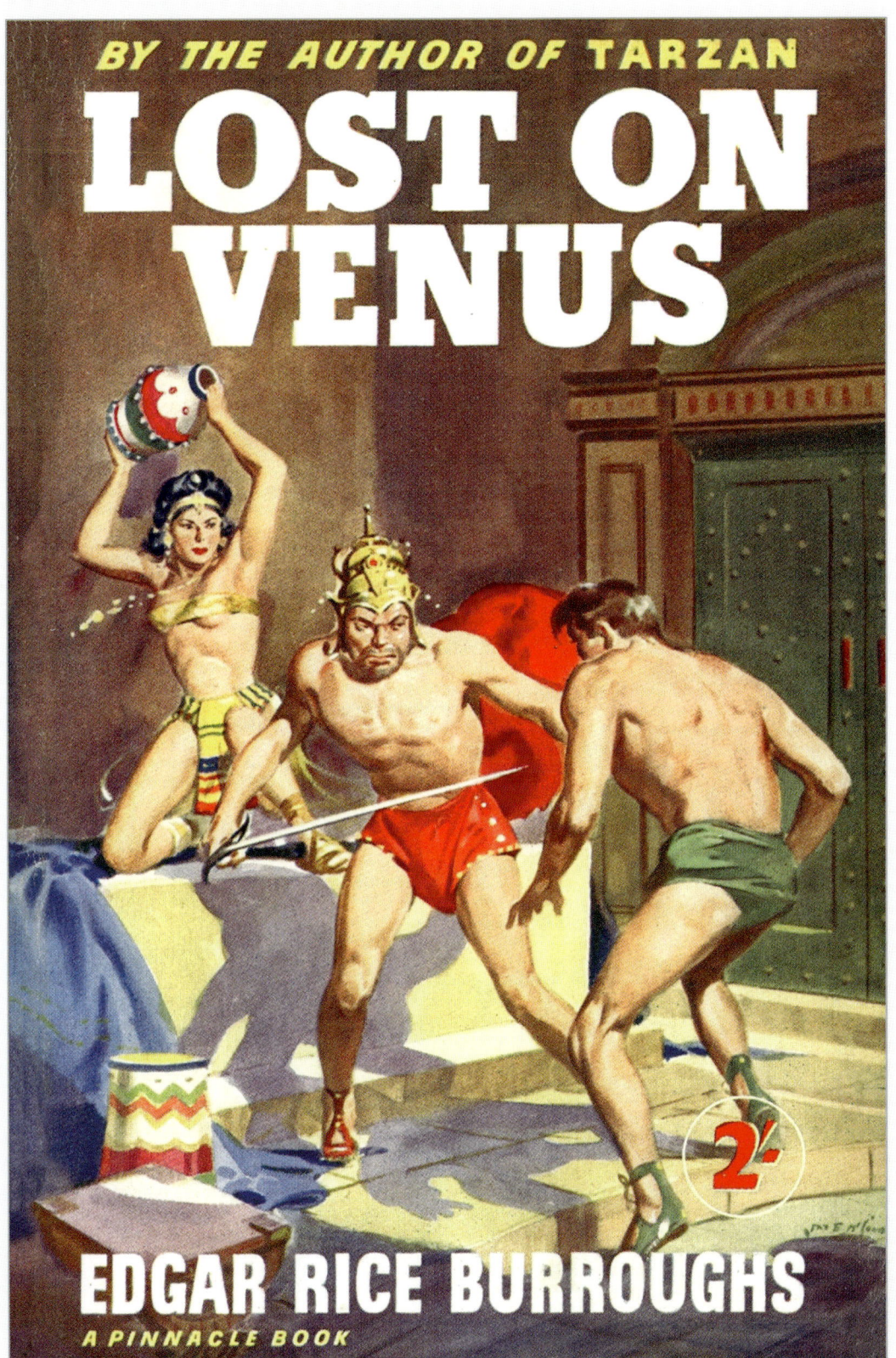

FANTASY AND EXOTICISM: *Lost on Venus* by Edgar Rice Burroughs (Pinnacle, 1953), painted August 1952. (Image courtesy Jim Kealy.)

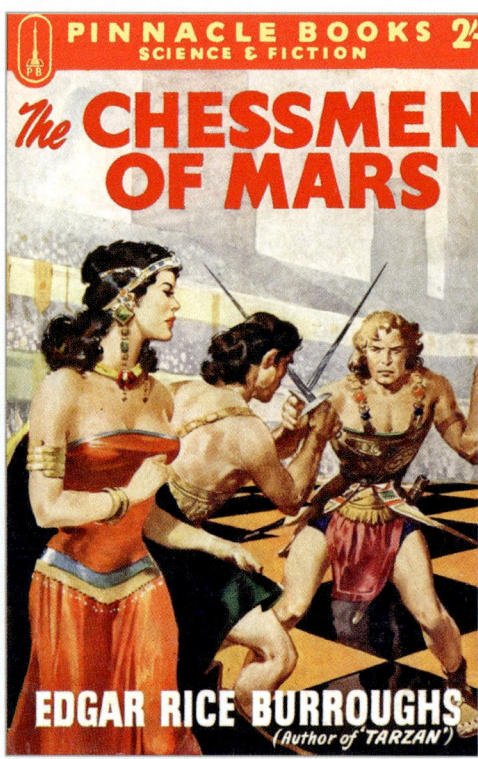
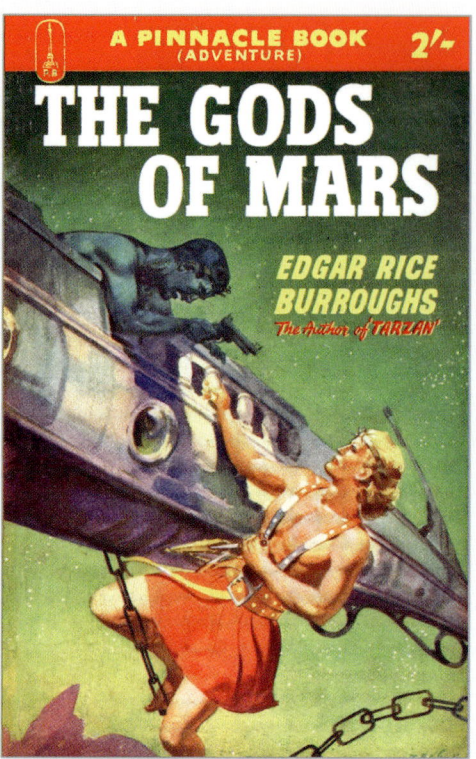
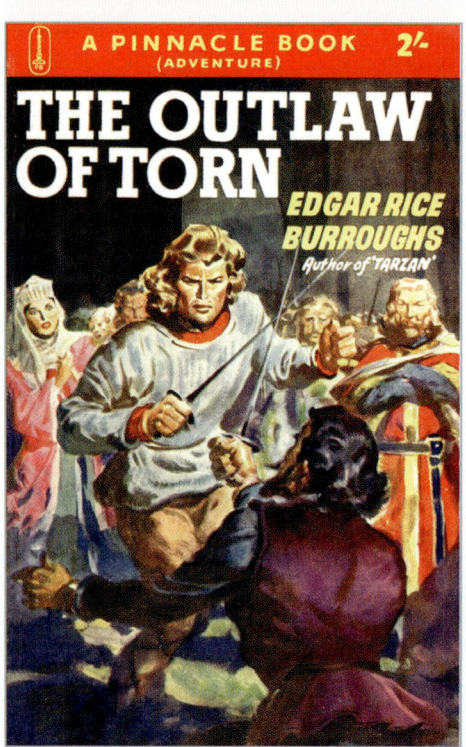
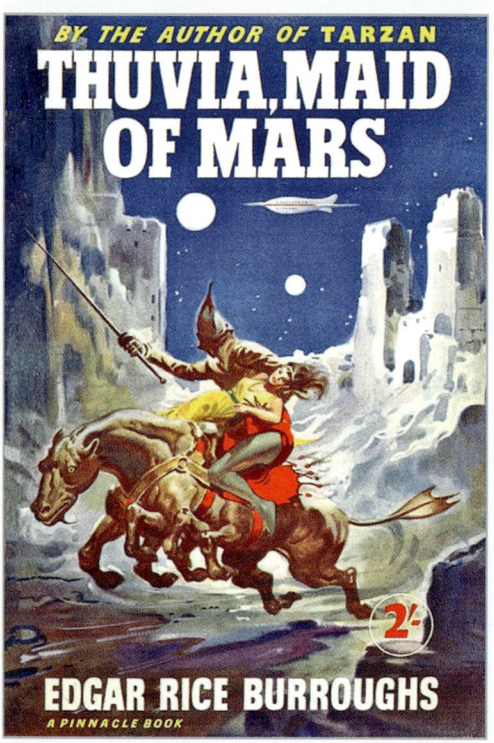

FANTASY AND EXOTICISM: Top left: *The Chessmen of Mars* by Edgar Rice Burroughs (Pinnacle, 1954); painted January 1954. Top right: *The Gods of Mars* by Edgar Rice Burroughs (Pinnacle, 1953); painted April 1953. Bottom left: *The Outlaw of Torn* by Edgar Rice Burroughs (Pinnacle, 1953); painted April 1953. Bottom right: *Thuvia, Maid of Mars* by Edgar Rice Burroughs (Pinnacle, 1953); painted August 1952.

GALLERY

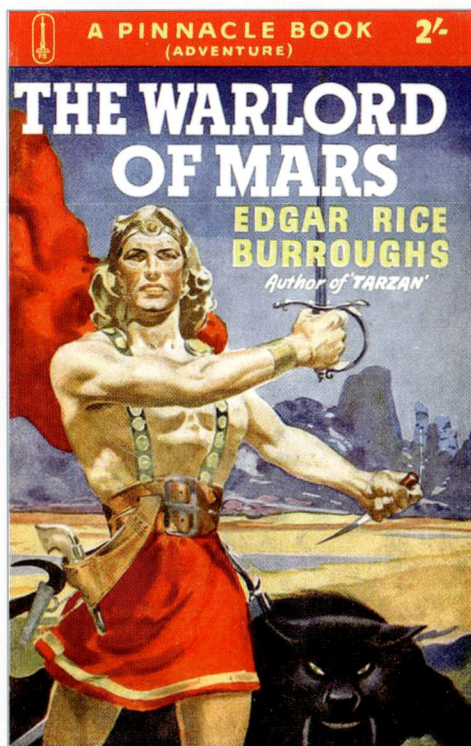
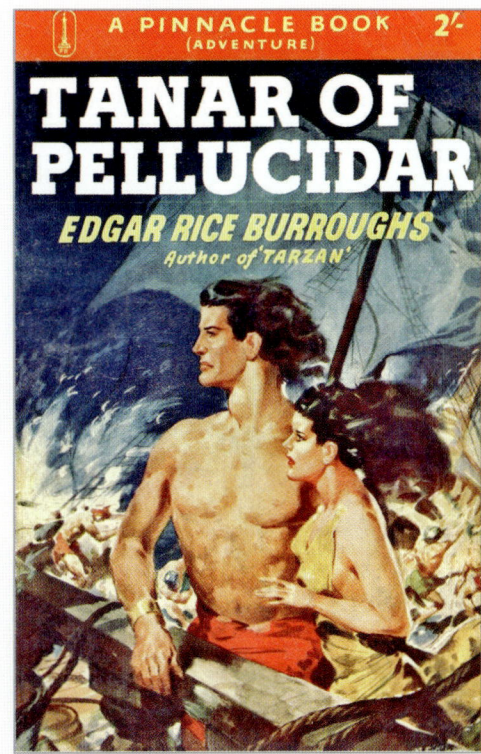
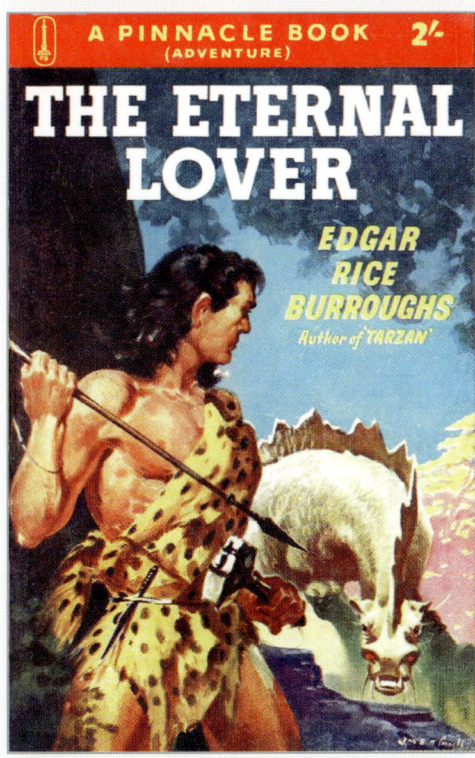
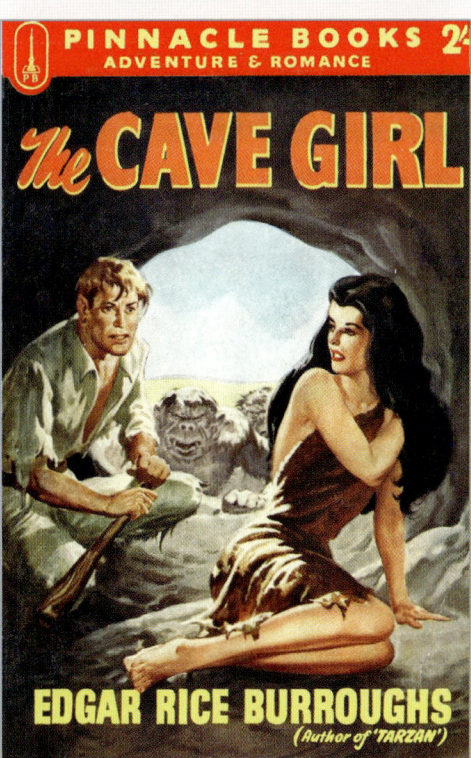

FANTASY AND EXOTICISM: Top left: *The Warlord of Mars* by Edgar Rice Burroughs (Pinnacle, 1953); painted April 1953. Top right: *Tanar of Pellucidar* by Edgar Rice Burroughs (Pinnacle, 1953); painted April 1953. Bottom left: *The Eternal Lover* by Edgar Rice Burroughs (Pinnacle, 1953); painted April 1953. Bottom right: *The Cave Girl* by Edgar Rice Burroughs (Pinnacle, 1954); painted January 1954. (*The Warlord of Mars* image courtesy Jim Kealy.)

Above: *Jacqueline Rides for a Fall* by Pat Smythe (Cassell, 1957); painted January 1957. Below *Three Jays Go to Rome* by Pat Smythe (Cassell, 1960); painted April 1960.

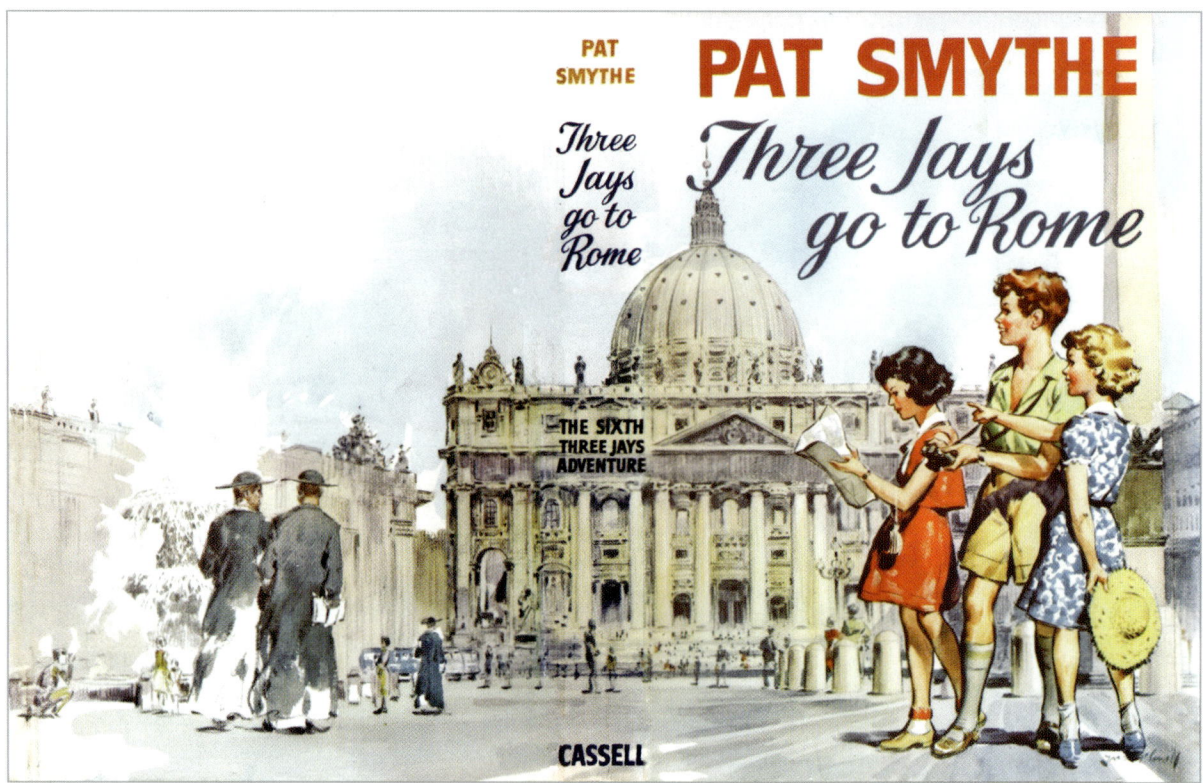

8: DOING IT FOR THE KIDS

'I am sometimes asked whether it is a good plan to get an artist to illustrate a story or whether it is a good plan to write a story around a series of pictures ... Speaking from experience, I think the illustrations should come after the story since the artist is, presumably, picturing certain incidents and can chose these as he wishes; to write a story round the pictures is very cramping to the author's imagination.'

Christine Campbell Thomson, 1946.[57]

The firm belief that children and young people need pictures to stimulate their appetite to

The Adventures of Robin Hood (anon) (Collins, 1947); painted December 1946. The following year, McConnell also produced colour plates for Stanley C Johnson's *Robin Hood and his Merry Foresters* (Foulsham, 1948).

Little Women by Louisa May Alcott (Ward Lock, 1952); painted February 1952.

read led to publications for the juvenile market being amongst the first to be given pictorial dust wrappers in the Edwardian era. Before long, the annual anthologies of children's stories published for the Christmas market featured line drawings, coloured frontispieces and plates, and dust jackets with their illustrations repeated on the cover boards. The proliferation of publications like these created lucrative opportunities for illustrators, and a whole regiment was kept busy on the tsunami of stories of public-school life that virtually defined children's literature in the inter-war years (despite those boarding schools being attended by only a small fraction of children). Therefore, it is perhaps surprising that, for the first decade of his career as a cover artist, James McConnell seems to have painted

The Cruise of the Condor by Capt W E Johns (Thames, 1949); painted December 1948.

almost exclusively for books intended for an adult readership. Things changed dramatically, however, in the early post-war years. Then, he began illustrating regularly for specialist juvenile publishers such as Raphael Tuck, Birn Brothers, Thames, and William Collins' Glasgow operation, working on covers and interior illustrations for boys' and girls' annuals and infant story books. He would also occasionally tackle classic stories, such as *The Adventures of Robin Hood* (Collins, 1947) and *The Last of the Mohicans* (Thames, 1957), but perhaps the most significant, from a book-collector's perspective, were his pieces for Thames's bestsellers by Captain W E Johns and featuring the adventures of his enduring flying ace, Biggles (James Bigglesworth). This work began in December 1948 with a wrap-around cover and five interior colour illustrations for *The Cruise of the Condor* (1949) and concluded seven years later with the eighth cover in the series, *Biggles of 266* (1956), depicting a scene of considerable precarity.

There were also illustrations for other adventure tales for youngsters. Perhaps the best-selling were Cassell's equestrian stories by show-jumper Pat Smythe and featuring the three Jays, the children of a rural horse-loving family reminiscent of McConnell's own. He also provided half-a-dozen paintings in the final months of 1953 for far more exotic adventure yarns published by Warne. But the large majority of his commissions were for Western subjects. McConnell produced distinguished work for Birn's annual *Wild West Book* (1952-54) and for spin-off annuals for Eagle's *Riders of the Range* (Thames, 1952-55); but his most regular client was Amalgamated Press, who published several long series of digest-size 'libraries' aimed at teenage readers – primarily boys.

McConnell started providing cover pieces for Amalgamated's Western Library from its inaugural title in February 1950. Four years later had completed another 81, along with 10 for other Amalgamated libraries, including

Biggles of 266 by Capt W E Johns (Thames, 1956); painted January 1956.

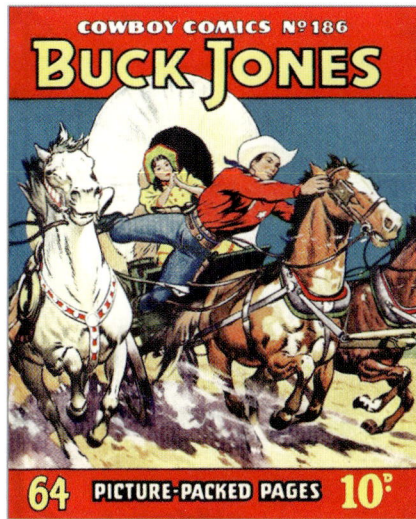

the Thriller Comics Library and the venerable Sexton Blake Library – a remarkable output.

When the Western Library bit the dust in 1954, the indefatigable artist jumped horses and rode away with its sister publication Cowboy Comics Library (later Cowboy Picture Library), adapting his style to suit the harder and cleaner lines of comic-book illustration – although he stuck strictly to the covers rather than tackling interior strips. The Cowboy Comics series featured some of his most dynamic compositions, three of many examples being Buck Jones leaping between speeding horses on #186 (1956); the Kansas Kid lassoing a mountain lion on #200 (1957); and Kit Carson dodging a scything war-club on #229 (1957) (see left). In all, McConnell dashed off at least 93 covers for titles in this Library, with still more for its associated hardback annuals featuring Kit Carson and Buck Jones.

As if that wasn't enough, there were more covers for the Thriller Picture Library, including a few for the exploits of the spitfire ace Battler Britton; and between 1957 and 1960 there were at least 44 (a few unused) for the Super Detective Library. Although McConnell was on familiar territory with dashing detective Rip Kirby, he was forced out of his comfort zone in visualising the dangerous interplanetary adventures of astronaut Rick Random. Actually, his sci-fi illustrations turned out to be surprisingly effective, particularly on the 'to infinity and beyond' cover for #129, *Perilous Mission*, and the canted composition for #111, *Sabotage from Space* (see page 315).[58]

But McConnell had not abandoned Wild West covers; he simply transferred to a different publisher. Between summer 1958 and summer 1959, he painted the first 24 covers for Arthur Pearson's (Newnes/Pearson's) Western Picture Library, swapping Kit Carson, Davy Crockett and friends for Mustang Gray, Jim Bridger, Jim Bowie and the more famous Buffalo Bill.

The end of McConnell's work on the Super Detective series in March 1960 roughly corresponded with Cecil King gaining control of Amalgamated Press and changing its name to Fleetway Publications; but this rebranding was far from the end of McConnell's employment with the firm. He continued to supply occasional illustrations for Fleetway's children's annuals, and from 1962 became one of the principal cover artists for their new educational magazine, *Look and Learn*, together with shorter-lived companion magazines *The Bible Story* (1964) and *Ranger* (1964-65) (both of which proved commercially unviable and were merged with the former title).[59] Thus McConnell's work on Amalgamated/ Fleetway's publications for young people endured for the final two-and-a-half decades of his career and provided his most important income stream during those years.

GALLERY

THE BIGGLES BOOKS: *The Black Peril* by Capt W E Johns (Thames, 1950); painted autumn 1949.

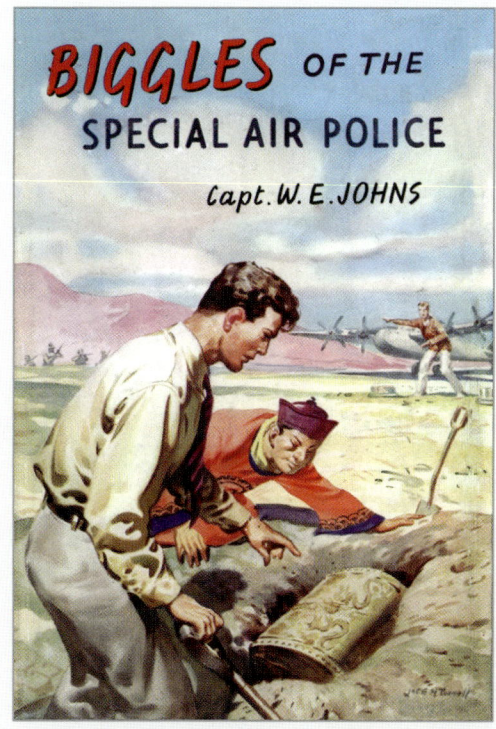

THE BIGGLES BOOKS: Top left: *Biggles Flies Again* by Capt W E Johns (Thames, 1954); painted April 1953. This was a title for which McConnell also supplied an earlier, 1952 edition jacket (see page 349). Top right: *Biggles of the Special Air Police* by Capt W E Johns (Thames, 1954); painted May 1953. Bottom left: *Biggles Pioneer Air Fighter* by Capt W E Johns (Thames, 1954); painted February 1954. Bottom right: *Biggles of the Camel Squadron* by Capt W E Johns (Thames, 1954); painted February 1954.

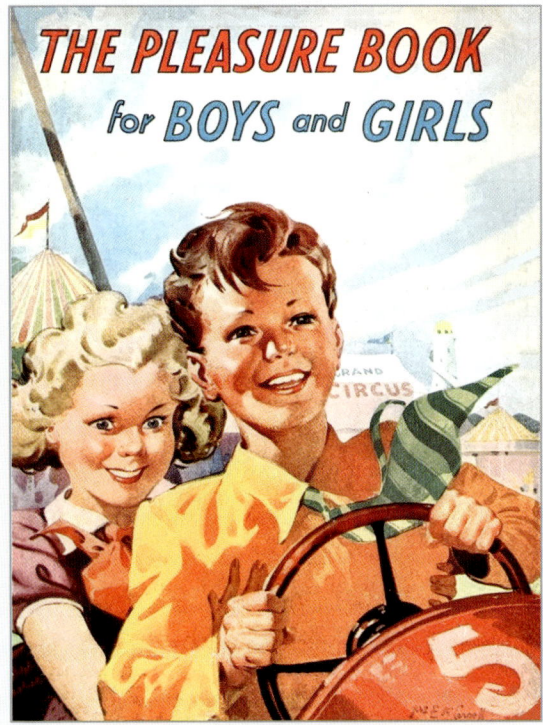

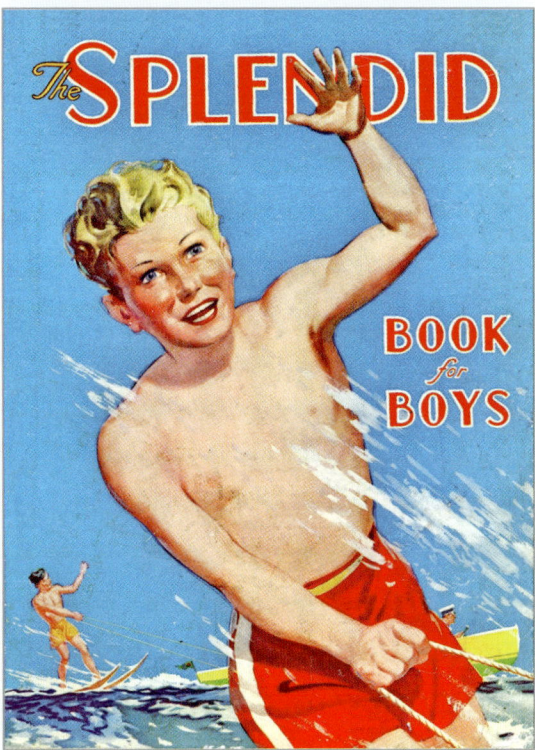

THE ANNUALS: Top left: *The Pleasure Book for Boys and Girls* (Thames, 1952); painted November 1951. Top right: *Every Boys Annual* (Thames, 1947); painted November 1946. Bottom left: *The Book for Boys* (Thames, 1955); painted July 1954. Bottom right: *The Splendid Book for Boys* (Birn Brothers 1948), painted December 1947.

GALLERY

THE ANNUALS: Top: *Flights into the Future* (Thames, 1948); painting not recorded. Bottom left: *Lion Book of Speed* (Fleetway, 1962); painted November 1961. Bottom right: *Lion Annual 1965* (Fleetway, 1964); painting not recorded. (Bottom two images courtesy Jim Kealy.)

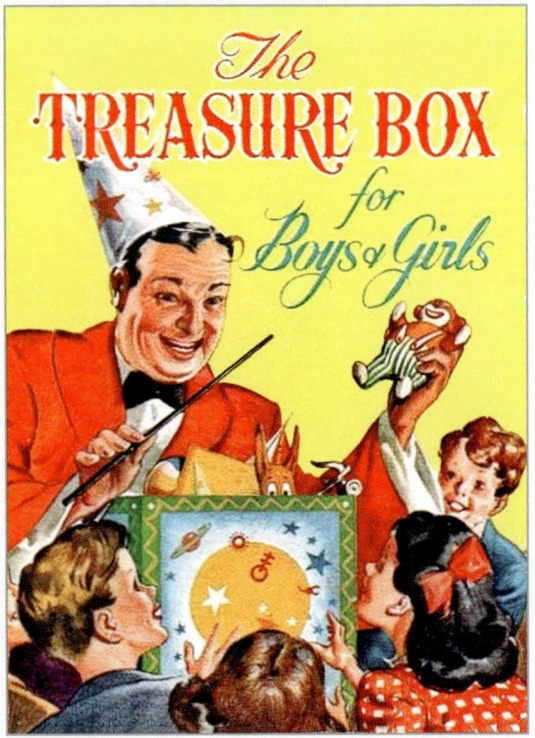

THE ANNUALS: Top left: *Riders of the Range* by Charles Chilton (Thames, 1952); painted March 1952. Top right: *Riders of the Range* by Charles Chilton (Thames, 1955); painted winter 1954-55. Bottom left: *The Treasure Box for Boys & Girls* (Collins, 1950); painted June 1949. Bottom right: *The Treasure Box for Boys and Girls* (Collins, 1951), painted August 1950. (*Riders of the Range* images courtesy Jim Kealy.)

GALLERY

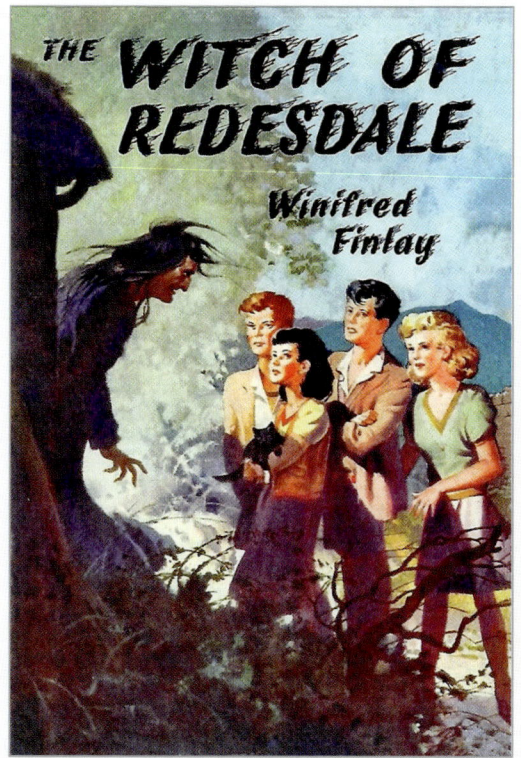
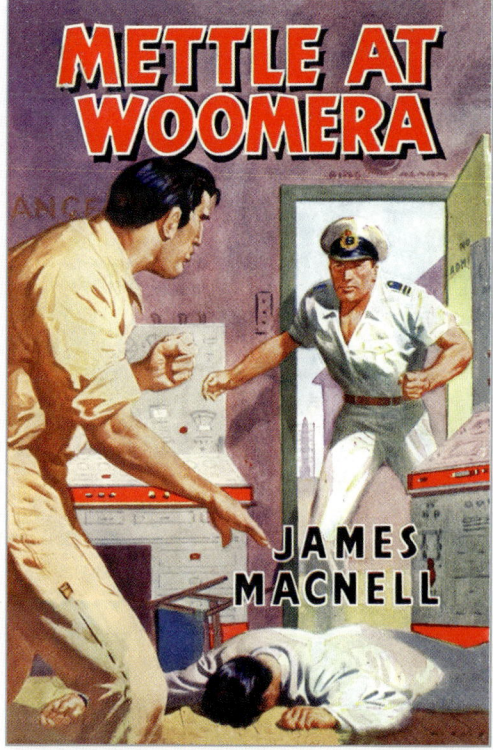

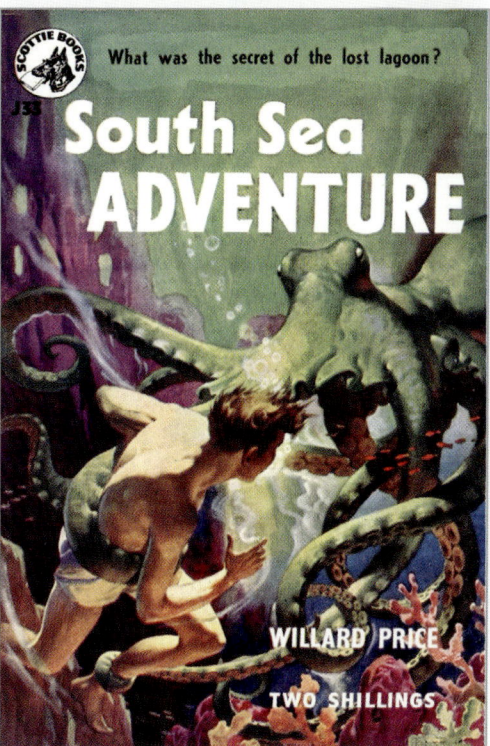

NOVELS: Top left: *The Witch of Redesdale* by Winifred Finlay (Harrap, 1951); painting not recorded. Top right: *Mettle at Woomera* by James Macnell (Collins, 1961); painted July 1959. Bottom left: *The 3 Pebbles* by Richard Parker (Scottie J27, 1956); painted November 1955. Bottom right: *South Sea Adventure* by Willard Price (Scottie J33, 1956); painted January 1955.

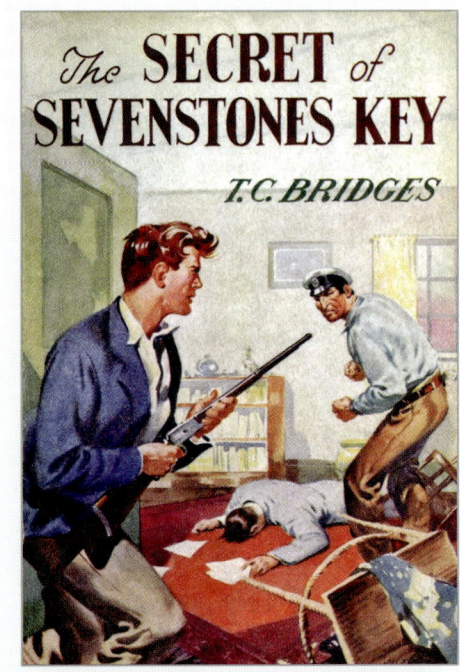
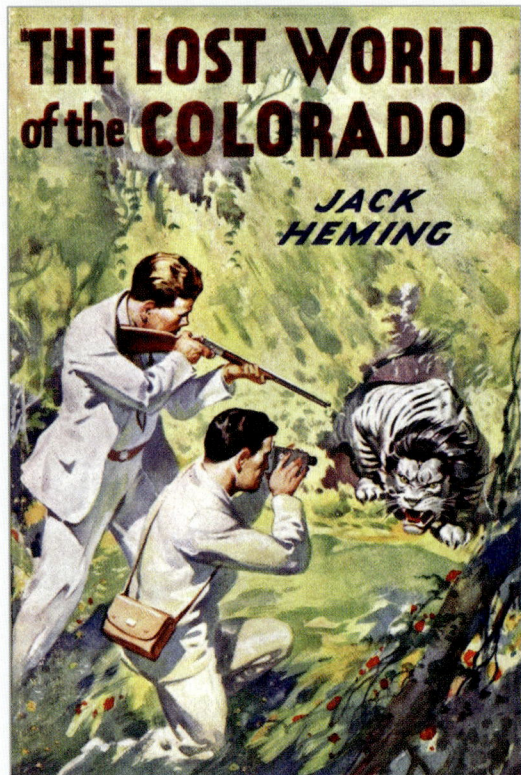
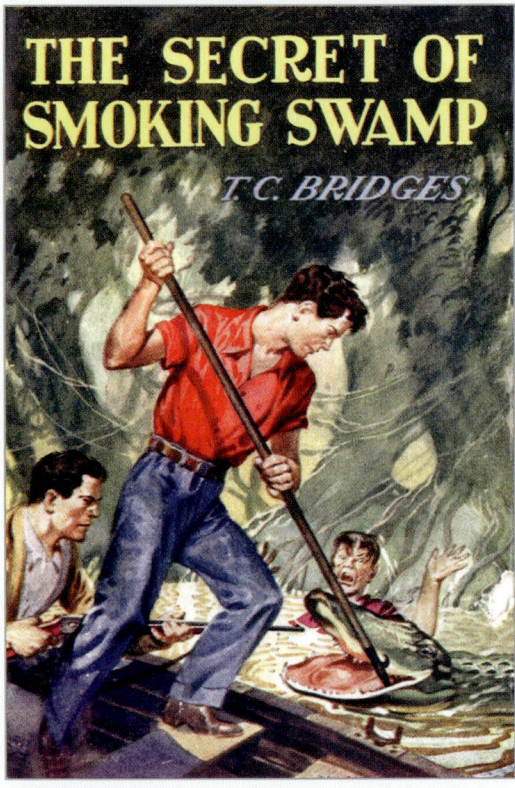

NOVELS: Top left: *Four at Falconbridge* by Winifred Norling (Ward Lock, 1950), painted October 1949. Top right: *The Secret of Sevenstones Key* by T C Bridges (Warne, 1954); painted December 1953. Bottom left: *The Lost World of the Colorado* by Jack Heming (Warne, 1954); painted October 1953. Bottom right: *The Secret of Smoking Swamp* by T C Bridges (Warne, 1954); painted November 1953.

GALLERY

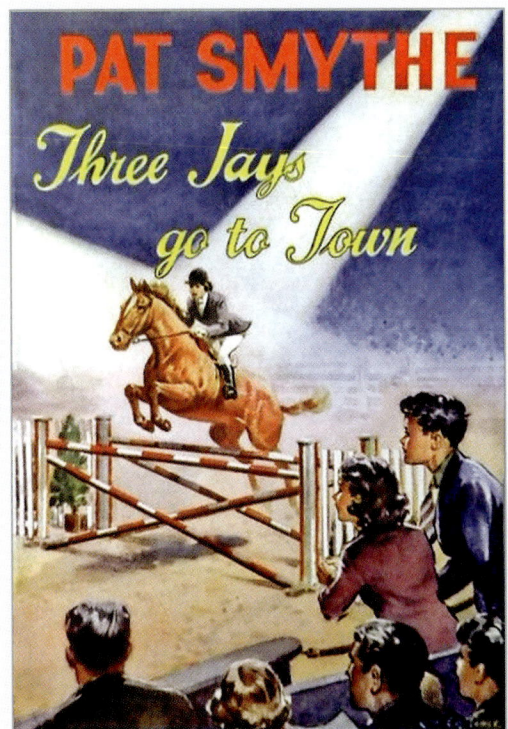
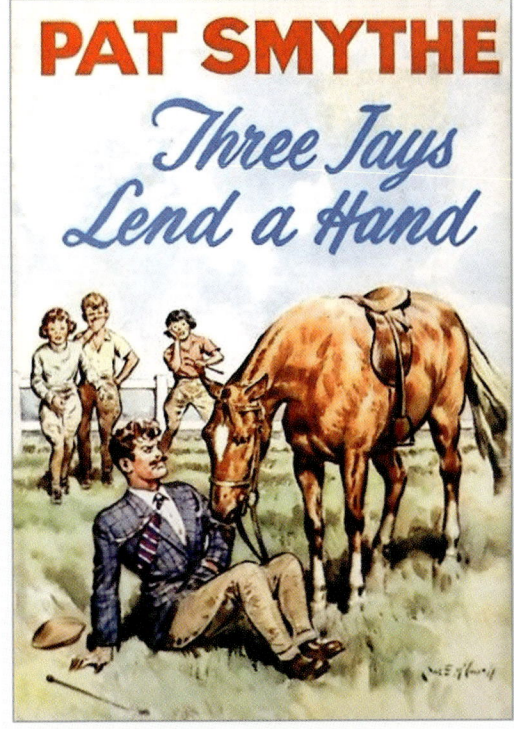
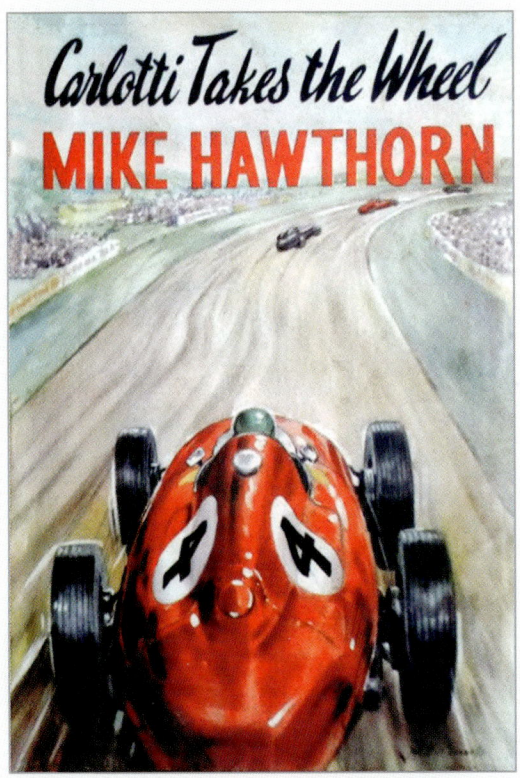
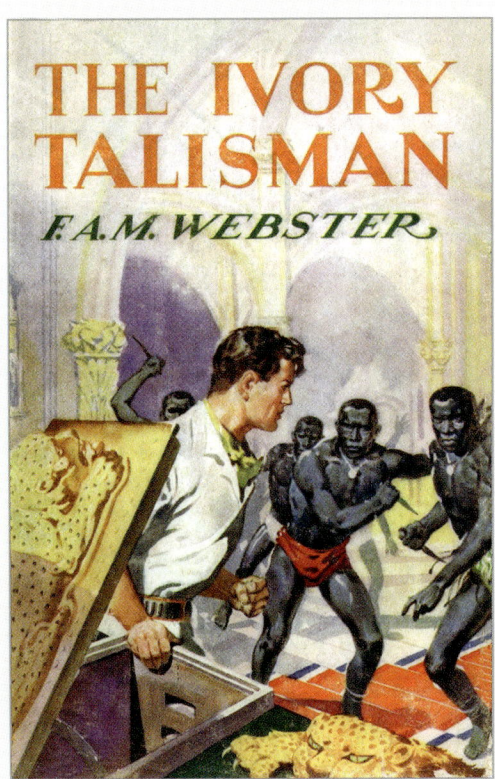

NOVELS: Top left: *Three Jays Go to Town* by Pat Smythe (Cassell, 1959); painted December 1958. Top right: *Three Jays Lend a Hand* by Pat Smythe (Cassell 1961); painted May 1961. Bottom left: *Carlotti Takes the Wheel* by Mike Hawthorn (Cassell, 1959); painting not recorded. Bottom right: *The Ivory Talisman* by F A M Webster (Warne, 1954); painted November 1953.

NOVELS: *SOS from Mars* by John Keir Cross (Hutchinson, 1954); painted September 1953.

GALLERY

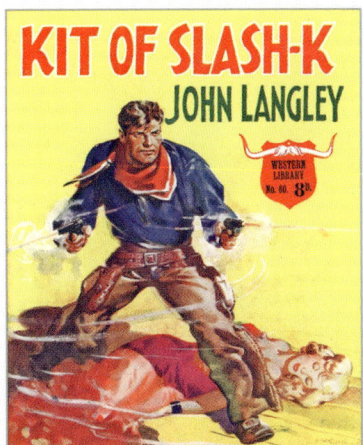
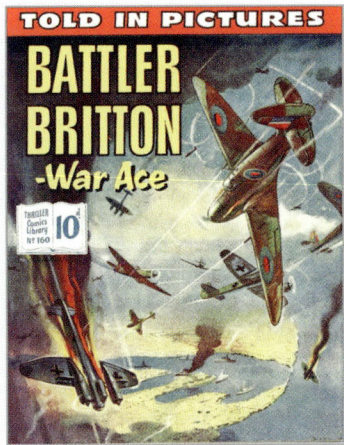
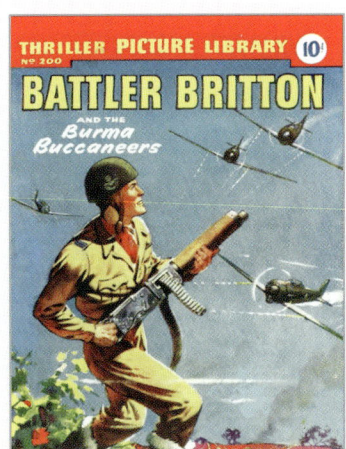
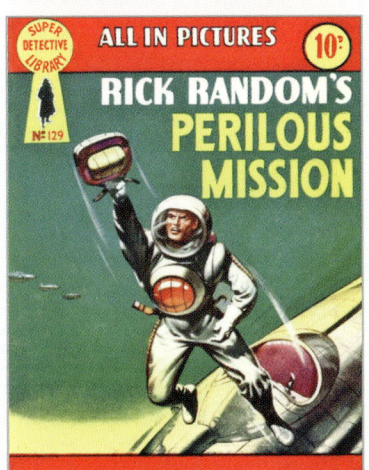

THE LIBRARY SERIES: Bottom right: Trade advertisement for Newnes-Pearson's Western Picture Library, featuring two McConnell covers; September 1958. Other images: five examples of the dozens of covers McConnell provided for Amalgamated's library series. Top left: *Kit of Slash-K* by John Langley (Western Library #60, 1952); painted June 1952. Top centre: *Battler Britton – War Ace* (Thriller Comics Library #160, 1957); painted July 1956. Top right: *Battler Britton and the Burma Buccaneers* (Thriller Comics Library #200, 1958); painted November 1957. Centre left: *Rick Random's Perilous Mission* (Super Detective Library #129, 1958); painted March 1958. Bottom left: *Rick Random in 'Sabotage from Space'* (Super Detective Library #111, 1957); painted June 1957. (Advertisement image from author's collection.)

The Case of the Vanishing Artist by Frank King (Robert Hale, 1956)

EPILOGUE

James McConnell's retirement as a commercial artist after 50 years in the business was marked by a well-earned exhibition of some of his paintings for Corgi at the Illustrators' Gallery in London's Covent Garden, close to one of his studios. The show was enthusiastically reviewed by Barry Fantoni in *The Times* on 17 November 1976. That same year, McConnell was also given honorary membership of the Association of Illustrators.

He continued to take on occasional private commissions for horse portraits, and to paint landscapes and equestrian scenes for his own pleasure, through much of the 1980s, at a new home in Milford, Surrey. He had decided to move from his house in Bookham after the death of his wife. The old property, on which he had laboured so hard, came to hold too many poignant memories. Ann McConnell recalls that her father took with him cuttings from the bush of miniature roses that had provided the blooms for her mother's wedding bouquet. She did the same when she moved to Spain, and the bush continues to flourish in her garden. The miniature rose is a touching symbol of family love, but it is also an appropriate emblem of the beauty and modest scale of so much of James McConnell's artwork. It never shouted from gallery walls; it was small and perfectly formed – designed for prolonged private contemplation as much as for instant sales appeal.

When I visited James McConnell at his home in the autumn of 1991, he told me that

A bloom from McConnell's rose: the miniature marvel.

James E McConnell, photographed by his daughter Ann.

the deterioration of his eyesight had forced him to abandon painting a couple of years earlier. For someone who had drawn or painted almost every day since childhood, it must have been a devastating blow. As he entered his nineties, he had outlived his wives and nearly all of his friends, including Bob, with whom he had spent so many pleasant hours in The Cricketers. Bob had ended his days in a care home, and McConnell feared a similar fate. He valued his independence and the domestic haven that he had always laboured to create. It was fitting, then, that when he passed away on 4 May 1995 aged 91, it was at his own home. That thought was certainly a comfort to his daughter Ann:

> 'I was both heartbroken and relieved for him, that he died at his home, in his lovely garden, independent to the last. I guess that's what any of us want in the end but most are not so lucky. He died as he lived. An incredible free spirit, with an amazing talent.'

MINIATURE MARVELS

Three examples of the types of paintings that McConnell produced, as private commissions or for his own pleasure, in the years following his retirement from commercial illustrating. The picture at the top he titled 'Bucephalus'.

REFERENCES

[1] *T P's and Cassell's Weekly*, 1924. Quoted in Charles Rosner, *The Growth of the Book-Jacket*, London: Sylvan Press, 1954.

[2] V L Danvers, *Training in Commercial Art*, London: Sir Isaac Pitman and Sons, 1926.

[3] Colin Larkin, *Cover Me: The Vintage Art of Pan Books 1950-1965*, Canterbury: Telos Publishing, 2020, chapter 6.

[4] All quotes from McConnell are taken from his interview at his home in Surrey with the author on 28 September 1991.

[5] Christian Barman, 'The Return of Illustration', R B Fishenden (ed), *Penrose's Annual* 47, London: Lund-Humphries, 1953.

[6] Quoted in A J Hoppe, 'Book-Wrappers', A paper read to the Society of Bookmen, published in *The Publisher and Bookseller*, 5 August 1932.

[7] James McConnell's siblings were Norman (born c1900), Lewis (born c1902), Anthony (born c1905) and Elsie (born 1910).

[8] Notes on the Fox and Hounds supplied by West Newcastle Picture History Collection.

[9] benwell-and-scotswood-in-the-early-20th-century.pdf (wordpress.com)

[10] W R Maxwell-Foster, *Drawings for Advertisements, Book Illustrations etc.: How to prepare and sell them*, London: A.C. Black, 1928, p.48.

[11] W R Maxwell-Foster, *Drawings for Advertisements,* op cit.

[12] V L Danvers, *Training in Commercial Art*, London: Sir Isaac Pitman and Sons, 1926.

[13] John Harrison, 'Realism: The Art of Septimus Scott', *Commercial Art*, no.21, March 1928.

[14] F A Mercer and W Gaunt, *Posters and Publicity 1928*, London: The Studio, 1928, pp 4-5.

[15] Robert J Kirkpatrick, 'Nat Long', https://bearalley.blogspot.com/2018/09/nat-long.html

[16] Maxwell-Foster, *Drawings for Advertisements,* op cit, p.47.

[17] K O Fearon, 'The Book-Jacket as a Sales Aid', *Commercial Art* no. 39, September 1929.

[18] A J Hoppe, 'Book-Wrappers', op cit.

[19] *The Advertising Art Annual and Art Buyer's Guide 1939*, London: Business Publications, 1938.

[20] Donovan Candler, 'The Artist and his Agent', *The Penrose Annual* 39, London: Lund-Humphries, 1937.

[21] Maxwell-Foster, op cit, p 49.

[22] Tom Bookman, *National Newsagent, Bookseller and Stationer* 10 June 1939.

[23] Tom Bookman, *National Newsagent, Bookseller and Stationer* 11 November 1939.

[24] Virginia Woolf, *A Writer's Diary*, 10 September 1941 (London: The Hogarth Press, 1953).

[25] John Feather, *A History of British Publishing*. London: Routledge, 2006, p 196.

[26] Christine Campbell Thomson, *The Right Way to Write Successful Fiction*, London: Andrew George Elliot, 1946, p 86.

[27] John Sutherland, *Reading the Decades: Fifty Years of the Nation's Bestselling Books*, London: BBC, 2002, p 16.

[28] Sir Max Beerbohm, *The Observer*, 1949, quoted in Charles Rosner, *The Growth of the book-Jacket*, London: Sylvan Press, 1954.

[29] The police offensive against alleged obscenity in pulp paperbacks, which peaked decisively in 1954, is comprehensively documented in Steve Holland, *The Trials of Hank Janson*, Tolworth: Telos Publishing, 2004.

[30] See Steve Holland, 'Margot Bland', https://bearalley.blogspot.com/2013/11/margot-bland.html

[31] Stephen Mogridge, 'Get into this growing market: Paper Backs', *Newsagents Booksellers Review* 2 April 1955.

[32] 'Big boom in paper-backs – new market', *Newsagents Booksellers Review* 14 January 1956.

[33] *Paperbacks: A Reference Catalogue* June 1960 and *Paperbacks in Print May 1961: A Reference Catalogue*, London: J Whitaker.

[34] Interview with the author, September 1991.

[35] Historical Picture Archive – 'McConnell' historical pictures, Look and Learn.

[36] K O Fearon, 'The Book-Jacket as a Sales Aid', op cit.

[37] Geo A Stephen (City Librarian, Norwich), 'Publishers' Book-Jackets', *Penrose's Annual,* vol 26, 1924.

[38] G S Sandilands, 'Book Jackets', *Commercial Art*, vol 2, Jan-June 1927.

[39] A J A Symons, 'How the Jacket Sells the Book', *Art and Industry*, June 1937.

[40] In 1927, the going rate for the printing of 1,500 four-colour book jackets was £25 – or 4d each for a book probably retailing for 50-60d. Sandilands, 'Book Jackets', op cit.

[41] Donovan Candler, 'The Artist and his Agent', op cit.

[42] I M Parsons, 'Book Production To-day', *The Penrose Annual*, 40, London: Lund-Humphries, 1938.

[43] J J Seeley, *The Profitable Lending Library: How it should be run*, London: J J Seeley, 1937,

[44] Tom Bookman, *National Newsagent, Bookseller and Stationer,* 16 April 1938.

[45] Tom Bookman, *National Newsagent, Bookseller and Stationer,* 15 November 1937.

[46] Tom Bookman *National Newsagent* 28 January 1939.

[47] www.peterchaney.com/chapter-two

[48] Christine Campbell Thomson, *The Right Way to Write Successful Fiction*, London: Andrew George Elliot, 1946, p 72

[49] Colin Wilson, *Snobbery with Violence: English Crime Stories and their Audiences*, London: Eyre and Spottiswoode, 1971, p 95.

[50] Colin Wilson, *Snobbery with Violence*, op cit, p 98.

[51] The illustration of jackets for Hale's series of John D MacDonald novels was shared with John Pollack.

[52] Stephen Mogridge, 'There's profit in Paperbacks: Westerns are on the way up', *Bookseller and Stationer*, 27 September 1958.

[53] Rachel Anderson, *The Purple Heart Throbs: the sub literature of love*. London: Hodder and Stoughton, 1974, p 11.

[54] *The Writers and Artists' Year Book 1938*, London: A & C Black, 1938, p 26.

[55] Christine Campbell Thomson, *The Right Way to Write Successful Fiction*, op cit, p 50.

[56] Christine Campbell Thomson, *The Right Way to Write Successful Fiction*, op cit, p 81.

[57] Christine Campbell Thomson, *The Right Way to Write Successful Fiction*, op cit, p 94-5.

[58] David Ashford and Steve Holland compiled 'Illustrated Guides' to *Thriller Picture Library* (1991), *Super Detective Library* (1992) and *Cowboy Comics Library* (1993), all published in Colne, Lancashire by A & B Whitworth.

[59] Steve Holland, *Look and Learn: A History of the Classic Children's Magazine*, first published 2006 in PDF form on www.lookandlearn.com

BIBLIOGRAPHY

Presented below is a listing of all of McConnell's currently known book covers, arranged by publisher (with associated publishers grouped together) and then chronologically. Dates are given for when each piece was painted, where known from McConnell's work-book, and published. If a particular painting was used for more than one book, generally only the first use is listed, although a few significant exceptions are also noted. Where rows in the table have a grey background, this means the entry in question is either unconfirmed – i.e. the cover is listed in the artist's work-book but the author has been unable to locate a copy – or unidentified – i.e. the information in the work-book is insufficient to identify a publication. A hardback format book is indicated in the 'Published' column by 'h/b', a paperback by 'p/b' and a reprint by 'r/p'; pieces believed to have been unpublished are marked 'u/p'.

W H ALLEN, MARK GOULDEN and PINNACLE

AUTHOR	TITLE	PAINTED	PUBLISHED
Stetson Cody	Wolf Trail	11/1951	9/1953 p/b
Kurt Singer	Gentlemen Spies	11/1951	1952 h/b + 3/1953 p/b
Walter Gibson	The Boat	12/1951	(u/p – 1952 h/b is by another hand)
Stetson Cody	Cactus Justice	4/1952	1952 h/b + 5/1954 p/b
Harry Hervey	Red Ending	4/1952	1952 h/b
G W Henderson	Jule	6/1952	12/1952 p/b
Leonard Matters	Jack the Ripper	6/1952	12/1952 p/b
Horace Wyndham	Guilty or Not Guilty?	6/1952	1952 p/b
John Brown	Murder Each Way	6/1952	1953 p/b
Edgar Rice Burroughs	Tarzan and the Golden Lion	7/1952	11/1952 p/b
Edgar Rice Burroughs	Son of Tarzan	7/1952	11/1952 p/b
Edgar Rice Burroughs	Lost on Venus	8/1952	2/1953 p/b
Edgar Rice Burroughs	Thuvia Maid of Mars	8/1952	6/1953 p/b
Edgar Rice Burroughs	Tarzan the Terrible	9/1952	2/1953 p/b
Stetson Cody	Overland Guns	10/1952	1953 h/b
Edgar Rice Burroughs	Tarzan and the Ant Men	11/1952	6/1953 p/b
Leonard Gribble	Death Racket	12/1952	6/1953 p/b
Paul Evan Lehman	Range Justice	12/1952	1953 h/b
Burt Arthur	Action at Spanish Flats	12/1952	1953 h/b
Archie Lynn Joscelyn	Texas Outlaw	12/1952	1953 h/b
Art Nolan	The Jockey wore Black	1/1953	6/1953 p/b
Frances Barker	Peace my Daughters	3/1953	1953 p/b
Charles Francis Coe	Pressure	3/1953	9/1954 p/b
Freddy Ford	King of the Crooks	4/1953	9/1953 p/b
Frank Laskier	Unseen Harbour	4/1953	10/1953 p/b
Edgar Rice Burroughs	Outlaw of Torn	4/1953	9/1953 p/b
Edgar Rice Burroughs	The Warlord of Mars	4/1953	9/1953 p/b
Edgar Rice Burroughs	The Eternal Lover	4/1953	12/1953 p/b
Edgar Rice Burroughs	Tanar of Pellucidar	4/1953	10/1953 p/b
Edgar Rice Burroughs	Bandit of Hell's Bend	4/1953	1953 p/b
Edgar Rice Burroughs	The Gods of Mars	4/1953	12/1953 p/b
Lee Floren	Four Texans North	5/1953	1953 h/b
Bryn Jordan	War at Muffled Hoof	5/1953	1954 h/b
Frances Evans Baily	Love Rules the World	11/1953	1954 h/b
Edgar Rice Burroughs	Jungle Tales of Tarzan	11/1953	4/1954 p/b
Maurice Dekobra	The Man who Died Twice	12/1953	1954 h/b
Edgar Rice Burroughs	The Chessmen of Mars	1/1954	6/1954 p/b
Edgar Rice Burroughs	The Cave Girl	1/1954	5/1954 p/b
l Sprague De Camp	Rogue Queen	4/1954	9/1954 p/b
Ray Dorien	Light the Bright Candles	4/1954	1954 h/b
Frederic Goldsmith	Murder in Mayfair	4/1954	1954 h/b
Bryn Jordan	The Westering Kid	5/1954	1954 h/b
Lee Floren	Pistol Partners	5/1954	1954 h/b
Edgar Rice Burroughs	Pellucidar	5/1954	1/1955 p/b
Edgar Rice Burroughs	Mastermind of Mars	5/1954	1/1955 p/b
Francis Evans Baily	Lovely Lady	5/1954	1955 h/b
Warren O'Riley	Forbidding Canyons	8/1954	1955 h/b
Frederic Goldsmith	The Smugglers	9/1954	1955 h/b
Gladwell Richardson	Desperado's Range	10/1954	1955 h/b
Ray Dorien	Heart's Content	2/1955	1955 h/b

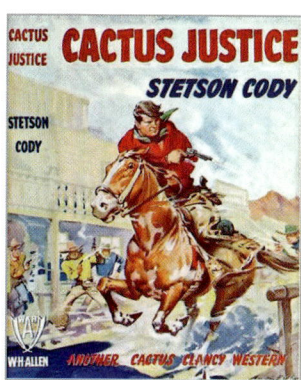

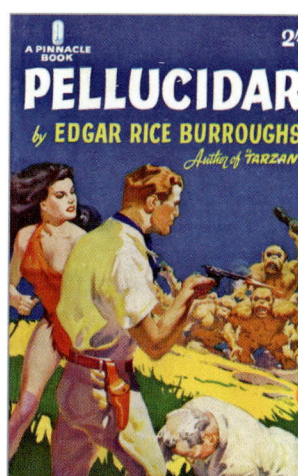

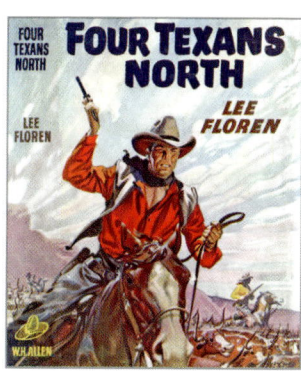

MINIATURE MARVELS

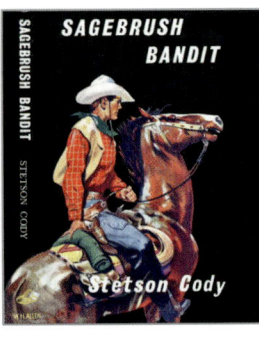

Stetson Cody	Branding Bullets	9/1955	1956 h/b
Lee Floren	Riders in the Storm	3/1956	1956 h/b
Stetson Cody	Moon River Outlaw	3/1956	1957 h/b
Gladwell Richardson	Western Justice	12/1956	1957 h/b
Warren O'Riley	Mountain Ambush	12/1956	1957 h/b
Stetson Cody	Gunsmoke at Necktie	4/1957	1957 h/b
Gladwell Richardson	Monument Pass	4/1957	1958 h/b
Warren O'Riley	Wild Vermilion	4/1957	1957 h/b
Russ Hardy	Hidden Gold	5/1957	1957 h/b
Edgar Rice Burroughs	Tarzan the Invincible	12/1957	1958 p/b
Edgar Rice Burroughs	Tarzan Lord of the Jungle	12/1957	1958 p/b
Edgar Rice Burroughs	Tarzan and the Lost Empire	12/1957	1958 p/b
Edgar Rice Burroughs	Tarzan and the Foreign Legion	12/1957	1958 p/b
Viola Castang	The Invisible Cord	4/1958	1958 h/b
Stetson Cody	Double X Ranch		1958 h/b
Stetson Cody	Sagebrush Bandit		1959 h/b

AMALGAMATED PRESS and FLEETWAY

Key: WL = Western Library; TCL = Thriller Comics Library, later TPL = Thriller Picture Library; SBL = Sexton Blake Library; CCL = Cowboy Comics Library, later CPL = Cowboy Picture Library; SDL = Super Detective Library. All are p/b.

AUTHOR	TITLE	LIBRARY/ NUMBER	PAINTED	PUBLISHED
Ernest Haycox	Whispering Range	WL 1	2/1950	4/1950
John Hunter	Quick on the Trigger	WL 2	2/1950	4/1950
John Hunter	The Guns of Lannagan	WL 3	2/1950	5/1950
Ernest Haycox	Trail Smoke	WL 4	3/1950	5/1950
George Owen Baxter	The Long Trail	WL 5	3/1950	6/1950
T C H Jacobs	Texas Stranger	WL 6	4/1950	6/1950
Ernest Haycox	Starlight Rider	WL 7	4/1950	7/1950
George Owen Baxter	Wooden Guns	WL8	5/1950	7/1950
Frank C Robertson	Rustlers on the Loose	WL 9	5/1950	8/1950
	(Romance title)	Oracle Library?	4/1950	
John Hunter	The Trail Leads to Lannagan	WL 10	5/1950	8/1950
Barry Ford	Gun-Shy!	WL 11	5/1950	9/1950
Ernest Haycock	Deep West	WL 12		9/1950
John Hunter	Lannagan's Luck	WL 13	7/1950	10/1951
Amos Moore	Danger Rides the Desert	WL 14	7/1950	10/1950
John Hunter	Go For Your Guns, Lannagan!	WL 15	8/1950	11/1950
Ernest Haycox	Smoky Pass	WL 16		11/1950
Denver Bardwell	Coyote Hunter	WL 17	8/1950	12/1950
Stone Cody	Dangerous Gold	WL 18	11/1950	12/1950
John Hunter	Look Behind You, Lannagan!	WL 22	11/1950	2/1951
Stone Cody	Five Against the Law	WL 24	10/1950	3/1951
John Hunter	Lannagan's Law	WL 25	1/1951	4/1951
William Colt MacDonald	The Riddle of Ramrod Ridge	WL 26		4/1951
George Owen Baxter	Red Hawk	WL 27	2/1951	5/1951
Denver Bardwell	Storm Ranch	WL 28	2/1951	5/1951
John Hunter	Lannagan Strikes it Rich	WL 29	3/1951	6/1951
Peter Field	Law Badge	WL 30	3/1951	6/1951
Frank Howe	Call for Colt Carey	WL 31	4/1951	7/1951
William Mcleod Raine	Square Shooter	WL 32	4/1951	7/1951
John Hunter	Lannagan's Hunch	WL 33	5/1951	8/1951
William K Reilly	Riders of Dry Gulch	WL 34	5/1951	8/1951
Ernest Haycox	Sundown Jim	WL 36	6/1951	9/1951
John Hunter	Lannagan Gets Hired	WL 37	7/1951	10/1951
Stone Cody	Desert Silver	WL 38	7/1951	10/1951
John Langley	Riders of Red Range	WL 39	8/1951	11/1951
William Mcleod Raine	Sorreltop	WL 40	8/1951	11/1951
	Dick Turpin – King of the Road *	TCL 22	8/1951	9/1952
Rex Quintin	Wildcat's Folly	WL 41	9/1951	12/1951
Charles Alden Seltzer	The Range Boss	WL 42	9/1951	12/1951
John Hunter	Lannagan Loads His Guns	WL 43	10/1951	1/1952
Ernest Haycox	Rim of the Desert	WL 44	10/1951	1/1952
Stone Cody	Outlaw Posse	WL 45	11/1951	2/1952
Mike M'Cracken	The Bounty Man	WL 46	11/1951	2/1952
James Marshall	Border Gold	WL 47	11/1951	3/1952
Clarence E Mulford	Bar 20 Days	WL 48	11/1951	3/1952
John Langley	Heir to Bar 60	WL 49	1/1952	4/1952
Claude Rister	Trail of the Blood-Mark	WL 50	1/1952	4/1952
Buck Billings	Lawless Guns	WL 51	2/1952	5/1952

* Intended for TCL2, but used later?

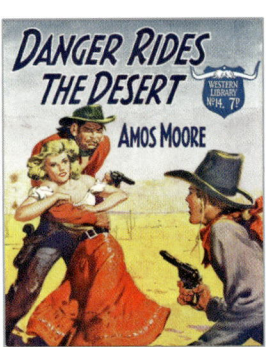

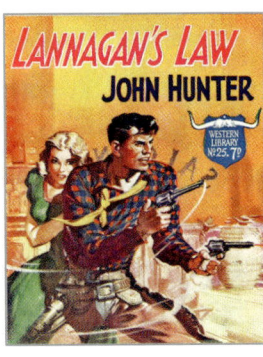

John Hunter	Lannagan Versus Trouble	WL 52	2/1952	5/1952
Jackson Cole	Black Gold	WL 53	3/1952	6/1952
Rex Quintin	Marked Bullets	WL 54	3/1952	6/1952
Mike M'Cracken	Cheyenne Joe	WL 55	4/1952	7/1952
Max Patrick	One-Way Trail	WL 56	4/1952	7/1952
John Hunter	Odds Against Lannagan	WL 57	5/1952	8/1952
James Marshal	Black Rider	WL 58	5/1952	8/1952
T C H Jacobs	Guns for Hire	WL 59	6/1952	9/1952
John Langley	Kit of Slash-K	WL 60	6/1952	9/1952
Stone Cody	Gun Smoke Cure	WL 61	7/1952	10/1952
John Hunter	Lannagan Horns In	WL 62	7/1952	10/1952
Clarence E Mulford	The Outlaw Orphan	TPL 17		07/1952
Hugh R Oldham	Carson's Girl	WL 63	8/1952	11/1952
Mike M'Cracken	The Dog Men	WL 64	8/1952	11/1952
Rex Quinton	Round-Up	WL 65	9/1952	12/1952
Max Patrick	Hold-Up Guy	WL 66	9/1952	12/1952
Richard Doddridge Blackmore	Lorna Doone	TCL 47	9/1952	1953
James Marshal	Outlaw Buttes	WL 67	10/1952	1/1953
Walter Tyrer	Stampede!	WL 68	10/1952	1/1953
J Vincent Nolan	The Lucky Chance	WL 69	11/1952	2/1953
Jackson Cole	Lone Star Legion	WL 70	11/1952	2/1953
Anthony Parsons	The Case of The Prince's Diary	SBL 285	12/1952	1953
Rex Hardinge	The Secret of The Fated Family	SBL 286	12/1952	1953
T C H Jacobs	Lone Adventure	WL 75	2/1953	5/1953
John Langley	Colorado Trail	WL 76	2/1953	5/1953
Mike M'Cracken	Kiowa Man	WL 79	4/1953	7/1953
Geo E Rochester	The Guy From Kansas	WL 80	4/1953	7/1953
Anthony Parsons	The Case of The Unknown Heir	SBL 295	4/1953	1953
Hugh Clevely	The Girl from Toronto	SBL 296	4/1953	1953
Max Patrick	Last Drive	WL 83	6/1953	9/1953
J Vincent Nolan	Range Rider	WL 84	6/1953	9/1953
John Hunter	Lannagan's Loot	WL 85	7/1953	10/1953
Stan Kenny	The Cheat	WL 87	8/1953	11/1953
John Hunter	Lannagan Hits Trouble	WL 88	8/1953	11/1953
Charles Wrexe	Vengeance Trail	WL 89	9/1953	12/1953
T C H Jacobs	Perilous Quest	WL 90	9/1953	12/1953
Anthony Parsons	The Secret of Sinister Farm	SBL 305	9/1953	1954
Rex Hardinge	The Lodging-House Mystery	SBL 306	9/1953	1954
	Hopalong Cassidy Rides In	TCL 55	8/1953	2/1954
James Marshal	Gunsmoke Valley	WL 93	11/1953	2/1954
Hugh R Oldham	The Six-Gun Dude	WL 94	11/1953	2/1954
Mike M'Cracken	The War Trail	WL 97	12/1953	4/1954
J Vincent Nolan	Gunsmoke at Sundown	WL 98	12/1953	4/1954
Rex Quintin	Say It with Guns	WL 99	1/1954	5/1954
John Hunter	Lannagan Fights Through	WL 101		6/1954
Max Patrick	Lynch Law	WL 102	1/1954	6/1954
	Buck Jones	CCL 126	12/1954	3/1955
	Kit Carson	CCL 128	12/1954	4/1955
	Buck Jones	CCL 132	2/1955	5/1955
	Buck Jones	CCL 135		6/1955
(Peter Meriton)	Captain Dack and the Mystery of Peril Island	SDL 55	4/1955	6/1955
	Forward, The Musketeers!	TCL 93	4/1955	7/1955
	Kit Carson	CCL 137		7/1955
	Buck Jones	CCL 141	5/1955	8/1955
	Buck Jones	CCL 144	6/1955	9/1955
	Buck Jones	CCL 147	7/1955	10/1955
	Buck Jones	CCL 150	8/1955	11/1955
	Buck Jones	CCL 153	9/1955	12/1955
	Buck Jones	CCL 156	10/1955	1/1956
	Buck Jones	CCL 159	10/1955	2/1956
	Buck Jones	CCL 162	11/1955	3/1955
(Robert W, Chambers)	Frontier Fury	TCL 120	10/1955	3/1956
	Buck Jones	CCL 164	12/1955	4/1956
	The Jaws of Terror	TCL 129	1/1956	5/1956
	Buck Jones	CCL 167	2/1956	5/1956
	Davy Crockett	CCL 168	2/1956	5/1956
	Buck Jones	CCL 170	2/1956	6/1956
	Under the Golden Dragon	TCL 132	2/1956	6/1956
	Davy Crockett	CCL 171	3/1956	6/1956
	Kit Carson	CCL 172	4/1956	6/1956
	Buck Jones	CCL 174	4/1956	7/1956
	Kansas Kid	CCL 176	4/1956	7/1956
	Buck Jones	CCL 178	4/1956	8/1956

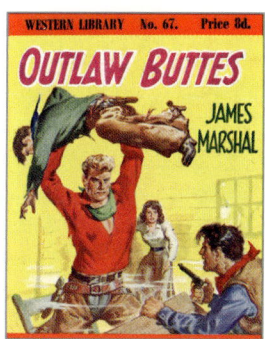

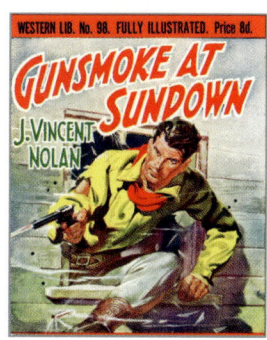

MINIATURE MARVELS

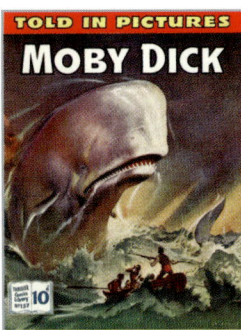

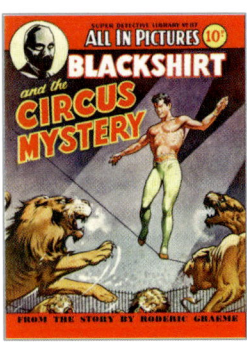

	Title	Ref		
	Kansas Kid	CCL 180	5/1956	8/1956
	Kit Carson	CCL 181	5/1956	9/1956
	Buck Jones	CCL 182	5/1956	9/1956
	Kansas Kid	CCL 184	6/1956	9/1956
	Kit Carson	CCL 185	6/1956	10/1956
	Buck Jones	CCL 186		10/1956
	Battler Britton – War Ace	TCL 160	7/1956	2/1957
	Kansas Kid	CCL 188	7/1956	10/1956
	Kit Carson	CCL 189	5/1956	11/1956
	Buck Jones	CCL 190	7/1956	11/1956
	Kansas Kid	CCL 192	7/1956	11/1956
	Kit Carson	CCL 193	8/1956	12/1956
	Buck Jones	CCL 194	8/1956	12/1956
	Davy Crockett	CCL 195	9/1956	12/1956
	Kansas Kid	CCL 196	8/ 1956	12/1956
	Moby Dick	TCL 157	8/1956	1/1957
	Buck Jones	CCL 198	10/1956	12/1956
	Kit Carson Annual 1957		10/1956	12/1956
	Davy Crockett	CCL 199	10/1956	1/1957
	Kansas Kid	CCL 200	9/1956	1/1957
	Kit Carson	CCL 201	8/1956	2/1957
	Cry Vengeance		9/1956	
	Buck Jones	CCL 202	10/1956	2/1957
	Davy Crockett	CCL 203		2/1957
	Captain Blood Sails Again	TPL 168	10/1956	2/1957
	Kansas Kid	CCL 204	9/1956	2/1957
	Kit Carson	CPL 205	12/1956	3/1957
	Davy Crockett	CPL 207	12/1956	3/1957
	Kansas Kid	CPL 208	1/1957	3/1957
	Kit Carson	CPL 209	1/1957	4/1957
	Buck Jones	CPL 210	1/1957	4/1957
	Davy Crockett	CPL 211	1/1957	4/1957
	Buck Jones Annual 1957 (cover + 5 col illus)		1-3 /1957	
	Knight of the Red Eagle	TPL 172		1957
	Kansas Kid	CPL 212	1/1957	4/1957
	Kit Carson	CPL 213	1/1957	5/1957
	Buck Jones	CPL 214	2/1957	5/1957
	Davy Crockett	CPL 215	2/1957	5/1957
	Kansas Kid	CPL 216	2/1957	5/1957
	Battler Britton Flies Again	TPL 179	3/1957	1957
	Buck Jones	CPL 218	3/1957	6/1957
	Davy Crockett	CPL 219	4/1957	6/1957
	Kansas Kid	CPL 220	4/1957	6/1957
	Kit Carson	CPL 221	5/1957	6/1957
	Buck Jones	CPL 222	4/1957	7/1957
	Davy Crockett	CPL 223	4/ 1957	7/1957
	Kansas Kid	CPL 224	5/1957	7/1957
	Kit Carson	CPL 225	5/1957	8/1957
	Buck Jones	CPL 226	5/1957	8/1957
	Davy Crockett	CPL 227	5/1957	8/1957
	Kansas Kid	CPL 228	5/1957	8/1957
	Kit Carson	CPL 229	6/1957	9/1957
	Buck Jones	CPL 230	6/1957	9/1957
	Rick Random in 'Sabotage from Space'	SDL 111	6/1957	9/1957
	Davy Crockett	CPL 231	7/1957	9/1957
	Kansas Kid	CPL 232	7/1957	9/1957
	Buck Jones Annual (cover + illus)		7-10 /1957	1957
	Kit Carson's Cowboy Annual 1958 (cover + illus)		7-10 /1957	1957
	Kit Carson	CPL 233	7/1957	10/1957
	Buck Jones	CPL 234	7/1957	10/1957
(Roderic Graeme)	Blackshirt and the Secret of Corey's Castle	SDL 113	8/1957	10/1957
Conrad Frost	Lesley Shane and the Jungle Treasure	SDL 114	7/1957	10/1957
	Rick Random and the S.O.S. from Space	SDL 115	8/1957	11/1957
	Davy Crockett	CPL 235	8/1957	10/1957
	Kansas Kid	CPL 236	8/1957	10/1957
	Buck Jones	CPL 238	8/1957	11/1957
	Battler Britton – Sky Commando	TPL 192	8/1957	1957
	Davy Crockett	CPL 239	8/1957	11/1957
	Kansas Kid	CPL 240	9/1957	11/1957
	Vic Terry and the Photo-Finish Mystery	SDL 116	9/1957	11/1957
	Kit Carson	CPL 241	9/1957	12/1957
	Buck Jones	CPL 242	9/1957	12/1957
	Davy Crockett	CPL 243	9/1957	12/1957

AUTHOR	TITLE		PAINTED	PUBLISHED
	Kansas Kid	CPL 244	9/1957	12/1957
(Roderic Graeme)	Blackshirt and the Circus Mystery	SDL 117	10/1957	12/1957
Conrad Frost	Lesley Shane and the Mystery of the Masks of Manton	SDL 118	10/1957	12/1957
	Kit Carson	CPL 245	10/1057	1/1958
	Buck Jones	CPL 246	10/1957	1/1958
	Davy Crockett	CPL 247	10/1957	1/1958
(Roderic Graeme)	Blackshirt and The King's Treasure	SDL 119	10/1957	1/1958
	Rip Kirby and The Man Who Stole a Million Dollars	SDL 120	11/1957	1/1958
	Kansas Kid	CPL 248	11/1957	1/1958
	Buck Jones	CPL 250	11/1957	2/1958
	Davy Crockett	CPL 251	11/1957	2/1958
	Rip Kirby in 'Duel with Danger'	SDL 122	11/1957	2/1958
	Kansas Kid	CPL 252	11/1957	2/1958
	Battler Britton and the Burma Buccaneers	TPL 200	11/1957	1958
(Roderic Graeme)	Blackshirt and the Island of Fear	SBL 121	12/1957	2/1958
	Kansas Kid	CPL 256	12/1957	3/1958
	Rick Random and the Planet of Terror	SDL 123	12/1957	3/1958
	Rip Kirby in 'Desert Fury'	SDL 124	1/1958	3/1958
(Roderic Graeme)	Blackshirt's Jungle Adventure	SDL 125	1/1958	4/1958
	Rip Kirby and the Runaway Lady	SDL 126	1/1958	4/1958
	Buck Jones	CPL 258	1/1958	4/1958
	Kansas Kid	CPL 264	1/1958	5/1958
Harry Harrison	Rick Random and the Space Pirates	SDL 127	2/1958	5/1958
	Robin Hood	TPL 243	2/1958	1958
	Buck Jones	CPL 266	2/1958	6/1958
	Rip Kirby and the Fatal Target	SDL 128	4/1958	5/1958
	Kit Carson	CPL 269	3/1958	7/1958
Harry Harrison	Rick Random's Perilous Mission	SDL 129	3/1958	6/1958
	Rip Kirby and the Race of Death	SDL 130	3/1958	6/1958
(Roderic Graeme)	Blackshirt and the Secret of the Devil's Ravine	SDL 131	4/1958	7/1958
	Kansas Kid	CPL 280	4/1958	9/1958
	Rip Kirby on Terror Island	SDL 132		8/1958
R Keston	Rick Random and the Mystery of the Frozen World	SDL 133	4/1958	8/1958
	Rip Kirby and the Clue of the Vanishing Gun	SDL 134	5/1958	8/1958
(Roderic Graeme)	Blackshirt and the Secret of the Sahara	SDL 135	6/1958	9/1958
	Rip Kirby's Dangerous Manhunt	SDL 136	6/1958	9/1958
	(Rip Kirby saving girl from car)		7/1958	(u/p?)
	(Rip Kirby escaping prison)		7/1958	(u/p?)
Harry Harrison	Rick Random and the Mystery of the Robot World	SDL 137	8/1958	10/1958
	Rip Kirby and the Trail of Terror	SDL 138	8/1958	10/1958
B Cocker and Conrad Frost	Rick Random and the Mystery of the Knights of Space	SDL 139	8/1958	11/1958
	Rip Kirby and the Man from Nowhere	SDL 142	9/1958	12/1958
	(Rip Kirby rolling boulder)		9/1958	(u/p?)
Harry Harrison	Rick Random and the Terror from Space	SDL 143	10/1958	1/1959
	Rip Kirby's Invitation to Danger	SDL 144	10/1958	1/1959
	Rip Kirby in 'Design for Murder'	SDL 146	12/1958	2/1959
	Rip Kirby and The Devil's Henchman	SDL 148	1/1959	3/1959
	Vic Terry and the case of The Haunted Racecourse	SDL 149	1/1959	4/1959
	Rip Kirby and the case of the Crooked Mile	SDL 150	1/1959	4/1959
	Rip Kirby and The Playground of Fear	SDL 152	2/1959	5/1959
	Rip Kirby and the Case of the Phantom Film star	SDL 154	3/1959	6/1959
	Buck Ryan in 'The House of Fear'	SDL 166	11/1959	1/1960
	Buck Ryan and the Secret Enemy	SDL 168	12/1959	2/1960
	Buck Ryan and the Four Faced Bandit	SDL 170	1/1960	3/1960
	Buck Ryan in 'Island of Refuge'	SDL 174	2/1960	5/1960
	Buck Ryan in 'Tunnel of Gold'	SDL 176	3/1960	6/1960
	Boys Annual (scouting, flags etc)	Fleetway	7/1960	
Various	The Lion Book of Speed	Fleetway	11/1961	1962
Various	Sue Day Annual	Fleetway	11/1961	1962
	Girls' Annual (holiday camp)	Fleetway	5/1962	
	Girls' Crystal Annual 1964	Fleetway	6/1962	1963
	Lion Annual 1965	Fleetway		1964
	Donald Campbell's Book of Record Breakers*	Fleetway		9/1965

* *Ranger* magazine gift

ERNEST BENN

AUTHOR	TITLE	PAINTED	PUBLISHED
James Rennie	Maverick Blood	3/1956	1956 h/b

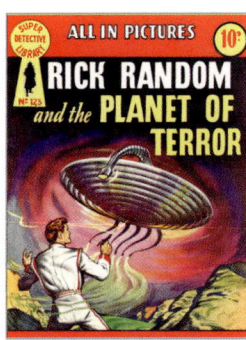
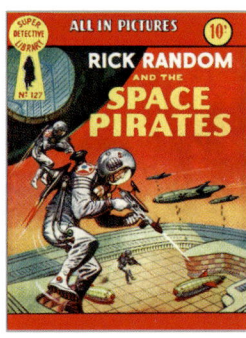

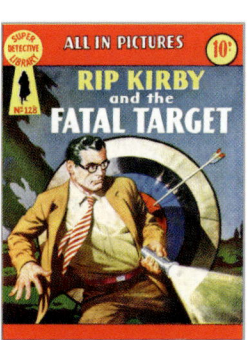
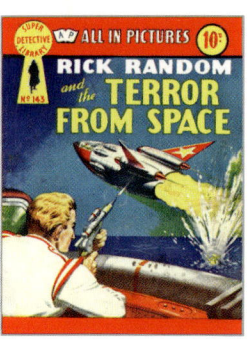

MINIATURE MARVELS

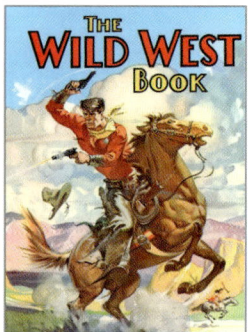

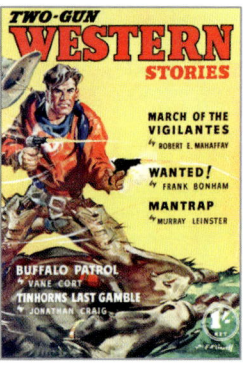

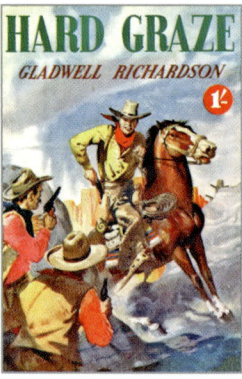

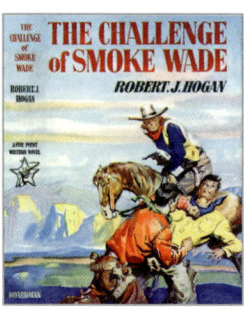

BIRN BROTHERS

AUTHOR	TITLE	PAINTED	PUBLISHED
Various	The Splendid Book for Boys	12/1947	1948 h/b
Various	Boys' Annual *	12/1947	
Various	The Circus Annual (Circus book) (cover + illus)	8/1948	1949
Anon	Farmyard Pictures	10/1949	1951
Arthur Groom	The Wild West Book (cover (gunman) + frontis)	11/1951	1952 h/b
Arthur Groom	The Wild West Book (cover (stage coach) + frontis)	9/1952-1/1953	1953 h/b
Arthur Groom	The Wild West Book (cover (brave) + frontis)	10, 11/1953	1954 h/b + ? p/b

* Possibly *The Modern Book for Boys*, with table-tennis player on cover

WILLIAM BLACKWOOD

AUTHOR	TITLE	PAINTED	PUBLISHED
John Thomas	Obstruction-Danger		1937 h/b
Gilbert Hackforth-Jones	No Less Renowned		1939 h/b

T V BOARDMAN

AUTHOR	TITLE	PAINTED	PUBLISHED
Rex Whitechurch	Renegade Road	4/1950 + 3/1952	1950 h/b + 8/1952 p/b
Tom Curry	The Comstock Lode	5/1950 + 7/1951	1950 h/b + 3/1952 p/b
Weston Clay	Range Town Renegade	5/1950	1950 h/b + 2/1952 p/b
Frank O'Rourke	Thunder on the Buckhorn	5/1950 + 3/1952	1951 h/b + 8/1952 p/b
Abel Short	Silver Spurs		1952 p/b
Gladwell Richardson	Rustlers' Moon	6/1950	1950 h/b + 2/1952 p/b
Gladwell Richardson	Sagebrush Sal	7/1950 + 7/1951	1951 h/b + 6/1952 p/b
Calico Jones	Foxfire Creek	7/1950 + 7/1951	1951 h/b + 6/1952 p/b
Frank O'Rourke	Blackwater	9/1950	1951 h/b
Lee Floren	Pioneer Printer	9/1950	11/1951 p/b
Bill Martin	Night Riders of Tonopah	10/1950	1951 h/b
Weston Clay	Boot Hill	10/1950 + 7/1951	1951 h/b + 2/1952 p/b
Murray Leinster	Fighting Horse Valley	10/1950	11/1951 h/b
Jackson Cole	The Death Riders	12/1950	11/1951 h/b
Murray Leinster	The Kid Deputy	1/1951	11/1951 h/b
Howard W Troyer	The Salt and the Savor	1/1951	1951 h/b
Chuck Martin	The Lobo Breed	1/1951	1951 h/b + 5/1954 p/b
Dave Waldo	The Man from Thunder River	2/1951	1951 h/b
Burt Arthur	Nevada	3/1951	1951 h/b
Weston Clay	Gunsmoke Bonanza	3/1951	12/1951 p/b
Various	Two-Gun Western Stories	3/1951	1952 pulp
Burt Arthur	Stirrups in the Dust	4/1951	1951 h/b
Gladwell Richardson	Hard Graze	5/1951	1951 h/b + 5/1954 p/b
Various	Six-Gun Western Stories	5/1951	1952 pulp
Weston Clay	Range Town Renegade	5/1951	1951 h/b + 2/1952 p/b
Lew Smith	Raiders of the White Pine	6/1951	12/1951 h/b
Weston Clay	Bar-M Boss	7/1951	1951 h/b
John Sims	The New Cowhand	7/1951	1951 h/b
Tom Gordon	The Fence Busters	8/1951	1952 h/b
Roe Richmond	Riders of Red Butte	10/1951	1952 h/b
Roe Richmond	Maverick Heritage	10/1951	1952 h/b
Mark Donovan	The Killer of K-Bar	10/1951	1952 h/b
Various	Six-Gun Western Stories	11/1951	2/1952 pulp
Rex Whitechurch	The Steel of the Torgons	12/1951	1952 h/b
Robert J Hogan	Two-Gun Law	1/1952	1952 h/b
Robert J Hogan	The Challenge of Smoke Wade	3/1952	1952 h/b
W F Bragg	Sagebrush Lawman	3/1952	1952 h/b
Duke Patterson	Block Diamond Round-Up	5/1952	1952 h/b
Frank O'Rourke	The Gun	6/1952	1952 h/b + 1952 p/b
Dave Waldo	Warbonnet	6/1952	1952 h/b
Rex Whitechurch	West of Wichita	10/1952	1953 h/b
Lee Wells	The Big Die	10/1952	1953 h/b
Gladwell Richardson	Paradise Range	10/1952	1953 h/b
Burt Arthur	The Killer	10/1952	1953 h/b
Roe Richmond	Mojave Guns	10/1952	1953 h/b
Paul Evan Lehman	This is my Range	11/1952	1953 h/b
Mark Donovan	Ticket to Remington	1/1953	1953 h/b
Dave Waldo	Ride on Stranger	1/1953	1953 h/b
Floyd Day	Call of the Owlhoot	3/1953	1953 h/b

BIBLIOGRAPHY

Gladwell Richardson	Quick Trigger	4/1953	1953 h/b
Kevin O'Malley	Copper Smoke	5/1953	1953 h/b
Lee E Wells	The Long Noose	7/1953	1953 h/b

BODLEY HEAD

AUTHOR	TITLE	PAINTED	PUBLISHED
	Trigger Slim	2/1955	
John Langley	Riders of the Red Range	2/1955	1955 h/b
Buck Coleman	Big Tracks	11/1955	1956 h/b

CASSELL

AUTHOR	TITLE	PAINTED	PUBLISHED
Christopher Bush	The Case of the Monday Murders		1936 h/b
Buck Billings	Trigger Pardners*		1937 h/b
Roy Norton	Big Jim		1937 h/b
Vingie E Roe	Guns of the Round Stone Valley		1937 h/b
Jackson Cole	Guns of the Silver Valley		1937 h/b
Tevis Miller	Riders of the Broken Circle		1937 h/b
C L Edholm	The Lone Cowboy		1937 h/b
Tobias Wagner	Turbulent Pendrayles		1937 h/b
Lucy Egerton	Courage in Gold		1937 h/b
Joan Sutherland	Thirsty Land		1937 h/b
Ned Andrews	Jerky		1938 h/b
Ethel M Dell	The Juice of the Pomegranate		1938 h/b
Charles Stoddard	North of the Stars		1938 h/b
Charles Stoddard	Trooper MacLean		1938 h/b
Renee Shann	Time to Go (pen and ink band)		1938 h/b
Christopher Bush	The Case of the Green Felt Hat		1939 h/b
Christopher Bush	The Case of the Flying Ass		1939 h/b
Q Patrick	Death and the Maiden		1939 h/b
Don Portbury	Brief Hour		1939 h/b
Tevis Miller	The Badman of VX Ranch		1939 h/b
Grant McAlpin	Shootin' Star		1939 h/b
Charles Stoddard	Wilderness Patrol		1939 h/b
Hugh Clevely	Archer Plus Twenty		1939 h/b
Hugh Clevely	Zero the 14th		1939 h/b
Hugh Clevely	Three Wooden Overcoats (same painting as above)		1939 h/b, 1941 r/p
Sax Rohmer	Salute to Bazarada*		1939 h/b
Hugh Clevely	The Gang Smasher Again*		1940 h/b
Erle Stanley Gardner	The Case of the Rolling Bones		1940 h/b
Charles North	Out of the Dog House		1940 h/b
Peter Field	The Man from Thief River		1941 h/b
John H Barrington	McCann the Rebel		1941 h/b
Clyde Davis	Nebraska Coast		1941 h/b
Ursula Bloom	Dinah's Husband		1941 h/b
Anne Duffield	The Inscrutable Nymph		1942 h/b
Anne Duffield	Sunrise		1944 h/b
Erle Stanley Gardner	Case of the Buried Clock	8/1945	1945 h/b
Vingie Eve Roe	Yukon Danger	6/1946	1947 h/b
Theodore Pratt	Mercy Island	9/1946	1946 h/b
	Old George	10/1946	
Brigid Knight	I Struggle and I Rise	12/1946	1947 h/b
G K Chesterton	The Father Brown Stories	1/1947	1949 h/b
	Song of the Years	1/1947	
Beryl Moore	Rapture of the Sea	1/1947	1947 h/b
Paul I Wellman	Angel with Spurs	2/1947	1948 h/b
Herbert Gorman	The Wine of San Lorenzo	4/1947	1948 h/b
Kenneth M Ellis	Guns Forever Echo	9/1947	1949 h/b
Louis Bromfield	Kenny	11/1947	1949 h/b
H L Davis	Harp of a Thousand Strings	11/1947	1949 h/b
Carol Ryrie Brink	Buffalo Coat	2/1948	1949 h/b
	The Builders	2/1948	
Barry Perowne	The Tilted Moon	4/1948	1949 h/b
Vingie E Roe	The Teamstress	11/1948	1949 h/b
R C Hutchinson	Elephant and Castle	12/1948	1949 h/b

* Unsigned; probably by McConnell

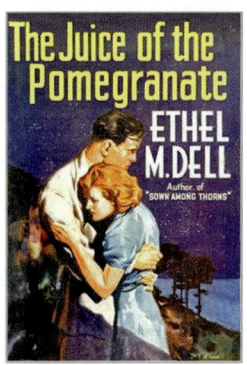
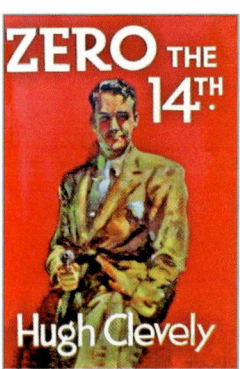
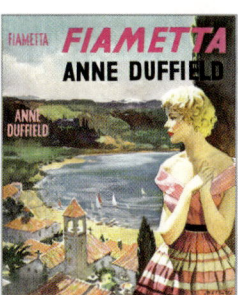
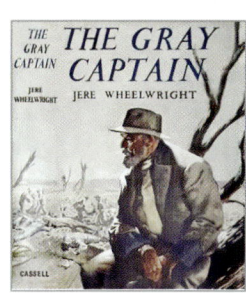

MINIATURE MARVELS

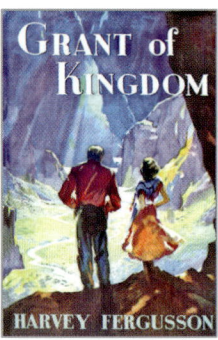
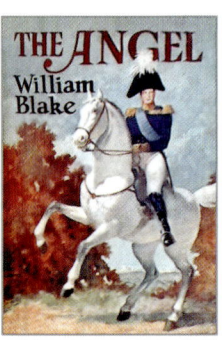
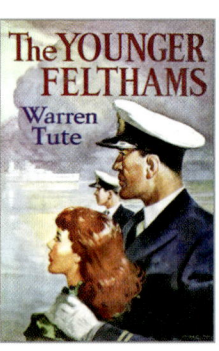

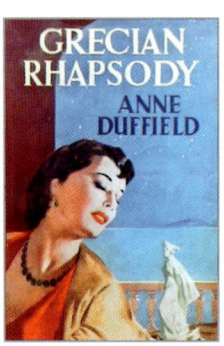

Author	Title	Date	Edition
Cecilie Leslie	Award of Custody	12/1948	1949 h/b
Louis Bromfield	The Wild Country	3/1949	1950 h/b
Constantine Fitz Gibbon	The Iron Hoop	6/1949	1950 h/b
Warwick Deeping	Old Mischief	6/1949	1950 h/b
Bernard Dryer	Port Afrique	6/1949	1950 h/b
Dorothy Black	The One I Love	6/1949	1950 h/b
Vingie E Roe	Slow White Oxen	7/1949	1950 h/b
Dorothy Black	The Stag at Bay	8/1949	1950 h/b
Ricardo Sicré	A Tap on the Left Shoulder	9/1949	1950 h/b
Warren Tute	The Felthams	9/1949	1950 h/b
Ross Macdonald	The Three Roads	9/1949	1950 h/b
Richard Jeremy	The Gale Brought Adventure	10/1949	1950 h/b
Thirza Eagle Nash	For Passion in Darkness	4/1950	1951 h/b
Beryl Moore	The Disenchanted	5/1950	1951 h/b
Harvey Fergusson	Grant of Kingdom	5/1950	1951 h/b
Nigel Morland	The Lady had a Gun	6/1950	1951 h/b
William Blake	The Angel	8/1950	1952 h/b
Warwick Deeping	Time to Heal	11/1950	1952 h/b
Nigel Morland	Call Him Early for the Murder	1/1951	1952 h/b
Neil McCallum	Fountainfoot	4/1951	(u/p – 1952 h/b is by another hand)
Sheila Kaye-Smith	Joanna Godden	6/1951	(u/p ?)
Sheila Kaye-Smith	Tamarisk Town	6/1951	1951 h/b
Glenda Spooner	Minority's Colt	9/1951	1952 h/b
Richard Ellington	Stone Cold Dead	10/1951	1952 h/b
Evelyn Eaton	By Just Exchange	10/1951	1952 h/b
Vingie E Roe	West of Abilene	10/1951	1952 h/b
Diana Raymond	Joanna Linden	11/1951	1952 h/b
Sheila Kaye-Smith	The Ploughman's Progress	12/1951	1952 h/b
Reginald Campbell & Peter Motte	Murder She Says	1/1952	1952 h/b
Ernest Raymond	The Corporal of the Guard	2/1952	1952 p/b
Sheila Kaye-Smith	The Hidden Son	2/1952	1952 p/b
G K Chesterton	Four Faultless Felons	2/1952	1953 p/b
Nigel Morland	Sing a Song of Cyanide	3/1952	1953 h/b
Anne Duffield	The Grand Duchess	9/1952	1953 h/b
Dorothy Black	The Blackthorn Winter	1/1953	1953 h/b
Peter Motte	Fell Clutch	2/1953	1956 h/b
Alec Waugh	Unclouded Summer *	2/1953	1953 h/b
Ethel M Dell	The Juice of the Pomegranate *		1953 h/b
Ethel M Dell	The Top of the World *		1954 h/b
Douglas V Duff	The Miracle Man	3/1953	1953 h/b
Paul Frischauer	The Shepherd's Crook	4/1953	1953 h/b
Warren Tute	The Younger Felthams	4/1953	1953 h/b
Tom Ronan	Vision Splendid	8/1953	1954 h/b
Vingie E Roe	Lost Trail	8/1953	1954 h/b
Peter Motte & Reginald Campbell	A Dog's Death	8/1953	1954 h/b
Anne Duffield	The Golden Summer	9/1953	1954 h/b
Mary Roberts Reinhart	The Frightened Wife	9/1953	1954 h/b
Igor Gouzenko	The Fall of a Titan †	12/1953	1954 h/b
Paul Ernst	The Bronze Mermaid	1/1954	1954 h/b
Rowland Winn	Carmela	2/1954	1954 h/b
Yvonne Seager	No Tears for Yesterday	6/1954	1954 h/b
Desmond Flower	Louis XIV at Versailles †	6/1954	1954 h/b
Nina Epton	The Valley of Pyrene	7/1954	1955 h/b
Ernest Raymond	The Nameless Places	7/1954	1954 h/b
Vincent Sheean	Lily	8/1954	1955 h/b
Elizabeth Eliot	Starter's Orders	10/1954	1955 h/b
Vingie E Roe	Tall Wheels of Oregon	11/1954	1955 h/b
Harvey Fergusson	The Conquest of Don Pedro	11/1954	1955 h/b
Anne Duffield	Come Back Miranda	12/1954	1955 h/b
T Rumsey Hamber	Closed Area	1/1955	1955 h/b
Frank O'Grady	The Golden Valley	1/1955	1955 h/b
Arthur L Hayward	A Book of Kings and Queens	2/1955	1955 h/b, 1960 r/p
Margaret Pratt	Show Them the Way to Go Home	2/1955 + 3/1955	1955 h/b ‡
	Portrait of George Gently **	2/1955	
Ethel M Dell	The Obstacle Race	4/1955	1955 h/b
Marjorie Stace	Blaze Royal	4/1955	1955 h/b
John Watson	Johnny Kinsman	4/1955	1955 h/b
Jere Wheelwright	The Gray Captain	4/1955	1955 h/b

* The jackets of these 1/- reissue editions of Cassell-published romances featured a generic McConnell illustration of Cupid.
† Scraper board illustrations.
‡ McConnell produced two different jacket paintings for this novel; it is assumed the second was used and the first was unpublished.
** This line drawing was for use on the back covers of a number of Alan Hunter's Inspector George Gently series crime novels.

AUTHOR	TITLE	PAINTED	PUBLISHED
F T Giles	A Rose for Marianne	5/1955	1955 h/b
Oreste Pinto	The Boys' Book of Secret Agents	6/1955	1955 h/b
George Greenfield	At Bay	7/1955	1955 h/b
Richard Ellington	It's a Crime	7/1955	1956 h/b
Derrick Nabarro	The Chariot of Desire	7/1955	1956 h/b
Tom Ronan	Moleskin Midas	7/1955	1956 h/b
Dorothy Black	Gentle Stranger	8/1955	1956 h/b
Sloan Wilson	The Man in the Grey Flannel Suit	8/1955	1956 h/b *
Anne Duffield	Glittering Heights	10/1955	1956 h/b
E Phillips Oppenheim	The Double Four	12/1955	1956 h/b
Anne Duffield	Fiametta	1/1956	1956 h/b
Sax Rohmer	The Island of Fu Manchu	1/1956	1956 h/b
Sax Rohmer	The Bride of Fu Manchu	1/1956	1956 h/b
Sax Rohmer	The Drums of Fu Manchu	2/1956	1956 h/b
Vingie E Roe	A Woman of the Great Valley	2/1956	1956 h/b
Theresa Charles	The Burning Beacon	2/1956	1956 h/b
Frank O'Grady	Goonoo, Goonoo	3/1956	1956 h/b
Neil Heaton	Home from the Office	5/1956	1956 h/b
Walter Westerfield Depew	Breakaway	6/1956	1958 h/b
Wallace Reyburn	Port of Call	7/1956	1957 h/b
Sax Rohmer	President Fu Manchu	8/1956	1957 h/b
Sax Rohmer	The Trail of Fu Manchu	8/1956	1957 h/b
Joan Pepper	Carola	8/1956	1957 h/b
Felix Jackson	So Help Me God	9/1956	1957 h/b
Anne Duffield	Karen's Memory	11/1956	1957 h/b
Anne Duffield	Grecian Rhapsody	1/1957	1957 h/b
Vingie E Roe	The Silver Herd	1/1957	1957 h/b
Pat Smythe	Jacqueline Rides for a Fall (cover + illus)	1/1957	1957 h/b + 1963 Armada p/b
Dorothy Black	The Loveless Marriage	4/1957	1958 h/b
Alan Phillips	The Living Legend	6/1957	1958 h/b
Elizabeth Harrower	The Long Prospect	7/1957	1958 h/b
Anne Duffield	Castle in Spain	10/1957	1958 h/b
Pat Smythe	Three Jays Against the Clock	11/1957	1958 h/b + 1963 Armada p/b
Thomas Armstrong	A Ring Has No End (cover + 6 illus)	1/1958	†
Pat Smythe	Three Jays on Holiday	4/1958	1958 h/b + 1963 Armada p/b
R M Bowker	A Boat of Your Own ‡	9/1958	(u/p)
Daniel Mannix	Kiboko	10/1958	1959 h/b
Jim Peters & Robert J Hoare	Spiked Shoes	10/1959	1959 h/b
Pat Smythe	Three Jays Go to Town	12/1958	1959 h/b + Armada p/b
Mike Hawthorn	Carlotti Joins the Team	1/1959	1959 h/b
Mike Hawthorn	Carlotti Takes the Wheel		1959 h/b
Pat Smythe	Three Jays Over the Border	10/1959	1960 h/b + 1966 Armada p/b
Anne Duffield	Violetta	11/1959	1960 h/b
Pat Smythe	Three Jays go to Rome	4/1960	1960 h/b
Pat Smythe	Three Jays Lend a Hand	5/1961	1961 h/b
Tom Ronan	Deep of the Sky	12/1961	1962 h/b
Robert Woollcombe	Winds of March	2/1962	1962 h/b
Wallace Reyburn	Good and Evil	2/1962	1962 h/b
Robert Murphy	The Haunted Journey	4/1962	1962 h/b
Sax Rohmer	Daughter of Fu Manchu	8/1962	1963 h/b
Charles Flood	Barren Hill	8/1962	1963 h/b
Patrick Raymond	A City of Scarlet and Gold	9/1962	1963 h/b
Kenneth Royce	The Angry Island	10/1962	1963 h/b
	Elephant Lover	1/1963	
Lord Montagu of Beaulieu	The Gordon Bennett Races	1/1963	1963 h/b
Sax Rohmer	The Mask of Fu Manchu	3/1963	
Douglas Lockwood	Fair Dinkum	5/1963	
Sax Rohmer	The Day the World Ended	11/1963	
Maggie Davis	The Far Side of Home	12/1963	1964
Kenneth Royce	Bones in the Sand	1/1967	1967 h/b

* Published jacket may not be by McConnell.
† Published with a cover by a different artist.
‡ Unused alternative cover.

CHAPMAN & HALL

AUTHOR	TITLE	PAINTED	PUBLISHED
Hugh Arnott	Mr Hyde		1939 h/b
Albert Payson Terhune	The Mystery of Grudge Mountain		1939 h/b
Philip Inman	Straight Runs Harley Street		1942 h/b
	Divorce of Course	8/1945	

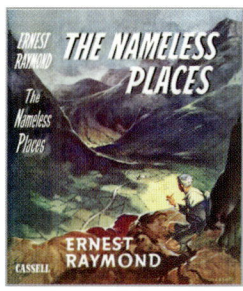
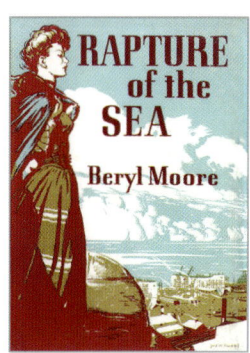
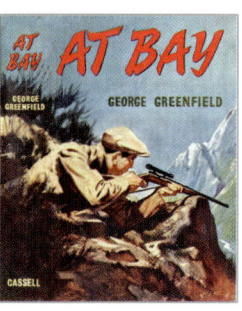

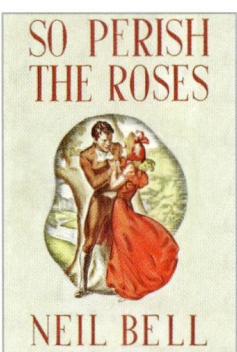
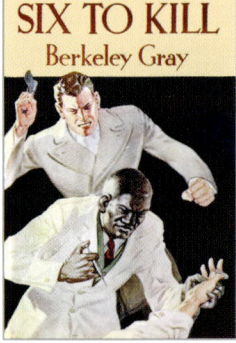
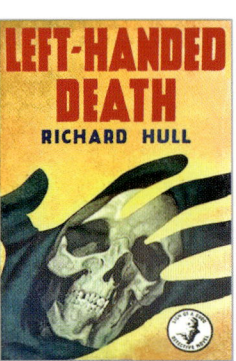
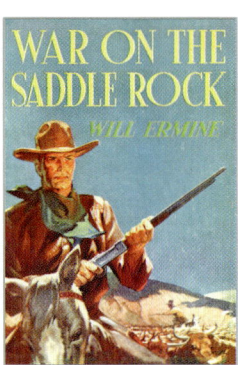

COLLINS

AUTHOR	TITLE	PAINTED	PUBLISHED
Peter Cheyney	This Man is Dangerous *		1936 h/b, 1950 r/p
David Hume	Call in the Yard †		1936 h/b
Stuart Cloete	Turning Wheels		1937 h/b
Clifford Dowdey	Bugles Blow No More		1937 h/b
Mary Howard	Partners for Playtime		1937 h/b
Charles Wesley Saunders	He Packed a Gun		1937 h/b
Rex Stout	Too Many Cooks		1938 h/b
Robert Ames Bennet	Cowboy Caballero		1938 h/b
Berkeley Gray	Mr Mortimer Gets the Jitters		8/1938 h/b, r/p x3
Berkeley Gray	Vultures Ltd		12/1938 h/b, r/p x2
A D Divine	Terror in the Thames		1938 h/b
Renee Shann	Time to Go *		1938 h/b
Evelyn Winch	Mankiller		1939 h/b
Neil Bell	The Abbot's Heel		7/1939 h/b
Berkeley Gray	Leave it to Conquest		10/1939 h/b, r/p x2
Berkeley Gray	Conquest Marches On		6/1939 h/b, r/p x3
Berkeley Gray	Miss Dynamite		3/1939 h/b, r/p x3
J M Walsh	Bullets for Breakfast		4/1939 h/b
J M Walsh	The King's Enemies		1939 h/b
Peter Cheyney	Dangerous Curves		1939 h/b
R W Thompson	Portrait of a Patriot		1939 h/b
James Barke	The Land of the Leal		1939 h/b, 1952 r/p
David Rame	Wine of Good Hope		7/39 h/b
Eugene Cunningham	Texas Triggers		1939 h/b
Eugene Cunningham	The Ranger Way		1939 h/b
B M Bower	A Starry Night		1939 h/b, 1940s r/p
Agnes Sligh Turnball	Remember the End		1939 h/b
David Hume	Death Before Honour ‡		1939 h/b
Victor Gunn	Footsteps of Death *		9/1939 h/b, 1940 r/p
Victor Gunn	Ironsides of the Yard *		4/40 h/b, r/p x2
David Hume	Invitation to the Grave *		1940
David Hume	Five Aces		1940
Miles Burton	Murder in the Coal Hole		1940 h/b
Neil Bell	So Perish the Roses		1940 h/b
Berkeley Gray	Meet the Don		5/1940 h/b, 1941 r/p
Berkeley Gray	Conquest Takes All		1/1940 h/b, r/p x2
Berkeley Gray	Six to Kill		8/1940 h/b, 1949 r/p
Frederick Niven	Mine Inheritance		1940 h/b
Peter Cheyney	You'd be Surprised *		1940 h/b, 1945 r/p
Pamela Wynne	Splendour of Love		1940 h/b
Betty Trask	The Sun Fades the Stars		1940 h/b
Thelma Strabel	Reap the Wild Wind		1941 h/b
Betty Trask	From Here to a Star		1941 h/b
Tom Gill	Jungle Harvest		1944 h/b
Ranger Lee	Just Dusty		1944 h/b
Ranger Lee	Outlaws of Ophir Creek	8/1945	1946 h/b
Will Ermine	Buckskin Marshal	9/1945	1946 h/b
Frank C Robertson	Hoofbeats in the Night	10/1945	1946 h/b, 1948 r/p
	Killer of Deusline Bar	11/1945	
Ranger Lee	The Valley Before Me	12/1945	1946 h/b, 1949 r/p
Richard Hull	Left-Handed Death (Crime Club)	12/1945	1946 h/b
Will Ermine	War on the Saddle Rock	12/1945	1946 h/b
Wade Smith	Rattlesnake	12/1945	1946 h/b
Berkeley Gray	Mr Ball of Fire	1/1946	6/1946 h/b
Ranger Lee	Short Grass Range	1/1946	1946 h/b, 1950 r/p
Marjorie Price	I Take What I Want	1/1946	1946 h/b
	Heads for romance cover	3/1946	
Norman Fox	Silent in the Saddle	4/1946	1946 h/b, 1949 r/p
Charles Franklin	Exit Without Permit	5/1946	1946 h/b
W C Tuttle	The Trouble Trailer	5/1946	1947 h/b
Gary Marshall	Mountain Money	5/1946	1947 h/b
Victor Gunn	Death on Shivering Sand	6/1946	1/1947 h/b
Hammond Innes	The Lonely Skier	7/1946	1947 h/b
Norman A Fox	The Valley of Vanishing Riders	7/1946	1947 h/b
Norman A Fox	Riders in the Rain		1947 h/b
Gary Marshall	Riding for the Diamond S	8/1946	1947 h/b

* Unsigned.
† Unsigned, possibly by McConnell.
‡ Unsigned, probably by McConnell.

Author	Title	Date	Reprint
Wade Smith	Three Masked Men	8/1946	1947 h/b
Ranger Lee	Flames in the Forest	8/1946	1947 h/b
Frank C Robertson	Boomerang Jail	9/1946	1947 h/b, 1949 r/p
Stephen Maddock	Exit Only	10/1946	1947 h/b
Laurence Meynell	The Evil Hour	11/1946	1947 h/b
Berkeley Gray	Killer Conquest	11/1946	4/1947 h/b, 1951 r/p
Arthur Hobart Mills	Don't Touch the Body	12/1946	1947 h/b
Norman Fox	Dead End Trail	12/1946	1947 h/b
Jackson Gregory	Lonely Trail	12/1946	1947 h/b
	The Adventures of Robin Hood	12/1946	1947 h/b
Chester Wills	Loot	3/1947	1947 h/b
Wade Smith	Land Beyond the Law	3/1947	1947 h/b
Gary Marshall	The Outsider	3/1947	1947 h/b
Jackson Gregory	Two in the Wilderness	4/1947	1947 h/b
Peter Dawson	High Country	4/1947	1947 h/b
Luke Short	Station West	4/1947	1947 h/b
Frank C Robertson	Man Bait	4/1947	1948 h/b
Berkeley Gray	The Conquest Touch	8/1947	1/48 h/b, 1951 r/p
Norman Fox	Cactus Cavalier	9/1947	1948 h/b
W C Tuttle	Straws in the Wind	12/1947	1948 h/b, 1951 r/p
Victor Gunn	Ironsides on the Spot	2/1948	8/1948 h/b
Gary Marshall	Copper Belt	2/1948	1948 h/b
Berkeley Gray	The Spot Marked 'X'	2/1948	10/1948 h/b, 1951 r/p
Frank C Robertson	Rope Crazy	3/1948	1948 h/b
	Children's Annual	4/1948	
Luke Short	High Vermilion	6/1948	1949 h/b
Victor Gunn	The Road to Murder	6/1948	1/1949 h/b
Wade Smith	Five Fingered Valley	7/1948	1949 h/b
Chester Wills	Silver on the Sage	7/1948	1949 h/b
Gary Marshall	Buffalo Valley	8/1948	1949 h/b
Frank C Robertson	Way of an Outlaw	8/1948	1949 h/b
Ranger Lee	Crimson Dust	10/1948	1949 h/b
Jackson Gregory	The Man from Painted Rock	10/1948	1949 h/b
Jackson Gregory	The Silver River	11/1948	1949 h/b
Berkeley Gray	Duel Murder	11/48	1949 h/b, 1952 r/p
J M Walsh	Time to Kill	2/1949	1949 h/b
Norman Fox	The Thirsty Land	4/1949	1950 h/b
Elizabeth Seifert	Pride of the South	5/1949	1950 h/b
Frank C Robertson	Road to Paint Rock	6/1949	1950 h/b
Various	The Treasure Box for Boys and Girls (cover + frontis)	6/1949	1950 h/b
Berkeley Gray	Dare-Devil Conquest	7/1949	2/1950 h/b, 1952 r/p
Luke Short	Ambush	7/1949	1950 h/b
Chester Wills	Shoot-up at Two Rivers	10/1949	1950 h/b
Ranger Lee	The Ranch in the Canyon	11/1949	1950 h/b
Gary Marshall	The Old Breed	12/1949	1950 h/b
Berkeley Gray	Seven Dawns to Death	3/1950	9/1950 h/b, 1953 r/p
Elizabeth Seifert	The Doctor Dares	3/1950	1950 h/b
Helena Grose	Poor Man's Darling	4/1950	1950 h/b
Peter Dawson	Renegade Canyon	4/1950	1950 h/b
Bart Spicer	The Dark Light	4/1950	1950 h/b
Bat Spicer	Blues for the Prince	6/1950	1950 h/b
Stephen Maddock	Public Mischief	6/1950	1951 h/b
Gary Marshall	Old Panther-Foot		1950 h/b
Victor Gunn	Murder on Ice	6/1950	2/1951 h/b
Frank C Robertson	Idaho Range	7/1950	1951 h/b
Various	The Treasure Box for Boys and Girls (cover + end paper + 11 illus)	8/1950	1951 h/b
Berkeley Gray	Operation Conquest	9/1950	3/1951 h/b, 1953 r/p
Ranger Lee	Wild Range Country	10/1950	1951 h/b
Elizabeth Seifert	The New Doctor	11/1950	1951 h/b
Frank C Robertson	Riders Against the Sky	1/1951	1951 h/b
Victor Gunn	The Borgia Head Mystery	1/1951	8/1951 h/b
	Treasure Box (cover + end paper)	2/1951	1951 h/b
Berkeley Gray	Conquest in Scotland	3/1951	10/1951 h/b, 1954 r/p
Frank C Robertson	Reach for the Skies	4/1951	1951 h/b
Wade Smith	Outlaws of Clover Valley	4/1951	1951 h/b
Bart Spicer	The Golden Door	5/1951	1951 h/b
Ranger Lee	The New Marshal	7/1951	1952 h/b
Norman A Fox	Tall Man Riding	7/1951	1952 h/b
Berkeley Gray	The Lady is Poison	10/1951	5/1952 h/b
Charles Franklin	No Other Victim	10/1951	1952 h/b
Stephen Maddock	Close Shave	11/1951	1952 h/b
Norman A Fox	Roughshod	11/1951	1952 h/b
Bart Spicer	Black Sheep, Run	12/1951	1952 h/b

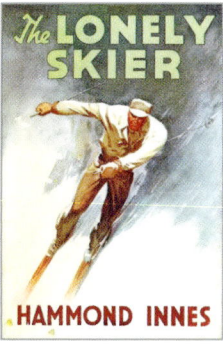

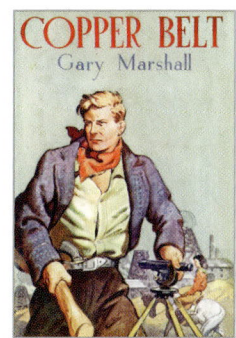
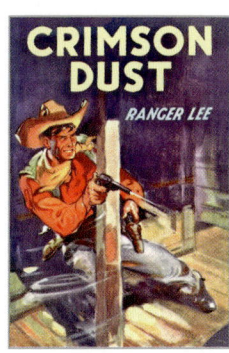
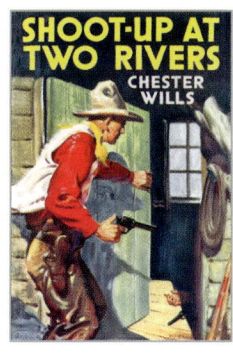

MINIATURE MARVELS

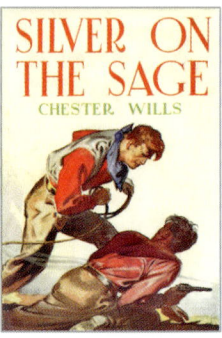

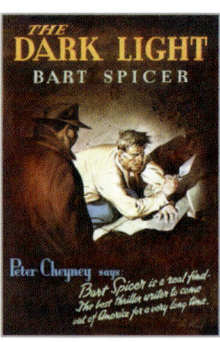

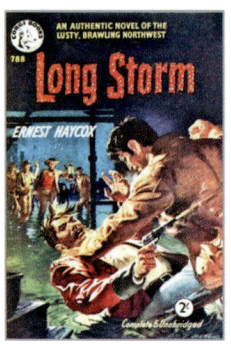

Chester Wills	The Devil's Trail	1/1952	1952 h/b
Gary Marshall	Mountain Gold	1/1952	1952 h/b
Frank C Robertson	Ride Out and Die	1/1952	1952 h/b
Victor Gunn	Death Comes Laughing	2/1952	8/52 h/b
Bart Spicer	Shadow of Fear	6/1952	1953 h/b
Berkeley Gray	The Half-Open Door	6/1952	2/1953 h/b, 1955 r/p
Frank C Robertson	Crooked Water	7/1952	1953 h/b
Chester Wills	Empty Guns	8/1952	1953 h/b
Bliss Lomax	Riders of the Buffalo Grass	10/1952	1953 h/b
Victor Gunn	The Whistling Key	12/1952	15/1953 h/b
Berkeley Gray	Target for Conquest	3/1953	10/1953 h/b, 1955 r/p
J Jefferson Farjeon	The Double Crime (Crime Club)	3/1953	1953 h/b
Victor Gunn	The Crooked Staircase	6/1953	1/1954 h/b
James Cody Ferris	X Bar X Ranch	6/1953	1954 h/b
Laurence Meynell	Give Me the Knife	8/1953	1954 h/b
Frank C Robertson	The Double Brand	8/1953	1954 h/b
Marjorie Warby	Kay Comes Home	8/1953	1954 h/b
Various	Whopper Cowboy Book	8/1953	1953 p/b
Various	Bumper Cowboy Book (same painting as above)	8/1953	1953 p/b
Mason Macrae	Coffin Canyon	8/1953	1954 h/b
Gary Marshall	Live Fence	10/1953	1954 h/b
Charles Franklin	Perchance to Kill	11/1953	1954 h/b
Berkeley Gray	Follow the Lady	11/1953	5/1954 h/b
Frank C Robertson	The Cruel Winds of Winter	2/1954	1954 h/b
Victor Gunn	The Crippled Canary	2/1954	8/1954 h/b, r/p x2
Berkeley Gray	Turn Left for Danger		5/1955 h/b, 1957 r/p
W C Tuttle	Thunderbird Range	4/1954	1955 h/b
Norman Fox	Broken Wagon	4/1954	1954 h/b, 1956 r/p
Berkeley Gray	Conquest Goes West	6/1954	11/1954 h/b
Ranger Lee	Panther Canyon	6/1954	1955 h/b
Peter Dawson	Dead Man's Pass	8/1954	1955 h/b
Gary Marshall	Lost Loot	8/1954	1955 h/b
Victor Gunn	The Laughing Grave	9/1954	3/1955 h/b
Ben Benson	Target in Taffeta	2/1955	1955 h/b
Lyndon Snow	Love Me Forever	3/1955	1955 h/b
Victor Gunn	The Painted Dog	3/1955	9/1955 h/b, 1958 r/p
Laura Conway	Enchantment	6/1955	1956 h/b
Hartley Howard	The Bowman Touch	6/1955	1956 h/b
Berkeley Gray	Conquest in Command	6/1955	1/1956 h/b, 1958 r/p
Ben Benson	The Burning Fuse	6/1955	1956 h/b
George Milner	The Scarlet Fountains	6/1955	1956 h/b
Marjorie Harding	Mask of Friendship	8/1955	1956 h/b
Victor Gunn	Dead Men's Bells	10/1955	5/1956 h/b, 1958 r/p
	The Adventures of Robin Hood (cover + illus?)	9/1956	1956 h/b
James Macnell	Mettle at Woomera (cover + illus)	7/1959	1961 h/b
Various	Collins Boys' annual (cover (possibly) + front papers)	7/1959	1960 h/b
Nelson Mapple	The Port Meriel Mystery	7/1960	1961 h/b

CONSTABLE

AUTHOR	TITLE	PAINTED	PUBLISHED
A t'Serstevens	Naked Gold *		5/1937 h/b
F Tennyson Jesse & H M Harwood	London Front		1940 h/b

* Possibly by McConnell.

CORGI

AUTHOR	TITLE	PAINTED	PUBLISHED
E E Halleran	Gunsmoke Valley (T56)	10/1952	7/1954 p/b
Clarence B Kelland	Desert Law (726)	10/1953	1954 p/b
Ernest Haycock	No Law and Order (T45)	11/1953	5/1954 p/b
Eleazar Lipsky	The People Against O'Hara (T51)	1/1954	6/1954 p/b
Walter Noble Burns	The Saga of Billy the Kid (T88)	8/1954	2/1955 p/b
Ernest Haycox	Long Storm	5/1955	1956 p/b
Hanley Wellman	Fort Sun Dance (T138)	7/1955	12/1955 p/b
E E Halleran	The Outlaw (T172)	8/1955	6/1956 p/b
Oliver La Farge	Cochise of Arizona (J20)	9/1955	3/1956 p/b
Richard Parker	The 3 Pebbles (J27)	11/1955	6/1956 p/b
Henry Treece	Legions of the Eagle (J31)	12/1955	7/1956 p/b

Willard Price	South Sea Adventure (J33)	1/1955	8/1956 p/b
Ernest Haycox	Return of a Fighter (T193)	3/1956	9/1956 p/b
Frank Crisp	Devil Diver (J39)	3/1956	9/1956 p/b
Ernest Haycox	Canyon Passage (T215)		12/1956 p/b
Max Brand	Smiling Desperado (T221)	6/1956	1/1957 p/b
	Book of Cowboys	8/1956	(u/p?)
Lee Wells	The Raw Country (The Big Die) (T469)	5/1957	10/1957 p/b
Dorothy Gardiner	The Great Betrayal (G483)	6/1957	12/1957 p/b
L P Holmes	Somewhere They Die (T496)	7/1957	1957 p/b
Max Brand	The Jackson Trail (S510)	8/1957	2/1958 p/b
Will Cook	Apache Ambush (T519)	9/1957	3/1958 p/b
MacKinlay Kantor	Arouse and Beware (S563)	10/1957	7/1958 p/b
Lee Leighton	Beyond the Pass (T540)	12/1957	5/1958 p/b
Clay Fisher	The Blue Mustang (562)	12/1957	7/1958 p/b
Max Brand	The Galloping Broncos (T550)	12/1957	8/1958 p/b
Lee Leighton	Law Man (T573)	12/1957	8/1958 p/b
Paul I Wellman	Death on the Prairie	1/1958	1958 p/b
Bennett Foster	Man Tracks (T601)	3/1958	10/1958 p/b
A B Guthrie	These 1,000 Hills (S600)	4/1958	10/1958 p/b
A B Guthrie	The Big Sky	4/1958	(u/p?)
A B Guthrie	The Way West	4/1958	1958 p/b
Paul I Wellman	Death in the Desert (S610)	4/1958	11/1958 p/b
Max Brand	South of the Rio Grande (T623)	5/1958	12/1958 p/b
Gene Markey	Kingdom of the Spur (S621)	6/1958	12/1958 p/b
Helga Moray	Dark Fury (G640)		3/1959 p/b
W R Burnett	Pale Moon (S660)	7/1958	3/1959 p/b
Richard Llewellyn	Flame of Hercules (S623)	9/1958	3/1959 p/b
Conrad Richter	The Light in the Forest (T672)	9/1958	4/1959 p/b
Ernest Haycox	Riders West (S685)	9/1958	5/1959 p/b
Bennett Foster	Dust of the Trail (S694)	9/1958	6/1959 p/b
Luke Short	Summer of the Smoke (T696)	11/1958	6/1959 p/b
C William Harrison	Unarmed Killer (T708)	1/1959	7/1959 p/b
David Lavender	Bent's Fort	1/1959	9/1959 p/b
Max Brand	The Tenderfoot (SW719)		9/1959 p/b
Walter Van Tilburg Clark	The Ox-Bow Incident (SW720)	1/1959	9/1959 p/b
Conrad Richter	The Sea of Grass (SW732)	2/1959	11/1959 p/b
E E Halleran	Wagon Captain (SW730)	2/1959	11/1959 p/b
Charles Marquis Warren	Only the Valiant (GW750)	2/1959	11/1959 p/b
Charles Marquis Warren	Valley of the Shadow (SW749)	2/1959	11/1959 p/b
Chad Merriman & Lee Leighton	Colorado Gold (SW771)	5/1959	1/1959 p/b
Hans Habe	Agent of the Devil (GN754)	5/1959	12/1959 p/b
Ernest Haycox	The Earthbreakers (SW788)	6/1959	2/1960 p/b
Max Brand	Outlaw Breed (SW782)	6/1959	2/1960 p/b
Max Brand	The Big Trail (SW836)	6/1959	6/1960 p/b
Fred Grove	Sun Dance (SW803)	7/1959	3/1960 p/b
Felix Holt	Big Eli (The Gabriel Horn) (SW808)	7/1959	4/1960 p/b
Clay Fisher	River of Decision (The Crossing) (SW802)	8/1959	3/1960 p/b
John Prebble	The Spanish Stirrup (SW805)	9/1959	3/1960 p/b
Jackson Burgess	Pillar of Cloud (GW815)	9/1959	4/1960 p/b
E E Halleran	The Hostile Hills (SW814)	9/1959	4/1960 p/b
Western Writers of America	Holsters and Heroes (SW830)	9/1959	5/1960 p/b
Chad Merriman	The Avengers (SW831)	9/1959	5/1960 p/b
Irwin R Blacker	Westering (GW838)	10/1959	6/1960 p/b
Elmore Leonard	Stand on the Saber (Lawless River) (SW847)	11/1959	7/1960 p/b
Ernest Haycox	Trail Town (SW864)	12/1959	7/1960 p/b
Ernest Haycox	The Long Storm (SW866)	12/1959	7/1960 p/b
Ernest Haycox	Whispering Range (SW867)	1/1960	7/1960 p/b
Ernest Haycox	The Wild Bunch (SW865)	1/1960	7/1960 p/b
Wade Everett	Fort Starke x 2 (SW878)	2-4/1960	1960 p/b
Ernest Haycox	Man in the Saddle (SW877)	2/1960	8/1960 p/b
Ernest Haycox	Trail Smoke (SW876)	2/1960	8/1960 p/b
Will Henry	The Seven Men at Mimbres Springs (SW849)	3/1960	7/1960 p/b
Thomas B Costain	Black Rose (FN870)	3/1960	8/1960 p/b
Will Henry	No Survivors (GW887)		1960 p/b
Merle Constiner	Last Stand at Anvil Pass (SW888)	4/1960	9/1960 p/b
Max Brand	Trail Partners (SW905)	5/1960	10/1960 p/b
Dale Van Every	The Scarlet Feather (GW906)	5/1960	10/1960 p/b
Wade Everett	First Command (SW935)	5/1960	12/1960 p/b
A B Guthrie	The Way West (GW908)	5/1960	10/1960 p/b
Lorenzo Madalena	Gino (Confetti for Gino) (GN920)	5/1960	11/1960 p/b
Ethel Hueston	Star of the West (GW915)	6/1960	11/1960 p/b
Forrester Blake	Johnny Christmas (GW923)	6/1960	11/1960 p/b
Oliver Strange	Sudden (GW941)	7/1960	1/1961 p/b

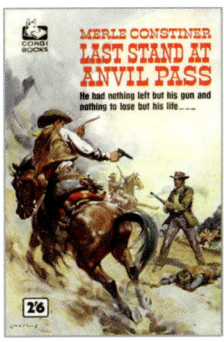
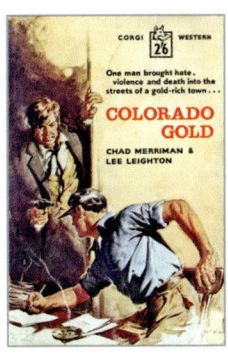

MINIATURE MARVELS

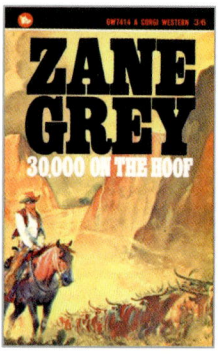

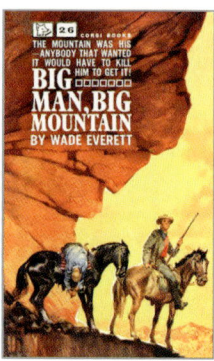

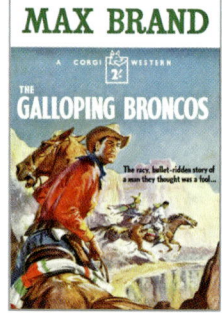

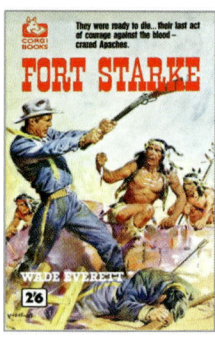

Eric Allen	The Man Who Chose Death (SC947)	8/1960	1/1961 p/b
E E Halleran	Spanish Ridge (SW963)	8/1960	1961 p/b
Fredric Brown	One for the Road (SC884)	8/1960	1/1961 p/b
Jack Schaefer (ed)	Out West: Volume One (GW964)	8/1960	1961 p/b
Milton Lott	The Last Hunt	8/1960	1961 p/b
Oliver Strange	Sudden – The Marshal of Lawless (SW975)	9/1960	1961 p/b
M E Chaber	A Hearse of Another Colour (SC972)	9/1960	1961 p/b
Logan A Forster	Proud Land (GW974)	9/1960	1961 p/b
William Everett Cook	Killer Behind a Badge (SW986)	10/1960	1961 p/b
Mike Brewer	Man in Danger (SC984)	10/1960	1961 p/b
Oliver Strange	Sudden Plays a Hand (SW991)	11/1960	1961 p/b, r/p x 6
Chad Merriman	Stampede (SW999)	11/1960	1961 p/b
Clay Fisher	Warbonnet (SW1001)	11/1960	1961 p/b
Max Brand	Blood on the Trail (SW1012)	12/1960	1961 p/b
Llewellyn Perry Jones	Hill Smoke	12/1960	1961 p/b
Oliver Strange	Sudden - Goldseeker (SW1026)	1/1961	1961 p/b
Jack Schaefer (ed)	Out West: Volume Two (GW1038)	2/1961	1961 p/b
Oliver Strange	Sudden Makes War (SW1050)	2/1961	1961 p/b
John Prebble	The Buffalo Soldiers (GW1049)	3/1961	1961 p/b
James Keene	Iron Man, Iron Horse (SW1062)	3/1961	1961 p/b
Dorothy M Johnson	Indian Country (SW1061)	3/1961	1961 p/b
Oliver Strange	Sudden Rides Again (GW1082)	3/1961	1961 p/b
Kenneth E Shiflet	The Valiant Strain (SW1093)	3/1961	1961 p/b
Lowell Bair (ed)	The Memoirs of Casanova (GG1071)	5/1961	1961 p/b
Robert Wilder	God has a Long Face	5/1961	1961 p/b
Borden Chase	Red River (SW1081)	5/1961	1961 p/b
Max Brand	Lucky Larribee (SW1094)	6/1961	1961 p/b
Paul I Wellman	Bronco Apache (SW1105)	7/1961	1961 p/b
James B Hall	Racers to the Sun (GN1099)	7/1961	1961 p/b
Oliver Strange	Sudden Takes the Trail (SW1116)	8/1961	1961 p/b
William R Cox	Comanche Moon (SW1106)	8/1961	1961 p/b
Oliver Strange	Sudden – The Range Robbers (GW1141)	9/1961	1962 p/b
Mike Brewer	Man on the Run	10/1961	1962 p/b (u/p? – photo cover used)
Oliver Strange	Sudden – The Law of the Lariat (SW1165)	11/61	1962 p/b
Wade Everett	Big Man, Big Mountain		1962 p/b
Zane Grey	30,000 on the Hoof *		1966 p/b
Zane Grey	The Thundering Herd (GW7344) †		1966 p/b
Frank O'Rourke	Latigo (0-552-10407) ‡		1977 p/b
Frank O'Rourke	Violence at Sundown (0-552-10430) **		1977 p/b
Frank O'Rourke	Gun Hand (0-552-10461) ††		1977 p/b

* Repurposed from the cover for *Man Tracks* by Bennett Foster.
† Repurposed from the cover for *Red River* by Borden Chase.
‡ Repurposed from the cover for *Spanish Ridge* by E E Halleran.
** Repurposed from the cover for *Sudden – The Marshal of Lawless* by Oliver Strange.
†† Repurposed from the cover for *The Saga of Billy the Kid* by Walter Noble Burns.

DAKERS

AUTHOR	TITLE	PAINTED	PUBLISHED
Thomas B Dewey	As Good as Dead	2/1952	1952 h/b
William O'Farrell	Harpoon of Death	10/1952	1953 h/b
Thomas B Dewey	Every Bet's a Sure Thing	5/1953	1953 h/b

JOHN DENNIS

AUTHOR	TITLE	PAINTED	PUBLISHED
Margaret Cameron	The Wilful Jade	5/1951	1952 h/b
Margaret Cameron	Blaze of Glory	12/1951	1952 h/b

DIGIT

AUTHOR	TITLE	PAINTED	PUBLISHED
Vernon Warren	Appointment in Hell *		1/1957 p/b
Lozania Prole	The King's Pleasure *		4/1957 p/b
Harold Robbins	A Stone for Danny Fisher		5/1957 p/b
Mansell Black	Steps in the Dark		7/1957 p/b
Vernon Warren	Brandon Returns *		8/1957 p/b
Vernon Warren	Brandon Takes Over *		9/1957 p/b

* Adapted cover.

AUTHOR	TITLE	PAINTED	PUBLISHED
Robert Cole	Vengeance Trail		9/1957 p/b
Vivian Connell	The Chinese Room		9/1957 p/b
Vernon Warren	Brandon in New York *		10/1957 p/b
Gerard Phillips	Rustler's Rule		11/1957 p/b
Vernon Warren	No Bouquets for Brandon *		11/1957 p/b
Charles Walters	Marshal from Dodge City (D272)		7/1959 p/b
Cliff Howe	Lovers and Libertines (G403)	7/1960	1960 p/b
F Yeats Brown	Bengal Lancer (R409)	7/1960	11/1960 p/b
Vivian Connell	The Chinese Room (R419)	8/1960	12/1960 p/b
Norman Gear	The House of Ruby Wogan (R418)	8/1960	12/1960 p/b
Frank Swinnerton	The Woman from Sicily (G439)	9/1960	1/1961 p/b
Marguerite Steen	The Bulls of Parral (G453)	11/1960	10/1961 p/b
Thomas Burke	Limehouse nights (R486)	1/1961	5/1961 p/b
Jasper Croft	Pagan City (G483)	1/1961	5/1961 p/b
Arthur Freeman	Cleopatra: Queen of Kings (R496)	2/1961	6/1961 p/b
George Moore	Esther Waters (G500)	2/1961	6/1961 p/b
D M Priestley	The Sinking Sands (R502)	2/1961	7/1961 p/b
George Foster	The Oldest Profession (R510)	2/1961	7/1961 p/b
Edgar Wallace	The Lone House Mystery (R517)	3/1961	8/1961 p/b
John Lodwick	Myrmyda (R516)	3/1961	1961 p/b
Edgar Wallace	Eve's Island (R528)	5/1961	9/1961 p/b
Brian Connell	Return of the Tiger (R524)	5/1961	9/1961 p/b
Jack Caplan	From Gorbals to Jungle (R530)	6/1961	10/1961 p/b
Ellery Anderson	Banner over Pusan (R534)	6/1961	10/1961 p/b
Olivia Leigh	Nell (R537)	7/1961	11/1961 p/b
Francis Reid	Resistance Fighter (R541)	7/1961	11/1961 p/b
Edgar Wallace	The Woman from the East (R566)	10/1961	10/1962 p/b
Pearl S Buck	Bright Procession (R569)	10/1961	6/1962 p/b
Pearl S Buck	Voices in the House (R568)	10/1961	6/1962 p/b
Robert Louis Stevenson	Dr Jekyll and Mr Hyde (R581)		1962 p/b
Edward Gaitens	The Gorbals Story (R582) †		5/1962 p/b
H G Wells	The Sea Lady (R592) †		5/1962 p/b
Guy De Maupassant	The Best of Maupassant (R594)		5/1962 p/b
Sir Arthur Conan Doyle	A Study in Scarlet (R604)		7/1962 p/b

* Adapted cover.
† Unsigned, probably by McConnell.

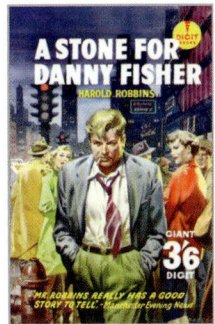
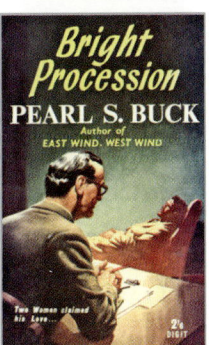
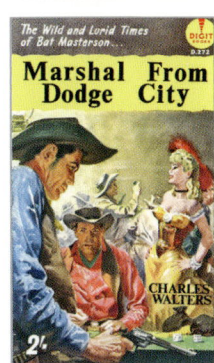

ELDON

AUTHOR	TITLE	PAINTED	PUBLISHED
Thornton Hill	Rory Grant Rodeo King	4/1946	(u/p – 1946 h/b is by Nat Long)
Ruth Alexander	The Wrecker	5/1951	1951 h/b

FABER & FABER

AUTHOR	TITLE	PAINTED	PUBLISHED
Colin de la Mare (ed)	The Ghost Book		1931 h/b, r/p x 3
Various	My Best Detective Story		1931 h/b, r/p x 8
Hanns Gobsch	Death Rattle		1932 h/b
Ronald Knox & H Harrington (eds)	Best Detective Stories (First Series)		1933 (2nd ed) h/b, r/p x 7
Various	Best Detective Stories (Second Series)		1933 (2nd ed) h/b, r/p x 7
F O Mann	Young George		1934 h/b
Norman Lindsay	Redheap		1934 h/b
Various	Best Mystery Stories		1937 h/b
William Roughead	Famous Crimes		1935 h/b
Julia Hart Lyon	Women Must Love		1937 h/b, r/p x 4

FEATHERSTONE

AUTHOR	TITLE	PAINTED	PUBLISHED
E T Portwin	The Limping Wolf	10/1945	1946 h/b

FICTION HOUSE

AUTHOR	TITLE	PAINTED	PUBLISHED
Webb Anders	Tornado Range (#nn)		5/1951 p/b
Webb Anders	Hell-Town Buster		7/1951 p/b

MINIATURE MARVELS

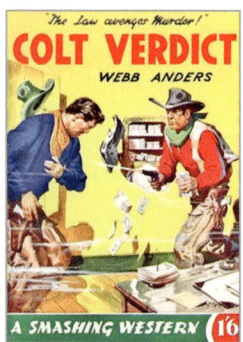
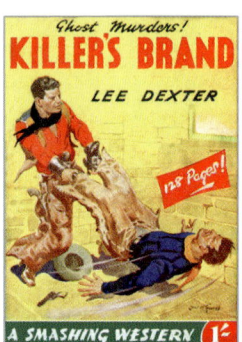
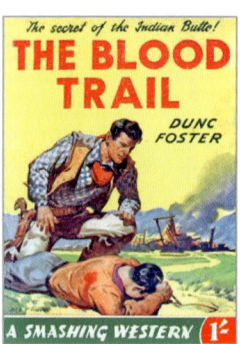
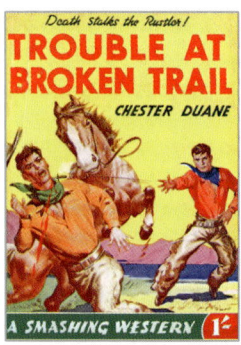

Author	Title		
Bryn Jordan	Trail Fever		7/1951 p/b
J Vincent Nolan	Gun-Toter	3/1951	9/1951 p/b
Jamie Boyd	Owl-Hoot Trail (#nn)	4/1951	9/1951 p/b
Webb Anders	Lawless Valley Feud	5/1951	10/1951 p/b
Bryn Jordan	Border Bandit	5/1951	11/1951 p/b
Chester Duane	Vengeance Trail (#nn)	6/1951	11/1951 p/b
Webb Anders	Rattlesnake Ranch (#188)	7/1951	1/1952 p/b
Pete Tolson	Dead Mule Valley	7/1951	1/1952 p/b
Pctc Tolson	Gold-Strike Range (#187)	8/1951	1/1952 p/b
Lee Anderson	Treachery Trail		2/1952 p/b
Dunc Foster	Gun Toting Prodigal	10/1951	2/1952 p/b
Wal Leonard	Nevada Pay-Off (#nn)	10/1951	2/1952 p/b
Pete Tolson	The Gringo Kid	12/1951	4/1952 p/b
Ross Dexter	Guns of the Black Duke (#197)	1/1952	4/1952 p/b
Lee Damaron	Snake in the Mesquite (#198)	1/19952	4/1952 p/b
Lee Dexter	Whistling Ranger	1/1952	6/1952 p/b
Dunc Foster	Six-Gun Vengeance	2/1952	6/1952 p/b
Dunc Foster	Trouble Shooter		6/1952 p/b
Ross Dexter	Man from Montana (#nn)	3/1952	6/1952 p/b
Trent McCoy	Justice in the Canyon	3/1952	6/1952 p/b
Dunc Foster	Colt Justice	3/1952	9/1952 p/b
Webb Anders	Bandit Gold	3/1952	9/1952 p/b
Dunc Foster	The Blood Trail	3/1952	9/1952 p/b
Lee Anderson	Killer's Gold	4/1952	9/1952 p/b
Wes Saunders	Lone Rider	4/1952	10/1952 p/b
Webb Anders	Hangnoose Law	5/1952	10/1952 p/b
Ross Dexter	Two-Gun Deputy		10/1952 p/b
Chester Duane	Trouble at Broken Trail	5/1952	10/1952 p/b
Ross Dexter	The Black Duke Rides Again	5/1952	1953 p/b
Wes Saunders	Vengeance Valley	6/1952	1/1953 p/b
Don Lawrence	Triangle T (nn)	8/1952	1/1953 p/b
Webb Anders	Colt Verdict	8/1952	1/1953 p/b
Chester Duane	Gallows Rock Guardian		1/1953 p/b
Ross Dexter	Killer's Brand	9/1952	2/1953 p/b
Chester Duane	Gunsmoke Guardian (#213)	10/1952	2/1953 p/b
Trig Elroy	Thunder Mesa	10/1952	2/1953 p/b
M LeBrun	The Corpse Clocks In	11/1952	1953 p/b, 1959 r/p
Don Lawrence	Gun Wizard	11/1952	2/1953 p/b
Webb Anders	Rail-Road Rustlers (#151)	11/1952	6/1953 p/b
Ross Dexter	Dead Man's Dinero (#152)	12/1952	6/1953 p/b
Chester Duane	Boss of Bullhide (#153)	1/1953	6/1953 p/b
Lee Dexter	Bandit's Booty (#154)	1/1953	6/1953 p/b
Webb Anders	Killer's Canyon (#156)	3/1953	9/1953 p/b
Pete Tolson	Pardners (#155)	3/1953	9/1953 p/b
Wal Leonard	The Buckaroo Rides Out (#157)	3/1953	9/1953 p/b
Lee Anderson	Trigger Pay Off (#158)	4/1953	9/1953 p/b
Wes Saunders	Texas Gunfighter (#160)	5/1953	10/1953 p/b
Cleve Canfield	Border Marshal (#159)	5/1953	10/1953 p/b
Lee Dexter	The Lawless Breed (#161)	7/1953	10/1953 p/b
F Allan Dunn	Prairie Justice (#162)	7/1953	10/1953 p/b
Webb Anders	20 Bar Outcast (#164)	9/1953	1/1954 p/b
Dunc Foster	Montana Showdown (#163)	9/1953	1/1954 p/b
E Z Frank	Dead City Round-Up (#165)	10/1953	1/1954 p/b
Tex Brander	Coyote Valley Pay-Off (#166)	10/1953	1/1954 p/b
Don Lawrence	Trigger Trouble (#167)	11/1953	3/1954 p/b
N Wesley Firth	Guns of Caliope (#168)	11/1953	3/1954 p/b
Roy L Meyers	The Man They Couldn't Kill	11/1953	1954 p/b
Ross Dexter	Scout in Buckskin (#237)	11/1953	5/1954 p/b
Webb Anders	Outlaw Round-Up (#169)	1/1954	5/1954 p/b
Earl Garrett	The Law Man (#170)	1/1954	7/1954 p/b
Lee Dexter	High, Wide and Handsome (#171)	2/1954	7/1954 p/b
Lee Anderson	Outlaws' Gulch (#174)	4/1954	7/1954 p/b
Earle Garrett	Herd Patrol (#179)	8/1954	1/1955 p/b
Trent McCoy	Rail Road Renegade (#180)	8/1954	1/1955 p/b
Webb Anders	Trouble Mesa	10/1954	6/1955 p/b
Vern Hanson	Trail Wolves	10/1954	6/1955 p/b
Earle Garrett	The Tinhorn (#189)	11/1954	8/1955 p/b
Don Lawrence	Lawless Legion (#190)	11/1954	8/1955 p/b
J Vincent Nolan	Trail Drive (#192)	4/1955	9/1955 p/b
Vern Hanson	The Sundown Riders (#191)	4/1955	9/1955 p/b
Wes Sanders	Poison Springs Feud (#1956)	6/1955	11/1955 p/b
Bud Williams	Double-Crossing Ramrods (#195)	6/1955	11/1955 p/b
Trent McCoy	Outlaws of the Range	8/1955	1/1956 p/b

BIBLIOGRAPHY

John Hornby	Red-Hot Triggers	8/1955	1/1956 p/b
Blair Wesson	In the Badlands	9/1955	2/1956 p/b
Earle Garrett	Range War	9/1955	2/1956 p/b
Vern Hanson	Colt Harvest (#209)	11/1955	7/1956 p/b
Webb Anders	Wyoming War Cry	11/1955	7/1956 p/b
Wes Sanders	The Canyon Killer	1/1956	9/1956 p/b
Mike Fallon	The Honest Texan	1/1956	9/1956 p/b
Lee Anderson	Dead Man's Gold	2/1956	11/1956 p/b
Earle Garrett	Saddletramp	2/1956	11/1956 p/b
Trig Elroy	Brand of the Sixty-Seven	3/1956	1/1957 p/b
Rex Horton	Blue Feather	3/1956	4/1957 p/b
Pete Tolson	Badman (#220)	3/1956	1/1957 p/b
Don Lawrence	The Straight 8 Segundo (#224)	3/1956	4/1957 p/b
Wes Sanders	Gunhand (#228)	11/1956	1957 p/b
George Hampden Edwards	Blue Sage and Gunsmoke (#227)	11/1956	1957 p/b
	Stagecoach to Santa Fe	3/1957	(u/p?)
	Guns of Lobo	3/1957	(u/p?)
	Arizona Feud	3/1957	(u/p?)
	Gun Trap Valley	3/1957	(u/p?)

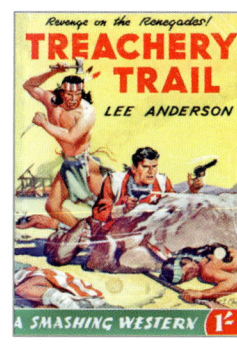

FOULSHAM

AUTHOR	TITLE	PAINTED	PUBLISHED
Chuck Stanley	The San Antonio Mail	9/1945	1946
Barry Cord	Trail Boss from Texas	4/1948	1948 h/b
Hugh Holman	Up This Crooked Way	6/1949	1951 h/b
Hugh Holman	Another Man's Poison	6/1949	1950 h/b + 1951 p/b
Lynn Westland	Texas Red	1/1951	1951 h/b + p/b
Calico Jones	Prairie Wind	1/1951	1951 h/b
Tom Roan	Lawless Old Wyoming	9/1951	1952
Tom Roan	The Gun Ghost	9/1951	1952 h/b
Charles Stoddard	Oregon Highroad	5/1954	1954
Barry Cord	Trail to Sundown	5/1954	1954
Charles Stoddard	The Golden Arrow	7/1954	1956 p/b
Larry Regan	Prairie Pioneer	7/1954	1956 h/b + 1957 p/b
Charles Stoddard	The Rider of Pecos Valley	4/1956	1957
Barry Cord	The Rustlers of Dry Range	4/1956	1956 p/b
Larry Regan	Oregon Trail Rider	11/1956	1957 p/b
Lauran Paine	Texas Revenge	4/1957	1957
Charles Stoddard	The Caribou Patrol	4/1957	1957 h/b
Chuck Stanley	Trouble in Texas *		1961

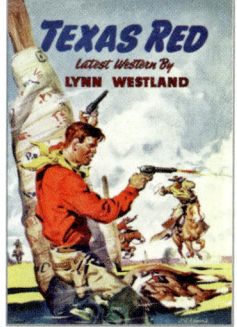

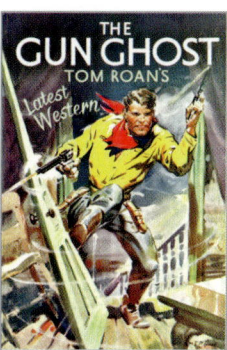

* Reuses art from T*he Gun Ghost* by Tom Roan

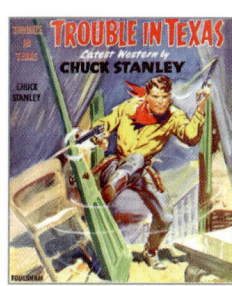

FOUR SQUARE (Landsborough Publications)

AUTHOR	TITLE	PAINTED	PUBLISHED
Pearl S Buck	The Patriot (#98)	12/1957	2/1959 p/b
Alex Weissberg	Advocate for the Dead (#131)	12/1957	6/1959 p/b
Pearl S Buck	Dragon Seed (#90)	12/1957	1958 p/b
Arthur Koestler	Darkness at Noon (#86)	12/1957	1959 p/b
Mary Durack	Keep Him My Country (#111)	10/1958	4/1959 p/b
Bill Parks	The Mestizo (#148)	2/1959	8/1959 p/b
Frank Yerby	The Treasure of Pleasant Valley (#160)	2/1959	9/1959 p/b
Hilary St, George Saunders	The Green Beret (#153)	4/1959	8/1959 p/b
Jan De Hartog	The Spiral Road (#173)	3/1959	10/1959 p/b
Thomas Armstrong	A Ring Has No End	6/1959	1960 p/b
Dan Cushman	The Silver Mountain (#203)	8/1959	2/1960 p/b
James D Horan	The Wild Bunch (#210)	8/1959	3/1960 p/b
John Gilbert	Zig-Zag (#272)	12/1959	1/1961 p/b
Howard Fast	The Last Frontier (#666)	1/1962	1962 p/b
Elmer Kelton	Donovan	2/1962	1962 p/b
Frank Yerby	The Garfield Honour	3/1962	1964 p/b
	Nigger Dan	4/1962	
	Hordingen's Fire	4/1962	

MINIATURE MARVELS

GANNET

AUTHOR	TITLE	PAINTED	PUBLISHED
Brett Cameron	The Cautious Caballero	2/1954	9/54 p/b
Brett Cameron	Guns of San Rosala	2/1954	9/54 p/b
	Weird Stories	2/1954	(u/p?)
	Dick Turpin	3/1954	(u/p?)
'Corporal'	Desert Sortie	3/1954	1954 p/b
	Foreign Legion cover	3/1954	(u/p?)
Hank McCoy	Wild Horse Range	5/1954	1954 p/b
	Death Wagon	5/1954	(u/p?)

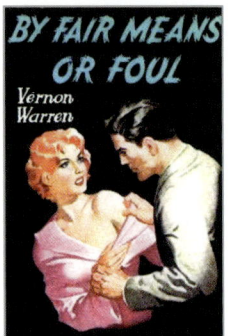

GAYWOOD

AUTHOR	TITLE	PAINTED	PUBLISHED
Tex Ryland	Bushwhacked	4/1948	1948 p/b

JOHN GIFFORD (JG) and FOYLES THRILLER BOOK CLUB (TBC)

AUTHOR	TITLE	PAINTED	PUBLISHED
Vernon Warren	Brandon Takes Over	1/1953	JG 1953 h/b, TBC r/p
Vernon Warren	Brandon in New York	4/1953	JG 1953 h/b, TBC r/p
Vernon Warren	Brandon Returns	7/1953	JG 1954 h/b, TBC r/p
Vernon Warren	The Blue Mauritius	9/1953	JG 1954 h/b, TBC r/p
Alexander Alderson	The Subtle Minotaur	10/1953	JG 1954 h/b, TBC r/p
Vernon Warren	No Bouquets for Brandon	10/1954	JG 1955 h/b, TBC r/p
Zane Grey	Wyoming	2/1955	(u/p?)
Vernon Warren	Bullets for Brandon	3/1955	JG 1955 h/b, TBC r/p
Vernon Warren	Appointment in Hell	11/1955	JG 1956 h/b, TBC r/p
Vernon Warren	Three Steps to Hell	11/1955	JG 1957 h/b, TBC r/p
Vernon Warren	By Fair Means or Foul	4/1956	JG 1956 h/b, TBC r/p
Vernon Warren	Mister Violence	3/1957	JG 1957 h/b, TBC r/p
Vernon Warren	Runaround	8/1957	JG 1958 h/b, TBC r/p

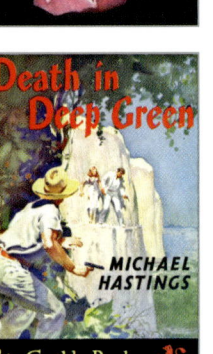

GUILD

AUTHOR	TITLE	PAINTED	PUBLISHED
Frank Harris	Montes the Matador	11/1951	1952 p/b
Michael Hastings	Death in Deep Green	1/1953	1953 p/b
George Arnaud	The Wages of Fear	2/1953	1953 p/b
C S Forester	Death to the French	3/1953	1953 p/b
Hugh Clevely	No Peace for Archer	4/1953	1953 p/b
Sax Rohmer	The Mystery of Fu-Manchu		1953 p/b
Gypsy Rose Lee	The Striptease Murders	5/1953	1953 p/b

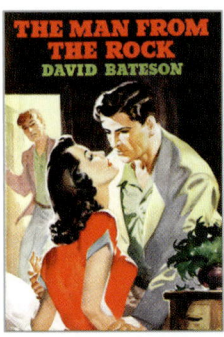

ROBERT HALE

AUTHOR	TITLE	PAINTED	PUBLISHED
Rob Eden	Love or Money		1936 h/b
Ivor Brown	Marine Parade *		1937 h/b
Hermina Black	Break with the Past		1939 h/b
Joan Kennedy	Paradise Calling *		1939 h/b
Margaret Ferguson	Blossom in the Dust		1939 h/b
Margaret Ferguson	The Man She Trusted		1939 h/b
Mary Richmond	Barbed Wire		1941 h/b
Rob Eden	Carol's Love Affair		1941 h/b
Rob Eden	Trapped by Love		1941 h/b
Ursula Bloom	The Golden Flame		1941 h/b
Hilda Hewett	Joy's Bonfire		1942 h/b
Ursula Bloom	Marriage in Heaven		1943 h/b, 1949 r/p
Christine Jope Slade	The Enchanted Swan		1952 h/b
Lozania Prole	The King's Pleasure	1/1954	1954 h/b
James M Cain	Past All Dishonour	4/1954	1954 p/b
James M Cain	Love's Lovely Counterfeit	4/1954	1954 p/b
John P Marquand	Think Fast Mr Moto	5/1954	1954 p/b
Claire Ritchie	Mending Flower	6/1954	1955 h/b
Ernest Dudley	The Blind Beak	6/1954	1954 h/b

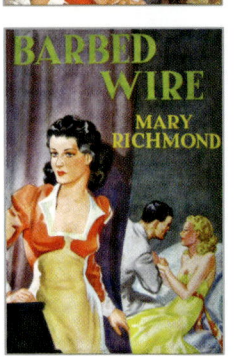

* Unconfirmed, but probably by McConnell.

BIBLIOGRAPHY

Author	Title	Painted	Published
Henrietta Mason	White Orchid	7/1954	1955 h/b
Marjorie Alan	Murder Looks Back	9/1954	1955 h/b
James M Cain	Jealous Woman	9/1954	1955 h/b
John P Marquand	Laugh Last Mr Moto	9/1954	1955 p/b
Rudolf Neidert	The White Citadel	9/1954	1955 h/b
Lozania Prole	The Enchanting Courtesan	9/1954	1955 h/b
Max Peacock	Dark Rosaleen	9/1954	1955 h/b
David Bateson	The Man from the Rock	9/1954	1955 h/b
John D MacDonald	Contrary Pleasure	10/1954	1955 h/b
Claire Ritchie	Gift of the Heart	10/1954	1955 h/b
Vicky Lancaster	Lovers in Darkness	10/1954	1955 h/b
Hermina Black	It Happened in Arabia	11/1954	1955 h/b
Faith Baldwin	The Golden Shoestring	12/1954	1955 h/b
Vicky Lancaster	In Search of Love	5/1955	1955 h/b
Josephine Lawrence	The Gates of Living	6/1955	1956 h/b
Max Peacock	Death to the Orange	6/1955	1956 h/b
Elizabeth Fenton (Kathleen Lindsay)	Song of India	6/1955	1956 h/b
Catherine Page	The Quiet Flame	7/1955	1956 h/b
Helen Eastwood	The Golden Slipper	7/1955	1956 h/b
Evadne Price	What the Heart Says	7/1955	1956 h/b
F Van Wyck Mason	The Barbarians	7/1955	1956 h/b
Frank King	The Case of the Vanishing Artist	7/1955	1956 h/b
Marjorie Alan	Murder in a Maze	7/1955	1956 h/b
Claire Ritchie	The White Violet	8/1955	1956 h/b
Theresa Charles	The Burning Beacon		1956 h/b
Lozania Prole	My Wanton Tudor Rose	10/1955	1956 h/b
Kathleen Picken	Uneasy Paradise	11/1955	1956 h/b
Harold Robbins	Never Leave Me	2/1956	1956 h/b
Elizabeth Fenton (Kathleen Lindsay)	Allah be with Us	2/1956	1956 h/b
Lozania Prole	A Queen for England	3/1956	1957 h/b
Ernest Dudley	Dr Morelle Takes a Bow	5/1956	1957 h/b
Max Peacock	Unconquered Marshal	7/1956	1957 h/b
Ernest Dudley	Callers for Dr Morelle	8/1956	1957 h/b
Lozania Prole	The Little Victoria	10/1956	1957 h/b
Kenneth Hayles	Trader Brook	11/1956	1957 h/b
Charles Franklin	Darling Murderess	12/1956	1957 h/b
John D MacDonald	Hurricane	12/1956	1957 h/b
Michael F Page	The Innocent Bystander	12/1956	1957 h/b
T B Morris	Blind Bargain	1/1957	1957 h/b
Lozania Prole	The Stuart Sisters	2/1957	1958 h/b
John D MacDonald	Death Trap	6/1957	1958 h/b
Charles Franklin	Death on my Shoulder	7/1957	1958 h/b
Lozania Prole	Henry's Last Love	10/1957	1958 h/b
Kenneth Hayles	Volcano	11/1957	1958 h/b
Max Peacock	No Law on Lundy	11/1957	1958 h/b
John D MacDonald	The Price of Murder	2/1958	1958 h/b
John D MacDonald	A Man of Affairs	2/1958	1958 h/b
Lozania Prole	Consort to the Queen	1/1959	1959 h/b
Lozania Prole	The Tudor Boy	11/1959	1960 h/b
Lozania Prole	My Love! My Little Queen!	6/1960	1961 h/b
Lozania Prole	For Love of the King		1960 h/b
Lozania Prole	The Queen's Midwife	7/1960	1961 h/b
Lozania Prole	Queen Guillotine	6/1961	1962 h/b
Lozania Prole	A King's Plaything	8/1961	1962 h/b
Lozania Prole	Daughter of the Devil	1/1962	1962 h/b
Lozania Prole	The Ghost that Haunted a King	10/1962	1963 h/b
Lozania Prole	The Wild Daughter	3/1963	1963 h/b
Lozania Prole	Henry's Golden Queen	8/63	1964 h/b

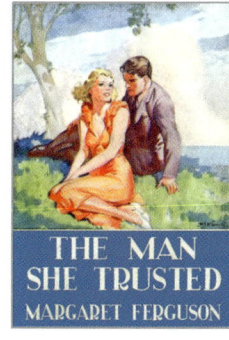

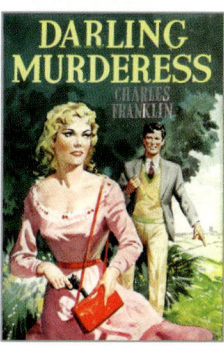
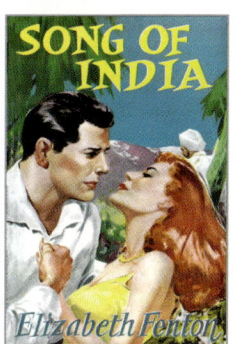

HAMILTON'S and PANTHER

TITLE	AUTHOR	PAINTED	PUBLISHED
Webb Anders	Renegade Canyon	12/1949	3/1950 p/b
W R Hutton	Injun Brand	12/1949	5/1950 p/b
Scott Brady	Boothill Posse (Panther Cub) (reuses the above painting)		
Glen Morton	Gunhawk Code		6/1950 p/b
W R Hutton	Gunslinger's Luck	5/1950	9/1951 p/b
R L May	Trigger Treachery	5/1950	9/1951 p/b
Chuck Lloyd	Santa Fe Trail	7/1950	11/1950 p/b
Doug Enefer	Ghost Town	7/1950	11/1950 p/b
J Vincent Nolan	Colt Law	7/1950	11/1950 p/b

MINIATURE MARVELS

Mike M'Cracken	Lynch Law	7/1950	3/1951 p/b
Richard Conroy	Injun Justice	7/1950	3/1951 p/b
Mike M'Cracken	Flaming Frontier	8/1950	1/1951 p/b
J Vincent Nolan	Gunman from Tombstone	8/1950	1951 p/b
Shaun O'Hara	Four Guns to Porcupine		1/1952 p/b
R L May	King Colt	10/1950	7/1951 p/b
Mike M'Cracken	Hombre from Tombstone	10/1950	1951 p/b
Thornton Dale	Rope Law	10/1950	9/1951 p/b
Tex Bland	Lead Poison	10/1950	10/1951 p/b
Shaun O'Hara	Rollin' Wheels	11/1950	10/1951 p/b
Shaun O'Hara	Solo to Rattlesnake	11/1950	10/1951 p/b
Jim Mack	Alaskan Gold	12/1950	9/1951 p/b
	Alaskan cover	12/1950	
Duke Montana	Lynch Law in Perdition	2/1951	9/1951 p/b
Chuck Lloyd	Guns Along the Brava	2/1951	
Shaun O'Hara	Four Guns to Porcupine	10/1951	1/1952 p/b
Shaun O'Hara	The Epic of Gloryrise	10/1951	9/1952 p/b
Dean Morgan	Assassin Trail	2/1952	9/1952 p/b
Mike M'Cracken	Law of the Lariat (Panther 41)	10/1952	1953 p/b
Russ Ames	Colt Lightning (Panther 42)	10/1952	1953 p/b
Scott Jefferson	Buffalo Bill Cody	10/1952	3/1953 h/b + p/b
Russ Ames	Blood on Powder Creek	12/1952	5/1953 p/b
Russ Ames	Guns Wild	12/1952	5/1953 p/b
Shaun O'Hara	Kazan the Killer	12/1952	1953 p/b
Frank Yerby	The Golden Hawk (Panther 825)	11/1957	1958 p/b
Harry Sanford	Spearhead (Panther 833)	12/1957	1958 p/b
Duncan Mackinlock	Island of Hell (Panther 1347)		1962 p/b

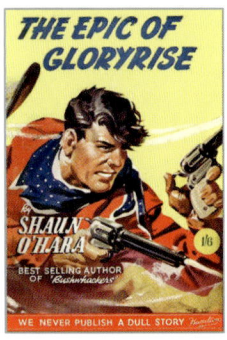

HARRAP and HENNEL LOCKE (HL)

AUTHOR	TITLE	PAINTED	PUBLISHED
William Victor Cook	Adventure Under Arms	8/1950	1951 h/b
Roy Manning	The Marshal of Vengeance Valley	9/1950	1951 h/b
Arthur Henry	Diamond D for Danger	9/1950	1951 h/b
Stanley Porteus	Providence Ponds	11/1950	1951 h/b
Winifred Finlay	The Witch of Redesdale		1951 h/b
Paul Evan Lehman	Redrock Gold	2/1951	HL 1951 h/b
Escott Wyatt	Clean-Up		HL 1952 h/b
Robert Lund	Hour of Glory	5/1951	1951 h/b
Hellmut Kirst	The Lieutenant Must be Mad	7/1951	(u/p – 1952 h/b is by another hand)
Janet Whitney	Intrigue in Baltimore	1/1952	1952 h/b
James Weygand	Legionnaire	7/1952	1952 h/b
Michael Patrick	Tommy Hawke's Third Case	9/1952	1953 h/b
Paul Evan Lehman	The Devil's Doorstep	3/1953	HL 1953 h/b
Gordon Lennox	Filibuster	6/1955	HL 1955 h/b
Paul Evan Lehman	The Bandit in Black	2/1956	HL 1956 h/b
George Vaizey	Or by Default	1/1957	1957 h/b

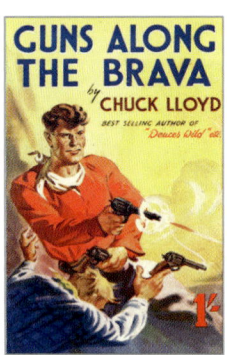

HODDER & STOUGHTON

AUTHOR	TITLE	PAINTED	PUBLISHED
Jackson Gregory	High Hand at Rocky Bend		1939 h/b, r/p
Charles Alden Seltzer	Boss of the Lazy Y	11/1946	1947 h/b, 1949 r/p
William MacLeod Raine	Saddletramp	7/1949	1949 h/b
Loula Grace Erdman	The Far Journey	2/1956	1956 h/b
Max Brand	Riders of the Plains *		1964 p/b
Michael Gilbert	After the Fine Weather	2/1965	1965 p/b

* Repurposes the cover for *High Hand at Rocky Bend* by Jackson Gregory.

GRANT HUGHES

AUTHOR	TITLE	PAINTED	PUBLISHED
Dennis T Hughes	Scourge of the Badlands	12/1948	1949 p/b
Richard W Hutton	Outlaw of Lost Canyon	12/1948	6/1949 p/b
Bert Ford	Laughing Cowboy	1/1949	4/1949 p/b
Bruff Curfew	Killer's Breed	1/1949	2/1949 p/b
	Death to Owlhoots	1/1949	

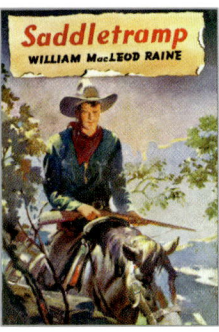

BIBLIOGRAPHY

HULTON/EAGLE

AUTHOR	TITLE	PAINTED	PUBLISHED
Macdonald Hastings	Men of Glory	6/1958	1958 h/b
	Western Annual	1/1959	

THE HUTCHINSON GROUP: Hutchinson (H), Hurst & Blackett (HB), Jarrolds (J), John Long (JL), Leisure Library (LL), Stanley Paul (SP), Rich & Cowan (RC), Skeffington (S), Arrow (A)

AUTHOR	TITLE	PAINTED	PUBLISHED
John Jay Chichester	Sanderson: Master Rogue		H 1934 h/b
Sydney Horler	The Man from Scotland Yard		H 1934 h/b
Isabel C Clarke	Roman Year		H 1935 h/b
Dorothy Black	The Spring Returns		H 1935 h/b
E W Savi	A Question of Honour		H 1937 h/b
Owen A Williams	Colorado Jones		JL 1937 h/b
Sanford Lock	Mail for McNair		H 1940 h/b
Eric Rober	Law and Order		LL 25 1940 p/b
Marten Cumberland	Everything He Touched		J 1945 h/b
Eliot Crawshaw-Williams	The Wolf from the West	8/1946	JL 1947 h/b
Roderick Owen	Easier for a Camel	6/1949	H 1950 h/b
Eric Leyland	Case for Red Lawson	7/1950	H 1951 h/b
Eric Leyland	Calling Red Lawson	6/1951	H 1952 h/b
	The School in England	8/1951	H
Horace Annesley Vachell	The Lamp of Golconda	11/1951	H 1952 h/b
Kathleen Groom	The Recoil	3/1952	H 1952 h/b
Frank Warner	Mountain Boss	9/1952	RC 1954 h/b
	The Angry Planet	10/1952	H
Brigid Knight	The Sun Climbs Slowly	11/1952	H 1953 h/b
Brigid Knight	The Covenant	11/1952	H 1953 h/b
Frank Warner	Outlaws of Jade Creek	3/1953	RC 1953 h/b
Jefferson Fraser	Renegade Ambush	5/1953	RC 1953 h/b
Tom Johnson Hopkins	Horsethief Crossing	7/1953	RC 1954 h/b
Penn Dower	Indian Moon	8/1953	JL 1954 h/b
Richard Goyne	The Gravel Patch	8/1953	SP 1953 h/b
John Keir Cross	SOS from Mars	9/1953	H 1954 h/b
Various	Treasure Trail (cover + front papers)	10/1953	H
Jefferson Fraser	Sombrero Ramrod	10/1953	RC 1954 h/b
Ethel M Dell	Storm Drift		H 1954 h/b
Kathleen Lindsay	Madonna of Hell (Valentine Romance Club)	1/1954	H 1954 h/b
Ethel M Dell	The Unknown Quantity	2/1954	H 1954 h/b
Dorian Lee	Prisoner Go Free	2/1954	JL 1954 h/b
Ethel M Dell	The Altar of Honour	3/1954	H 1954 h/b
Raymond Armstrong	Midnight Cavalier	3/1954	JL 1954 h/b
F Van Wyck Mason	The Silver Leopard		J 1954 h/b
Kathleen Lindsay	Dark Destiny	5/1954	H 1955 h/b
May Sutherland	The Wild Olive	5/1954	H 1954 h/b
Claire Emsley	The True Physician	5/1954	SP 1954 h/b
Nancy Cosette Keeling	One Master Passion	5/1954	SP 1955 h/b
C V Terry	Buccaneer Doctor	5/1954	J 1955 h/b
T C H Jacobs	Results of an Accident	7/1954	SP 1955 h/b
Gordon Ashe	The Kidnapped Child	7/1954	JL 1955 h/b
John Muir	The Devil's Post Office	7/1954	H 1955 h/b + A 444H 2/1957 p/b
Margaret Archer	See a Fine Lady	8/1954	J 1955 h/b
Marjorie Vernon	Fair Ladies Ltd	8/1954	JL 1955 h/b
Eric Leyland	Red Lawson and Sons of the Desert	9/1954	H 1955 h/b
Robert Neill	Mist Over Pendle	10/1954	H 1955 h/b + A 376 5/1955 p/b
F Van Wyck Mason	Blue Hurricane	10/1954	J 1955 h/b
Anne Vernon	The Depths of the Country	10/1954	SP 1955 h/b
John Courage	The House with a Past	11/1954	SP 1955 h/b
Dorian Lee	The Bad Companions	11/1954	JL 1955 h/b
Rafael Sabatini	Scaramouche	12/1954	A 386H 7/56 p/b
Brian Flynn	The Toy Lamb	2/1955	JL 1955 h/b
Gordon Ashe	The Man Who Stayed Alive	2/1955	JL 1955 h/b
Andrew Spiller	Ring Twice for Murder	2/1955	SP 1955 h/b
Peter Bourne	Black Saga	2/1955	A 386H 11/1955 p/b
Kathleen Lindsay	Tomorrow We Die	2/1955	H 1955 h/b
L W Emerson	Desert Violence	2/1955	RC 1955 h/b
Sylvia Thorpe	Smugglers' Moon	2/1955	RC 1955 h/b
Ismay Lee	Bandits of the Hidden Valley	3/1955	RC 1956 h/b
C V Terry	Darien Venture	4/1955	J 1955 h/b
John Clagett	Buckskin Cavalier	5/1955	A 410H 4/1956 p/b

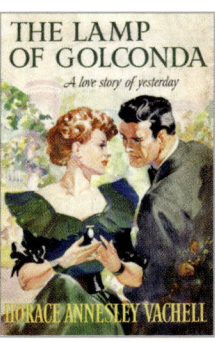
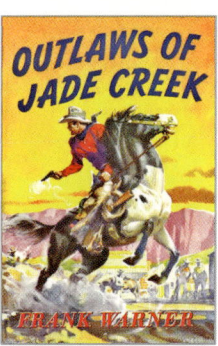
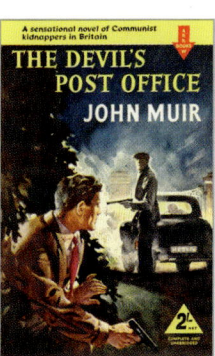
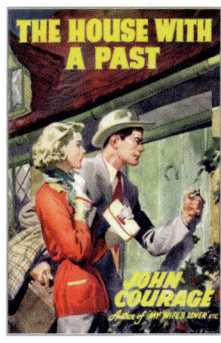

MINIATURE MARVELS

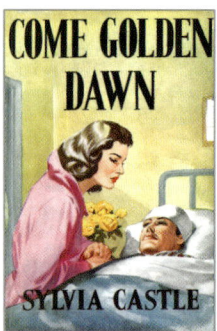
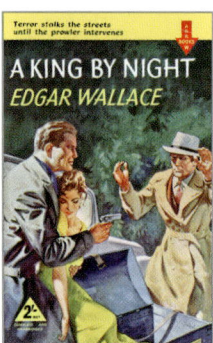
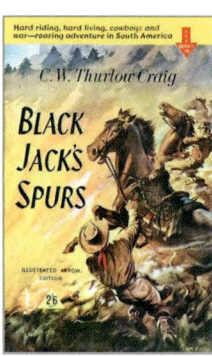
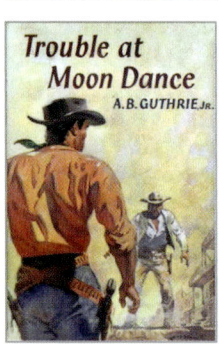
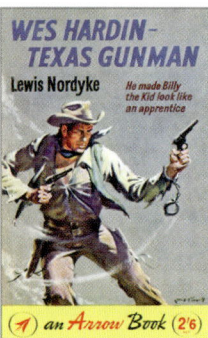

Author	Title	Date	Edition
Jean Marsh	Death Among the Stars	5/1955	JL 1955 h/b
Sutherland Scott	Doctor Dodds' Experiment	5/1955	SP 1956 h/b
Sylvia Thorpe	The Golden Panther	6/1955	RC 1956 h/b
Raymond Armstrong	Cavalier of the Night	7/1955	JL 1956 h/b
Harriet Gray	Bride of Doom	7/1955	RC 1956 h/b
Andrew Spiller	Black Cap for Murder	9/1955	SP 1956 h/b
Richard Goyne	The Fentons	9/1955	SP 1956 h/b
Kathleen Lindsay	Dangerous to Know	10/1955	H 1956 h/b
Edwin Radford	Look in at Murder	10/1955	JL 1956 h/b
F Van Wyck Mason	Cutlass Empire	11/1955	A 416J 7/1956 p/b
William Dawson Hoffman	The Bearcats' Brand	11/1955	H 1956 h/b
Arnold Mayo	Marshal of Toledo	11/1955	JL 1957 h/b
Ewart Brookes	To Endless Night	12/1955	A 408J 4/1956 p/b
Ewart Brookes	Nor on What Seas	12/1955	J 1956 h/b + A 510J 8/1958 p/b
Frank Usher	The Lonely Cage	12/1955	JL 1956 h/b
Sylvia Castle	Come Golden Dawn	12/1955	SP 1956 h/b
Frank G Slaughter	The Scarlet Cord	1/1956	J 1956 h/b
Wallace Elton	The Dark Gunman	2/1956	JL 1957 h/b
	Goodbye to Sunstroke (?)	2/1956	JL
Andrew Davidson	The Golden Lode	2/1956	H 1956 h/b
Sylvia Thorpe	Sword of Vengeance	2/1956	RC 1957 h/b
Edgar Wallace	The Hand of Power	3/1956	A 413JL 1956 p/b
Naomi Jacob	Antonia	4/1956	A 421JL 1956 p/b
T C H Jacobs	Broken Alibi	4/1956	SP 1957 h/b
Billy Wright	The World's My Football Pitch		SP 1956 h/b + A 424SP 1957 p/b
Kathleen Lindsay	The Devil's Dominion	5/1956	H 1956 h/b
Lewis Broad	The Adventures of Sir Winston	5/1956	H 1956 h/b + A 436H 1957 p/b
Frank G Slaughter	The Flaming Frontier	6/1956	J 1957 h/b
Andrew Spiller	Brains Trust for Murder	6/1956	SP 1956 h/b
Colin Robertson	The Eastlake Affair	7/1956	JL 1957 h/b
Norgrove Thurley	Giants of Darkness	7/1956	SP 1957 h/b
Ismay Lee	Lynchlaw Vengeance	7/1956	JL 1957 h/b
Frank Crisp	The Manila Stranger	8/1956	SP 1957 h/b
Shirley Seifert	Let My Name Stand Fair	8/1956	SP 1957 h/b
Edgar Wallace	A King by Night	8/1956	A 441JL 1957 p/b
Conroy Lea	The Treasure of Red Gulch	9/1956	JL 1957 h/b
John Myers Myers	Doc Holliday	9/1956	J 1957 h/b
Neta Muskett	Red Dust	10/1956	A 445H 1957 p/b
Frederick R Van De Water	Wings of the Morning	10/1956	J 1957 h/b
C W Thurlow Craig	Black Jack's Spurs	10/1956	A 457 1957 p/b
F Van Wyck Mason	To Whom Be Glory	11/1956	J 1957 h/b
Barbara Cartland	The Captive Heart	12/1956	H 1957 h/b + A 454H p/b
Ray Lindwall	Flying Stumps	12/1956	A 452 1957 p/b
Peter Bourne	Twilight of the Dragon		A 1957 p/b
Norah C James	Silent Corridors	1/1957	A 462 1957 p/b
Harriet Gray	Gold for the Gay Masters	2/1957	A 469 8/1957 p/b
Jefferson Fraser	Stage City	4/1957	JL 1957 h/b
John Harlow	Trail into Mexico	4/1957	JL 1957 h/b
Peter Krott	Tupu-Tupu-Tupu	7/1957	H (u/p – 1958 h/b uses photo)
Elsa McCormick Barker	Showdown at Penasco Pass	8/1957	JL 1958 h/b
Ismay Lee	Guns Across the Border	8/1957	JL 1958 h/b
Rafael Sabatini	The Sea Hawk		A 488 1958 p/b
Penn Dower	Frontier Marshal	10/1957	JL 1958 h/b + A 1958 p/b
Elton Wallace	Avenger's Trail	10/1957	JL 1958 h/b + A 1958 p/b
Laramine Colson	Silver Dollar Mine	11/1957	JL 1958 h/b + A 1958 p/b
Tom Curtis	Gun Business	2/1958	JL 1958 h/b
F W Kenyon	Emma	2/1958	A 498 1958 p/b
Andrew Davidson	The Wilderness Road	4/1958	J 1958 h/b + A 1958 p/b
Robert Neill	Hangman's Cliff	4/1958	A 518 11/1958 p/b
Robert Alexander	The Killing at Broken Wheel	4/1958	JL 1958 h/b + A 574 1958 p/b
Ismay Lee	Trouble Territory	5/1958	JL 1958 h/b + A 1958 p/b
Wallace Elton	The Killer Gun	5/1958	JL 1958 h/b + A 1958 p/b
Frank Warner	Red River Showdown	7/1958	JL 1959 h/b + A 1959 p/b
Elsa McCormick Barker	War on the Big Hat	7/1958	JL 1959 h/b
Tom Curtis	Lone Star Law	9/1958	JL 1959 h/b
Lion Feuchtwanger	Jew Suss	10/1958	A 517 2/1959 p/b
Eric Leyland	The Colorado Kid	3/1959	H 1959 h/b + A 1959 p/b
Elsa McCormick Barker	Secret of the Badlands	8/1959	H 1960 h/b + A 1960 p/b
Will C Brown	Laredo Trail	10/1959	JL 1960 h/b
A B Guthrie Jnr	Trouble at Moon Dance	10/1959	JL 1960 h/b
Lewis Nordyke	Wes Hardin – Texas Gunman		A 555 1960 p/b
Carl W Breihan	Outlaws of the Old West		A 589 1960 p/b

Kathleen Lindsay	A Lady for Botany Bay	12/1960	H 1961 h/b
Edgar Wallace	Face in the Night		A 593 1961 p/b
Kingsley West	South to Gunsight Pass	4/1961	JL 1961 h/b
Norah Lofts	Scent of Cloves	4/1961	A 607 1961 p/b
Joan Nicholson	The Sea Pearl	5/1961	HB 1961 h/b
Kathleen Lindsay	Paulette	8/1961	HB 1962 h/b
Frank Wilson Kenyon	I Eugenia	11/1961	H 1963 h/b
Anne Hepple	Touch-Me-Not	11/1961	A 1963 p/b
Anne Hepple	Can I Go There?	11/1961	A 689 1962 p/b
Carse Boyd	Ride the Man Down	1/1962	JL h/b 1962
Dennis Wheatley	The Quest of Julian Day		A 632 1962 p/b
Naomi Jacob	White Wool	2/1962	A 1962 p/b
Kathleen Lindsay	There is no Yesterday	4/1962	HB 1962 h/b
Naomi Jacob	A Passage Perilous	5/1962	A 684 1962 p/b
Naomi Jacob	The Morning Will Come	5/1962	A 686 1962 p/b
Kingsley West	Ride West to Pueblo	5/1962	JL 1962 h/b
Anne Hepple	Sally Cockenzie	10/1962	A 694 1963 p/b
Peter Bourne	Black Saga	11/1962	H
Anne Hepple	Janet Forsythe	12/1962	A 1963 p/b
Kathleen Lindsay	Love's Atonement	12/1962	HB 1963 h/b
Anne Hepple	The North Wind Blows	1/1963	A 708 1963 p/b
Anne Hepple	Sigh No More	2/1963	HB 1963 h/b + A 710 1963 p/b
Kathleen Lindsay	Less than the Dust	3/1963	HB 1963 h/b
Kathleen Lindsay	Theodora	8/1963	HB 1964 h/b
Margaret Cameron (Kathleen Lindsay)	A Devil from Muscovy	7/1964	HB 1964 h/b
Kathleen Lindsay	Loyal Lady	8/1964	HB 1965 h/b
Kathleen Lindsay	Enchantress of the Nile	1/1965	HB 1965 h/b
Margaret Cameron (Kathleen Lindsay)	Kitty of Russia	5/1965	HB 1965 h/b
Kathleen Lindsay	Song of the Dawn	6/1965	HB 1965 h/b
Margaret Cameron (Kathleen Lindsay)	Katouska	11/1965	H 1966 h/b
Kathleen Lindsay	Queen of the Mirage	2/1966	HB 1966 h/b
Margaret Cameron (Kathleen Lindsay)	Fanfare for Margaret	7/1966	HB 1967 h/b
Kathleen Lindsay	Incomparable Doll	8/1966	HB 1967 h/b
Kathleen Lindsay	Rustle of Spring	2/1967	HB 1967 h/b
Margaret Cameron (Kathleen Lindsay)	Anastasia	2/1967	HB 1967 h/b
Margaret Cameron (Kathleen Lindsay)	My Dearest Dear	1/1968	HB 1968 h/b
Kathleen Lindsay	She was my Beloved	1/1968	HB 1968 h/b

KEMSLEY NEWSPAPERS: CHERRY TREE BOOKS

AUTHOR	TITLE	PAINTED	PUBLISHED
Frank H Shaw	Atlantic Gold!	3/19	1953 p/b
Russ Hardy	The Saga of Gory Gold	4/1952	1953 p/b
Frank H Shaw	Sea Watch	7/1952	1953 p/b
	Outlaws of Loan-Wolf City	9/1852	(u/p?)

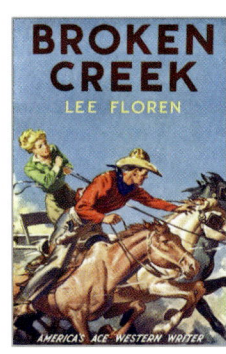

LIVINGSTONE PRESS

AUTHOR	TITLE	PAINTED	PUBLISHED
Gladys Rumpus	Six Coloured Marbles	1/1947	1947

R & L LOCKER: ARCHER BOOKS

AUTHOR	TITLE	PAINTED	PUBLISHED
Various	American Western Magazine No 5	4/1948	1948 p/b
Various	American Western Magazine No 6	4/1948	1948 p/b
Lee Floren	Riders in the Night	4/1948	12/1948 p/b
Lee Floren	Rifles on the Rimrock	8/1948	1948 p/b
Lee Floren	Broken Creek	8/1948	11/1948 p/b
Russell Storm	Guns for the Valley	8/1948	1948 p/b
Don Wilcox	Too Soon to Die	8/1948	1948 p/b
Charles H Snow	Bandits of Bed Rock		1948 p/b
Charles H Snow	The Trail to Abilene	8/1948	1948 p/b
Charles H Snow	Roaring Guns	11/1948	1/1949 p/b
Charles H Snow	Cardigan Cowboy	11/1948	1/1949 p/b
Charles H Snow	The Black Riders of the Range	11/1948	3/1949 p/b
Charles H Snow	Argonaut Gold	11/1948	3/1949 p/b
H B Hickey	Saddles West	1/1949	2/1950 p/b
William Hopson	A Thousand Head North	1/1949	2/1950 p/b

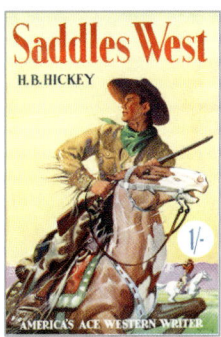
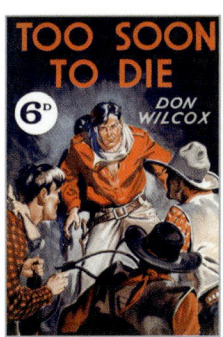
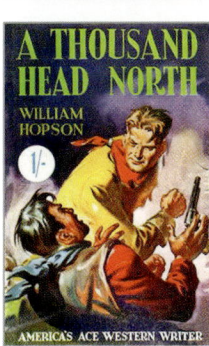

MINIATURE MARVELS

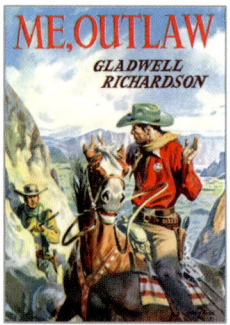

LONGMANS GREEN

AUTHOR	TITLE	PAINTED	PUBLISHED
Iris Bromige	The Traceys	7/46	1946 h/b

LUTTERWORTH

AUTHOR	TITLE	PAINTED	PUBLISHED
	24 Wash Days	10/1949	
Jane Rogers	Fires in Montana	6/1950	1951 h/b

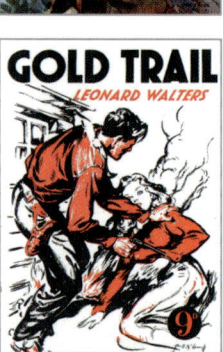

MACDONALD

AUTHOR	TITLE	PAINTED	PUBLISHED
Marten Cumberland	Everything he Touched		1945 h/b
Julia Hitchens	Beat Back the Tide	7/1954	1955 h/b
Frank McLowery	Missouri Man	11/1954	1955 h/b
John Newton Chance	Jason Goes West	1/1955	1955 h/b
George Bagby	The Body in the Basket	11/1955	1956 h/b
Gladwell Richardson	Me, Outlaw	11/1955	1956 h/b

MARTIN & REID: ARROW and MASCOT (M)

AUTHOR	TITLE	PAINTED	PUBLISHED
Nigel Morland	The Hatchet Murders	10/1945	1947 p/b
Nigel Morland	26 Three Minute Thrillers	10/1945	1947
Nigel Morland	The Case of the Innocent Wife	11/1945	1947 p/b
Stanley Russell	Romance of Denstone Bar	11/1945	1947 p/b
Howard Jackson	Soho Pay Off	12/1945	1946 p/b
Leonard Walters	Gold Trail	1/1946	1946 p/b
Jean Sinclair	Girl Trap	1/1946	1947 p/b
Various	Complete Stories No1	2/1946	1946 p/b
Leonard Walters	Yellow Streak	3/1946	1946 p/b
Lee Kimberley	By Love Repaid	4/1946	1946 p/b
John Theydon	Dead Man's Spread	8/1948	M 1948 p/b
John Theydon	Black Wolf Trail	8/1948	M 1948 p/b

MILLS and BOON

AUTHOR	TITLE	PAINTED	PUBLISHED
Joan Blair	The Glitter and the Gold		1940 h/b
Lilian Chisholm	Afraid to Dream		1941 h/b
Calico Jones	Vermillion Outlaw	12/1952	1953 h/b
Gladwell Richardson	Ranger Round-up	1/1953	1953 h/b
Clem Colt	No Tomorrow	1/1953	1953 h/b
Johnston McCulley	Texas Showdown	7/1953	1954 h/b
Gladwell Richardson	Open Range	7/1953	1954 h/b
Nelson C Nye	Smoke Talk	7/1953	1954 h/b
Tevis Miller	Gun-play in Killer Canyon	7/1953	1954 h/b
Johnny Ringo	Lonely Gun	12/1953	1954 h/b
Will Ermine	Longhorn Empire	3/1954	1954 h/b
Gladwell Richardson	Renegades' Den	5/1954	1954 h/b
Gladwell Richardson	X-Handled Gun	5/1954	1954 h/b
John R Winslowe	ZERO Range	6/1954	1954 h/b
Maurice Kildare	Stormy	6/1954	1954 h/b
John Shane	Along the Yermo Rim	6/1954	1955 h/b
Mark Donovan	Gunsmoke in Crosbie	7/1954	1954 h/b
Maurice Kildare	Emigrant Gap	8/1954	1955 h/b
John R Winslowe	Tinhorn Gambler	9/1954	1955 h/b
Gladwell Richardson	Lightning Lomax	10/1954	1955 h/b
Paul Durst	Die Damn You	11/1954	1955 h/b
Nelson Nye	Quick Trigger Country	2/1955	1955 h/b
Jeff Cochran	Guns of Circle 8	2/1955	1955 h/b
Gladwell Richardson	Sorry Cowtown	3/1955	1955 h/b
Clem Colt	The Lonely Grass	3/1955	1955 h/b
Calico Jones	Dancing Rabbit Creek	5/1955	1955 h/b
Maurice Kildare	Lariat Law	6/1955	1955 h/b
Nelson Nye	The Parson of Gunbarrel Basin	6/1955	1955 h/b

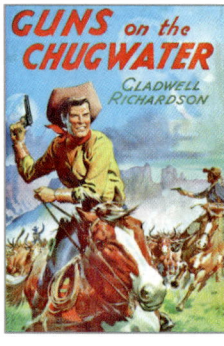

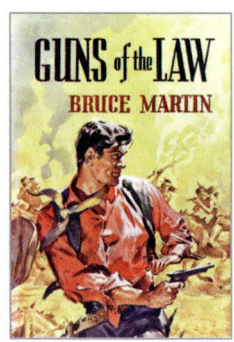

John R Winslowe	Dry Gulchers Creek	8/1955	1956 h/b
John Shane	Sundown in Sundance	8/1955	1956 h/b
Tex Houston	The Sheriff of Hammer County	10/1955	1956 h/b
Gladwell Richardson	Guns on the Chugwater	10/1955	1956 h/b
Mark Donovan	Jail Break	11/1955	1956 h/b
Gladwell Richardson	Hang the Cowboy High	1/1956	1956 h/b
John Shane	Six-Gun Thursday	3/1956	1956 h/b
Nelson Nye	Blood Sky	3/1956	1956 h/b
Tex Huston	Gunman Deputy	5/1956	1956 h/b
Mark Donovan	Gunshots in Hambone	5/1956	1956 h/b
Gladwell Richardson	Ride Yonder	8/1956	1956 h/b
Calico Jones	Six-Shooter Country	8/1956	1956 h/b
Nelson Nye	South Fork	9/1956	1957 h/b
Christopher Wigan	Mossyhorn Trail	2/1957	1957 h/b
Bruce Martin	Guns of the Law		1962 h/b

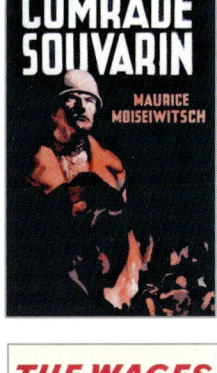

ALEXANDER MORING

AUTHOR	TITLE	PAINTED	PUBLISHED
Tex Ryland?	Bushwacked	11/1956	(u/p)
	A Grave for a Coyote	11/1956	(u/p)

FREDERICK MULLER

AUTHOR	TITLE	PAINTED	PUBLISHED
Bliss Lomax	The Leather Burners		1941 h/b, 1945 r/p
S Fowler Wright	The Siege of Malta		1942 h/b
Maurice Moiseiwitsch	Comrade Souvarin	8/1945	1945 h/b
Babs Lee and Clare Castler Saunders	Measured for Murder	1/1946	1946 h/b

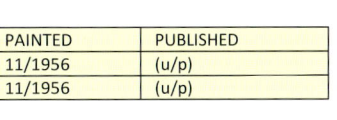

JOHN MURRAY

AUTHOR	TITLE	PAINTED	PUBLISHED
A E W Mason	The Four Feathers	3/1960	1960 p/b
C P Wrenn	The Wages of Virtue	6/1960	1960 p/b

MUSEUM PRESS

AUTHOR	TITLE	PAINTED	PUBLISHED
S C George	The Reluctant Infidel	3/1953	1954 h/b
Howard Swiggett	March or Die	4/1954	1955 h/b
Helen Reilley	The Velvet Hand	5/1954	1955 h/b
S C George	The Witch Doctor	8/1954	1955 h/b

PETER NEVILL

AUTHOR	TITLE	PAINTED	PUBLISHED
Stanley Vestal	Dodge City, Queen of the Cowtowns	10/1954	1955 h/b

NEWS OF THE WORLD (Pocket)

AUTHOR	TITLE	PAINTED	PUBLISHED
George Harmon Coxe	Murder in Havana (#B90)	1/1952	1953
Eleazar Lipsky	The People Against O'Hara	1/1952	(u/p)
Lytle Shannon	Rimrock Red (#B82)	2/1952	1953
John Keith Bassett	Trailers of the Sage (#B88)	3/1952	1953
Stuart Hardy	Arizona Justice (#B106)	10/1952	1953
	The Department of Death	10/1952	
Peter Danvers	The Lone Wolf Trail	10/1952	
	Trouble at the Lazy S	10/1952	

IVOR NICHOLSON & WATSON

AUTHOR	TITLE	PAINTED	PUBLISHED
Grace Elliott Taylor	She Grew Up		1934

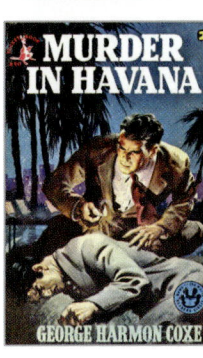

MINIATURE MARVELS

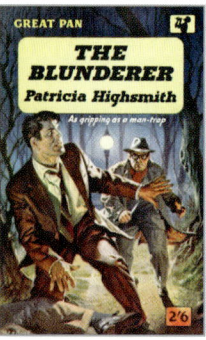
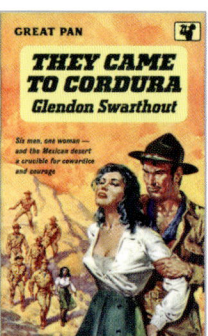

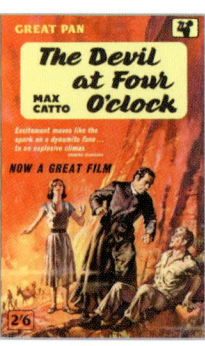
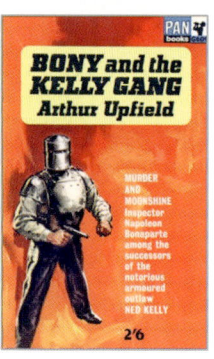

PAN

AUTHOR	TITLE	PAINTED	PUBLISHED
Frank O'Rourke	Violence at Sundown (G147)		1958 p/b
Patricia Highsmith	The Blunderer (G153)	11/1957	1958 p/b
John Wyllie	Riot (G159)	11/1957	1958 p/b
Charles Neider	Guns Up (G228)	12/1957	1958 p/b
Lew Wallace	Ben-Hur (X32)	10/1958	1959 p/b
Jack Finney	House of Numbers	11/1958	(u/p? – 1960 p/b may be by another hand)
Annamarie Selinko	Désirée (M6)	11/1958	1959 p/b
Harold Sinclair	The Horse Soldiers (G239)	11/1958	1959 p/b
Robert S Close	Eliza Callaghan (G293)	11/1958	1959 p/b
Gerald Sparrow	Opium Venture (G333)	2/1959	1959 p/b
Eric Ambler	The Night-Comers	5/1959	(u/p – 1959 p/b is by Boldero)
Cecil Saint Laurent	Clotilde (M7)	5/1959	1959 p/b
John Steinbeck	The Log from the Sea of Cortez	5/1959	(u/p – 1960 p/b is by Tayler)
Georgette Heyer	The Talisman Ring (G311), (X200)	5/1959	1959 p/b, 1963 r/p
Alexander Fullerton	The White Men Sang (G364)	5/1959	1959 p/b
A M Harris	The Tall Man	6/1959	(u/p – 1960 p/b is by Tayler)
William Humphrey	Home from the Hill	9/1959	(u/p – 1960 p/b is photographic)
Glendon Swarthout	They Came to Cordura (G405)	9/1959	1960 p/b
	Terrible Beating	9/1959	
Rafael Sabatini	Scaramouche	9/1959	1960 p/b
Heinz Schroter	Stalingrad (X58)	9/1959	1960 p/b
Georgette Heyer	The Grand Sophy (X64)	12/1959	1960 p/b
Georgette Heyer	Friday's Child (X70)	12/1959	1960 p/b
J A Hunter	Hunter's Tracks (G485)	6/1960	1960 p/b
Joseph Wechsberg	Avalanche (G432)	7/1960	1961 p/b
Christopher Landon	The Shadow of Time (G449)	7/1960	1960 p/b
Georgette Heyer	An Infamous Army (X88)	10/1960	1961 p/b
Max Catto	The Devil at Four O'Clock (G434)	11/1960	1961 p/b
Georgette Heyer	The Reluctant Widow (X108)	11/1960	(u/p – 1951 p/b is by Sheldon)
Kylie Tennant	The Battlers (X87)	11/1960	1961 p/b
Rafael Sabatini	Fortune's Fool (X120)	7/1961	1962 p/b
Robert Lewis Taylor	Travels of Jamie McPheeters	7/1961	1962 p/b
Georgette Heyer	These Old Shades (X119)	9/1961	1962 p/b
Georgette Heyer	The Corinthian (X285)	10/1961	1962 p/b
John Buchan	John Burnet of Barns (X116)	10/1961	1962 p/b
Ruth Park	The Frost and the Fire (G560)	10/1961	1962 p/b
Arthur Upfield	Bony and the Black Virgin (G574)	10/1961	1962 p/b
Alexander Cornell	The Hosts of Rebecca	1/1962	1962 p/b
Lawrence Williams	The Fiery Furnace (X149)	2/1962	1962 p/b
Rafael Sabatini	The Black Swan (G591)	2/1962	1962 p/b
Peter Freuchen	Vagrant Viking (2)	3/1962	New edition u/p?
Peter Freuchen	Ice Floes and Flaming Water	3/1962	
Rafael Sabatini	Chronicles of Captain Blood (X171)	4/1962	1962 p/b
Arthur Upfield	Bony and the Kelly Gang	5/1962	1963 p/b
Georgette Heyer	The Foundling	10/1962	1963 p/b

PARTRIDGE

AUTHOR	TITLE	PAINTED	PUBLISHED
Chester William Harrison	Boothill Trail	9/1945	1946 h/b
Michael Dare	Murder Incognito	4/1946	1947 h/b
William Beyer	Murder by Arrangement	4/1946	1947 h/b
Anne Powers	The Gallant Years	6/1946	1949 h/b
Vivian Beynon-Harris	Trouble at Hanard	9/1946	1948 h/b
Sidney E Porcelain	The Purple Pony Murders	4/1946	1948 h/b
Lee Floren	Guns of Wyoming	5/1950	1950- h/b
Calico Jones	A Ranger from Texas	8/1951	1952 p/b
Jefferson Fraser	Down the Trail	2/1952	1952 h/b
	The Border Gangs	10/1952	1953 h/b
Jefferson Fraser	Fightin' Outlaw		1952 h/b

ARTHUR PEARSON – Western Picture Library

AUTHOR	TITLE	PAINTED	PUBLISHED
	Mustang Gray: Comanche War Drums #1		10/1958 p/b
	Jim Bridger: Danger in the Mountains #2		10/1958 p/b
	Mustang Gray: The Fury of Geronimo #5	6/1958	11/1958 p/b

346

	Jim Bridger: The Taming of Dark Eagle #4	6/1958	11/1958 p/b
	Jim Bridger: By Wagon to Santa Fe #6		11/1958 p/b
	Mustang Gray: Badmen and Comanches #7	7/1958	12/1958 p/b
	Jim Bridger: The Iron Horse #9	7/1958	1/1959 p/b
	Jim Bridger: Son of Red Cloud #18	9/1958	5/1959 p/b
	Mustang Gray: Gunsmoke on the Pecos #13	9/1958	3/1959 p/b
	Jim Bridger: The Highland Hunter #8	9/1958	12/1958 p/b
	Jim Bridger: Storm on the High Sierras #10	9/1958	1/1959 p/b
	Mustang Gray: Apache Peril #11	10/1958	2/1959 p/b
	Jim Bridger: The Wilderness Fort #12		2/1959 p/b
	Jim Bridger: The Danger Trail #14	10/1958	3/1959 p/b
	Mustang Gray: Ambush at Red Butte Pass #3	11/1958	11/1958 p/b
	Mustang Gray: Under Custer's Flag #15		4/1959 p/b
	Jim Bridger: The Enchanted Mesa #16	1/1959	4/1959 p/b
	Mustang Gray: The Battle at San Carlos #17	1/1959	5/1959 p/b
	Buffalo Bill: Black Thunder of the Apaches #19	3/1959	6/1959 p/b
	Jim Bowie: Massacre at Medicine Bow #20		6/1959 p/b
	Jim Bowie: Voice of the Mountain #22	3/1959	7/1959 p/b
	Buffalo Bill: Indian Fighting #23	5/1959	9/1959 p/b
	Jim Bowie: Perils of the Pioneers #24	5/1959	9/1959 p/b
	Buffalo Bill: Trail Driving in the Badlands #21		7/1959 p/b

PICKERING & INGLIS

AUTHOR	TITLE	PAINTED	PUBLISHED
Ann Millar	Kids' Corner (cover + frontis + 12 illus)	3/1946	1946 h/b, 1948 r/p, 1950 r/p
David Morris	The Castle of Hope	2/1949	1949 h/b

POPULAR PRESS

AUTHOR	TITLE	PAINTED	PUBLISHED
George C Henderson	Alias the Tornader	8/1950	1951 p/b
George C Henderson	Hawk of the Rio Grande	8/1950	1951 p/b

ALVIN REDMAN

AUTHOR	TITLE	PAINTED	PUBLISHED
Rosamond Marshall	Rogue Cavalier	7/1955	1956 h/b
Walter O'Meara	The Spanish Bride	9/1955	1956 h/b
Zola Ross	Cassy Scandal	12/1955	1956 h/b
Rosamond Marshall	Kitty	1/1956	1956 h/b
Rosamond Marshall	Captain Ironhand	5/1957	1957 h/b
Helen Topping Miller	After the Glory	2/1959	1959 h/b
Carter A Vaughan	The Devil's Bride	3/1959	1960 h/b
Carter A Vaughan	The Wilderness	7/1959	1960 h/b
Helen Topping Miller	Witch Water	12/1959	1960 h/b
Carl J Spinatelli	Baton Sinister	12/1959	1960 h/b
Helen Topping Miller	Slow Dies the Thunder	6/1960	1960 h/b
Robert F Mirvish	Two Women, Two Worlds	12/1960	1961 h/b
Donald Barr Chidsey	The Wickedest Pilgrim	6/1961	1961 h/b
Mary Astor	The Incredible Charlie Carewe	7/1961	1962 h/b
Robert F Mirvish	Cleared Narvik 2000	8/1961	1962 h/b
Robert F Mirvish	Point of Impact	11/1961	1962 h/b
Barbara Levy	The Idol of Paris	12/1961	1962 h/b
Neil Bell	Weekend in Paris	1/1962	1962 h/b
Jeanne Montupet	The Red Fountain	2/1962	1963 h/b
Noel B Gerson	The Land is Bright	3/1962	1962 h/b
Carter A Vaughan	Scoundrels' Brigade	3/1962	1963 h/b
Mary Astor	The Image of Kate	5/1962	1962 h/b
Noel B Gerson	The Trojan	7/1962	1963 h/b
Claire Kenneth	The Love Riddle	11/1962	1963 h/b
Edward Rowe Snow	Women of the Sea	2/1963	1963 h/b
Jan Westcott	The Mercenary	4/1963	1963 h/b
Eugene B Block	Great Stagecoach Robbers of the West	4/1963	1963 h/b
Noel B Gerson	The Golden Lyre	5/1963	1963 h/b
Samuel Dembo	The Amber Eyes of the Lion	5/1963	1963 h/b
John Jennings	The Emden	8/1963	1964 h/b
Philip Vail	The Sea Panther	9/1963	1964 h/b
Barnaby Ross	The Scrolls of Lysis	10/1963	1964 h/b

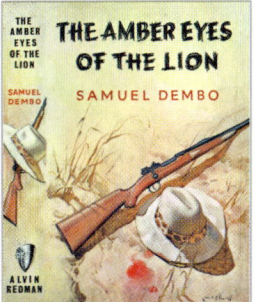
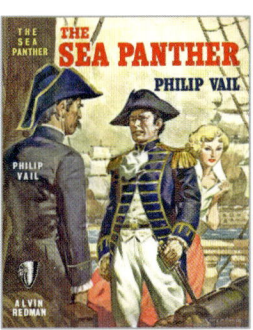
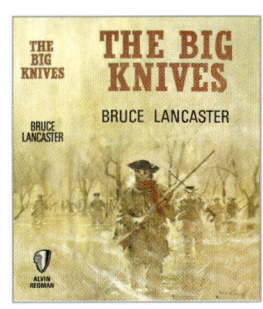

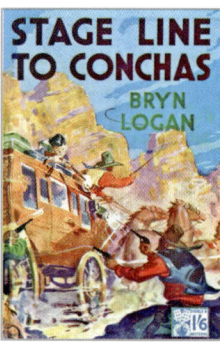

Garland Roark	Witch of Manga Reva	12/1963	1964 h/b
Cynthia Stewart	Jethro's Daughters		1964 h/b
Neil Bell	Immortal Dyer	1/1964	1964 h/b
Neil Bell	Love and Julian Farne	2/1964	1964 h/b
Henry Gaston	Strongest Enemy	6/1964	1964 h/b
Carter Vaughan	Dragon Cove	7/1964	1964 h/b
Bruce Lancaster	The Big Knives	9/1964	1965 h/b
Noel B Gerson	Old Hickory	9/1964	1964 h/b
Noel B Gerson	Kit Carson, Folk Hero and Man	11/1964	1965 h/b
Donald Barr Chidsey	Edge of Piracy	3/1965	1965 h/b
William Charles Anderson	Adam M-I	3/1965	1965 h/b
Neil Bell	The Ninth Earl of Whitly	9/1965	1966 h/b
	Comrades of War	3/1966	

ROBIN HOOD and PEVERIL (P)

AUTHOR	TITLE	PAINTED	PUBLISHED
Clinton Wayne	Tinhorns on the Tilted-K	12/1948	5/1949 h/b + p/b
Lance Carson	Dan Furber – Outlaw	2/1949 + 7/1951	1949 h/b + 1951 p/b
Bryn Logan	Deputy of Squaw Rock		1/1950 p/b
Bryn Logan	The Trail from Boom Town (above cover repurposed)		P 1952 p/b
Bryn Logan	Sin Ross – Trouble Shooter		1949 p/b
Bryn Logan	Gullytown Gets a Marshall	2/1949	1951 h/b
Paul Evan Lehman	Vengeance Valley	2/1949	9/1951 h/b + p/b
Paul Evan Lehman	The Cold Trail (above cover repurposed)		1951 h/b + p/b
Paul Evan Lehman	The Cold Trail (alternative cover)	5/1950	1951 p/b
Bryn Logan	Stage Line to Conchas	11/1949	9/1950 h/b + p/b
Clinton Wayne	Hell-Driver on Nowhere Trail	11/1949	1950 p/b
Clinton Wayne	The Grass Killers (above cover repurposed)	11/1952	P 1953 p/b
Paul Evan Lehman	The Siren of Silver Valley	5/1950	2/1951 h/b + p/b
Lance Carson	The Trouble-Kid Quits	7/1951	11/1951 h/b + 1/1952 p/b
Clinton Wayne	End of a Feud	7/1951	1/1952 h/b + p/b
Bryn Logan	Gunfighters Die Young	7/1951	4/1952 h/b
	Ten Million Hoofs	11/1952	

SCION

AUTHOR	TITLE	PAINTED	PUBLISHED
V Joseph Hanson	Blue Lightning	6/1950	9/1950 p/b
John Russell Fearn	Skeleton Pass	7/1950	10/1950 p/b
Kim Hope	The Man from 'Box Four'	7/1950	12/1950 p/b
Dean Kelly	Feud Fury	9/1950	1/1951 p/b
V Joseph Hanson	Troubleshooter!	10/1950	2/1951 p/b
V Joseph Hanson	Red Silver!	10/1950	1/1951 p/b
Webb Anders	Roughriders!	10/1950	2/1951 p/b
V Joseph Hanson	Bushwhacker!	10/1950	1/1951 p/b
Webb Anders	Saddlebow!	10/1950	9/1951 p/b
V Joseph Hanson	Smoke in the Valley	11/1950	2/1951 p/b
Jim Bowie	Paydirt!	12/1950	4/1951 p/b
Jim Bowie	Gun-Shot Grief!	12/1950	4/1951 p/b
Webb Anders	Range Wolves	1/1951	4/1951 p/b
Kim Hope	The Arizona Terror	1/1951	4/1951 p/b
	Boxing	1/1951	
Jim Bowie	The Drifter	2/1951	8/1951 p/b
Jim Bowie	Dakota Badlands	2/1951	8/1951 p/b
Jim Bowie	Buffaloed!	2/1951	9/1951 p/b
Webb Anders	Saddlebow!	2/1951	9/1951 p/b
Webb Anders	Wild Bunch	3/1951	10/1951 p/b
Jim Bowie	Apache Kid	3/1951	10/1951 p/b
	Boxing	3/1951	
Jim Bowie	Gun Flash!	4/1951	10/1951 p/b
Tom Moynihan	The Wild Trail	4/1951	10/1951 p/b
Jim Bowie	Scarred Leather	5/1951	1/1952 p/b
Jim Bowie	Red Hellions	5/1951	1/1952 p/b
Jim Bowie	Colt Country	6/1951	1/1952 p/b
Webb Anders	Drygulched!	6/1951	1/1952 p/b
V Joseph Hanson	The Bishop Riders	8/1951	1/1952 p/b
Webb Anders	Thunder Guns	8/1951	2/1952 p/b
Jim Bowie	Trigger Music	8/1951	2/1952 p/b
V Joseph Hanson	Lawless River	8/1951	3/1952 p/b

BIBLIOGRAPHY

Webb Anders	Dinero Trail	9/1951	3/1952 p/b
V Joseph Hanson	The Gunhawks!	9/1951	3/1952 p/b
Webb Anders	Desert Cross Fire	11/1951	4/1952 p/b
Jim Bowie	Raw Deal	11/1951	1952 p/b
Jim Bowie	Renegade Ranger	11/1951	12/1952 p/b
Webb Anders	Buzzard Bait	11/1951	1/1953 p/b
Webb Anders	Rawhide Reckoning	1/1952	3/1953 p/b
Jim Bowie	Showdown in Lead	1/1952	8/1953 p/b

SELWYN & BLOUNT

AUTHOR	TITLE	PAINTED	PUBLISHED
David J Murphy	Inspector Malone Sails In	9/1946	1947 h/b

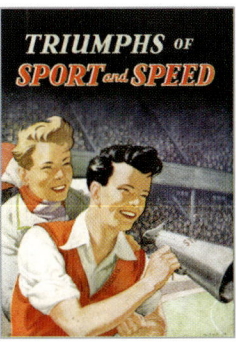

THAMES/JUVENILE (J)

AUTHOR	TITLE	PAINTED	PUBLISHED
Various	Every Boy's Annual	1/1946	1946 h/b
Various	The Book for Boys (canoeing)	1/1946	1946 h/b
Ann Tucker et al	Winning Through: Stories for Girls (cover + illus)	3/1946	1947 h/b
Various	Every Boy's Annual	11/1946	1947 h/b
Reginald Digby	Triumphs of Sport and Speed (cover + illus)	12/1947	1948 h/b
Various	Flights into the Future		1948 h/b
H Brandon-Cox	Wanderings with the Woodman		1948 h/b
Various	Every Boy's Annual (cover + frontis) (skiing)		1948 h/b
Various	Every Boy's Annual	12/1948	1949 h/b
Capt W E Johns	The Cruise of the Condor: A Biggles Story (cover + illus)	12/1948	1949 h/b
Capt W E Johns	The Black Peril: A Biggles Story (cover + illus)	8-11/1949	1950 h/b
	Jolly Book	2/1950	J
Various	Every Girl's Annual (skating girls)	5/1950	1950 h/b
Various	My Pictureland ABC		1950 h/b
Phyllis Briggs	The Secret Garden (cover + illus)	12/1950	1951 h/b
	Curley (cover + illus)	2/1951	J 1951 h/b
Capt W E Johns	Biggles Flies Again (cover + illus) (with gun)	10/1951-2/1952	1952 h/b
Various	The Pleasure Book for Boys and Girls	11/51	1952 h/b
	Coronation book	10/52	J
	Pecos Bill	11/1952	J
Charles Chilton	Riders of the Range (cover + illus)	3/1952	1952 h/b
Capt W E Johns	Biggles Flies Again (new ed)	4/1953	1954 h/b
Capt W E Johns	Biggles of the Special Air Police	5/1953	1954 h/b
Capt W E Johns	Biggles Pioneer Air Fighter (cover + frontis)	2/1954	1954 h/b
Capt W E Johns	Biggles of the Camel Squadron (cover + frontis)	2/1954	1954 h/b
Various	Riders of the Range (cover + illus)	1-2/1954	1954 h/b
Various	The Book for Boys (cover + frontis)	6/1954	1955 h/b
Charles Chilton	Riders of the Range (cover + illus)	9/1954-3/1955	1955 h/b
Capt W E Johns	Biggles of 266	1/1956	1956 h/b
J Fenimore Cooper	Last of the Mohicans	4/1957	1957 h/b
	Western	2/1958	
	Treasure Trove	2/1958	

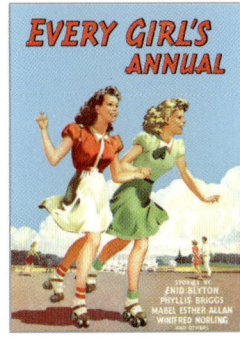

RAPHAEL TUCK

AUTHOR	TITLE	PAINTED	PUBLISHED
	My Farm Colouring Book (My Farm ABC)	11/1945	1947
William Macdowell	My Picture Book of Trains (Railway ABC)	2/1946- 4/1947	1947

WARD LOCK

AUTHOR	TITLE	PAINTED	PUBLISHED
	Mother's Little Girl	7/1949	
Winifred Norling	Four at Falconbridge	10/1949	1950 h/b
Isabel Peacocke	No More Tears	9/1950	1951 h/b
Dorothy Quentin	The Winds of Love	12/1950	1951 h/b
Patricia Young	Beyond Reach	1/1951	1951 h/b
Dorothy Quentin	The Honest Heart	6/1951	1952 h/b
Laura Whetter	Made for Joy	6/1951	1952 h/b
Mabel Esther Allan	Return to Derrykereen (cover + frontis)	9/1951	1952 h/b
	A Girl and Her Ways	10/1951	

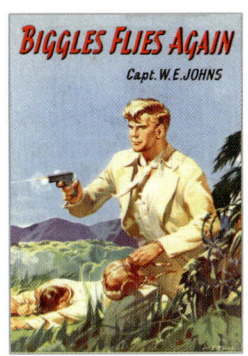

MINIATURE MARVELS

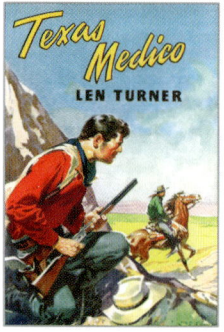

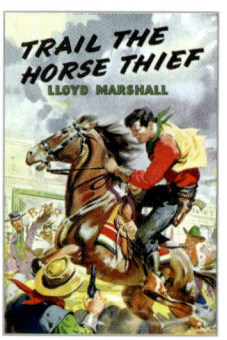

Margaret Locherbie-Cameron	Nurse Kathleen	11/1951	1954 h/b
John Winslowe	Marshal of Diablo	12/1951	1953 p/b
Louisa M Alcott	Little Women	2/1952	1952
E Stone	The Boy's Book of Conjuring	5/1952	1952 h/b
William K Reilly	Range Vengeance	6/1952	1954 h/b
Laura Whetter	Flash of Youth	6/1952	1953 h/b
Clifford Allen	The Untroubled Wolves	6/1952	1953 h/b
Kay Winchester	Melody of the Heart	9/1952	1953 h/b
Hal Dunning	White Wolf's Outlaw Legion	10/1952	1953 h/b
Nye Tredgold	Desert Doublecross	10/1952	1953 h/b
Alan Holmes	Quick on the Draw	10/1952	1953 h/b
Kathleen Treves	The Glowing Heart	12/1952	1953 h/b
Patricia Young	A Man and his Country	12/1952	1953 h/b
Effie A Rowlands	The Heart Line		1953 h/b
Clem Colt	Strawberry Roan	2/1953	1953 h/b
Shayne Morris	The Golden Hooves	3/1953	1953 h/b + p/b
Kathleen Treves	No Time for Romance	5/1953	1954 h/b
	Ca…ello Wild Bunch (partially illegible)	7/1953	
Ethel Turner	The Cub	7/1953	1954 h/b
	A Woman's Temptation	8/1953	
Kay Winchester	My Heart is Yours	9/1953	1954 h/b
Diana Ridley	Someone to Love	1/1954	1954 h/b
Lloyd Marshall	Trail the Horse Thief	1/1954	1954 h/b
Valentine	Would She Were Mine	3/1954	1954 h/b
Isabel M Peacocke	Incompatibles in Love	4/1954	1955 h/b
Dorothy Quentin	Inheritance of Love	6/1954	1955 h/b
Arnold Mayo	Heritage of Hate	7/1954	1955 h/b + p/b
Kay Winchester	The Heart Besieged	7/1954	1955 h/b
Doris Howe	I Give You My Heart	7/1954	1955 h/b
Len Turner	Texas Medico	9/1954	1955 h/b
Bryn Logan	When the Long Trail Calls	11/1954	1956 h/b + 1957 p/b
Kathleen Treves	The Brave of Heart	12/1954	1955 h/b
Doris Howe	Somewhere My Love	12/1954	1955 h/b
Mark Cross	The Best-Laid Schemes	2/1955	1955 h/b
Dorothy Quentin	Reflection of a Star	6/1955	1956 h/b
Patricia Young	Silence is the Sinner	8/1955	1956 h/b
Kathleen Treves	Richer than Wealth	1/1956	1957 h/b
Kay Winchester	Escape to Romance	6/1956	1957 h/b
Kay Winchester	Arnella	9/1956	1957 h/b
Paula Allardyce	The Lady and the Pirate	10/1956	1957 h/b
Kathleen Treves	I'll Wait Beloved	8/1957	1959 h/b
Matt Stuart	Wild Summit	3/1958	1959 h/b

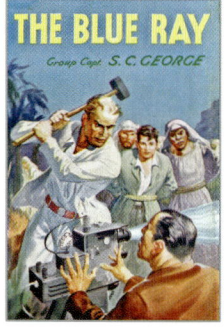

WARNE

AUTHOR	TITLE	PAINTED	PUBLISHED
S C George	The Blue Ray	10/1953	1954 h/b + p/b
Jack Heming	The Lost World of Colorado	10/1953	1954 h/b + p/b
F A M Webster	The Ivory Talisman	11/1953	1954 h/b + p/b
T C Bridges	The Secret of the Smoking Swamp	11/1953	1954 h/b + p/b
T H Scott	The Treasure Trail	12/1953	1954 h/b + p/b
T C Bridges	The Secret of Sevenstones Key	12/1953	1954 h/b + p/b

WARNER LAURIE

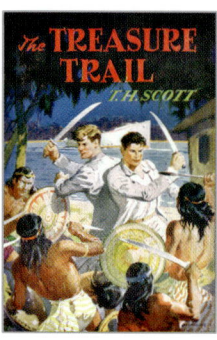

AUTHOR	TITLE	PAINTED	PUBLISHED
Prynne Hutton	Pastures New		1949 h/b
Paul I Wellman	The Iron Mistress		1952 h/b
Margot Bland	Julia	12/1952	1953 h/b

WORLD DISTRIBUTORS / CONSUL

AUTHOR	TITLE	PAINTED	PUBLISHED
Walt Grove	Down (N1026)	7/1961	1961 p/b
Rafael Sabatini	The Hounds of God (N1033)	7/1961	1961 p/b
Jack Schaefer	The Canyon	7/1962	1963 p/b
Mark Corrigan	Sin of Hong Kong (1223)	9/1962	1963 p/b

BIBLIOGRAPHY

WORLD'S WORK

AUTHOR	TITLE	PAINTED	PUBLISHED
John Russell Fearn	The Golden Amazon Returns		1948 h/b
Fulton Oursler & Will Oursler	Father Flanagan of Boys Town		1950 h/b
	The Unlucky One	3/1961	

WRIGHT & BROWN

AUTHOR	TITLE	PAINTED	PUBLISHED
Rosemary Rees	Sackcloth for Susan		1941 h/b, 1945 r/p

OTHER

AUTHOR	TITLE	PAINTED	PUBLISHED
	Boys' Annual	1/1946	Radolfo
	Fireside Annual for Boys	5/1946	Attwood
	I was Roosevelt's Shadow	10/1946	Attwood
	Second Love	2/1947	Attwood
	2 Westerns	4/1948	Attwood
	3 Westerns	6/1949	Attwood
	Western	12/1949	PP
	2 Westerns	2/1950	PP
	2 Westerns	3/1950	PP
	Golden Canyon	8/1950	PP
	Riders of the Desert Trail	11/1951	PP
	No Range is Free	11/1951	PP
	Guns of Ghost Valley	11/1951	PP
	Arizona Ranger Courage (cover + 3 colour illus)	11/1951	
	The Masked Rider	2/1952	Preston
	Six-Gun Luck	2/1952	Purnell
	Daily Mirror Annual	7/1954	
	Attack!	12/1956	
	Western cover	9/1959	
	6 covers for Swedish books	4/1962	

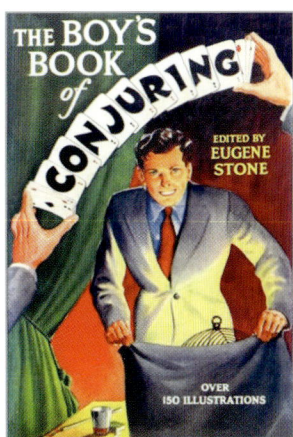

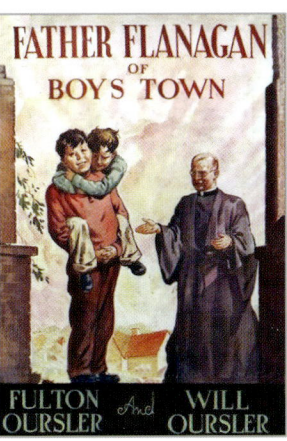

Below: McConnell's original paintings for *Smiling Desperado* by Max Brand (Corgi, 1957) (left), *Guns for Hire* by T C H Jacobs (Amalgamated, 1952) (top right) and *Lannagan Horns In* by John Hunter (Amalgamated, 1952) (bottom right). (Images courtesy Jim Kealy.)

The Golden Flame by Ursula Bloom (Robert Hale, 1941)